DATE DUE

BUY AMERICAN

Buy American

The Untold Story of Economic Nationalism

DANA FRANK

Beacon Press

BOSTON

Beacon Press
25 Beacon Street
Boston, Massachusetts 02108-2892
www.beacon.org

Beacon Press books
are published under the auspices of
the Unitarian Universalist Association of Congregations.

Union Label Song, written by Paula Green on behalf of the International
Ladies' Garment Workers' Union. Reprinted by permission.

Saturday Night Live excerpt courtesy of Broadway Video Entertainment
and NBC Studios.

05 04 03 02 01 00 99   8 7 6 5 4 3 2 1

Text design by Elizabeth Elsas
Composition by Wilsted & Taylor Publishing Services

Library of Congress Cataloging-in-Publication Data
Frank, Dana.
    Buy American : the untold story of economic nationalism / Dana
Frank.
        p.   cm.
    Includes bibliographical references and index.
    ISBN 0-8070-4710-4
        1. Consumers—United States.   2. Consumers' preferences—United
States.   3. Buy national policy—United States.   I. Title.
    HC110.C6F734   1999
    658.8'343'0973—dc21   98-50066

TO MARGE FRANTZ AND
ELEANOR ENGSTRAND

CONTENTS

During the late 1980s and early 1990s, the same story kept popping up in the nation's newspapers. It went something like this: The main character—let's call her Ms. American Consumer—went out shopping one day, innocently enough. On her way in the car she started musing about the disappearance of good American jobs, and, with thoughts of plant shutdowns tugging at her conscience, she arrived at the local mall. Passing into its cool, climate-controlled passages, she moved from store to store, looking casually at VCRs, television sets, radios, home appliances. Suddenly she realized that all the goods she had examined were made in China, Japan, or Korea. Rushing through the mall, she peered at label after label and discovered to her great horror that she couldn't find a TV or a VCR or a toaster made in the U.S.A.

Stunned, she sped home and swept through her house, tearing through the living room, the kitchen, the closets. Her best shoes, she discovered, were from Korea, her favorite dress from Taiwan, her son's toys from China. Almost everything was imported. Unbeknownst to her, foreign products had infiltrated the inner sanctum of her home—and of the nation. In a state of shock, Ms. Consumer put two and two together: because people like herself were buying imports, American workers were losing their jobs. From now on, she would Buy American and assiduously inspect every single label on every purchase, making sure it read "Made in the U.S.A."[1]

Although the story typically exaggerated the drama of Ms. Consumer's epiphany—we might call it an "import panic attack"—it resonated throughout the United States. All over the country during the 1970s, '80s, and '90s, ordinary people were worried about unemployment, increased economic inequality, and the future of the United States in a rapidly globalizing economy. Above all, they were alarmed by economic processes that seemed well beyond their control and concerned about their own futures and those of their children and the people in their communities. They chose to Buy American as a way of asserting at least a small measure of influence.

In the 1970s, the International Ladies' Garment Workers' Union first ran a series of immensely popular television advertisements asking shoppers to "Look for the Union Label" and make sure their clothes were made in the U.S.A. Then autoworkers, laid off by the hundreds of thousands in the early 1980s, started to swing sledgehammers at Toyotas and ask car buyers to "Buy American—The Job You Save May Be Your Own." Textile manufacturers ran their own television ads, insisting that Americans who bought imports caused plant shutdowns. Wal-Mart dangled red, white, and blue bunting in its stores, promising to Buy American and "Keep America Working and Strong." Spurred on by continuous national promotional campaigns, the idea that Americans could use their purchasing dollars to chart their economic future spread steadily but dramatically.

Buy American campaigns were not a new idea, though—they extend back to the very founding of the nation. The Boston Tea Party, after all, was a demonstration against British imports, organized by colonial protesters who vowed to wear American clothing and reject all foreign tea. A major Buy American movement erupted again during the Great Depression of the 1930s, organized by newspaper mogul William Randolph Hearst and others seeking to relieve unemployment by rejecting both foreign products and immigrant workers, especially those from Asia. From that point to the present, the Buy American movement has been inextricably interwoven with fears of alleged economic infiltration by Asians and their goods.

This book examines the history and politics of Buy American campaigns from the American Revolution to the 1990s. It asks why people have turned to nationalist shopping again and again, and how effective Buy American campaigns have been at addressing their concerns. Are imports to blame for the decline of working people's standard of living? The history of the Buy American movement turns out to be full of surprises, including misguided heroes, chilling racism, and more than a few charlatans who have used economic nationalism to mask private interests.

But this book is not just the story of Buy American campaigns. It is about the politics of foreign trade and about how ordinary Americans have tried to understand difficult questions of foreign economic relations.

The mainstream press usually presents foreign trade policy as two diametrically opposed choices. On one side lies the free trade position: if barriers to trade, such as tariffs, are removed and goods are free to move from nation to nation unfettered, its proponents promise, all Americans prosper. This camp reigns triumphant in the press, the economics profession, and recent global trade pacts such as the North American Free Trade Agreement (NAFTA) and the General Agreement on Tariffs and Trade (GATT). On the other side lie the protectionists. They support high barriers to trade, hoping to protect American jobs and people by preventing the entry of foreign goods and, usually, foreign people. Their most prominent advocates in recent times have been presidential candidates Ross Perot, who garnered 19 percent of the popular vote in 1992 by opposing NAFTA, and especially Patrick Buchanan, who combines avid protectionism with Christian fundamentalism.[2]

Are these our only choices? During the battle around NAFTA's passage in 1993, environmentalists and trade unionists came together to ask if another approach to trade policy, addressing working people's concerns, was possible. Since then, they have tried to build more effective networks among labor activists across national borders and to reconceptualize foreign economic relations from below.[3]

We have had a difficult time devising alternative approaches to the politics of trade in part because we are taught that only "experts" and professional economists can, or should, understand foreign trade. We are told that "natural" economic laws dictate trade policy. Yet at the same time, those "natural" laws repeatedly seem to serve only corporate and elite economic interests. We have groped toward alternative economic policies, but except for a few trade union staffers, university-based academics, and think-tank denizens, most of us know little about the politics of trade.

This book shows how both the free trade and the protectionist positions have been historically created—along with the illusion that only two choices are possible. It reveals all sorts of alternative notions of foreign and domestic economic relations that working people have proposed. And it shows the ways in which foreign economic relations have been repeatedly cast in terms of race, especially regarding Asians both within and beyond the U.S. border.

This is not, however, a history of public policy on trade matters. Although I do introduce the broadest of histories of national trade policy, I do so only as background to the story of ordinary people's opinions about foreign products. I spend relatively little time on the free trade position, in order to focus on popular economic nationalism and its strengths and weaknesses as a response to the economic challenges facing working people in U.S. history.

We are used to thinking of the nation as a political entity or as a geographical place. Here, I use the concept of the "economic nation" to explore the meaning of the United States as an economic entity. The "American" economy has never stopped at the official border—it has always extended far and wide over the globe through investment, trading, and manufacturing relationships. And it has always been the product of deep conflicts between rich and poor, between natives and newcomers, and between people who see themselves as white and people they define as racially different and often unwelcome. This book explores the history of popular economic nationalism to see what diverse Americans have meant by their economic nation and how they have sought to construct and define it. It is thus about the way in which Americans have defined the nation's people and society at the most basic level.

This is ultimately a story about democracy. By buying American products, people of all sorts have tried to exercise democratic control over their nation and their economic lives. And they have usually been thwarted in the process. With this book I hope to change that picture, to help build a more democratic economy and empower ordinary working Americans by bringing trade relations out of the obscure realm of experts who tell us what to think, and into our own union halls, kitchens, and living rooms—where the enemy might turn out to be not Asians allegedly infiltrating with VCRs, but someone else altogether.

BUY AMERICAN

Part One

CHAPTER I

Whose Economic Nation?
Buy American Campaigns and the American Revolution

The streets of Boston on December 16, 1773, were so tense you could hear a tea cup spill five blocks away. "Twould puzzle any person to purchase a pair of p[isto]ls in town," one businessman wrote a friend in Philadelphia, "as they are all bought up, with full determination to repel force by force."[1] Three ships sat moored in the city's inner harbor, packed full of British tea. Governor Thomas Hutchinson insisted that the ships unload. But for weeks, leaflets ominously signed "THE PEOPLE" had warned that any verminous sorts who unloaded the ships would be denounced as "Wretches unworthy to live and will be the first victims of our just Resentment."[2] The pamphlets' authors knew very well that Hutchinson was deliberately trying to defy their boycott of British tea and, more broadly, to crack their determination to purchase only goods made in the colonies.[3]

Late in the evening of the 16th, somewhere between fifty and a hundred men met up in secret little groups throughout the neighborhood near the Boston docks. John Crane, Thomas Bolton, and Samuel Fenno, carpenters, arranged to rendezvous at Crane's house at Hollis and Tremont streets. Others, including merchants, common sailors, artisans, and assorted apprentices, met at prearranged street corners or taverns. Paul Revere, the silversmith, was one; so was Thomas Melvill, a young graduate of Princeton and Harvard; so was the more humble shoemaker George Robert Twelves Hewes, who, blackening his face along with rest, "fell in with" other anonymous protesters in a silent march to the dock.[4] Supposedly, Samuel Adams, the radical intellectual, wasn't there; nor was John Hancock, the rich merchant. But everyone knew they were behind the whole thing.[5]

For one brief evening, at least—if not in the years soon to come—rich and poor alike joined hands.

At the dock the men broke into three gangs under predesignated leaders. Boarding the *Dartmouth,* the *Beaver,* and the *Eleanor,* they used a block and tackle to haul out 342 heavy chests of tea, then hacked the chests open with hatchets and plopped the tea overboard. They had a little problem with the tide: it was so low the water level was only two or three feet, and the enormous quantity of tea—90,000 pounds, worth £9,000—kept piling up, so other men were assigned to push it aside. Throughout the night a huge silent crowd of two or three thousand people stood at the wharf side, watching, as did officials aboard a cordon of armed British ships in the harbor.[6]

The protest took three hours. "We then quietly retired to our several places of residence, without having any conversation with each other, or taking any measures to discover who were our associates," Hewes, the shoemaker, recalled.[7] By dawn the tide had risen and long thick streams of tea stretched far out across the harbor. "This Destruction of the Tea," future president John Adams reflected in his diary that day, "is so bold, so daring, so firm, intrepid & inflexible, and it must have so important Consequences and so lasting, that I cannot but consider it as an Epocha in History."[8]

Thus a Buy American campaign gave birth to the United States of America. The Boston Tea Party climaxed a decade-long movement against British imports, known at the time as "nonimportation," "nonconsumption," or, by the outbreak of the Revolutionary War, "nonintercourse." Beginning in the 1760s, its adherents not only swore to give up imported goods but for the first time began to celebrate what they called domestic manufactures—what we would today call American products. The Boston Tea Party escalated the movement for independence to a new stage, as the tea partygoers defiantly declared the colonies independent of imports and, in the process, began to build a new state and a new economic nation, inextricably bound together. Through the nonimportation movement the colonists declared economic sovereignty, embraced economic nationalism, and began to express their vision of the ideal economic nation.

But, to borrow Linda Colley's phrase, whose nation was it?[9] The question of democracy lay at the very center of the colonists' vision of an economic nation. The nonimportation movement depended upon truly popular enforcement, as colonists collectively tried to enforce nonimportation's strictures down to the last cup of tea. People of very different economic positions enthusiastically joined in the movement—all the carpenters, shoemakers, sailors, apprentices, and rich merchants at the Tea Party, for example. But each protester had his or her own vision of the economic nation and how to sustain it. And, as often as not, their visions of the just economy, unleashed by the Revolution, were in conflict with each other.

The nonimportation movement set into motion not just colonists' challenges to British rule but, equally important, deep challenges to established authority within the colonies. As historian Carl Becker put it in a famous formulation in 1909, the American Revolution was not just a question of "home rule" but of "who would rule at home."[10] Class tensions seethed throughout the colonies; and the colonists' definitions of "fair trade," "free trade," and freedom itself were all up for grabs. Samuel Adams and John Hancock had one thing in mind. Popular committees seeking to enforce the boycott, poor women fleeing almshouses, patriotic sailors resisting the British navy, and George Washington's slaves had something else in mind altogether, as we shall see. A "Buy American" movement gave birth to the economic nation, and the question of foreign trade loomed large in the nation's future. But who was that economy for? And how would "the people" decide?

BUY COLONIAL

The story of the nonimportation movement begins, modestly enough, almost a decade before the Tea Party in an ordinary Boston Tavern in August 1764. Fifty upstanding merchants, pledging their sacred honor, signed a collective pact to give up laces, ruffles, and cloths imported from England, except at designated prices, and to wear only simple outfits at funerals. Soon, groups of individuals popped up all over New England to announce similar vows. A group of Boston artisans, for example, swore only to wear work clothes made in Massachusetts. A group of Yale students unanimously swore off foreign liquors.

Then the governments of cities and towns across the region started pronouncing they, too, were eschewing British imports. In

October 1768, the Boston town meeting first vowed to give up a long list of British imports, hold cheaper funerals, and encourage the production and purchase of local products. Within three months, twenty-four other Massachusetts towns had signed on to Boston's agreement. The movement leaped across colonial borders; by the fall of 1769, merchants in New York and Philadelphia had sworn to an even stricter nonimportation agreement. By 1770 these pacts coalesced into a boilerplate formula in which protesters publicly swore to eschew all imports and wear only American-made clothes. Soon the legislative assemblies of every colony except New Hampshire had signed on, if with a bit of foot-dragging on the part of Maryland, South Carolina, and other Southern colonies. [11]

Giving up imports was suddenly immensely popular. Through nonimportation, the colonists were trying to address the classic grievances that produced the American Revolution. At their core, those grievances boiled down to fury at Britain's efforts to constrain the colonists' economic independence. First, Parliament had imposed the Stamp Act of 1764, which assigned a new tax on all printing and legal documents and mandated elaborate paperwork to go with it. Colonists, ranging from lowly boardinghouse keepers to the highest and mightiest of international merchants, were incensed. They devised nonimportation, in response, to try to wound British trading interests, which, they believed, would in turn pressure Parliament to repeal the Act. And, for its own circuitous reasons, Parliament did indeed repeal the tax in February 1766.

Then it slammed down the still more hated Townshend Duties of 1767, a package of legislative measures calling for a reorganized, more vigilant customs office; the reassertion of imperial control over colonial government; and new taxes on lead, paint, paper, glass, and tea. Colonists of many political stripes reacted in fury and frustration, and a second, far broader nonimportation movement swept like wildfire through the colonies. Imports to New England dropped dramatically, by almost 50 percent between 1768 and 1769. In some colonies the figure was two-thirds (although in a few backsliding colonies the numbers actually went up).[12] Once again, Parliament repealed all the measures, except one—the tax on tea—and in late 1770 the colonial boycotters officially lifted their strictures.

Not having quite learned its lesson, in 1773 Parliament announced it would circumvent colonial merchants and bring tea into the colonies solely through officially designated, British-controlled agents of the East India Company monopoly, and that it would enforce the hated tea tax. As John Adams predicted, colonial opposition to these "tea acts" was so widespread, and the Boston Tea Party defying it so dramatic, that nonimportation quickly exploded into the full American Revolution against British authority.[13]

The rejection of imports and celebration of American products stayed right at the center of the revolutionary movement all the way through the Declaration of Independence in 1776 and the Revolutionary War (1775–1783). Most Americans know that the first transcolonial political body was the First Continental Congress, formed in Philadelphia in October 1774. Few know that its main order of business was a nonimportation agreement called "The Association," a colony-wide alliance to enforce a boycott of British products. Famous patriots such as John Jay, George Washington, Patrick Henry, and John Adams signed this biggest nonimportation agreement of all. Its language spoke of economic grievance, of demanded redress, and of confident effect:

> To obtain redress of these grievances, which threaten destruction of the lives, liberty and property of His Majesty's subjects in North America, we are of opinion that a non-importation, non-consumption, and non-exportation agreement, faithfully adhered to, will prove the most speedy, effectual and peaceable measure.

The delegates vowed "under the sacred ties of virtue, honour, and love of country" to give up a long list of specific British goods and to "encourage frugality, economy, and industry, and promote agriculture, arts and the manufactures of this country."[14]

Through the nonimportation movement these colonists knit together their economic interests for the first time into a common vision: of trade free from British strictures and of the economic freedom to develop "domestic manufactures" out from under the thumb of imperial domination. A little less than two years later, with the Declaration of Independence, they explicitly asserted political independence from Great Britain. But the Association preceded it by two years with a declaration of economic independence.[15]

Yet precisely as it purported to express a singular colonial will, the

Association's manifesto also contained a few clues to the roiling internal politics of the Revolution to come. Two of its seemingly inexplicable clauses—repeated from hundreds of previous vows—had little, directly, to do with independence from Great Britain and everything to do with politics at home: First, the Founding Fathers promised to abandon ostentatious display. And second, they swore "That all manufactures of this country be sold at reasonable prices."[16] Soon it will be clear what those two vows were all about.

THE PEOPLE'S ENEMIES LIST

The nonimportation movement involved a lot more than official agreements signed by patriots whose names we recognize today. The real adventure took place at the grassroots level, in communities all up and down the colonies. The Association, as had previous agreements, set up an official enforcement system, specifying "That a committee be chosen in every county, city, and town, by those who are qualified to vote for representatives in the legislature, whose business it shall be attentively to observe the conduct of all persons . . ." If the committee members found that anyone had "violated this association," they were required to publish the individual's name in the local newspaper, "to the end that all such foes to the rights of British-America may be publicly known, and universally contemned as the enemies of American liberty."[17]

The members of "The Committee of Sixty-Six" in Philadelphia, for example, divided their city up into six districts. They assigned a member from each "to inspect the arrival of vessels" in their district and report the results at the London Coffee House every morning.[18] The committee then posted offenders' names and tried to shame them publicly. In towns and cities all over the colonies, local committees used ancient rituals of public shaming to create a climate of community-based political and economic morality. In New York September 19, 1769, for example, a crowd erected a scaffold and called forward Thomas Richardson, a jeweler whom the local committee had charged with importing British goods. "Mounted on the rostrum, he discovered a readiness to ask the forgiveness of the public and to agree to store his goods."[19]

As Richardson's groveling indicates, violators often publicly renounced their previous behavior and vowed to observe the boycott.

Thomas Lilly of Marblehead, Massachusetts, got caught importing tea in March 1775. He burned the offending leaves before a big crowd and then signed a confession that "I do now in this publick manner ask their pardon, and do solemnly promise I will not in future be guilty of a like offence." The local committee then pronounced Lilly once again "justly entitled to the esteem and employ of all persons as heretofore."[20]

A large part of the nonimporters' power came from ostracizing violators. The idea, as one group in Massachusetts put it, was to "Expose to shame and Contempt all persons" trafficking in British goods.[21] Members of the local committee in Cumberland, New Jersey, for example, couldn't convince one resident not to drink British tea with his family; so they "br[oke] off all dealings with him," and published his name, "so that he may be distinguished from the friends of American liberty."[22]

The process of spurning these folks was not always so polite. Boycott enforcers threw dirt, broke windows, and scrawled the eighteenth-century equivalent of graffiti on violators' businesses and homes. "Signs, Doors, and Windows were daub'd over in the Night time with every kind of Filth," wrote one businessman, "and one of them particularly had his person treated in the same manner."[23]

Part of what is so important here is that through the importation committees, ordinary people were forming new systems of colonial government, independent of British control, which were in many ways more democratic than previous colonial governments. Unlike the colonial assemblies or Parliament, the committees were based on popular vigilance, collective morality, and grassroots enforcement. They interlocked with, and in theory supported, the work of the Continental Congress. But they also reflected the diverse opinions of small farmers, local business people, and skilled workers—those whom historians call the "middling sorts"—whose economic lives and political concerns were distinct from the more well-off delegates to the new Congress and who were quite capable of independent action as the Revolution moved forward.

DRESSED FOR REDRESS

The nonimportation movement was all very public. Much boycott activity centered around elite men and women who loudly proclaimed what they were giving up and made sure everyone knew it. The first thing to go, beginning in 1765, was lavish funereal display, in which the rich had increasingly indulged during the early 1760s. "None of us . . . will go into any further mourning-dress, than a black crape or ribbon on the arm or hat, for gentlemen, and a black ribbon and necklace for ladies, and we will discontinue the giving of scarves and gloves at funerals," read a typical vow.[24] Depending on the particular list to which they subscribed, boycotters also abandoned "Loaf Sugar," "Chaises and Carriages of all Sorts," "Gold and Silver Buttons," "Clocks and Watches," "Womens and Childrens stays," "Malt Liquors and Cheese," "Silversmiths work of all Sorts," "Linseed Oyl," "Furs and Tippets, and all Sorts of Millinery Wear," "Silks of all kinds," "looking glasses," as well as fire engines, mustard, candy, chairs, tables, and, of course, tea, for which they declared their intention to substitute local herb tea.[25] Five fire companies in Philadelphia swore they wouldn't touch lamb—since wool was necessary to produce domestic cloth—and boycotters all up and down the colonies joined them. Songs, cartoons, and assorted bad poems all celebrated the boycott of imports and promoted domestic products:

> Farewell the Tea Board, with its gaudy Equipage
> because I'm taught (and I believe it true)
> Its use will fasten slavish Chains upon my country.[26]

Or another from Bridgewater, Massachusetts:

> Foreign productions she rejects
> With nobleness of mind,
> For Home Commodities, to which
> She's properly inclined.[27]

Nonimportation also involved an equally ostentatious celebration by the elite of American-made products. This side of the movement revolved around the symbolic wearing of homespun, the colonists' name for domestically produced cloth. George Washington, Thomas Jefferson, and other leading patriots strode about in homespun garb. Elite ladies vowed to "set aside gaudy . . . expensive Dresses Brought from Europe" in favor of "decent plain Dresses made in their own Country."[28] Harvard and Yale students appeared at their graduations wearing homespun.[29] The boycott committee in Prince George's County, Maryland, announced, "To be clothed in manufactures fabricated in the Colonies ought to be considered as a badge and distinction of respect and true patriotism."[30]

In order to obtain all that colonial-made fabric, patriotic men of the elite exhorted their womenfolk to spin and weave more. A popular poem, frequently reprinted in the press, advised women in 1767:

> First then throw aside your high top knots of price
> Wear none but your own country linen.
> Of economy boast. Let your pride be the most
> Show cloaths of your own make and spinning.[31]

The only problem was that the wives, daughters, girlfriends, and widows of the protesting merchants and planters had given up spinning and weaving at least a generation before, to instead buy thread and cloth made by the working people of Britain or the colonies. Now they took up the spinning wheel again in patriotic fervor and, as two girls wrote, "felt Nationly" doing so.[32]

In 1769, especially, a rage for spinning bees swept through the proper ladies of the colonies. At the bees they ritualistically and very, very publicly (one bee in Rhode Island drew six hundred spectators) engaged in patriotic spinning. Typically, the women costumed themselves in homespun and gathered in groups of about forty at the home of a local minister, to spend the day together spinning furiously, all the while engaging in edifying and patriotic conversation. At one such bee the spinners drank colonial herbal tea and ate only "American produce prepared which was more agreeable to them than any foreign Dainties and Delicacies."[33] At another, in Berwick, Maine, the women "made their Breakfast on Rye coffee" and ate "a Carrot which after it was trim'd weighed two Pounds and a half" and which we can presume had been germinated in American dirt.[34]

But elite women did not intend to actually spend all their time spinning and weaving the massive amounts of cloth that would be necessary if the colonists were going to give up imports. The bees were merely a ritual. Instead, their menfolk unveiled plans for the development of the colonies' first factories to produce the requisite homespun. In 1767, the New York Society for the Promotion of Arts, Agriculture and Oeconomy, for example, offered bonuses to local manufacturers, set up spinning schools and a biweekly market for New York–made products, and hired three hundred poor women to make linens.[35] Inspired by New York, Philadelphia put three hundred of its own poor women to work spinning flax and sold "linens, sha-loons, flannels, ink-powder and the wares of Pennsylvania" at a market three times a week.[36] These new manufacturing enterprises were not designed for the ladies at the spinning bees. They were designed as poor relief for unemployed women, as the name of one such group proclaimed: "The New York Society for employing the Industrious Poor and Promoting Manufactory."[37] For all the rich ladies' demonstrative labor at their spinning bees, it was poor women who would, in the elite's plans, make the actual homespun and thus liberate the nation. In effect, the merchants proposed to sustain the Buy American movement with an eighteenth-century version of 1990s workfare for poor women and their children.[38]

But the enterprises kept failing. The impoverished women fled the spinning factories as fast as they could, quickly figuring out that the patriots paid wages below starvation level. The women preferred the more practical alternative of take-home sewing work, which not only paid better but which also allowed them to continue child rearing and household responsibilities.[39] Investors, for their part, fled equally swiftly. As historian Arthur Schlesinger, Sr., summarized, "Manufacturing enterprises, which would, in all probability, collapse the moment trade with England was renewed, did not appeal as attractive investments to men of capital; and as a class they refused to lend support."[40]

ENLIGHTENED SELF-INTEREST

Schlesinger's assessment offers us a hint that powerful economic interests hummed inside those who suddenly "felt nationly" and chafed at imperial constraints. Noble declarations of independence and indignation aside, the most prominent boycotters also had their own self-interested reasons for pushing nonimportation.

Two key groups of men were particularly drawn to the nonimportation movement. First were urban artisans—known at the time as "mechanics"—such as Paul Revere, Thomas Paine, and George Robert Twelves Hewes. Highly skilled craftsmen, these men followed a hierarchical system through which boys proceeded in status from apprentice to journeyman to master artisan. In theory, each would eventually achieve his own independent household with a wife, family members, apprentices, and journeymen all under his control. This system produced most colonial manufactured goods in the era before the Revolution. But British hostility to the independent development of colonial production held the artisans back. Meanwhile, the beginnings of the Industrial Revolution in Britain meant that cheaper imported goods consistently undercut colonial products. As a result, colonial artisans such as Paine, Revere, Hewes, or the three carpenters at the Tea Party enthusiastically welcomed nonimportation because it meant better markets for their products; and indeed, they did prosper in every period during which imports were banned.[41] Yet their support was neither unanimous nor without sacrifice, since many artisans utilized imported materials in their production processes. (Even at the time of the Revolution, a purely "American product" could be hard to find.)[42]

But a second, far more elite group really drove the nonimportation movement and produced its strongest leaders: men who made their wealth from large-scale merchant operations, from buying and selling colonial goods, foreign imports, and, in many cases, people from Africa. The merchants' concerns began in 1763 when, at the conclusion of the French and Indian Wars, a flood of British imports swept through the colonies, producing a deep depression. "Trade was dull, money scarce, credit poor, and debt the common burden of farmers, country storekeepers, merchants in the cities, and people generally," notes Charles McLean Andrews, the first historian to analyze the merchants' position.[43] "The current of indebtedness," he notes, "was always toward Great Britain."[44] In the northern and middle port cities, imported goods piled up on overstocked shelves. On the plantations of the South, slave masters sustained elaborate lifestyles only by borrowing heavily from Scottish and English merchants.[45]

As the established colonial merchants sank ever deeper in this quagmire of indebtedness and oversupply, nonimportation offered a way out. By cutting off imports, it decreased supplies, cleared overstocked shelves, and raised profit levels. As one advocate promised in the *Pennsylvania Gazette* of November 1767, "You will have a good price for all your dead goods which have always been unprofitable."[46] Another less satisfied patriot complained that merchants who refused to carry imports forced customers "to take old moth-eaten cloths that had lain rotting in the shops for years and to pay a monstrous price for them."[47] The boycott also meant that merchants could make a great deal of money from smuggling. As a result, Schlesinger concluded, the tea boycott in particular "corresponded as much to self-interest as devotion to principle."[48]

The motivations behind individuals' observation of the boycott were equally revealing. Before the boycotts, most imports were bought by the rich. Material life for the poor, working people, and most farmers, by contrast, was crude, depending upon goods produced locally or bartered within elaborate systems of noncash exchange. Middling people—artisans, farmers, small merchants—bought a few imported goods but could afford few of the luxury goods consumed by the rich.

In the 1750s and especially the 1760s, the colonial rich were getting richer, the poor poorer. Class differentiations were growing rapidly. Increasingly, the rich worked hard to distinguish themselves from those below through elaborate displays of consumption. And the luxury goods they displayed were largely imported. By the mid-1760s, their spending habits were spiraling out of control, and wealthy people were sinking further into debt to keep up with the proverbial Joneses.[49]

The nonimportation movement offered a way out for them, too. On the one hand, it defused class resentments, as elites publicly countered charges from those below that they were indulging in "luxury" or ostentation, by ostentatiously giving things up in the name of patriotism. On the other hand, boycotting and nonconsumption gave individuals a public excuse to cut back and thus relieve their debt problems. It was a form of conspicuous nonconsumption that let everyone off the hook. When the *Massachusetts Gazette* exhorted, "of economy boast," it captured the dynamics perfectly. The nonimportation movement, then, wasn't just about spurning imports and supporting domestic goods; it was also about rejecting "gaudy equipage"—such as all those free gloves and scarves the rich had given out at funerals—which the elite could no longer afford.[50]

George Washington understood this well. Writing to George Mason in 1769, he enthused about nonimportation: "There are private, as well as public advantages to result from it," he noted. "The penurious Man," by cutting back his living expenses, "saves his money, & . . . saves his credit;" while "The extravagant & expensive man has the same good plea to retrench his Expenses." As a result, "He is thereby furnished with a pretext to live within bounds." As for "the poor & needy man," Washington concluded, he is left the same, but with one advantage: "as he judges from comparison, his condition is amended in Proportion as it approaches nearer to those above him." Or, in other words, the poor man would see that the gap between rich and poor had narrowed—and be potentially less angry about it.[51]

A slogan in the *Pennsylvania Gazette* of December 10, 1767, summed up the motivations behind elite support for nonimportation exactly: "If we mean still to be free, let us unanimously lay aside foreign superfluities, and encourage our own manufacture. SAVE YOUR MONEY AND YOU WILL SAVE YOUR COUN-TRY."[52] Self-interest, a new economic nationalism, and the emerging ideology of freedom: here was the essence of the elite's Revolution. Noble grievances and ostentatious nationalism marched arm in arm with a private, more pecuniary politics.

PRICES AND PATRIOTISM

The story of the poor women fleeing the spinning factory suggests, though, that not all Americans had the same idea of what the Buy American movement or the new economic nation itself might mean. Class tensions permeated the nonimportation movement, and defusing them proved nowhere near as simple as Washington's plan for placating the man at the bottom looking upward. "THE PEOPLE," charged with enforcing the boycott, could prove just as enthusiastic as the upper classes about nonimportation. But they had their own notions of where it began and ended. Here the revolutionary plot thickens, and the question of democracy looms.

As a successful strategy, nonimportation depended upon enforcement, which, in turn, depended upon broad popular support. In the eighteenth century that meant the crowd. As one historian put it, "Without crowd action, there would have been no resistance movement."[53] For centuries, Europeans and then the European colonists had expressed their opinions through carefully organized crowd actions. When the patriots called for the creation of local committees to enforce nonimportation, they consciously mobilized such crowd action, as in the Boston Tea Party. But the question at the center of the Revolution was whether they could subsequently control it. As Cadwallader Colden, the lieutenant governor of New York, put it at the time, the issue was "Whether the men who excited this seditious spirit in the People have it in their power to suppress it."[54]

Most crowds were neat, brisk, and effective. In Wrentham, Massa-

chusetts, in December 1774, after the local nonimportation committee published the name of N. Aldis as a boycott violator, four or five
hundred people rallied outside his house and charged him with buying tea. Aldis and four friends promptly apologized before the crowd
for making "exasperating speeches" that had "boldly opposed" the
Continental Congress, and the crowd drifted home, irritated but
satisfied.[55]

Other crowds were less tidy. On three Thursdays in a row in
March 1770, mysterious signs appeared in the commercial district of
Boston, naming importers who had violated the agreements. The
third day, a group of young boys, out of school because it was market
day, started threatening customers who tried to enter the alleged importers' shops and warned off anyone who tried to take down the
signs charging the violators. Then William Jackson, one of the accused, tried to pull the signs down. "A Number of Idle people . . .
standing by, with Clubs and sticks in their Hands" stopped him. Then
soldiers tried to remove the signs; the crowd stopped them, too. The
situation escalated when a well-known customs informer, Ebenezer
Richardson, tried to take one of the signs down. The crowd chased
him home, throwing rocks all the while. When he turned and shot
eleven-year-old Christopher Sneider, the crowd finally pulled Richardson forcibly through the streets of Boston, at one point trying to
"put a rope about his Neck and . . . execute him themselves."[56]

As the elite who formed the Association had intended, members
of these crowds targeted those who violated the nonimportation
agreements. But by the time of the Revolutionary War, crowd participants added to their enforcement activities a new, independent concern all their own. Listen to the story Abigail Adams wrote to her husband, John, on July 31, 1777:

Abigail began by reminding John of the "great Scarcity of Sugar
and Coffe [sic]" in Boston,

> "the merchants having secreted a large Quantity. . . . It was rumourd that
> an eminent, wealthy stingy Merchant (who is a Batchelor) had a Hogs-
> head of Coffe in his Store which he refused to sell to the committee under
> 6 shillings per pound.

His customers thought he was price gouging—that is, taking unfair
advantage of scarcities produced by the cut-off in imports.

A Number of Females some say a hundred, some say more assembled with a cart and trucks, marched down to the Ware House and demanded the keys, which he refused to deliver, upon which one of them seazd him by his Neck and tossd him into the cart. Upon his finding no Quarter he delivrd the keys, when they tipd up the cart and dischargd him, then opend the Warehouse, Hoisted out the Coffe themselves, put it in the trucks and drove off.

Throughout, "A large concourse of Men stood amazd silent Spectators." (She added: "It was reported that he had a Spanking among them, but this I believe was not true.") A Boston selectman in his own account added that the protesters "were not your Maggys but reputable Clean drest Women some of them with silk gownes on."[57]

The women attacked this particular merchant not because he imported, but because he jacked up prices. Nonimportation produced scarcities, opening up lucrative possibilities for hoarding and profit-gouging, exacerbated by wartime inflation. In response, local committees swiftly merged nonimportation with price controls. "This is the very same oppression we complain of Great Britain," "A Farmer" wrote in to the *Connecticut Courant* in February 1778.[58] Daniel Roberdeau, a high-ranking militia officer and merchant chosen to chair the Philadelphia price committee in 1779, explained: "I have no doubt but combinations have been formed for raising the prices of goods and provisions, and therefore the community, in their own defense, have a natural right to counteract such combinations, and to set limits to evils which affect themselves."[59] These colonists, in the words of historian Barbara Clark Smith, merged "prices and patriotism."[60]

Price controls, Smith has shown, grew out of locally based ideas of mutuality, neighborliness, and fair trade. In colonial towns and villages, "exchange did not occur in an insulated or separate realm where 'the rules of the market' reigned supreme," she notes.[61] People conceptualized market relations to be embedded in day-to-day networks of community and obligation. "It made sense to understand the purpose of trade as 'mutual' benefit for all parties," Smith found, "and not—as a minister stressed in the 1770s—the advantage of one party over others."[62]

Smith estimates that during the 1770s, somewhere around seven thousand people participated in official committees, enforcing nonimportation and price controls. As Abigail Adams's story suggests, the leaders of price control crowds were often female or mixed male and female. And as her story also suggests, they came from elite as well as middling backgrounds. In Fishkill, New York, in 1776, one such group of women gathered to attack Jacobus Lefferts, who had been accused of profiteering on tea. They first asked three "gentlemen" passing by to help. When the men refused, the women put them under guard, marched to Lefferts's store, confiscated the tea, weighed it out carefully, and sold it at the price of six shillings approved by the Continental Congress. They intended to send the proceeds to the Congress.[63]

Was this a "food riot" or a carefully regulated "crowd"? A month earlier, in Longmeadow, Massachusetts, a crowd seized banned imports held by a man named Samuel Colton, hid them, and relinquished them only when Colton claimed to repent of his ways. When he again raised prices, they broke into his store and took molasses, sugar, rum, and salt. Colton charged that the crowd also "ransacked" his house "from top to bottom," producing "great Fear and Terr'r." But a local minister insisted, instead, that the crowd was orderly and careful and gave over the goods to the town clerk to sell at approved prices. When Colton wouldn't accept the proceeds, they walked into his house, left the money on a table, and departed, making sure witnesses saw it all.[64]

These strategic "rioters" targeted only those merchants who they believed had violated popularly understood norms of fairness in the marketplace. In their own words, the transgressors were "atrocious V[illain]s," "vile Miscreants who, thro' the avaricious Humour of raising a private Fortune on the Ruins of the Public," had violated the nonimportation agreement *and* raised prices.[65] For the women and men who enforced price controls, the economic nation thus began at home, in a local community, where a moral economy of just price and fair trade came first. Just as important to them as the birth of a new, independent nation-state was the maintenance of a domestic economy of local interdependence and respect.

CHEATERS NEVER PROSPER?

The price controllers had plenty to police, it turns out. The necessity of such regular and concerted vigilance underscores that throughout the nonimportation period, there was a whole lot of cheating going on. If the boycotts were enormously popular, at the same time their boundaries were often vague and, for many colonists, interpretation of their strictures loose. After all, as one historian put it, "homespun was neither becoming nor fashionable, and the pleasures of the table, the tavern, and the race-course were not easily resigned."[66] Any boycott is only effective if people have a desire for the boycotted goods in the first place, or there would be no power involved in giving it up.

The nonimportation movement elicited a sea of private transgressions on the part of otherwise vehement nonimporters. As Abigail Adams noted in another letter, even highly patriotic ladies were sure to put by "a small stock" of potentially boycotted goods, in case they might soon be banned from use.[67] Once an imported good had been outlawed, the ladies had their ways. "For it was possible to obtain tea by such stratagems as whispering across the merchant's counter and obtaining falsely labelled packages of tea."[68]

If the patriotic small fry fudged a bit, so did the big fish. A perusal of Thomas Jefferson's biography in search of his nonimportation activities reveals that in 1771 he ordered from London a long list of British goods for his new house. He acknowledged that they were prohibited but anticipated that Parliament would soon repeal the hated Townshend Acts, ending the boycott—and ordered them anyway. Frustrated in June that the restrictions were still in place, he wrote his London agent to send "some shoes and other prohibited articles," proposing to store them if, upon their arrival, the ban wasn't lifted. He then added an order for a fancy pianoforte of "fine mahogany, solid, not veneered . . . the workmanship very fine" for his new wife.[69] This from a man who had abandoned luxury, extravagance, and British imports.

George Washington had a similar problem with the fine distinctions of nonimportation. In July 1769 he, too, sent his London agent a long order specifying imports. In his cover letter he took care to point out that he had signed the Association and "was fully determined to adhere religiously to it, and may perhaps have wrote [sic] for some things unwittingly which may be [banned] under these circumstances." His list, though, included "trinkets" and an array of banned British manufactured goods, including "hardware and equipment" for his carriage. His biographer concludes rather charitably: "Either he drew some close distinctions or else he forgot that certain commodities were not to be imported so long as a tax remained on tea, glass, paint, and pigments." Forgot? Washington, along with his friend George Mason, had written the boycott list himself.[70]

One final story involves yet another famous patriot. In the spring and summer of 1769, John Mein, a prominent Boston newspaper editor opposed to nonimportation, decided to undercut the movement and deflect charges of his own disloyalty by publishing the names of prominent local signers of the Association who, he alleged, continued to import banned goods. Beginning in August, every two weeks he published a copy of the incoming cargo lists of violators' ships, listing their exact contents. The accused included John Hancock, the "merchant prince" and well-known advocate of nonimportation, who would later be famous for his flowery signature on the Declaration of Independence and the insurance conglomerate bearing his name. Mein insisted that three ships owned by Hancock, the *Lydia,* the *Last Attempt,* and the *Paoli,* had contained banned goods, including five bales of "British Linen" on board the *Lydia.* Hancock was out of town, but his manager denied the charges, claiming that the offending cloth was in fact "Russia Duck," to which Mein countered by producing a certified copy of the customs certification listing British linen. The *Newport Mercury* reflected: "one of the foremost of the Patriots in Boston . . . would perhaps shine more conspicuously . . . if he did not keep a number of vessels running to London and back, full freighted, getting rich, by receiving freight on goods made contraband by the Colonies."[71]

John Hancock was only the lofty tip of an iceberg of violators quietly profiting in banned goods. As one historian put it, "There was much running of forbidden commodities by night, and the charge was freely made that the warehouses had two doors, one in front and one behind" through which to smuggle imports. Mein's opposition reminds us, moreover, that many businessmen and merchants were against nonimportation from its inception. The colony of Georgia, for example, never signed onto the Association and was therefore spurned by the patriots,[72] as was "that dirty little colony of Rhode Island," whose merchants preferred not to eschew the imports on which their colony's economy depended. Beyond them lay all the colonists—perhaps as many as one-third—eventually known as the Loyalists, who opposed independence altogether.

Wealthy patriots like Jefferson and Washington embraced economic nationalism because it promised a larger, freer scope for their economic endeavors. But at a personal level, well, all those irritating—and expensive—sacrifices were for the little folk. For men like John Hancock, a concerted "Buy American" campaign could serve as a useful nationalist smoke screen through which to increase one's profit rate, as prices rose in response to shortages. His ilk will reappear throughout our story: exceedingly wealthy men who speak forcefully about nationalism in public but who, in private, use economic nationalism to feather their own economic nests, while privately violating the very boycotts they so vehemently pronounce.

A NATION CONCEIVED IN LIBERTY

The price controllers weren't the only ones whose vision of the economic nation clashed with that of the Founding Fathers. Other colonists similarly envisioned a moral economy enforced from below, designed to empower not those at the top, but those in the middle or at the bottom. Seamen were one of the most prominent of such groups and served as key players in the economic drama of the Revolution.

By the 1760s sailors and dockworkers were the largest single body of workers in the colonial port cities. Most sailors were technically "free" laborers, but the men who loaded and unloaded the ships at the wharves included indentured servants, bound apprentices, and slaves. While at sea, sailors' lives were grueling and rough. Captive for anywhere from three days to three years on a cramped, wet, wooden box, they were subject to the arbitrary authority of vicious ship captains—caught, as Marcus Rediker has put it, "between the devil and the deep blue sea." The sailors' most deeply felt grievance was impressment. Throughout the eighteenth century, the British navy met labor quotas on its ships by employing infamous press gangs, or crimps, who were well known to roam the streets of port cities across the Atlantic and kidnap sailors in dark alleys.[73] In one notorious 1757 raid on New York City, British officials captured eight hundred men, or one-quarter of the city's entire adult male population.[74]

By the 1760s sailors and their friends in port had learned to employ crowd action to crimp the press gangs themselves. In New York in July 1764, for example, a "mob" attacked a press gang aboard the *Chaleur,* "drawed its boat before the City Hall and there burnt her," liberated a forced impressee, and forced the captain to apologize.[75]

Sam Adams was impressed (in a different meaning of the word) by a famous 1747 incident when an irate Boston mob, swelling to several thousand and using "clubs, swords, and cutlasses," took one offending officer from the HMS *Lark* hostage, threw another in the town stocks, and placed guards at the city's piers to keep the rest from fleeing back to the ship. Adams later used the Knowles Riot, as it became known, to justify direct action in defense of freedom, including the Boston Tea Party.[76]

As colonists' hostility to British control grew, sailors merged anti-impressment with Stamp Act resistance. In October 1765 eighty enraged sailors, "armed with Cutlasses and Clubs" and shouting, "Liberty, Liberty & Stamped Paper," swarmed to the house of Henry Laurens, a wealthy Charleston merchant who they believed possessed hated imperial stamps, and only dispersed when they became convinced he was innocent.[77] In Wilmington, North Carolina, "A furious Mobb of Sailors" forced the local stamp official to resign.[78] In 1768 in Boston, as in ports throughout the colonies, sailors attacked customs ships in the exact way they had punished impressers: as Governor Thomas Hutchinson recounted one incident with horror, "a boat, belonging to the custom-house was dragged in triumph through the streets of the town, and burnt on the Common."[79]

These sailors were not dull, mindless brutes following more "broad-thinking" leaders whose names are familiar today. Not only did Revolutionary strategists such as Sam Adams, instead, follow and learn from the sailors, but seamen had well-developed political philosophies based on an intimate knowledge of global affairs. It was their labor, after all, that made possible the vast Atlantic trade of which the colonial merchants wanted a bigger, more independent piece, and they knew a lot about the trade question from the bottom up. They saw how the Stamp Act restricted the commerce upon which their livelihoods depended and resented it when customs officials suddenly started raiding the private caches in which they had traditionally secreted a few items for private trading.[80]

Historians Marcus Rediker and Peter Linebaugh have shown how swirling networks of mobile seamen—including escaped slaves and indentured servants—circulated throughout the Atlantic economy, crossing back and forth between England, Africa, the Caribbean, and the colonies. Of dozens of different national origins and ethnic backgrounds, speaking hundreds of different languages, they shared a popular language of freedom. As one seaman insisted to a crimp, you have "come with a press-gang to deprive me of my liberty. You have no right to impress me."[81]

They freely traded in tactics about how to achieve liberty, moreover. As Rediker and Linebaugh demonstrate, seamen briefly on shore in Boston, Philadelphia, or Charleston employed methods—such as the strike, invented in London in 1768—that they learned either while on shore in Liverpool, Bristol, or London, or from fellow-sailors while on ship. Escaped slaves, many of whom found work on ships, added their own ideas about rebelling against unjust authority.[82]

Sailors' ideas of the Revolution were in many ways complementary to those of the Founding Fathers. They hated repressive colonial officials. They believed in liberty and believed the British sought to deprive them of it. And they were the first past the post in rebelling against the Stamp Act, the Townshend Act, and eventually the British military in the 1760s and 1770s. But they weren't nationalists. Unlike the Fathers, they conceptualized their Revolution in international terms, and their economic nation could transcend boundaries of nation, colony, language, and often even race—if not gender—in a transnational solidarity of seafaring men and their shoreside comrades. They, too, hated trade restrictions but of a different sort altogether: the confining bonds of ship captains, naval officers, and corrupt recruiters. They, too, presage characters who will reappear: those who envision transnational alliances among working people, aligned against the wealthy and powerful—of whatever nation—who would push them downward.

FREE TRADE AND SLAVE TRADE

The colonists who knew best the full meaning of freedom were the half-million enslaved Americans and Africans, almost one-fifth of the colonies' entire population.[83] Their point of view on the Revolution reveals both the sharpest limits of Jefferson's, Washington's, and other slaveholders' vision of the economic nation and the deepest contradictions within it. Like the sailors, enslaved people challenged the Founding Fathers' definition of both free trade and of freedom itself.

"In every human Breast, God has implanted a Principle, which we call Love of Freedom," wrote the poet and former slave Phillis

Wheatley in Boston, exactly two months after the Tea Party. "It is impatient of Oppression, and pants for Deliverance." She captured perfectly the hypocrisy at the center of the Revolution: "the cry for Liberty, and the reverse Disposition for the exercise of oppressive Power over others," which, she concluded, "it does not require the Penetration of a Philosopher to determine."[84] Ex-slaves like Phillis Wheatley understood the contrast between Patrick Henry's cry "Give me liberty or give me death" and his insistence eight months later that "diligent patrols" try to stop runaway slaves.[85]

Slavery tainted the nonimportation movement from its inception. Northern merchants, when they wanted more homespun, had tried to get poor women to spin more in sweatshops. In the South, their patriotic counterparts assigned slave women to the task. In 1775, Virginia planter Robert Carter, for example, to acquire sufficient homespun "sett a part, Ten black Females the most Expert spinners belonging to me—they to be Employed in Spinning, solely."[86] By the war's end he had ten enslaved weavers and four spinners working at his plantation's "Linnen and Woolen Factory."[87] George Washington, similarly, put one free white woman and five "Negro Girls" to work spinning on his plantation.[88] The "American made cloth" in which the Founding Fathers from the Southern colonies strode about was largely the product of slave labor—and often, like that of the Northern factories, of child labor as well.

Enslaved people were also commodities themselves in the colonial economy, and the official nonimportation agreements explicitly discussed slaves as a traded item to be boycotted along with other goods. The Virginia agreement of 1770, for example, read:

> Fourthly. That we will not import or bring into the colony, or cause to be imported or brought into the colony, either by sea or land, any slaves, or make sale of any upon commission, or purchase any slave or slaves that may be imported by others after the 1st day of *November,* unless the same have been twelve months upon the continent.
>
> Fifthly. That we will not import any wines . . .[89]

Delegates to the First Continental Congress in 1774 likewise swore: "We will neither import nor purchase any slave imported after the first day of December next; after which time we will wholly discontinue the slave trade" until Parliament gave in to their demands.[90]

Were these vows to give up the traffic in human beings a first move to abolish slavery on moral grounds? Or were enslaved people just another boycotted product, like, say, the wine that followed on the list? W. E. B. Du Bois concluded in 1896 that it was a bit of both, identifying six factors behind the nonimportation movement's ban on the slave trade. First, since slavery had already failed economically in the middle and Northern colonies, many assumed it was on its last legs in the South. Second, Du Bois observed, "the new philosophy of 'Freedom' and the 'Rights of man,' which formed the corner-stone of the Revolution, made the dullest realize that, at the very least, the slave-trade and a struggle for 'liberty' were not consistent." Third, the signers were afraid of slave insurrections, especially if a war was about to break out. Fourth, in 1774 and '75 "nearly all the American slave markets were . . . overstocked"; as a result, "many of the strongest partisans" of nonimportation "were 'bulls' on the market, and desired to raise the value of their slaves by at least a temporary stoppage of the trade." Fifth, since the price of slaves was down, the slave-traders figured they would lose their investments in a war anyway, so they didn't oppose the measures. Finally, since the signers' goal was to punish Britain by withholding their trade, and the slave trade was a big part of it, a ban on slave trading would make the boycott all the more effective.[91]

The slaves themselves, like Phillis Wheatley, had no problem resolving the contradiction between slavery and the call for liberty. Soon after the Declaration of Independence, slaves began to petition for their legal freedom, artfully calling on the revolutionaries to adhere to their own principles. In January 1777, for example, Prince Hall, the founder of the first lodge of African American Masons, and seven other slaves appealed to the Massachusetts General Court. They claimed, "in Common with all other men a Natural and Unaliable Right to that freedom which the Grat Parent of the Unavers hath Bestowed equalley on all menkind" and asked the legislature to abolish slavery, so that the inhabitants of the states might be "No longer chargeable with the inconsistancey of acting themselves the part which thay condem and oppose in others."[92] Nineteen petitioners in New Hampshire similarly pleaded "that the name of slave may not more be heard in a land gloriously contending for the sweets of freedom."[93]

More often, slaves eloquently expressed their commitment to freedom by running away. The revolution offered an unprecedented opportunity, as the outbreak of war in 1775 produced huge troop movements involving British occupations, patriot reoccupations, and complex civilian relocations. British authority disintegrated, creating a chaos in which cracks for liberation suddenly opened up. Slaves' hopes rose dramatically. Individuals, families, and groups planned carefully the minute details of escape. They borrowed extra clothes or got literate friends to write false passes, secreted stockpiles in canoes and boats in which they planned to flee, and tapped into elaborate networks to learn about neighboring terrain, shipping schedules, and the location of friends or work in faraway places, as well as the war's exact progression.[94]

The rate at which slaves fled escalated dramatically after November 14, 1775, when Lord Dunsmore, the royal governor of Virginia, announced he would free any slaves or indentured servants who joined the British army.[95] An immense chaos of liberation erupted, as "boatloads of slaves" sought out British troops wherever they could, eventually to form an all-African American regiment with "Liberty to Slaves" emblazoned on their breasts.[96] In 1781, when British ships sailing up the Potomac reached George Washington's Mount Vernon estate, at least seventeen of his slaves seized the moment to run away.[97]

But armed terror surrounded all such efforts to flee, as South Carolina whites made clear in December 1775. Throughout the weeks after Dunsmore's pronouncement, dozens of escaped slaves had fled to Sullivan's Island in the mouth of the harbor at Charleston. There they took refuge in a small building known as the "pest house," which traders bringing slaves into the harbor had used to quarantine new imports. Some of the escapees passed on from there to nearby British ships. Others stayed, built shacks in the woods to live in, and used the island as a base for raids through which to free fellow slaves.

Late in the night of December 6 fifty or sixty white men, constituting the Charleston Council of Safety, swept in on the fugitives. At dawn, according to Charleston merchant Josiah Smith, Jr., they "sett Fire to the Pest House, took off some Negroes and Sailors Prisoners, Killed 50 of the former that would not be taken, and unfortunately lost near 20 that were unseen by them till taken off the Beach by the Men [of] Warrs Boats" (i.e., British ships).[98]

The white raiders were under the direction of Henry Laurens, president of the South Carolina Committee of Safety. A rich Charleston merchant, Laurens had made a fortune in the slave trade and himself estimated that his own slaves, "if sold at Public Auction tomorrow," would be worth at least £20,000. In November 1770, he had presided over the formation of the South Carolina Nonimportation Agreement and in 1777 would become president of the Continental Congress.[99]

The massacre at Sullivan's Island captures the rough odds slaves faced in achieving freedom and the outcome should they fail. That they tried, nonetheless, testifies to the depth of their commitment to freedom and to the horrors of enslavement at the hands of revolutionaries such as Laurens, Jefferson, and Washington. In South Carolina, Virginia, Eastern Pennsylvania, and all over the colonies somewhere around half of all adult enslaved men fled their masters during the war, women at a lower rate. In Virginia alone, Jefferson estimated, thirty thousand slaves escaped during the 1781 British invasion of the colony.[100]

For white patriots such as Patrick Henry, slavery was a vibrant metaphor for economic and political oppression at the hands of Britain. For enslaved African Americans, it was an all too real nightmare from which it was nearly impossible to wake up. Many leading white patriots grasped the contradiction inherent in their metaphorical cry for economic freedom. But most didn't. Jefferson, Washington, Laurens, these slaveholders were disturbed by slavery and discussed their ideas about how to end it—in the future. But they weren't so upset that they freed their slaves. Nor was their relationship to slavery a passive one. Washington and his paid agents successfully recaptured or bought back at least seven of his slaves who had run away during the war, and he spent years trying to kidnap back his wife Martha's favorite seamstress, Oney Judge, who escaped to New Hampshire after the war. He freed his slaves upon his death but not a moment before. Thomas Jefferson owned 175 people at the time of the Revolution; fifty years later, at the time of his death, he had added another 92.[101] The Founding Fathers' slaves judged correctly that the Revolution was only a brief opening in which to try to achieve freedom before the jaws of the Founders' new nation, its economy thriving on their enslaved labor, snapped shut around them like a vise.

TRADE AGREEMENTS

By the late 1770s the elite merchants, lawyers, and plantation masters who set the Revolution in motion had had enough of the messy democracy of popular control. Three years into the war, their slaves were running away, sailors were rioting rather than loading their ships, and poor women were refusing to spin their cloth. Artisans had their own ideas about how to manage society, and popular price control enforcers increasingly turned their sights on wealthy men just like themselves. The answer to Cadwallader Coldon's query as to "Whether the men who excited this seditious spirit in the People have it in their power to suppress it" was a resounding no.

Since the Declaration of Independence in 1776 the merchant and planter elite had been struggling to devise a new political system. These gentlemen had a vision for an American economic nation in which enlightened people like themselves—male, white, far-thinking—who had amassed tidy fortunes as merchants, landlords, slaveholders, or all three, would build a society that would further the development of their economic affairs, whether through burgeoning trade, the westward expansion of slavery, or incipient manufacturing enterprises. The new nation state would be their vehicle through which to achieve this and through which they would govern.

By the late 1770s that vision seemed to be slipping away. The Articles of Confederation, instituted in 1781, were proving unsatisfactory to their goals. Under the Articles, power rested with the state assemblies, which usually consisted of a single house, elected yearly. But individual states could easily veto pan-colonial agreements. Delegates to Congress often didn't show up or went home early. And, perhaps most important, artisans, small farmers, small traders, and other middling sorts kept getting elected to the state legislatures and then passing laws the big merchants and planters didn't like, such as debt relief. In 1784 an elite group of wealthy men came together in Philadelphia to solve their problems with a new Constitution. By 1790, they had persuaded the states to ratify it.

These wealthy men designed the Constitution to be deliberately less democratic than the Articles. Edmund Randolph, in his opening speech at the Constitutional Convention, openly acknowledged that "our chief danger arises from the democratic parts of our [state] constitutions. . . . None of the constitutions have provided a sufficient check against the democracy."[102] Randolph and the Framers designed the new document to shield the "better sort" of rich men from challenges by the less enlightened below. As Alexander Hamilton explained, "All communities divide themselves into the few and the many. The first are the rich and the well-born, the other the mass of the people. . . . The people are turbulent and changing; they seldom judge or determine right."[103] Amos Singletary, an elderly farmer who had been a member of the Massachusetts General Court, saw what was coming:

> These lawyers, and men of learning, and moneyed men, that talk so finely, and gloss over matters so smoothly, to make us poor illiterate people swallow down the pill, expect to get into Congress themselves; they expect to be the managers of this Constitution, and get all the power and all the money into their own hands, and then they will swallow up all us little folks.[104]

Indeed, power under the Constitution now resided in the centralized federal government, far away from the "little folks." The national government would have two legislative bodies. But each representative in the House now spoke for a sea of thirty thousand constituents, and he would now be elected every two years, not one (and he could only be a he). Senators got six-year terms, to shield the government still further from popular accountability, and they were elected not directly but by the state legislatures. A new, centrally powerful executive would be chosen not by the voters directly but by the electoral college. Now, only some of the people would decide, carefully shielded from the middling sorts and the riffraff.

The Founding Fathers also designed the Constitution to make possible federal economic policy. As historian Edmund S. Morgan has noted, the framers needed measures enabling "economic as well as political independence."[105] The Constitution gave the federal government new powers over currency, the relationship between debtors and creditors, and bankruptcy laws, for example. Equally important, it enabled Congress to make trade policy. From the merchants' point of view, two economic problems had emerged under the Articles of Confederation. First, state assemblies kept passing tariffs *between* the states, interfering with the merchants' flow of goods and profits. The Constitution abolished all inter-state trade barriers and instead created a new free trade zone among the former colonies—called the United States.

Second, under the Articles of Confederation, traders and diplomats had been frustrated by their inability to enact foreign trade policy. Especially after peace with Britain in 1783, merchants in the new United States had rushed to re-enter Atlantic trade, only to discover that the rules had changed. They had economic independence from Britain now, but they were on the outside of the British imperial system, no longer protected. To advance themselves, they wanted a powerful central government to negotiate new tariffs, trade treaties, and territorial acquisitions with Britain and the other European trading empires. The Constitution gave them that power.

The Revolution that began with an anti-import campaign, tying together colonial economic interests for the first time, thus ended with the consolidation of national trade policy. Concludes Edmund Morgan, "It is altogether fitting that the united states, which first acted together as a government when the Continental Congress undertook the non-importation, non-exportation, non-consumption Association of 1774, gained a permanent effective government when Americans again felt an urgent need to control trade."[106] And so the colonial Buy American movement climaxed in the new economic nation, and the merchants, lawyers, and planters largely succeeded in realizing their vision.

But the slaves did not. The Constitution, while it mandated the abolition of the slave trade by 1808, also created a fugitive slave agreement among the states that allowed slaveholders—such as George Washington—to kidnap runaway slaves who had crossed into states that had abolished slavery. Furthermore, by counting an enslaved American as three-fifths of a person in calculating congressional representation, the Constitution codified the disfranchisement of enslaved Americans.

Slaves were certainly not citizens of the new political nation. Nor were the poor spinning women or the female price controllers. Even the merchants and planters' wives, after all those spinning bees, didn't get to be fully enfranchised citizens. Nor did a vast chunk of the free male population, barred from voting because of property qualifications. The Buy American call was issued in the name of a new nation. But in the end, neither the sailors who moved its goods nor most of the working people—slave or free—who produced them could call the nation their own. Economic nationalism was for a different sort altogether.

One last group stood outside the borders claimed by the new nation, or newly entrapped within it, watching carefully and with alarm as its economic tentacles crept toward and around them. For Native American people, the new nation would mean genocide and the devastation of their own forms of economic life. "An empire is rising in America," Sam Adams declared two years before the Declaration of Independence, and proposed the swift annexation of Nova Scotia, Canada, and the fishing banks beyond.[107] For Adams and the other Founding Fathers, the new nation was from its inception designed as much to achieve conquest of lands and peoples to its North, West, and South, as it was to achieve liberation from across the seas to its East. Noah Webster published his first spelling book at the time of the Revolution, describing it as a tool for the intellectual ascendancy of "this infant Empire." Capturing perfectly the elite's unification of imperial ambition and Buy American sentiment, he proposed to "encourage genius in this country, [so that] the EMPIRE OF AMER-ICA will no longer be indebted to a foreign kingdom for books."[108]

ONE ECONOMIC NATION, INDIVISIBLE?

Those men who tiptoed onto the *Dartmouth,* the *Beaver,* and the *Eleanor* on the night of December 16, 1773, to dump British products into the sea thought they were just protesting British economic strictures. But within a few short years the tea protesters' defense of colonial products had produced an entirely new political entity, and with it the promise of a unified people. The rhetoric of the Revolution and the Constitution defined a new "Us"—Americans—and a new "Them," comprising not just the British, but the rest of the world. And it promised economic policies—including trade policies—for the benefit of all.

But the Constitution's evocative language of unity and perfection masked an imperfect democracy and deep ruptures of inequality. The "American products" it was designed, in part, to protect were as often as not produced by impoverished women working for sub-starvation wages or by enslaved people enriching the very men who wrote the Constitution. Price controllers, sailors, slaves—all brought notions of democratic control of the economy far broader and deeper than those of the Founding Fathers who ruled over them. The Revolution had settled little. It only launched the next two hundred years' debate over "whose economic nation?"

The Buy American movement of the Revolution had everything

to do with what would follow: it both set the political frame for discussions thereafter of the proper economy and placed trade relations at the center of the nation's self-definition. But before we rush to the present, we need to make a foray into the nineteenth century, to see how, as the nation gunned up to world industrial supremacy, Americans came to fight with such stunning ferocity over the seemingly dull question of foreign trade.

CHAPTER 2

The Class Politics of the Tariff
Or, Secrets of the Tariff Revealed

Ask any victim of a high school American history class what he or she thinks is the most boring subject imaginable in all U.S. history, and you will get the same reply: the tariff. Probably not a one could explain why the subject mattered or why the teacher had spent time on the subject. Yet for decades tariff debates remained central to the teaching of nineteenth-century U.S. history, and however much students might squirm or nap, "no generation of Americans has escaped the tariff controversy," as Sidney Ratner opened his 1972 history of the subject.[1] One well-known New York editor recalls how she made up little mnemonic devices in order to memorize all the requisite tariffs. Each was an imaginary rock-n-roll band, such as "Smoot Hawley and the High Barriers."

If we thought we would be spared in the late twentieth century, the controversies over the North American Free Trade Agreement (NAFTA) and the General Agreement on Trade and Tariffs (GATT) have brought home the continued centrality of trade policy and specifically the debate between protectionism, on the one hand, and free trade, on the other. In the nineteenth century, the tariff was, in truth, a hotly debated issue; only slavery and Reconstruction provoked more heated partisan debate. Following the Civil War, the tariff proved the single clearest issue demarcating the Democratic from the Republican Party, as the nation gunned up its manufacturing engines and emerged as an industrial powerhouse.

Most important for our story here, the nineteenth- and early-twentieth-century tariff conflict framed debates about the economic nation and its foreign relations ever since. Buy American campaigns disappeared during this period. But when they burst forth again in the 1930s and the 1970s, they would always be understood within the political debate over federal trade policy as it was cast in the nineteenth century. To understand that debate, then, a brief foray into the historical equivalent of lima beans is a necessary evil.

Those teachers don't turn out to be so misguided, after all. The tariff debate did strike at the center of the nation's basic economic vision. But the secrets of the tariff, revealed, show that the debate was not what it seemed. "The controversy was a maze of rhetoric, greed, and statecraft befogged by myth," one historian reflects.[2] When we clear off the fog, the tariff debate turns out to have been a clever smoke screen for the real issues at stake in the economic nation; and economic nationalism masked divergent class interests just as it had during the American Revolution. But the effectiveness of that smoke screen in obscuring the real dynamics of trade politics ever since makes it all the more important to understand.

PROTECTING INFANTS AND GIANTS

The trade debate began the moment the nation was founded, heated up over the course of the nineteenth century, and reached titanic proportions by its end. In one corner were the protectionists, whose position dated back to Alexander Hamilton's famous *Report on Manufactures* of 1791. Hamilton envisioned a nation of burgeoning domestic manufacturing enterprises, which would be protected from competition with British goods by a benevolent state subsidizing the growth of selected industries. He didn't advocate using tariffs to do so, but his report justified the use of the federal government to nurture private manufacturing interests.[3]

Congress imposed the first tariffs—taxes on imported goods—as soon as the Constitution was passed. These tariffs were designed not to protect industries, though, but to fund the federal government. Until the creation of a federal income tax in 1913, most of the federal budget came from tariffs. In 1790 they provided 99.9 percent of federal revenues, in 1860 94 percent. Between the Civil War and 1914, the federal government still obtained almost half of its income from tariffs.[4] This sort of tariff became known as a revenue tariff. Few politicians or business owners contested it.[5]

The fight erupted over what became known as a protective tariff. In the pre–Civil War era, its most famous proponent in the government was Henry Clay, the long-term Senator from Kentucky. One of those classic figures of nineteenth-century American history, Clay turns out to be more interesting than he might seem. Born in 1777, he had "a wonderful sense of style, a flare [sic] for the dramatic, a gift for the outrageous," one biographer writes.[6]

He was also a sharp and successful entrepreneur as well as politician. He liked to describe himself as having been left a penniless orphan after his father died, but in fact he grew up on a plantation with twenty-one slaves and, at the age of four, inherited two of his own slaves from his father. He built a thriving career as a lawyer, entrepreneur, and politician, eventually owning over six thousand acres of land sprawling across Kentucky, Illinois, Missouri, and Ohio; a variety of houses; a resort in Bath County; a hemp and cotton mill; a salt mine; and thirty-three enslaved people. He was also a director of, and lawyer for, Kentucky's two banks. Much of his Kentucky land was planted in hemp, grown for use in rope making, not entertainment. "Throughout his legislative career Clay never neglected what was necessary to benefit this industry," one biographer rhapsodizes. "He deserved his occasional title, the prince of hemp."[7]

The Prince of Hemp emerged by the 1820s as a strong proponent of economic nationalism enforced through high tariffs (including the tariff on hemp). Clay propounded his position most forcefully in a famous speech to Congress on March 30–31, 1824, that lasted two entire days. In it, he expounded the basic theory of a protective tariff supporting industrial development. Using the textile industry as his example, Clay argued that "The adoption of the restrictive system by the United States, by excluding the produce of foreign labor, would extend the consumption of American produce, unable, in the infancy and unprotected state of the arts, to sustain a competition with foreign fabrics."[8] This became known as the "infant industries" argument in favor of a high tariff.

Clay thought the government should take an active role in subsidizing industrial development. "There are few, if any governments which do not regard the establishment of domestic manufactures as a chief object of public policy."[9] In order to counteract British protectionism, in particular, he believed the United States needed to play the same game. "Let us counteract the policy of foreigners, and withdraw the support which we now give their industry and stimulate that of our own country."[10] Clay didn't reject the theory of free trade altogether but argued that "as long as other nations act on the protective system, [I will] continue in favor of this country taking care of its own industry in preference to fostering that of other nations."[11] He wanted high tariffs to establish "a genuine American System."[12] Clay soon became famous as the father of the "American System," of high protectionist tariffs and federal spending on internal improvements such as roads, canals, and railroads.

By the late nineteenth century protectionism had moved far beyond the infant industries argument. It was deeply entrenched at the center of American political theory and public policy. Not just infants and adults but industrial giants such as the iron and steel industry came to rely upon—and powerfully protect in Congress—a policy of high tariffs. Tariff rates on manufactured goods ranged between 40 and 50 percent; on iron, steel, and textiles they reached 100 percent.[13]

By the 1880s the strongest advocate of the protectionist position was Congressman William McKinley, the chair of the House Ways and Means Committee who would be elected president in 1896 on a high-tariff platform. McKinley's father and grandfather were both iron manufacturers, though McKinley himself was not. His congressional district in Ohio, however, was replete with coal mines, iron mills, blast furnaces, and manufacturing concerns.[14]

McKinley explained his support for protectionism succinctly in a speech to Congress on May 18, 1888:

> Our kind of tariff makes the competing foreign article carry the burden, . . . supply the revenue; and in performing this essential office it encourages at the same time our own industries and protects our own people in their chosen employments. That is the mission and purpose of a protective tariff.[15]

By contrast, "Free foreign trade admits the foreigner to equal privileges with our own citizens. It invites the product of cheap foreign labor to this market in competition with the domestic product, representing higher and better paid labor."[16] McKinley drew a strict line between Americans, "Us," and foreigners—"Them."

> Let American labor . . . manufacture American products. . . . This Government is made for Americans, native-born and naturalized; and every

pound, every bushel, every ton, every yard of foreign product that comes into this country to compete with ours deprives American labor of what justly belongs to it.[17]

McKinley also insisted class harmony would reign under the tariff: "There is no conflict of interests and should be none between the several classes of products, and consumers in the United States. Their interests are one, and interrelated and interdependent. That which benefits one benefits all."[18] Those who opposed the tariff, McKinley charged, fostered such conflict. Their speeches were "calculated to create an antagonism where none existed. The farmer, the manufacturer, the laborer, the tradesman, and the producer and consumer all have a common interest in the maintenance of a protective tariff. All are alike and equally favored by the system which you [i.e., tariff reductionists] seek to overthrow."[19]

The protectionist position, then, mushroomed from the simple "tariff for revenue only" at the beginning of the century, to Henry Clay's American system protecting "infant industries" by the 1820s, to McKinley's full-blown protection of powerfully entrenched industrial corporations by the 1880s. Both Clay and McKinley wanted an activist state developing an industrial nation. Clay with his hemp mill, McKinley with his constituents' iron mills—both also expounded economic theories whose outcome would directly benefit industrialists' interests. By the end of the century Clay's earlier advocacy of a protection of U.S. manufactures against the powerful imperialism of Britain had become protection of the nation's own powerful industrial giants who, in the theories of McKinley and most high tariff advocates of his time, would themselves protect U.S. workers from the cheapening of their labors.

IN TRADE WE TRUST

In the other camp lay the free traders and others who opposed high tariffs. The protectionists triumphed over them, politically, in the nineteenth century. But the free traders would come to dominate in the twentieth, in part through their colonization of the economics profession, which would come to heap volumes of scorn on the foolish, backward protectionists.

Two theorists of political economy, Adam Smith and David Ricardo, fathered the free trade position. In his famous book *The Wealth of Nations*—published with spectacular coincidence in 1776—Smith argued that societies functioned best when economic actors were free to pursue unfettered self-interest. The "invisible hand" of the market would then regulate supply and demand to achieve the optimum, laissez faire economy. What might look like unregulated individual greed was, rather, the common good.[20]

In 1817 David Ricardo extended Smith's free market principles to trade policy with the theory of comparative advantage. According to Ricardo, each country prospered best if it produced and traded those articles in which it held a "comparative advantage" relative to other countries, and then imported those goods in which it had a disadvantage. The key was each nation's *relative* advantage. Ricardo gave as his famous example, evoked in economics textbooks ever since, English cloth and Portuguese wine. Since England excelled at textiles, Portugal at wine, both would come out ahead if they specialized. If, instead, Portugal used tariffs to encourage a domestic textile industry, and England used tariffs to encourage vintners, all would suffer.[21]

Most nineteenth-century politicians who opposed protectionism were not orthodox free traders, although they invoked laissez-faire theories to justify their positions at times. They never proposed to abolish tariffs altogether, but they did want to reduce them. Gradually, during the 1870s and '80s low-tariff voices gained in strength and began to include powerful Northern economic interests. Then, in 1887, launching what became known as "The Great Tariff Debate of 1888," President Grover Cleveland dramatically broke with the protectionist orthodoxy to attack high tariffs directly and, more personally, their advocate William McKinley.

Unlike Henry Clay, Grover Cleveland does not turn out to be more interesting than he might seem.[22] A former sheriff from Erie County, New York, Cleveland rose in four swift years to become mayor of Buffalo in 1881 and then U.S. president in 1885. He is largely known to posterity as the only president to serve two terms not in succession (1885–1889 and 1893–1897).[23]

In a famous message to Congress on December 6, 1887, Cleveland dramatically attacked the tariff: "Our present tariff laws, the vicious inequitable and illogical source of unnecessary taxation, ought to be at once revised and amended."[24] Cleveland cast the tariff as an onerous tax imposed on all Americans as consumers, driving up the cost of living in order to feather the nests of a few powerful industries; "a burden upon those with moderate means and the poor, the employed and unemployed, the sick and well, and the young and old . . . a tax which with relentless grasp is fastened upon the clothing of every man, woman and child in the land."[25] High tariffs also impaired the advances of American business abroad, Cleveland cautioned Congress. Lowering the tariff wouldn't hurt manufacturers. Rather, he argued, "our people might have the opportunity of extending their sales beyond the limits of home consumption, saving them from the depression, interruption of business, and loss caused by a glutted domestic market," in the process "affording their employees more certain and steady labor with its resultant quiet and contentment."[26]

By the turn of the century, opposition to the tariff by politicians such as Cleveland had grown into a powerful reform cause in which opponents cast tariff advocates as special interests sucking the economic blood of the American people. Middle-class social reformers, joined into the Progressive movement of the 1890s and 1900s, attacked the monolithic "trusts"—monopolistic national corporations—that had amalgamated in the late nineteenth century. Investigative journalists known as "muckrakers" led the charge. Ida Tarbell, for example, in 1904 published a scathing attack on Standard Oil that swept the company into disrepute and Tarbell into public prominence.[27] Tarbell hated the tariff. When her editor at the *American Magazine* in 1906 asked her to write a series on the tariff, she said yes. "I so despised the prohibitive tariff that I was willing to try. . . . It looked in 1906 as if the Day of Judgment was near, and I asked nothing better than to be on the jury." She eventually published her judgment in 1911 as a book, *The Tariff in Our Times.*[28]

Tarbell saw the tariff as a creature of the trusts. "Freed from foreign competition . . . these home manufacturers have by a succession of guerrilla campaigns . . . corralled industry after industry so completely that they could control its output and at once cheapen the quality and increase its price."[29] Yes, she granted, wages and working conditions were better in the United States than in Europe. "But it is only the blind and deaf who do not realize that the same forces of allied greed and privilege which have made life so hard for so many in the Old World are at work, seeking to repeat here what they have done there."[30] The tariff-protected trusts were certainly no protectors of American workers. "The only chance of peace and of permanency in this country lies in securing for the laboring classes in this country an increasing share of increasing wealth."[31] For Tarbell and other reformers, the tariff was a hideous tax on consumers imposed to fatten the trusts.

Tarbell devoted the final installment of her series to Rhode Island. "Rhode Island to-day is a tariff-made state, and as such should offer us ample material for an easy analysis of what the American system of protection, given ample encouragement, does for a community." It did not, she made clear, benefit working people. She detailed the long hours, low wages, high turnover, filthy toilets, air choked with cotton dust, and child labor, all of which flourished in the "tariff-made" textile industry of Rhode Island. Tarbell also underscored that "the first feature of the textile industry of Rhode Island is that the operatives are not Americans; they are distinctly foreigners—new-come foreigners," from Italy, Scotland, Russian, Portugal, Canada, Ireland, and elsewhere. "We have the surprising fact then, that as far as the benefits of the textile tariffs are concerned in Rhode Island, if the laborer gets them, it is a foreign laborer." Tarbell saw how amorphous were lines between "Us" and "Them" in a nation whose economy was burgeoning precisely because of immigrant labor.[32]

Overall, tariff opponents in the nineteenth century were a messier lot than the protectionists with their tidy arguments proceeding in a logical progression. At the theoretical level tariff reductionists wanted the "free hand of the market" to arrange prosperity through unfettered natural processes, not the nurturance of ineffectual economic weaklings. At the practical political level at which Grover Cleveland operated, tariff reductionists attacked protection as an inappropriate subsidy for the profits of a few industrial giants, impeding the expansion of American markets abroad. All promised that freer trade would unleash a flood of harmony and prosperity. Only Tarbell hinted that more fundamental measures of redistribution might be necessary.

IMPERIAL CONSENSUS
Here we have, then, both sides of the conflict that wracked nineteenth- and early-twentieth-century national politics. It's hard, at this distance, to capture the vitriol and passion with which each side cast

its opponents and the lavish prosperity each promised its adherents. But as the personal histories of both Clay and McKinley illustrate, the tariff controversy—like the nonimportation movement—was not an abstract game in which individuals chose sides out of pure principle or entirely disinterested concern for others.

The tariff debate was always deeply embedded in nineteenth-century sectional political interests. To put it simply, before the Civil War, Northern manufacturers wanted high protectionist tariffs to subsidize industrial development; Southern slaveholding planters wanted low tariffs to keep agricultural exports flowing freely into foreign countries without corresponding tariffs at the other end. Southerner John Randolph, for example, during an 1824 debate accused Northerners of using the tariff to reduce the South to "a state of worse than colonial bondage."[33] John C. Calhoun viewed the tariff "as a lever for lifting extra profits out of the south's pockets," in the words of one historian. These slaveholders in Congress called the high 1828 tariff bill the "Tariff of Abominations."

In 1832 tensions between Northerners and Southerners over trade policy reached an early climax, known as the "nullification crisis." Incensed by another high tariff passed that year, South Carolina legislators held a convention in Charleston and announced that as far as South Carolina was concerned, the 1828 and 1832 federal tariff laws were null and void. Overtly defying the federal government, they refused to allow the collection of any tariffs within the state's borders. Eventually, in 1833, congressional Northerners blinked and passed a new bill that gradually reduced tariffs.

After the Civil War party alignments shifted, but the basic partisan conflict over the tariff remained. The Democratic and Republican Parties dominated national politics and lined up eagerly on either side of the tariff question. By the 1880s the Republicans—led by McKinley—were the "party of the tariff." The Democrats—led by Grover Cleveland—opposed it in the name of the people. Throughout the 1880s, 1890s, and the first two decades of the twentieth century, the tariff question was the single biggest issue demarcating the two parties.

But the first secret of the tariff was that underneath that titanic conflict lay a deep consensus. For all their bickering, both sides by the 1870s believed the nation's economy should be a capitalist one. Both sides believed in massive industrialization. Both sides believed in a model of ever-expanding growth. The question was not whether the infants should become giants, or whether the giants would produce prosperity, but which were the most efficient giants, which sectors of the economy they should harken from, and whether the state should help them or not. James L. Huston, reviewing the debate in the *Journal of American History,* concludes:

> Protectionists lauded property rights as the basis of civilization, urged the lower classes to climb the ladder of success, . . . and deprecated any attempt of laborers to form unions. . . . The free trade position . . . was not different from that of the protectionists. They too were stout supporters of capitalism, and they envisaged greater wages for the employee arising from the expansion of business.[35]

Party alignments and positions on the tariff did, to a certain extent, reflect the divergent interests of particular sectors of the economy. Export-dependent agricultural interests, for example, feared that high tariffs might prompt other nations to retaliate with their own tariffs against U.S. agricultural products. Manufacturers, for their part, did not always line up on the Republican, high-tariff side. Abram Hewitt, congressman and iron manufacturer, for example, wanted to import cheap raw materials for his rolling mills and backed the low-tariff Democrats.[36] Yet all camps assumed a larger framework of industrial capitalism led by corporate growth; and many corporate financial interests used both parties to pursue their goals. In fact, "there were bankers and finance capitalists on both sides of the [tariff] contest," as muckraker Matthew Josephson revealed in a 1938 exposé, *The Politicos.* "There were coal and iron industrialists on both sides. . . . In the case of Henry Havemeyer of the Sugar Trust, and the Standard Oil men, the practice of making contributions to both parties was . . . openly reported."[37]

The second secret of the tariff was that the debate was really about empire. The problem inherent in the model of industrial capitalist development with which both parties agreed, was that protected infants got big and started to saturate the market for their products within the United States. If they were to keep growing, they needed to expand. The corporations' solution was to expand overseas. "Many of our manufacturers have outgrown or are outgrowing their home markets . . . and the expansion of our foreign trade is their only promise of relief," Theodore Search, president of the National Association of Manufacturers, pleaded in 1897.[38] But to expand overseas, U.S.-based firms needed to leap over other nations' own protective tariffs, instituted to protect their economies from precisely such interloping giants from overseas.

In the early nineteenth century, the United States possessed only a small and not particularly competitive industrial base. It was in no position to compete, say, with Great Britain. Protectionism therefore constituted a win-win policy for manufacturers. But by the late nineteenth century the United States was emerging as one of the world's major industrial powerhouses. Its share of world trade grew from 6 percent in 1868 to 11 percent by 1913. By 1902 U.S. steel and iron production exceeded the combined output of Great Britain and Germany.[39] U.S. firms were bursting their domestic economic seams. They lusted after access to both the raw materials of other nations and markets for manufactured goods within those countries. Their problem, when it came to trade policy, was that they wanted the best of both worlds: they wanted the protection against imports that would be afforded by high tariffs and the ability to freely export that would be afforded by low tariffs. As historian Walter LaFeber describes McKinley, "He wanted it all."[40]

One economist sums up the tariff debate succinctly: "protectionism is for the weak, free trade is for the strong."[41] Now the United States was the strong, and the big firms wanted a way to keep getting stronger without giving up what had made them so strong. That was what they were really arguing about in 1888: how to tinker with the tariff to pull that off.

By the late nineteenth century U.S. corporate and financial interests came up with four solutions to their problem of foreign market access and economic growth; one old, three new. The old one was territorial expansion: take over new lands and peoples and make them into part of the United States. Following this path, in 1867 the United States bought Alaska from Russia for $7.2 million and in 1898 took over Hawaii. The second solution was to arrange individual trade deals with other countries known as "reciprocity agreements," in which the United States swapped specific tariff barriers—on sugar or coffee, for example—in exchange for market access or raw mate-

rials. In the mid and late nineteenth century the United States began
to experiment with short-lived reciprocity agreements—with Canada in 1854, for example, then with Brazil, Guatemala, Nicaragua,
and other Latin American nations in 1890.[42]

But the corporations that shaped U.S. trade and foreign policy
wanted more. They wanted broad access to markets and raw materials
all over Latin America and Asia, and to achieve that they were willing
to go to war. Battling Spain and the people of Cuba, Puerto Rico, and
the Philippines in 1898, the United States emerged as the victorious
"liberator" of all three islands. Eschewing both independence for
their peoples, on the one hand, and old-style direct colonialism, on
the other, it devised a new course: U.S.-dominated protectorates that
would guarantee the United States economic access to both Latin
America and Asia, ensured by a "friendly"—but permanent—military presence.

The big prize, though, for U.S. exporters and financiers, then as
now, was China. U.S. foreign policy strategists saw Alaska, Hawaii,
and the Philippines all as stepping stones to the vast market and resources potentially available, they believed, in China. But China was
too big to buy or invade. In an effort to claim China as its own, U.S.
corporations devised their fourth and final approach to economic
empire, known as the "Open Door" policy. In a series of 1899 missives to Great Britain, Germany, Russia, Japan, Italy, and France,
known as the "Open Door Notes," the United States unilaterally announced that thereafter all the imperial powers would have equal access to the China market, without interference.

The 1880s and '90s were the fulcrum, in sum, of a long shift in
U.S. trade relations. Imperial expansion itself wasn't new, as Native
Americans and Mexicans knew well. Trade expansion to nominally
independent nations at gunpoint was. As LaFeber summarizes:
"Americans were finished with land expansion from sea to sea. They
were confident now in supremacy over much of the Western Hemi-
sphere and embarked on an imperialist course in parts of Asia and Africa."[43] In the 1870s, "three hundred years of unfavorably balanced
American trade reversed . . . and the U.S. headed for world economic
supremacy."[44] Although the United States would not achieve full supremacy for fifty years, the trade policies necessary to do so were now
in place.

CLASS, DISMISSED

But the third and biggest secret obscured by the debate was that the tariff, while it reflected a real contest over economic advantages, was also a smoke screen for class conflict.

Listen, again, to the arguments both sides employed in the tariff debate: William McKinley assured Congress that "There is no conflict of interest and should be none between the several classes. . . . All are alike and equally favored by the [high tariff] system."[45] In the other corner, Grover Cleveland promised that lowering the tariff would simultaneously benefit manufacturers and guarantee "their employees more certain and steady labor with its resultant quiet and contentment."[46] Both men acknowledged seemingly divergent class interests, only to assert that their chosen trade policy would resolve them to create common interests. Both McKinley and Cleveland acknowledged that something was amiss in American society that the high or low tariff would solve.

These politicians preached harmony because, by the 1880s, class tensions were seething in the United States. The economic future of the country was up for grabs. There was no consensus in U.S. society regarding capitalism, industrialization, or empire, and certainly no consensus that the industrial giants were doing anything but trampling working people and farmers like so many grapes.

In a series of mass social movements known as the "Great Upheaval," conflict between working people, farmers, and small business people, on the one hand, and the new corporations and financiers, on the other, reached a climax in the late 1880s. In the Populist movement small farmers rose up against monopolistic railroads and financiers to demand currency reform. In newly formed national trade unions, skilled white male workers joined together to protect themselves against wage cuts, the speedup, and technological obsolescence. In 1886 they founded the American Federation of Labor (AFL). By that same year several hundred thousand working men and women had joined a more broadly conceived, multi-ethnic workers' organization called the Knights of Labor, with locals in almost every town in the United States. Acknowledging the scale on which the nation's economic future was being contested, in 1883 the U.S. Senate created a special Committee on Relations Between Labor and Capital, which traveled throughout the country, interviewed dozens of witnesses, and produced a four-volume, 4,000-page report.[47] Tensions climaxed in May 1886 when a saboteur's bomb went off at a peaceful rally for the eight-hour day in Chicago's Haymarket Square. In response the federal government and employers across the nation swept down in a brutal wave of repression that swiftly crushed both working people's organizations and their rising spirit of utopian reform.

Class conflict escalated, in other words, in precise correlation with the official insistence in national politics that the most important question was the tariff and that harmony would reign if only voters adhered to the correct position on trade policy. The point is not that class conflict caused the tariff debate, but that it was far safer to argue over trade policy than over class power, and the men who ran Congress were anxious to deflect the conversation away from fundamental questions about the premises and purposes of the economic nation. "The political uses of the tariff were infinite," concludes Tom Terrill in a study of tariff politics. "Both major parties employed the tariff issue to unify an increasingly discordant society."[48]

The last thing the party leaders wanted was the specter Tarbell raised: redistribution of wealth. The tariff, by diverting—if not diffusing—class tensions into acceptable channels, promised to ensure prosperity for workers and farmers alike but without the messy prospect of challenging the rich or the new corporations. As James L. Huston has argued in analyzing the Pennsylvania Republican Party's strategy in 1858, "the tariff provided a measure that could absorb working-class anger and channel the laborers' activities away from economic and social change and into acceptable political behavior."[49]

The proof was in the policies. Both sides promised that their respective approaches to trade policy would economically benefit all working people. But in practice both opposed the concrete measures and organizations through which working people sought to obtain their share of the national wealth. Protectionist Henry Clay, for example, promised economic growth but did not use the wealth he obtained from the hemp tariff to emancipate his slaves; rather, he emerged as one of the nation's most vocal defenders of slavery. William McKinley promised a "full dinner pail" of working-class prosperity, but he headed "the party of business" into which corporations and financiers poured millions. As congressman and then president, he sat back while the corporations merged into the monstrous trusts

of the late nineteenth century. In 1895 he was the featured speaker at
the founding convention of the National Association for Manufacturers in 1895, whose members spearheaded a national "open shop"
drive against trade unions.[50] As for Grover Cleveland, he turns out to
be famous for something, after all: he was the first president to call out
federal troops against the labor movement in the Pullman Strike of
1894. James L. Huston concludes, after a survey of both sides in the
national tariff debate, "Neither the protectionists nor the free traders
believed in labor unions or collective bargaining."[51]

US AND THEM

To fully grasp how narrow that consensus was, we need finally to look
at the tariff conflict from the other side of the class divide. Working
people—as they had during the American Revolution—had their
own ideas about the economic nation and the direction in which it
was developing.

A few workers joined the tariff debate at a national level, such as
John Jarrett. Ida Tarbell detested him: "There [was] no more hearty
and conscienceless supporter of prohibitive tariffs."[52] Born in 1843
in Wales, where he worked as an iron puddler, Jarrett emigrated to
Pennsylvania in 1862 and rose to the presidency of the Amalgamated
Association of Iron and Steel Workers, one of the new, national-level
trade unions that would later form the American Federation of Labor (AFL).[53]

Jarrett was one of the many unionists who testified in 1883 before
the Senate Committee on the Relations Between Labor and Capital.
He was unabashedly pro-tariff. "Our organization is strongly a tariff
organization, from the fact that we know that we do get better wages
on account of the tariff," Jarrett began.[54] "We claim as workingmen
that the object of the tariff is not merely to protect infant industries,
but to protect labor employed in carrying on those industries."[55] He
specifically contested the argument that the tariff subsidized trusts:
"It is all nonsense to say that the tariff builds up monopolies, because
what the tariff has done in this country free trade has done in England. In other words, the manufacturing concerns in England, as a
rule, are larger by far than those in this country."[56]

Jarrett endorsed a model of class harmony. "As a workingman I
have always maintained that there is no conflict between labor and

capital. . . . We recognize that the employer and the workingmen must come together. Their interests are identical."[57] At the same time he acknowledged employers' constant desire to undercut their employees' position: "The majority of them [i.e., iron and steel manufacturers], where they have the workingmen in their power, the tariff or anything else will make but very little difference as to the wages they pay. . . . Hence I favor organization among the workingmen of our country."[58]

But Jarrett's concept of the solidarity of "workingmen" was a narrow one. He allied himself harmoniously with "American capital," but his union admitted only skilled white male workers of Northern and Western European descent, shutting out even the hundreds of thousands of Southern and Eastern European immigrant men who by the 1880s labored in brutal unskilled jobs in the iron and steel industry. "The class of common labor that largely predominates in the mills . . . are foreigners—Hungarians, Poles, Italians, Bohemians," he told the Senate committee disdainfully, "men that really don't know the difference . . . between light work and heavy, or between good wages and bad wages."[59]

Jarrett's path as an economic nationalist led him deeper and deeper into the employers' camp. In 1887 he quit the union to work as a lobbyist for the Tin Plate Association, in which capacity he successfully lobbied Congress for a high tariff on Welsh plate—that is, against the products of his own former union brothers in Wales. He served as American consul in Birmingham, England, for three years and then returned to work as an executive for the Sheet Steel Association from 1892 to 1900.[60] John Jarrett's counterparts will appear again in the twentieth century: labor unionists who venture so far into nationalist partnerships with employers that they come to align themselves against workers, even unionized ones, abroad.

Even in the late nineteenth century Jarrett was not alone. Trade unionists from a range of industries formed partnerships with their employers to lobby for protection of their particular products, agreeing that high tariffs would redound to working people's benefit. New England textile workers, for example, emerged as vehement advocates of high tariffs to keep out the products of British textile workers. Skilled hat workers, too, joined with their employers to keep out foreign headwear. "Such activity reinforced the [hat finishers'] union's traditional motto, 'the interests of journeyman and employers are inseparable,'" historian David Bensman comments, "a belief that certainly militated against class consciousness."[61]

Samuel Gompers of the cigarmakers' union, who emerged in the 1880s as president of the new American Federation of Labor, liked protectionism, too. But he didn't think it went far enough. "If it performed what its advocates claim for it, the protection of labor, it is of the greatest importance and should be adopted," he argued in a report to his union on the founding convention of the Federation of Organization Trades and Labor Unions, the AFL's predecessor, in 1881. "But . . . while the industries are protected by preventing the importation of foreign manufactured articles, *it does not prevent the importation of the cheapest and most servile labor*" [emphasis in original]. Gompers equated foreign products with foreign workers, especially Asian ones, and wanted to keep out both. In his very next line he reported approvingly: "Resolutions were adopted declaring the presence of and competition of Chinese with free white labor as extremely dangerous and demanding the passage of laws entirely prohibiting their importation." Gompers, with his depiction of foreign workers as "imports" to be banned and his racial demarcations between working people, will also reappear in our story, all too soon.[62]

But other working people were utterly unimpressed by the promise of protectionism and were not about to trot out their votes on behalf of their employers' pro-tariff arguments, as an October 25, 1884, poem in the *Journal of United Labor,* entitled "My Vote," captured eloquently. The poem's narrator laments the "ten long years" he has labored "in old Jimmie [sic] Dobson's mill" while watching his children go shoeless and his beloved Mollie's hair turn gray:

> . . . the boss came round to-day
> With a ticket—I have torn it—
> Saying, "you must vote this way."

> "This," he said, "is for the tariff.
> And will keep your wages high;
> You can hold them where they are if
> You are true and stand right by."

> "Where they are?" I silent queried,
> But no least reply I made—
> Mollie, I am weak and wearied,
> And shall vote it, I'm afraid.

By the poem's end the narrator has determined to "keep a freeman's will" and vote according to his own, not his boss's command— against the tariff.[63]

Jarrett, Gompers, and the protectionist hat finishers—all founders of the AFL—represented only one set of workers who were building collective power in the 1880s. The AFL's great rival was the Knights of Labor, which counted between 700,000 and a million members in 1886. In contrast to the narrowly defined, exclusionary craft unions in the American Federation of Labor, the Knights admitted people of all occupations—housewives, shoemakers, domestic servants, un-skilled ditch diggers—everyone except lawyers, liquor dealers, spec-ulators, and bankers (whom they deemed "parasites," as opposed to "the producers"). The Knights rejected "the wages system," seeking instead "noble equality" advanced through education, arbitration, and alternative utopian institutions such as producers' and con-sumers' cooperatives.[64]

The Knights' newspaper was replete with forthright arguments about the tariff question, written with the wonderful literary flair of nineteenth-century oratory. Ralph Beaumont, the Knights' corre-spondent in Washington, D.C., for example, reported in April 1890 of his attendance in Congress at the opening of the usual heated parti-san debate on the tariff question. Beaumont's response was a big yawn. "I told these same politicians during the last session that the tariff issue had about as much to do with settling of the burdens that the working people of this country were struggling under as my yellow dog—and I did not have a yellow dog." When a reader subsequently queried what Beaumont had meant in saying "the tariff . . . was not the real is-sue before the country," Beaumont expanded: "The question of the tariff has nothing to do with settling the labor question as it is before the American people today."[65]

On October 25, B. C. Stickney of Brooklyn, New York, put it more bluntly. "Certain capitalists give it out that the tariff is a benefit to the workingmen. But since when have the workingmen been in the habit of looking to capitalists for advice? When was any nefarious scheme ever perpetrated upon any community without a lot of cant about benevolence to the workingman?" Stickney didn't buy em-ployers' pro-tariff arguments, didn't think rejecting foreign goods was necessary, and thought free trade was just fine—although he was no laissez-faire capitalist. He thought the government should abolish the Customs House but nationalize the railroads. "We are sometimes favored with the bugaboo that it is wicked for us to use foreign made goods because it makes less work for American workers," he mocked. "It is really too bad, isn't it, that with our big country, fabulously rich with unused natural resources, we can find nothing to do unless we first shut ourselves off from commerce with foreigners." Stickney concluded by quoting a "shining light" of the labor party in Minnesota: the tariff was "only a scheme devised by the old parties to throw dust in the eyes of laboring men."[66]

For William Saul, of Jersey City, New Jersey, writing in the *Journal of the Knights of Labor* that same year, the tariff was a scheme to fatten the rich at the workers' expense. In an article headlined "The Fetich of Protection. The Workers, Not the Drones, Pay the Tariff," he attacked "the wholesale plunder of the community under the name of protection." The tariff "neither protects those it claims to nor benefits those it professes to," he charged, because "the levy made upon the community . . . never reaches their hands, but filters into the pockets of individual manufacturers and bloated corporations." He estimated that the government had taken in $600 million in duties on imports in 1889, "not one penny of which goes into the pockets of the community, of all shades and grades who work for a living, but to swell the ranks of the sensuous rich, and add to the millions of starving poor, whose daily toil becomes worse and worse under the fetich of protection."[67]

As did Ida Tarbell, these Knights cast the tariff as a bloodsucking tax on the workers, profiting only the rich. Two years later, the famous Homestead Strike gave concrete form to their charges. By the 1890s, Andrew Carnegie's gigantic steel corporation had become a classic beneficiary of the high tariff. In 1892, just after receiving a new round of tariff protection from Washington, Carnegie, through his manager, Henry Clay Frick, announced a 22 percent pay cut at his Homestead steel mill in Pennsylvania. The mill's skilled workers, represented by the Amalgamated Association of Iron and Steel Workers, balked; so Frick simply shut down the plant, locking out the union. When the workers still wouldn't give in and successfully scared away strikebreakers, Frick hired three hundred Pinkerton detectives, armed them with rifles, and on July 6 sent them on barges upriver to the plant. When they tried to land, an armed battle broke out. The Pinkertons fired into a crowd of women and children, strikers fought back, and when the battle was over, nine strikers and three Pinkertons were dead. Eventually, the Pennsylvania state militia arrived and broke the strike. The steel workers' union was shattered for decades.[68]

Observers who took the strikers' side were quick to link Carnegie's treatment of his employees to his advocacy of high tariffs. Protectionism, the *Pittsburgh Catholic* concluded—with reference to Carnegie's famed philanthropic benevolence—"has become the instrument of the capitalist, while masquerading as a philanthropist and proclaiming its mission to be the protection of the American workman and American industries."[69] More graphically, a cartoon in *The World* two days before the battle, entitled "De-fence at Homestead," depicted a fence with a cannon mounted in it, labeled "protection." On the far side of the fence lay a steel mill with flags atop it marked "Reduced Wages" and "High Tariff" and a caricatured rich man in top hat. He pointed down at the cannon, which was aimed at a symbolic steel worker on the near side of the fence. A second cartoon, the day after the battle, more explicitly pictured Andrew Carnegie, with a Pinkerton behind him, pointing a rifle at a striker. Both sat on top of a wall marked " 'Homestead'!!! Mill. PROTECTED BY THE MCKINLEY TARIFF AND A PINKERTON ARMY." Below, the symbolic workman, standing nobly tall, had planted his boot on a notice reading, "Note to Protected American Workmen: . . . Wages Reduced 30%." All these commentators played off the concept of "protection": high tariffs ostensibly protected workers and employers alike; but in actuality, they only protected the bosses, and the bosses were using Pinkerton thugs to protect themselves from the workers. Protectionism didn't produce prosperity—it only provided a "defense" against workers asserting their democratic rights to act collectively, defend their standard of living, and, in the end, to define "protection" quite differently.[70]

John Jarrett, Samuel Gompers, and other protectionist trade unionists had drawn a different line between "Them" versus "Us": for them, American workers and employers were on one side, foreign products and foreign workers on the other. For them, protectionism led to a partnership of nationalist capitalists and native-born workers. The *Journal of United Labor's* correspondents and the Homestead strikers' defendants, by contrast, drew their line along a different axis:

"Them" meant the oppressive capitalists and their protectionist allies, "Us" meant working people. But members of their camp, while framing trade issues more explicitly on behalf of working people, could also be quick to exclude "foreigners" from their concept of "the workers" and to attack such foreigners whether within or beyond U.S. borders. Both Homestead cartoons, for example, attacked Carnegie not only for turning guns on U.S. workers but also for encouraging, on the sly, immigration of foreign labor. In the first cartoon, the boss in his top hat opens a door in his fence to admit "pauper labor"; in the second, a leaflet on Carnegie's protectionist wall reads "Wanted 4,000 Foreign Pauper Laborers."[71]

The cartoons' charges contained a grain of truth: Employers such as Carnegie were indeed eager to undercut domestic workers by recruiting immigrants. But many U.S. unions themselves rejected foreign-born fellow workers, once inside the United States, from their organizations, especially immigrants from Eastern and Southern Europe, Asia, or Mexico, along with native-born African Americans. The Amalgamated Association of Iron and Steel Workers—John Jarrett's union—which represented Homestead's striking skilled workers, for example, was notorious for excluding Eastern and Southern European workers. The Knights of Labor, too, could sink to the lowest of anti-immigrant lows. On the West Coast, the Knights blamed Chinese immigrants for white workers' plight and degenerated into a violent anti-Chinese movement.[72]

The great irony was that most of these immigrant-bashers were themselves immigrants. Samuel Gompers was born in London of Dutch-Jewish parents; John Jarrett was born in Wales; and the leaders of the anti-Chinese packs in San Francisco were Irish immigrants, proving themselves to be "good" Americans by turning around and attacking other immigrants. "American" workers and "immigrant" workers were in reality one and the same. By the 1880s and 1890s most working people in the United States had been born outside the United States or else their parents had. Herbert Gutman and Ira Berlin estimate that in four out of five American cities, "at least 75 percent of wage earners were either immigrants, the children of immigrants, or blacks."[73] As Ida Tarbell pointed out in the case of Rhode Island, the "American" workers who were allegedly to benefit from the tariff were themselves as often as not "foreigners."

Late-nineteenth-century workers faced a choice: of where to

draw the line between "Them" and "Us"; of who to protect and from
whom; of whether to ally with employers above or with other working people across national borders. That choice would never go away.
It would return when the Buy American question resurfaced in the
1930s and again in the late twentieth century, when the politics of
trade and the politics of immigration would fuse once again, and
both would come once more to effectively mask the politics of class.

SMOKE AND MIRRORS

That old tariff magic was powerful, after all. Sitting in classrooms all
those years, memorizing the tariff's ups and downs and following the
fiery debate rending American politics, students were being taught
that the real divide in nineteenth-century politics was between protectionists and free traders, between Republicans and Democrats. In
an incremental fog of boredom, amidst paper airplanes and notes
passed to the next desk, they were being wrapped in an ideological
haze known today as "consensus history." American history was a
story of consensus, it taught; capitalism, industrialization, and empire
were both inevitable and uncontested. Those Americans whose opinions mattered were presidents and senators.

Behind the fog all was contested, down to very roots of economic
relations, citizenship rights, and the border between "Americans"
and "foreigners." The American Revolution, far from establishing a
harmonious unity, had only set in motion new conflicts, as the social
and economic processes it unleashed brought millions of new people
to the country, enfolded thousands of people within its expanding
borders, and gave birth to new visions of the just economy. If Mc-
Kinley and Cleveland's vision of corporate growth and industrial empire produced one version of the economic nation, ensconced in
public policy and public memory, theirs was only one version. B. C.
Stickney, Ralph Beaumont, William Saul, and other Knights of Labor had quite another vision, even if they never got to realize it.

For the Knights, as for thousands of working people caught up in
a utopian moment, the axis of political and economic debate was not
over the tariff; it was over who would control their work and their
communities—whether it would be Jimmy Dobson, the mill owner
in the poem; or the poem's proud narrator and his wife, Mollie, and
their shoeless children. As Mollie's husband concluded, free trade

would not have freed them or protectionism protected them. "What is Free Trade under the present conditions of society? Freedom of Capital," Karl Marx argued in an 1848 speech in Brussels. "So long as you let the relations of wages-labor to capital exist, no matter how favorable the conditions under which you accomplish the exchange of commodities, there will always be a class which exploits and a class which is exploited."[74]

CHAPTER 3

Circling the Wagons

Buy American Campaigns During the Great Depression

Nine years into the Great Depression of the 1930s, an unassuming man named Francis X. A. Eble warned Congress that foreign products were sapping the nation's economic life-blood. With every year that passed, he insisted, the country was sinking deeper and deeper into an "economic morass," and imports were to blame. Only through a mass Buy American movement could the nation dig itself out. Facing the Senate Committee on Interstate Commerce in June 1939, Eble urged Congress to expand the Buy American Act of 1933, which required the U.S. government to purchase goods of domestic origin only. Otherwise, he announced with a dramatic flourish, "this country cannot survive half international and half American."[1]

Eble, a former druggist from Hazelton, Pennsylvania, told the committee he represented the Made in America Club, Inc., a "nation-wide institution" with "members in every State in the Union," representing eleven hundred companies in sixty-five industries, plus six million consumer members. He depicted his organization as "distinctly nonpartisan and non-profit." All its members served without pay, he said, and even paid their own way to attend meetings from "far-distant points." With self-effacing charm Eble reassured the committee, "I am not a politician but am an American citizen." The worst of times demanded a higher duty. "We have to face this situation, not as Democrats or Republicans, but . . . as Americans."[2]

Eble pointedly evoked the nonimportation movement of the American Revolution: "The demand for a bill of this kind is greater today than at any time heretofore in the history of our country, unless we go back to George Washington's time, when the Government was created and the Constitution was adopted." Washington, Eble reminded the assembled Senators, "refused to wear a suit of foreign clothing . . . because if this country was to survive and he wore such a suit it would set an example to others, and to purchase and to wear American-made clothing was one way by which this country could be developed and maintained."[3]

By contrast, those Americans who embraced foreign trade were aiding and abetting the forces of economic darkness crouching at the nation's borders. "Here is a document entitled 'Syllabus on Foreign Trade,' which was prepared for the high-school division, Board of Education, city of New York," he revealed to the committee. The syllabus spoke approvingly of the attractiveness of imports, which would encourage healthy trade between nations. "Why, gentlemen of the subcommittee," he concluded with McCarthyite chill, "that is economic treason."[4]

For all his zeal, Eble was himself a latecomer to a Buy American movement that swept the country in the early years of the Great Depression of the 1930s. Concerned with jobs in a time of unemployment, and immigration in a time of nationalist alarm, the movement presaged with startling similarity the Buy American sentiment that would burst forth in the 1970s and '80s. The biggest mover and shaker behind the 1930s movement was newspaper mogul William Randolph Hearst, Jr. In late 1932 and early 1933 Hearst marshaled all his enormous resources behind a Buy American campaign, which he blazoned across the headlines of his twenty-seven daily newspapers. The idea spread rapidly across the country, culminating in the Buy American Act of 1933, which President Herbert Hoover signed on his last day in office. The popularity of the Buy American movement of the 1930s rose in exact correlation with the economy's degeneration. At its core, it offered an answer to the enormous crisis of the Depression: "foreigners" and their economic incursions were the cause. An inward-looking protection of "Americans" was the solution.

DOMINO EFFECTS

One thing was clear by late 1932 and early 1933: The U.S. economy had completely collapsed. Around one-third of all wage-earners—or fifteen million people—were unemployed. Another third were underemployed and scraping by on part-time, temporary, or itinerant work. Wages for those lucky enough to have a job fell 16 percent.

Larger statistics on the economy reveal an equally stark picture: between the stock market crash of October 1929 and the bottom of the Depression in 1933, the GNP (Gross National Product) fell by 29 percent. Construction spending dropped 78 percent. Overall investment in the economy plummeted a whopping 98 percent. Then, as economic activity came to a standstill and jobs disappeared, banks started to go belly-up. By 1931 five thousand banks had collapsed, taking with them nine million savings accounts.[5]

President Herbert Hoover met this crisis with a paralysis of denial. He kept insisting that the economy was fundamentally sound and that the real problem was consumer and business confidence. If only investors and consumers would return to normal investment and spending activities, Hoover argued, then prosperity would return. Hoover believed that federal spending on relief for the unemployed would fatally undermine their moral fiber. Reluctantly, he finally authorized $700,000 in federal spending on public works in 1931; but otherwise, he felt that private volunteer efforts should help out the unfortunate. Meanwhile, the crisis deepened. By late 1932 private charities had exhausted their funds, and cities that tried to provide relief at the local level were going bankrupt.[6]

Into this vacuum stepped William Randolph Hearst, Jr., to present himself as savior of the nation. By 1932 Hearst was one of the most powerful people in the country. He owned twenty-seven major newspapers with a daily circulation of 5.5 million; dozens of magazines, including *Cosmopolitan* and *Good Housekeeping;* three luxury hotels in New York City, including the Ritz and the Warwick; and a copper mine in Peru. He lived in his own castle on a California mountain, around which he owned all the land his eyes could see, a total of 230,000 acres spreading from fifty miles of oceanfront property all the way to the Sierra Nevada. Hearst's art collection alone was worth somewhere around $20 million.[7]

For decades Hearst had always sought to translate his economic resources into political power. In 1902 and 1904 he got himself elected to Congress from New York, but for years after that he was known as a perpetual candidate who just couldn't win (William "also-ran"dolph Hearst). Undaunted, he continued to throw his weight around behind the scenes, in part through interlocking directorates tying him to powerful entities such as the Bank of America, Pacific Gas and Electric, and the California Republican Party. His politics reflected the eclecticism of the superrich man who believes he has the best interests of the working masses at heart. In some ways he was a Progressive, advocating government ownership of utilities and attacking the special "business interests" that sought to influence politics. But he was also a vicious propagandist for whom the phrase "yellow journalism" was invented. He helped produce the 1898 U.S. intervention in Cuba by printing falsified documents in his papers, for example.[8] One biographer referred to his coverage of the *Maine* incident as "the orgasmic acme of ruthless, truthless newspaper jingoism."[9]

In the fall of 1932 Hearst decided the answer to the Great Depression was a Buy American campaign. Every day for two months, beginning December 26th, the front pages of his twenty-seven newspapers trumpeted at least one, and often three or four, Buy American stories. Every day he wrote an editorial praising the idea. Every day he inserted the Buy American concept into smaller stories throughout his papers. His Hearst Metrotone News Service, meanwhile, carried the message into the nation's movie theaters. In one especially charming newsreel, entitled "CHILDREN ENLIST TO AID 'BUY AMERICAN,'" a bevy of endearing white children clutched American-made toys (including a black Mammy doll) and asked viewers to admire their "smart" American-made sailor suits. "My mother and dad say that everybody should buy American so lots of people will get jobs," a nervous little blond girl recited.[10]

Hearst's politics were so quirky that it is difficult to say exactly why he chose the campaign. Clearly, though, he had long been hostile to U.S. entanglements with Britain and France. After World War I he opposed the League of Nations, and in the months leading up to his Buy American campaign his papers were full of editorials lambasting Britain and France for reneging on their payment of war debts to the United States.[11]

"Cheap foreign goods," Hearst charged in December, 1931, were causing the Great Depression. "Alien manufacturers and merchants have practically wrested the American market away from us and appropriated it to themselves." If the American people bought only American goods, the money they spent would return on what Hearst called the "economic train:" money spent on American products would start up American factories whose employees, in turn, would spend their wages on American products at the store, and the merchant, in turn, would order more American products. Every day all twenty-seven Hearst papers ran a ten-point list of "Prosperity Politics for American Patriots," the first of which was "Buy American and spend American. See America first. Keep American money in America and provide employment for American citizens."[12]

In support of his campaign Hearst lined up an impressive array of endorsers, who testified as much to his power to get what he wanted as to the appeal of his Buy American arguments. Bank presidents, governors, members of Congress, senators, and manufacturers fell into line, offering a daily parade of celebrity quotations that rang with all the enthusiastic caution of the kept. Some did come across wholeheartedly, such as A. F. Hockenbeamer, president of Pacific Gas and Electric: "I think it is a brilliant idea and am for it 100 percent."[13] It was possible to read between the lines with others, such as Walter J. Kohler, former governor of Wisconsin: "The principal market for American goods has always been the domestic market, and it is upon that market that the revival of productive enterprise in this country must mainly depend."[14] It was all in the qualifiers. Will C. Wood, vice president of the Bank of America, even circled back round to Hoover's approach: "It is only good business for Americans to purchase American-made products whenever possible to do so. If all would do so, I believe it would do much to restore confidence throughout the country."[15]

Hearst also lined up prominent upper-class white women involved in the club movement, who exuded more eagerness. Grace Poole, president of the General Federation of Women's Clubs, specifically appealed to "American women" to support the campaign. "Let us do our best, we who constitute eighty-five percent of the purchasers of the nation."[16] Mrs. William A. Limbaugh, chairman of the outdoor art department of the California Club, answered "I Do, with a great big D, believe in the 'Buy American' movement."[17] Only Grace Boles Hedges, president of the San Francisco branch of the League of American Penwomen, wasn't quite so sure but pulled through: "In the abstract, the 'Buy American' movement may not be the most Christian thing, but it is the most intelligent. Self-preservation depends on it."[18]

Hearst's campaign had an enormous impact. The *Saturday Evening Post* had already taken up the Buy American idea in late 1932, and in early 1933 letters applauding the campaign flowed into newspapers and magazines across the country. The *San Francisco Examiner* claimed in February 1993 that in the previous six weeks over 250,000 people had signed Buy American pledge forms printed in the Hearst papers.[19] The *New York Times* reported that purchases of "Paris Styles" dropped 25 percent in January, in part because of "the influence of the 'Buy-American' movement" and "the strong emphasis lately put on American style creations and the smaller merchandising value of the foreign label under current economic conditions." Asked on January 26th if she planned to shop while visiting Paris, movie star Clara Bow replied "Oh, no. . . . I bought all my dresses and everything I need before I left home. We're doing that now in California, you know."[20]

BUY NATIONAL

Hearst did not alone a national movement make. The Buy American movement of early 1933 was possible only because his arguments landed in a fertile field—a nation in crisis, with its president in denial, and in which many people were already in the mood to turn inward.

After playing a leadership role in World War I, the United States had drawn back sharply from European diplomatic involvement in the 1920s, especially after Wilson withdrew from the League of Nations in 1920. An isolationist tone crept into national discussions of foreign relations, and many Americans recoiled from engagement with Europe. The biggest flashpoint was the World War I debt question. By 1922 the country's wartime allies owed the United States a total of $22 billion, including interest. Germany, for its part, owed $33 billion to the Allies in reparations. The Allies argued that they couldn't pay the United States until Germany first paid them. Complex negotiations partially resolved the crisis in 1924, but attacks on Britain and France for refusing to pay their debts continued in the U.S. press, and the tone was one of suspicion and distrust.[21]

Britain, meanwhile, had a real problem on its hands. In order to pay its debt to the United States, it needed a favorable balance of payments. To try to solve the problem, sporadic, privately sponsored "Buy British" campaigns sprang up in the 1920s. Then, on November 16, 1931—a year before Hearst's campaign—the British government launched a massive "Buy British" campaign. It plastered four million glossy posters onto the nation's buses, trains, subways, and government offices and put up a fifteen-foot high sign in London's Trafalgar

Square, lit by thirteen hundred lightbulbs, that proclaimed "Buy British." The Boy Scouts, BBC, National Union of Manufacturers, and thousands of small businesses threw themselves into the campaign. One Durham bottling company advertised, for example, "We are a *British* Firm, Employing *British Labour.* Our products are in *British Made Bottles.* By Buying from us you support the slogan *Buy British.*" Approvingly, the London *Times* reported that the Duke of Connaught was "spending the winter at Sidmouth instead of on the French Riviera." A scandal erupted when Tabasco sauce served in the House of Commons was revealed to bear a "Made in the U.S.A." label.[22]

By 1933, as the Depression rippled through Europe, the "buy national" idea spread to the continent. In France, thousands of women and trade unionists demonstrated on February 1, 1933, "in favor of French products and against foreign goods" and proposed nationalist shopping "as a means of economy recovery."[23] Two months later the French government announced that all knitted goods must henceforth bear labels naming their country of origin. "Like two previous rulings on shoes and porcelain it is intended to foster the 'Buy French' movement," the *New York Times* reported, "and indirectly to protect home industry by making the sale of foreign goods more difficult."[24] In October, fifty pro-Hitler business leaders launched a parallel "Buy German" movement.[25]

Hearst himself got the "buy national" idea from the British. He repeatedly referred to the "Buy British" campaign in his editorials, depicted it in cartoons, and even ran an enormous photo of the sign in Trafalgar Square.[26] Knowledge of the "Buy British" campaigns was widespread outside the Hearst press, moreover. In November 1933 the *Saturday Evening Post* ran a seven-page spread on the British campaign.[27] Americans also learned of the campaign when postage from Britain arrived with "British Goods are Best" stamped on the cancellation. "The prominence given to their movements abroad had excited deep concern in the minds of the American people," a U.S. Chamber of Commerce committee concluded in March 1933, "and has prompted a spirit of reprisal."[28] "M. L." of East Orange, New Jersey, in a letter to the *New York Times* two months before Hearst's campaign, queried: "If England can paint her cliffs and her cities with the slogan 'Buy British!' why can't the United States do something similar for this land?"[29]

This rising nationalism within the United States and hostility to Europe produced a wave of economic nationalism in the 1920s and early '30s, which Hearst both contributed to and was trying to sustain. By 1933 economic nationalism was so popular that James Goodwin Hodgson had compiled a debate handbook on the subject. Hodgson opened with a definition: "Economic nationalism is that governmental policy which aims to develop the nation as a closed unit, and to foster its ability to exist independently of other countries."[30] He then inserted a proposed outline for debate on the topic. Hodgson had his prospective debater ask, "Why economic nationalism is a current issue in the United States." The first answer was the country's shift from debtor to creditor nation (i.e., the war debt); the second,

> The severity of the depression has made the whole world reconsider its attitudes toward fundamental economic problems.
>   1. Nationalism developed by world war has reacted in a demand for national industrial development.
>   2. Local unemployment has concentrated attention on the needs of localities.[31]

Under the heading "Favoring Economic Nationalism," Hodgson then reprinted a March 23, 1933, speech by Wallace B. Donham, dean of the Graduate School of Business Administration at Harvard. "I believe the road to prosperity in the years ahead lies in making this great nation so far as possible self-sufficient," Donham argued, "maintaining a proper balance between agriculture, mining and manufacturing and supplying its own wants."[32]

Many of these arguments were familiar ones, deployed by our earlier cast of pro-tariff characters. In the 1930s, as before, popular economic nationalism legitimated protectionist interests that had long advocated high tariffs. In 1930 they pushed through the famously high Smoot-Hawley Tariff, which raised the average tariff on imported goods to 59 percent. Many at the time blamed it for causing the Great Depression—although the idea has since been discredited—because European nations retaliated with their own nationalist round of higher tariff walls in response, cutting down on international commerce.[33]

In its purest, strongest form, economic nationalism could move beyond protectionism to a call for autarchy, or complete national self-sufficiency. As the U.S. economy collapsed in the early 1930s, many found the idea of autarchy tremendously appealing. The Buy American movement fit its model exactly: by keeping U.S. purchasing power inside a neat national circle, it promised that the American people could take care of themselves. "It is getting too late to apply simply a higher protective tariff," Byron H. McCullough of New Bedford, Massachusetts, argued in a letter to the *New York Times,* evoking, once again, the American Revolution. "It would be better, in the words of Jefferson, [to] 'purchase nothing foreign where an equivalent of domestic fabric can be obtained, without regard to any difference of price.' American dollars for American-made goods."[34]

BUYING AMERICA

Buy American advocates immediately began to pressure the government at all levels to pass Buy American legislation. Their efforts help us begin to identify more explicitly the economic interests behind the Buy American movement, as well as trace its evolving political logic.

In 1933 cities, counties, and states across the country quickly passed resolutions endorsing the Buy American approach on general terms, including the Cook County (Illinois) Commissioners, Ohio Senate, Los Angeles County Supervisors, City and County of San Francisco, and Alameda County Supervisors. "Uncle Sam has been the boob of the world in international commerce," boomed Cleveland city councilman William R. Hopkins on behalf of his city's Buy American resolution. "The U.S. should retaliate against 'Buy British' and similar European trade-stimulating movements."[35]

Just as quickly, though, the Buy American movement also elicited calls to "buy state" or "buy city." "I go a step further and buy California products," Mrs. F. G. Law, president of the California League of Women Voters, told the Hearst *Examiner.*[36] In February, upstate New York canneries initiated a "Buy New York" campaign. A Madison, Wisconsin, paper reported in March 1933 that "Leading merchants in this city say that the most reasonable way to insure national business recovery is to start the movement in our own home town. A dollar can go a few miles on a business trip and come back in an hour, but when it travels far away, it may never get home again."[37]

Many of these campaigns antedated the Depression. In 1920, for example, the Chamber of Commerce in Richmond, Virginia, had initiated a "Buy Richmond-Made Goods" campaign, which it referred to as a "Buy-at-Home" movement.[38] The Depression, though, produced a much broader "buy state" and "buy city" movement. By May 1932, the *New York Times* reported not only "a trend toward economic isolation . . . in the policy of nations" but also that "various States in this country . . . are also drawing into their own shells."[39] Kansas, Minnesota, Missouri, Kansas, Wyoming, and North Dakota all passed laws mandating that supplies for public institutions be purchased from their state's firms whenever the price allowed.[40] In South Carolina, dairy farmers advertised that their cows had grazed only on forage grown in their state.[41] As a contemporary pamphlet observed, the Buy American movement "brought in its train a wave of local as well as national economic patriotism."[42]

Meanwhile, pressures mounted on the federal level in late 1932 and early 1933 to pass Buy American legislation. Efforts focused on the Buy American Act, which would require the federal government to purchase only goods made in the United States. As early as 1817 the United States, in similar fashion to European nations, had passed a "cabotage" law excluding foreign ships from engaging in trade between U.S. ports. Another law from the early twentieth century required that all army and navy vessels be made in the United States. But efforts to pass a more sweeping Buy American federal procurement law in 1928 failed.[43]

In late 1932 Buy American advocates in Congress tried again, attaching a Buy American provision to the 1934 Treasury and Post Office appropriations bill. On January 16, 1933, the bill passed the House; on February 4, the Senate passed it by a vote of 41 to 12. Eighteen Democrats crossed traditional party lines on trade to vote yes. "A majority of both parties joined in an effort to end the ridiculous system under which the Government undertook to encourage American industry and to create jobs for workless Americans, and then purchased a considerable portion of its supplies from foreign countries," reported the *Washington Post* in an editorial entitled "America First."[44] Hoover signed what became known as the Buy American Act on his last day in office, March 3, 1933.[45]

Who exactly was behind all this legislation? Reports on the state and city-level laws suggest their strongest advocates were businesses who stood most directly to gain from local purchases: for example, the South Carolina Dairy industry, the upstate New York canning industry, or the small business people who constituted the Richmond

Chamber of Commerce. At the national level, almost all the supporters of the failed Buy American Act of 1928 were manufacturers of materials for the construction industry, such as the Common Brick Manufacturers Association of America, the American Institute of Steel Construction, the United States Cast Iron Pipe & Foundry Co., and cement and window glass companies—that is, businesses that would harvest lucrative federal contracts should the law pass.[46]

The same interests show up in 1933. In his speech on the Senate floor on behalf of the Buy American Act, Senator William King of California referred specifically to the protection of American-made cement, lumber, and other building materials.[47] The bill's sponsor, Senator Hiram Johnson of California, a longtime collaborator of Hearst's, in his speech on behalf of the bill openly admitted that "the genesis" of his support for the Act had been a conversation with a group of interested manufacturers. "A month or more ago certain manufacturers in the State of California, and some in the State of Pennsylvania, called upon me in reference to bids that were to be opened on the 3d day of February at the Boulder Dam—bids for turbines, generating machinery, and the like," Johnson told the Senate. "They explained to me their fear . . . that they would be unable to compete . . . with bids that would come from Germany and perhaps another nation of Europe, too."[48]

If we return to Francis X. A. Eble, the man who warned Congress in 1939 that the nation could not endure "half international and half American," the economic interests driving the Buy American movement become even clearer. Despite obsequious protestations that he was "not a politician but an American citizen," Eble was no apolitical, anonymous citizen. He had been Commissioner of Customs in Hoover's Republican administration, in which he promoted high-tariff policies. Before that he had served as an economic adviser to the government of Poland. In November 1933 he took a position as director of the American Match Institute, "to direct its fight for greater tariff protection for American match manufacturers."[49]

Nor was the Made in America Club the spontaneous grassroots movement from below that Eble described. The club was founded in 1934 by executives from the match and chemical industries, who hired Eble away from the Match Institute to be their manager. Francis P. Garvan, president of the Chemical Foundation, served as the club's vice president. Its ten-member advisory council was composed entirely of executives from U.S. manufacturing corporations producing textiles, pottery, watches, and containers, who stood to benefit from high tariffs and who formed the club to mobilize opposition to Roosevelt's free trade policies. By 1936 they were joined by the building materials industry—cement, lumber, and shingle interests. The *New York Times* described the Made in America Club aptly in 1936: "A resurgence of nationalistic feeling on a scale several times as great as that of 1932 is promised by industrialists, raw material producers and others aligning themselves behind movements preaching a gospel of buying goods produced by American workmen."[50]

It was all carefully orchestrated to look "popular": Eble launched the club in 1935 with dozens of letters to match industry executives, then another fifty-two missives to the toy and lace industries, followed by the "Knitted Outwear" and "Grass and Fiber Rug" industries, totaling a hundred letters a week. In October he announced to the press that the club was distributing "Made in America Club" stickers and license plate holders. By the next spring he had set up a Buy American chain letter system of sorts, in which each member signed a pledge card and then promised to sign up five others.[51]

In January 1935 Francis Garvan, vice president of the Made in America Club, wrote to William Randolph Hearst asking him to join a "Nation-wide hook up" radio hour on behalf of the club on George Washington's birthday. Joining Hearst would be Matthew Woll, vice president of the American Federation of Labor. Garvan promised "a musical program of the highest order," with George M. Cohan—of "I'm a Yankee Doodle Dandy" fame—as master of ceremonies.[52] Whether the radio show actually took place and who might actually have joined it remain unclear. What is clear is that despite Garvan's insistence in his invitation—like Eble's in his congressional testimony—that the Made in America Clubs were "distinctly nonprofit," the corporations who funded it and directed its activities were distinctly not. Their effort to build a "grassroots" Buy American movement, it turns out, was mostly a front for our old friend, the tariff.

AMERICAN LABOR

The third man invited to that radio show, Matthew Woll of the American Federation of Labor (AFL), shows us, though, that business interests that stood to profit directly from nationalist consumption or high tariffs were not the only organized group behind the Buy American movement. Hearst's most basic argument was that the Buy American movement would create jobs for "American" workers. Woll, along with many others in the 1930s AFL, bought it.

At the onset of the Great Depression, the U.S. labor movement had sunk to its lowest point since the Civil War. Most organized workers belonged to international unions affiliated with the AFL, the same federation of which John Jarrett, the pro-tariff iron worker, had been a founder. During World War I millions of unskilled, immigrant, minority, female, and often radical workers had stretched the AFL's conservatism to challenge both employers' iron rule over the workplace and the entrenched leadership of more conservative AFL bureaucrats such as president Samuel Gompers. But vicious anti-union repression followed the war, and the unions that survived soon turned on and purged their own left-leaning members. By the mid-twenties most of those who remained were complacent business unionists who preached harmony with employers, made few demands, and represented only the most skilled, elite workers organized by craft. One observer summarized the AFL in 1928 as "a curious blending of 'defeatism' with complacency." Its members, overwhelmingly white and male, usually banned female or minority workers, with a few major exceptions such as the United Mine Workers and the International Ladies' Garment Workers' Union.[53] When the Depression hit, the AFL's leaders responded with a defeatism and paralysis that exceeded even Hoover's. They evinced little interest in organizing unorganized workers or in fundamental social change.[54]

Since the 1880s, when the tariff question had ripped apart the federation's national convention, the AFL's top leadership had agreed to take no stand on trade questions. Frustrated, Matthew Woll, joined by thirteen international unions, in 1928 had formed his own pro-tariff lobbying group called America's Wage Earners' Protective Conference.[55]

When unemployment devastated AFL unions in the 1930s, AFL members started blaming imports for the loss of their jobs and calling more loudly for tariff protection, without yet advocating Buy American. "Hundreds of our American match workers are walking the streets idle while the administration permits the importation of foreign matches made by very cheap labor," F. B. Gerhart, president of United Match Workers Federal Labor Union Local #18928 of Barberton, Ohio, wrote to AFL president William Green in July 1934. "Every imported match supplants an American match which American labor produces."[56] The National Council of United Cement Workers in 1937 demanded that the federal government raise tariffs on cement to stop "cheap foreign labor" and "avert an inevitable crisis in the American Portland Cement Industry which would subject thousands of American wage earners to unemployment and privation."[57] Perhaps not coincidentally, these unions represented workers in many of the same industries in which employers lobbied for the Buy American Act.

Well before Hearst's campaign, a few scattered AFL unionists then started adding a call to Buy American to their attacks on imports. At its annual convention in March 1928, the AFL-affiliated Florida State Federation of Labor, for example, protested the further use of "foreign-made material" in public buildings. "The use of this material has a tendency to lessen employment for workers in this country, engaged in the production of such materials," it charged. "This loss of opportunity to be employed during this period of depression is working a direct hardship on a large group of American-born workers."[58]

When Hearst launched his campaign in late 1932, he drew on this base to line up endorsements from AFL unionists around the country, ranging from Matthew Woll—already a friend of Hearst's—to A. W. Hoch, president of the California State Federation of Labor, to the Vallejo, California, local of the International Association of Machinists.[59] From then on, Buy American arguments and slogans cropped up consistently, if sporadically, within the AFL. In July 1938, for example, the American Flint Glass Workers passed a resolution at their convention that asked the government to "buy American to keep American factories going."[60] Around the same time Buy American references started to appear in the official AFL press, especially in the publications of the Union Label Trades Department, which began to add "American made" to its "union made" campaigns.[61] "There is no better method through which better times can be brought to America," exhorted the department's secretary-treasurer T. M. Ornburn in his 1938 Christmas message, "than through the buying of Union Label and America-made products. It will keep our money in our own land."[62] Two years later his department sponsored a union-label essay contest. "I buy union label goods because they are made in America," wrote Lillian Benco in her winning essay.[63] "This aids our home industries and helps make our future secure." "When people buy American all the labor is American," Ornburn summarized.[64]

Although exceptions abounded, since the nineteenth century the AFL's power in the workplace had been largely based on an inward-turning protection of the skilled few, who monopolized skills such as plumbing or tool-and-die making through tightly regulated apprenticeships and then used their monopoly to bargain hard with employers. In the late 1920s and early '30s many AFL unions, particularly those in the building trades, had already begun to join with employers in "local products" and "buy city" campaigns. In Seattle, for example, the AFL-affiliated Central Labor Council joined with local employers from 1925 onward to promote an annual "Northwest Products Exhibition" and exhorted its members to "Spend Northwest Dollars for Northwest Products." Individual AFL unions in Seattle then used the "local products" call to try to keep jobs within the city. In 1926 the Seattle Metal Trades Council advocated "the construction of Seattle's eighty new street cars in Seattle, by Seattle people."[65]

In Salinas, California, the Central Labor Council in 1930 printed up little cards that summarized exactly the convergence of AFL craft unionism with the promotion of local products:

> Principles and Aims of the Labor Movement of Salinas, California:
> Loyalty to our community . . . Our Magic Circle—Employment of local contractors who shall employ local labor to make a local payroll to be spent with local merchants and local professional men to make a more prosperous Salinas for all. Whatever we do, think of Salinas First, Last, and Always.[66]

Defensive, its ranks sharply closed, the early 1930s AFL's inward-turning self-protection by the skilled meshed exactly with the Buy American movement's call for national self-protection.

ALIEN INVADERS

The big question lurking within the Buy American movement, though, was who was inside the Magic Circle and who the movement pushed outside. "When people buy American all the labor is American," T. M. Ornburn ensured in his comments on the prize essays. Who exactly was the "American labor" whose jobs would be saved by the movement? Here the "Us" and "Them" question reared its head again; and it was ugly. The line, in the 1930s, was one of race as much as citizenship; and the fertile field into which Hearst's campaign landed was poisoned by racial hatred. Hearst himself had sown that poison for decades.

Repeatedly, in his 1932 and 1933 Buy American editorials, Hearst equated immigration to the United States with "foreign goods" that might enter as imports.

> We have as much RIGHT to REGULATE IMPORTS as we have to REGULATE IMMIGRATION.
> We have as much RIGHT TO EXCLUDE CERTAIN IM-PORTS, DANGEROUS to our AMERICAN STANDARDS AND IDEALS, as we have the right to EXCLUDE certain IMMIGRATION which is a MENACE TO OUR AMERICAN STANDARDS AND IDEALS.[67]

The product of "foreign labor," Hearst argued, was the same "menace" whether it was produced overseas or in the United States by an immigrant. "The product of [the foreign workman], if we buy it, is just as ruinous a competitor with our workman, and as successful a rival for his job, as if we had permitted the alien in person to pass our immigration barriers."[68] Both the "home market," and the "sacred" soil of the country, therefore, "MUST BE PROTECTED FROM INVASION, AND BOTH ALIKE MUST BE DEFENDED FROM WITHIN" (emphasis in original).[69] Hearst equated the two through "news" stories as well as editorials. "BAN ON ALIEN ACTORS SOUGHT," read a typical story: "Inspired by the Hearst 'Buy American' drive," it reported, "members of the Lambs Club today renewed their efforts to have the Alien Actors bill [restricting noncitizen actors] enacted into law."[70]

Almost always Hearst's "aliens" were Japanese. In a December 29, 1932, editorial, for example, he argued that the depreciation of the yen had "enabled the Japanese producer TO ANNEX THE AMER-ICAN MARKET."[71] News reports in his papers repeatedly disparaged Japanese imports or celebrated their cessation. " 'Buy American' Blocks Order for Jap Bulbs" read one such story about a firm in Baltimore that, in response to Hearst's campaign, had quickly canceled its order for a million light bulbs from Japan.[72] These stories were full of racist attacks on allegedly conniving Asians who supposedly preferred "low Asiatic living standards" and, Hearst charged, perpetually conspired to invade the United States. "We exclude Asiatics from our country for one reason, among others, that they tend to lower the American standards of living. But we do not exclude the products of these same Asiatics," B. C. Forbes, listed as a "noted financial authority," argued over a Hearst-owned radio station in New York on January 2, 1933.[73]

Hearst's coverage slid over into almost caricatured sensationalism, especially when it came to seafood. One story, entitled "Japanese Oysters for the U.S.," warned: "American oystermen are alarmed at what seems to them an invasion on their territory by Japanese concerns which are importing and transplanting millions of Oriental oysters in Pacific coast waters every year." "At least 150,000,000 'alien' oysters have been put in the waters of the West Coast to compete with the native product."[74] Another irresistible headline screamed, "SLIPPERY ALIEN FISH CLOSE UP OUR CANNERIES." "Little and big fish, abundant on both Americans [sic] coasts, are jumping in endless procession out of the ocean into foreign nets and cans headed down America's gullet."[75]

AFL advocates, too, used the Buy American call to draw a line within the American working class against immigrants. Matthew Woll, in his endorsement of the campaign for the Hearst press, for example, argued that buying American would "provide employment for American citizens."[76] The Florida State Federation of Labor, in its resolution, quoted earlier, argued that buying American would save jobs for "American-born workers"—moving beyond Woll to exclude not just noncitizens but naturalized U.S. citizens born abroad.[77] A. W. Hoch, president of the California State Federation of Labor, was even firmer in his endorsement: "Organized labor worked for the adoption of strict immigration laws in order that American citizens might have employment."[78] As Woll put it bluntly: "Merely to keep foreign workers from our shores, and then to purchase goods made by workers in foreign lands is to defeat the very purpose of restrictive immigration legislation;"[79] or, in the words of Congressman Cooper (R-Ohio) at the height of Hearst's campaign, a " 'Buy American' policy followed naturally from the restrictive immigration policies of the country."[80]

At the 1939 Senate Interstate Commerce Committee hearing on extensions to the Buy American Act—at which Eble warned that the nation was becoming "half international and half American"—the Act's proponents hammered this point home again and again: importation of foreign products and immigration of foreign labor were one and the same. Millard Rice, legislative representative of the Veterans of Foreign Wars (VFW), told Congress that the VFW, at its encampment in Columbus, Ohio, had passed a resolution asking the federal government to pass a Buy American law ensuring that all jobs paid for by federal funds "should be performed solely by American citizens and by those who owe allegiance to the U.S. and those aliens who had theretofore properly signified their intent to become American citizens." Senator Homer T. Bone agreed: "It would be stupid to employ Americans on the work and yet to use products made in other countries." He asked Rice if the VFW was "demanding that Americans be given jobs in America." Yes, Rice affirmed. "You would be in effect importing a job that should be performed by Americans, if you imported foreign materials." Testifying after Rice, E. F. Herr, of the Shingle Weavers' union of Washington and Oregon, charged that lowering tariff barriers would "turn our unionized industry over to a foreign, anti-union, and oriental-employing group."[81]

THE RISING TIDE OF RACISM

These attacks did not emerge in a vacuum. In responding to the Great Depression, all these people drew on a climate of vicious immigrant-bashing that had flourished in the 1920s. Anti-immigrant tensions had in fact been mounting since the late nineteenth century, as millions of immigrants flowed in from Europe, joined by tens of thousands from Asia and Mexico. World War I only heightened attacks on immigrants. A new nationalist alarmism called for "100% Americanism." Then, after the war, employers linked resurgent labor activism with "Bolshevism" and swooped down to deport allegedly radical immigrants. In the decade that followed, the Ku Klux Klan enjoyed an enormous resurgence, especially in the North and West. In this "Second Klan," Klan members added vicious attacks on immigrant Jews and Catholics to racism against African Americans, and Klan membership reached its all-time peak in 1925 at two million. In 1924 anti-immigrant sentiments triumphed with the National Origins

Act, which restricted overall immigration to 150,000 a year; imposed national quotas biased toward Northern and Western Europe; and banned all further immigration from Asia.[82]

On the West Coast, immigrant-bashers had since the 1850s particularly directed their ire against Asians. A first wave of anti-Asian violence in the 1870s and '80s drove Chinese immigrants out of most Western towns and into a compressed enclave in San Francisco, and produced the Chinese Exclusion Act of 1882. When Japanese immigration began after 1905—in tiny increments relative to European immigration—a new wave of attacks erupted. William Randolph Hearst was the leader of the pack, using his papers to alarm America about an imaginary "yellow peril" of Japanese perpetually plotting to invade the country. "JAPAN SOUNDS OUR COAST. Brown Men Have Maps and Could Land Easily" a typical headline in the *San Francisco Examiner* read.[83] The *San Francisco Chronicle* jumped on the bandwagon to ring its own racial alarms: "THE DEAR LITTLE BROWN MEN. How They do Things to White Folks When They Get the Power," it screamed in 1907.[84] "We repeat the warning which we have frequently given, that if Japanese coolies are allowed to get a monopoly of the work the employers will not be permitted to make a single dollar. The Japs will take it all."[85] Historian Roger Daniels concludes that "by the end of the First World War a great reservoir of anti-Japanese sentiment had been created throughout the country."[86] The reservoir soon filled law books. California and Washington State passed Alien Land Laws banning noncitizens from owning land in 1913 and 1921, respectively. Since the U.S. naturalization act of 1790 barred Asians from becoming citizens, the new laws effectively excluded Japanese and Chinese from owning land.[87]

In the broader anti-immigrant context of the 1920s these attacks only deepened. Anti-Japanese agitators in Hollywood, California, in 1922 and 1923 sponsored a "Swat the Jap" campaign, for example:

> JAPS
> You came to care for lawns,
>   we stood for it
> You came to work in truck gardens,
>   we stood for it
> You sent your children to our public schools,
>   we stood for it

You moved a few families in our midst,
   we stood for it
You proposed to build a church in our neighborhood
   BUT
We DIDN'T and WE WON'T STAND FOR IT
You impose more on us each day
   until you have gone your limit
WE DON'T WANT YOU WITH US
SO GET BUSY, JAPS, AND
GET OUT OF HOLLYWOOD.[88]

By the 1920s Asian-bashing had wormed its way to the center of mainstream American intellectual life. In 1920, Lothrop Stoddard, a Harvard Ph.D., published an enormously popular book called *The Rising Tide of Color Against White World-Supremacy,* which went through fourteen editions in the next four years.[89] Stoddard warned that a "rising tide of color" was ready to engulf the "white races," "menacing every part of the white world. . . . The whole white race is exposed, immediately or ultimately, to the possibility of social sterilization and final replacement or absorption by the teeming colored races." He carefully warned his readers that "Colored triumphs of arms are less to be dreaded than more enduring conquests like migrations which could swamp whole populations and turn countries now white into colored men's lands irretrievably lost to the white world." Readers could follow these incursions with the book's three maps printed in bright yellow, red, and brown, showing the "Distribution of the Primary Races," "Categories of White World-Supremacy," and "Distribution of the White Races." This was racism of the rawest sort: Stoddard divided up all the world's peoples into four biological races, ascribed racial characteristics to each, ranked them, and then assumed a global contest for racial supremacy. He wanted the whites to win.[90]

Hearst was cheering them on all the way. In 1932 and 1933, simultaneously with his Buy American campaign, he published a prominent five-part editorial series by Stoddard entitled "Lonely America," in which Stoddard espoused his theories of white supremacy and Asian racial evil.[91] Hearst, with his Buy American campaign, was trying to reap the "yellow peril" sentiment he had himself sown for thirty years. Now he could cast a wider net for his theories by trying to blame Asians for mass unemployment in the Great Depression. And sure enough, by February 9, the *Washington Post* had taken his bait: "Japanese producers" were trying "to capture the American market," a *Post* editorial dutifully echoed. "Americans are foolishly permitting foreign producers to flood this market with cheap goods." Buying American, the *Post* concluded, "is a measure as clearly intended for the national defense as if it provided an army to defend American shores against invasion."[92]

We can trace, lastly, the convergence of Stoddard's theories with the Buy American movement at the grassroots level in a November 28, 1934, letter from A. W. Mitchell of Houston, Texas, to AFL president William Green. "An embargo by the white races of the world and by the United States, against importing Japanese goods which come into competition with the United States employment, would heal much of the unemployment in the United States and other white races of the world," Mitchell advised Green. He combined Hearst with Stoddard to emerge with a racial theory of trade and employment: "An economic boycott of Japan by the white races of the world would create havoc among the yellow races in the much heard of struggle between the white races and the yellow races for world supremacy." Mitchell's solution? "Patronize home industry."[93]

As had earlier rounds of Asian-bashing, these racialized attacks on immigrants and foreigners led to concrete—and tragic—results in the 1930s and beyond. Immigrants from all over the world came under attack, especially those from Asia or Mexico, who were perceived as being non-white. In 1931, the California legislature passed a new law requiring that any firm doing business with the state must bar noncitizens from employment. Immediately, hundreds of Mexicans lost their jobs. During the first week of February 1933, just as Hearst's Buy American campaign peaked, so did agitation for legislation barring noncitizen actors from working in the United States. George Jessel, Eddie Cantor, and George M. Cohan (who was later slated to emcee the Buy American radio show) all signed petitions on the bill's behalf. That same week federal authorities seized eleven actors and activists in Hollywood who had allegedly failed to comply with immigration laws, and commenced deportation proceedings.[94]

Secretary of Labor William Doak signed eagerly onto Hearst's Buy American train. "There is another alien matter to which I wish to refer," he pressed in his endorsement for Hearst of buying American. "The United States Department of Labor is striving to keep from this country alien workers who would enter into competition with American workers."[95] This man had the power to impose his theories. Immediately after he took office in December 1930, Doak announced that the solution to unemployment in the United States was the deportation of illegal immigrants, and his office initiated a sweep of potentially "alien" seamen.[96] On an even greater and more disastrous scale, between 1930 and 1935 Doak supervised the deportation and repatriation of half a million Mexicans and Mexican Americans. Some were locked up and put on trains when they applied for relief. Others were rounded up by raids in Los Angeles and other cities, in which local and state officials scapegoated Mexicans for the Depression. More commonly, Mexicans responded to scare tactics and their own unemployment by leaving voluntarily. Many of those repatriated were American citizens.[97]

Ten years later, 110,240 Americans of Japanese descent, two-thirds of whom were U.S. citizens, would lose their businesses and homes and be locked up in internment camps in the name of the "yellow peril" within.[98] Stoddard's *Rising Tide of Color,* meanwhile, was discovered by the Third Reich and went through six editions in Germany.[99]

The enemy within and the enemy without were one and the same, Hearst, Woll, and Stoddard warned. Only white, native-born Americans of Northern European descent could be sure they were safely inside the nation. The Buy American movement of the 1930s promised prosperity for "American workers." But all too many American workers, it seemed, weren't included.

ECONOMIC TREASON

When the unassuming but clever Mr. Eble warned Congress in 1939 that buying American was the only way out of the Great Depression, he was quick to wrap himself in the American flag. George Washington, he insisted, was on his side, along with Abraham Lincoln, whose famous "house divided" speech he invoked by pronouncing "this country cannot survive half international and half American." By charging advocates of foreign trade with "economic treason," Eble not only likened economic affairs to wartime but hinted at a domestic enemy within, secretly aiding and abetting the forces of economic darkness abroad.

If the nation's economic house could not survive half international, half American, Hearst's solution was to cut out the international part. Drawing on Lothrop Stoddard, decades of Yellow Perilism, and deeply held notions that the true American could only be white, Hearst and his allies brought race to the center of foreign economic relations. What had earlier been the British oppression of the eighteenth century, or the foreign pauper labor of the nineteenth, became, under Hearst's tutelage in the 1930s, alien Asians espying the nation's economic resources. In Hearst's Manichean world of domestic good and foreign evil, alleged racial traits marked all "Asians" eternally "foreign." Their products were therefore evil, whether manufactured abroad or by their agents plotting within the borders of the United States.

To both incursions, the answer was a racialized excision of all products and persons "alien." All too eagerly, the American Federation of Labor—quick to figure out the confluence of racialized nationalism with its own restrictive defense of a narrow band of white American workmen—picked up the knife.

CHAPTER 4

No Thanks, Mr. Hearst

Alternatives to Buy Americanism in the 1930s

Like the nonimportation movement of the American Revolution, the Buy American movement of the 1930s invoked a united American people whose interests would all be served by economic nationalism, and which the people themselves would enforce through ferociously nationalist shopping. But the inequalities structured into the nation from its birth had only grown deeper by the 1930s. The American people had their own independent ideas about the economic nation, just as they had during the Revolution, and their own ideas as well about what the nation's root problems were during the Great Depression.

For many Americans, including those of African and Chinese descent, the answer to the economic crisis was to embrace international ties or to define their own economic community in transnational terms. For many, the solution was not to build higher walls around the nation but to tear down walls of racism within. Still others took up the Knights' earlier challenge and proposed to resolve the nation's crisis through a politics of redistribution. All of them talked back, sometimes directly, to Mr. Hearst.

DON'T BUY WHERE YOU CAN'T WORK
One of the clearest responses to Hearst's Buy American campaign came from the African American community. Editors of the country's major African American newspapers rejected it right off. In a January 28, 1933, editorial entitled "Buy America First," Robert Abbott, editor of the *Chicago Defender*—the nation's most prominent Af-

rican American newspaper, with a circulation of 180,000—retorted: "We're for it. . . . Certainly we'll buy America first, and we're happy to recommend this to our readers."

> And here are some of the things purely American which we shall hence-forth insist upon buying:
>> We'll buy Pullman tickets from Chicago to Atlanta . . .
>> We'll buy a night's lodging in hotels in Birmingham, Jacksonville, Memphis . . .
>> We'll buy a steak or a pork chop dinner in a restaurant in Baltimore, Philadelphia, Charleston . . .
>> We'll buy theater tickets . . .

"They can certainly count on us to start right now buying America first," he rounded off.[1] Of course, the whole reply was ironic: Jim Crow segregation barred African Americans from buying any of those things. As a poem in the February 25 *Defender,* entitled "Buy American (Oh, Yeah!)," submitted by "Ima Twin" from Urbana, Ohio, mocked:

> Swell hotels, cabarets, come dance and dine.
> Atta boy, let's all make whoopee, brother.
> What's that? No, you don't serve my kind.
> I said it; get out while you're all together.
>> "Buy American." . . .
> American transportation cannot be beat.
> Our ships, our trains, buses and airplanes.
> But when you buy a ticket it's take back seat.
> Segregation's lullabye, such sweet refrains.
>> "Buy American."[2]

On February 4, the *Defender* responded to Hearst more directly with a cartoon headlined "How Can We 'Buy American' When the Right to Work Is Denied Us?" It pictured an African American man in overalls, taking off his jacket and about to take up one end of a saw cutting into a log marked "American Industry." A white man at the saw's other end, wearing overalls marked "Labor," is holding up his palm to stop the first man. "Sorry, we don't hire your kind here," he says.[3] As long as discrimination by the AFL and employers contin-ued to ban African Americans from jobs, the cartoon argued, the "Buy American" call was irrelevant: only whites would get the jobs created by a purportedly patriotic call issued to *all* Americans. The Buy American call for job creation "seems to come from a heart that beats true brotherhood," Barney E. Page seconded in a March letter to the editor, but "when the petitioners entreat Americans to buy American and provide more jobs, they are deaf to the importunings of Race Americans [African Americans] who really buy American, and of right are entitled to their share of jobs. . . . The whole affair is too hypocritical for permanent relief."[4]

On January 28 Abbott responded with a "Chicago Defender Platform for America" designed to look exactly like Hearst's "Prosperity Politics" platform. Number one on the list, a direct stab at the AFL, called for "The opening up of all trades and trade unions to blacks as well as whites." Abbott and his African American readers understood that both as consumers and as workers seeking jobs, they were outside the circle Hearst and the AFL had in mind. From their perspective, white racism within the United States was the problem, not some far away "foreigners."[5]

African Americans were not immune, however, to the immigrant-bashing that was pervasive in the white mainstream press. The *Pittsburgh Courier*—like the *Defender,* a prominent African American paper with a national circulation—countered Hearst with an editorial entitled " 'BUY AMERICAN' and HIRE AMERICAN." "What Mr. Hearst needs to add to his suggestion is the necessity for hiring American as well as buying American," it argued.

> Hiring American . . . will tend to keep in this country millions of dollars earned every year by foreigners and shipped away as rapidly as it is earned. . . . Not only should we buy American, but we should see to it that we hire American, so that the money spent for labor, personal service and whatnot should be spent by Americans, with Americans, and, best of all, the money kept in America for Americans.[6]

The *Defender* also attacked immigrant workers: in its cartoon of the two men with the saw, off to the left a third, smaller man appeared, drawn as a stereotypical Chinese and speaking in squiggly lines representing Chinese characters. Behind him another stereotyped man appeared in a sombrero, symbolizing Mexican labor.[7] On January 26 a second *Defender* cartoon portrayed a white waiter with a mustache and longish hair—symbolizing European immigrants—serving a white couple in a posh restaurant, while pushing out an expensively dressed African American couple. "We don't serve your kind here!" he exclaims. The cartoon's headline asked: "How Can We 'Buy American' When These Foreigners Won't Let Us?"—renouncing the employment of immigrants, the Buy American call, and Jim Crow segregation all at the same time.[8]

Anti-immigrant arguments in the African American press in 1933 most often objected not to European immigrants, as in this restaurant cartoon, but to those from Asia, as in the saw cartoon. African Americans were particularly concerned with their displacement as Pullman porters by Japanese, Filipino, and sometimes Chinese immigrants. A *Pittsburgh Courier* editorial on January 18, for example, entitled "Foreigners and Pullman Service," attacked Asian employment in the United States and endorsed a bill under consideration in the Senate that would have barred employment in Pullman cars of non-citizens—that is, Asians, ineligible for citizenship. "They are foreigners, and our American industries owe it to the American man to hire him first, last, and always," the editorial argued.[9] Lillian Johnson, endorsing the same bill in a March 18 *Houston Informer* column, additionally expressed her concern over the displacement of African Americans by immigrants in domestic service jobs. "While these replacements apply mostly to men, the women have not been left out, Polish, German and many other women of foreign birth taking the place of nurse girls and household servants." Johnson then quoted the *Baltimore Afro-American:* "If 'Buy American' is a good slogan, why is not 'Employ Americans' equally as good?"[10]

We need to place these comments in careful perspective. Conditions for black people during the Great Depression were desperate. African American unemployment exceeded even that of the general population. Most people were surviving only through tightly knit kinship networks based on sharing meager resources obtained by those who were lucky enough to find work. As the Depression deepened, white employers increased their discrimination against African Americans. In a nationwide pattern, as white men and women lost their jobs, they bumped African Americans and other workers of color down the ladder of job hierarchy, until they bumped them off the bottom end of the employment ladder altogether. During the 1930s white women, both native- and foreign-born, started displacing African American women from the one job to which they had traditionally been relegated, domestic service. When unemployed African American people then applied for government aid, white relief officials overtly discriminated against them, usually denying them assistance.[11]

Tensions among those at the economic bottom mounted in response, as people fought over the only scraps allotted to them in a racialized job structure in crisis. White employers exacerbated the situation to their advantage by deliberately playing one group off against the other. African Americans felt threatened by Asian workers in 1933 for a very specific reason: the Pullman company had just hired dozens of Japanese workers in a conscious attempt to undercut African American men's new union, the Brotherhood of Sleeping Car Porters. When some African Americans in response blamed Asian immigrants for undercutting their economic position, a long line of white racism—such as Hearst's and the AFL's—and exploitation by employers, such as Pullman, had both created their plight and encouraged them to point the finger for it at "aliens."[12]

But most African Americans did not blame immigrants for their situation. Rather than jumping on Hearst's "Yellow Peril" bandwagon, in the 1930s they launched a wave of city-based campaigns advocating, instead, "Don't Buy Where You Can't Work." In at least thirty-five cities between 1929 and 1941, ordinary women and men responded to the Depression by demanding that white employers in African American neighborhoods begin to hire black workers. Like Hearst's Buy American campaign, they argued that purchasing power be put to work in the name of job creation. The difference was in their definition of the problem—and in their concept of "Us" and "Them."[13]

African Americans in the late 1920s were outraged that white retailers operating in black communities refused to hire African American workers. In Chicago, whites controlled 90 percent of retail trade in African American neighborhoods, for example, but only rarely employed African Americans.[14] In 1929 Chicago activists started calling on the worst offenders and asking that they change their ways. If the stores refused, the activists began to picket them, using the slogan "Don't Buy Where You Can't Work." The idea spread like wildfire in Chicago's black community, and by 1930 the campaign had obtained three to five thousand new jobs for African Americans.[15]

When the Depression hit, obliterating most of the jobs African Americans had been precariously hanging on to in the 1920s, Chicago's idea spread rapidly across the country. In Baltimore, for example, African American activists—including future Supreme Court justice Thurgood Marshall—started out in 1933 by demanding jobs at smaller, locally owned stores that had long catered to African Americans but always refused to hire them, and then moved on to larger chains like the A & P. When the larger stores balked, the "Don't Buy Where You Can't Work" movement threw up picket lines around them. Within a few days, "the stores were practically closed down," Evelyn Burrell, one of the picketers, recalled. "We had young people going from door to door, acquainting people. We had trucks and loudspeakers going all around the neighborhood."[16] The A & P quickly gave in and hired thirty-eight new black workers by the next April. "It was a tremendous victory," remembered Juanita Jackson Mitchell, one of the movement's leaders.[17]

In many cases these protests spilled over into campaigns to support local African American businesses under the parallel slogan "Buy Where You Can Work." "We must organize our purchasing power behind a demand for equal opportunity to work and also in support of those businesses in which Negroes can do work without discrimination," the New Negro Alliance, a Washington, D.C., boycott group argued.[18] The Reverend John Johnson of St. Martin's Protestant Episcopal Church in Harlem similarly preached, "We must spend our money among our own people."[19] Johnson and others advocated a "Buy Black" policy that called upon African Americans to spend their money within a race-conscious circuit, which would, in turn, create jobs for their people. These activists argued that money spent on white-owned businesses soon spiraled far away from the African American community. As a reader wrote to the *Houston Informer* in February 1933: "I buy my groceries from a Negro, but he buys them from a white jobber; the jobber buys them from a white manufacturer; and the white manufacturer buys them from a white grower."[20] In the process, African Americans were cut out of the employment loop.[21]

Much of the support for this second, "Buy Where You Can Work" approach came from the African American business community. In Harlem, a group of merchants distributed "Race Loyalty" buttons that read: "I hereby pledge myself to buy from Race Enterprises whenever and wherever practicable (or from stores employing Negro help) thereby helping to create MORE and BETTER jobs right here in Harlem."[22] In Harlem, Detroit, Baltimore, Cleveland, and throughout the country middle-class African American women formed new Housewives Leagues to support both the boycotts and black-owned businesses. Women performed much of the hard, daily work of knocking on doors, dissuading shoppers, and making the soup, historian Darlene Clark Hine has shown. By 1935 the Detroit Housewives League counted ten thousand members. "It is our duty as women controlling 85 percent of the family budget to unlock through concentrated spending closed doors," its members proclaimed, "that Negro youth may have the opportunity to develop and establish businesses in the fields closest to them."[23]

These arguments in support of a separate, racially defined economy overlapped within the boycott movement with overt black nationalist ideas, still widespread after the collapse of Marcus Garvey's Universal Negro Improvement Association (UNIA) in the early 1930s. Immensely popular, Garvey had advocated a Pan-Africanist program of black pride institutionalized through a separate black economy and a back-to-Africa migration. Several of the key leaders of the "Don't Buy Where You Can't Work" movement in the 1930s modeled themselves after Garvey and echoed his nationalist approach. They could be compelling street speakers who melded demands for African American employment with race pride. A former Garveyite named Kiowah Costonie, for example, set up shop in Baltimore in 1932 as a faith healer but soon organized a voter registration drive, gave lectures on "race pride and economics," and spearheaded the city's "Don't Buy Where You Can't Work" movement.[24]

In a new study of Cleveland's African American community during the interwar years, historian Kimberley Phillips gives us our closest glimpse into the rank-and-file world of the "Don't Buy Where You Can't Work" movement. Cleveland's "Don't Buy" campaign was above all a working-class movement, she shows, sustained from below by dedicated rank-and-file activists. In February 1935, inspired by the other cities' successes, seventeen women and men met up at the home of John Holly, a shipping clerk and former coal miner, chauffeur, and auto worker; formed a new organization, the Future Outlook League; and launched the country's most powerful "Don't Buy Where You Can't Work" campaign. By 1936 several hundred members had joined, most of them working people, including radicals, southern migrants, and the unemployed.[25]

A large percentage of the rank-and-file members of the Future Outlook League were female. As one member put it in an interview with Phillips, "Black women were the FOL." Phillips notes that working-class African American women were particularly anxious to find a way out of their seemingly permanent entrapment in domestic service employment—if they were lucky enough even to get those jobs in the 1930s. They had all the requisite skills to do clerical and sales work. They saw white women employed by the millions in clerical and sales jobs. And every day they saw white business owners throughout their community employ whites only.[26]

Increasingly, the league started functioning as a proto-trade union. As their campaign paid off, Cleveland African Americans began their new jobs working at white-owned businesses. The conditions could be horrific, the wages meager. In response, the league pivoted to address the workplace concerns of its newly employed members. In 1936 it formed a new sub-organization called the Employees' Association, which was soon racking up successes as impressive as the initial campaign to obtain jobs. At the Rainbow Cafe, for example, league members waitressing in new jobs were initially told to work a grueling twelve-hour day, seven-day week, for $5.00 a week. When the owner wouldn't agree to decrease their hours or raise their pay, the waitresses "put down aprons and trays," customers "put down their drinks and forks," and together they picketed the Cafe. Within an hour the owner capitulated.[27]

The Future Outlook League's campaign was a far cry from Hearst's Buy American movement. African Americans in Cleveland and throughout the country were well aware of the hypocrisy of those who claimed to protect "Americans" but excluded black people from most jobs within the country. Like other Americans, people of African descent could blame immigrants, especially Asian immigrants, for their plight. But more often they pointed the finger at racial discrimination by white Americans—practiced by those who refused to serve African Americans in restaurants, on trains, and in theaters; by those who were happy to sell to African Americans, but who refused to hire them; and by AFL unionists who kept them out of well-paid jobs.

BUYING AN EMPIRE

Elected president in late 1932, Franklin Delano Roosevelt talked back to Hearst, too. In early January 1933, Hearst dispatched an emissary, E. D. Coblentz, publisher of the *New York American*, to influence the newly elected president. Roosevelt "was very earnest in his expressed desire to talk with you personally," Coblentz reported back in a January 11 letter to Hearst. The president invited Hearst to meet with him in early February or late March 1933 at a spa in Warm Springs, Georgia. Coblentz reported that Roosevelt "disapproves of the 'Buy American' campaign as a long-term policy . . . saying that it would stifle all our foreign trade and would promote the erection of insurmountable tariff walls in other countries against us." But Roosevelt was far too clever to completely dismiss Hearst: "He did say, however, that it was a good club to hold over the heads of our European competitors at present."[28]

Roosevelt had no intention of following Hearst's program for recovery. His understanding of the problems sapping the nation's economy was fundamentally different from Hearst's. So were his solutions, and within days of his inaugural he had utterly reframed the nation's understanding of the Depression and how to end it.

Hearst's campaign turned out to be a flash in the pan. By mid-decade, Franklin Delano Roosevelt and the New Deal had utterly eclipsed the economic nationalism of Hearst's Buy American movement. Rather than sealing off the nation from foreign ties, the New Deal consciously sought to revive the U.S. economy by redistributing income to those at the bottom. Working people seized the moment, formed the Congress of Industrial Organizations (CIO), and built a mass movement of interracial solidarity that pointed the finger at corporate power, not at foreigners. Politics pivoted on the axis of class. At the same time, free trade interests triumphed in the Roosevelt administration. Eble was too late: by the time he addressed Congress in 1939, free traders, the New Deal, and the CIO had left Hearst and his nationalist allies in the economic dust.

Roosevelt took on the Depression on two fronts; first and foremost, the domestic one. For Roosevelt and his advisers, the Great Depression had been caused in part by domestic "underconsumption": The gap between the volume of goods produced by U.S. industry and the

American people's ability to consume them had widened so far that the economy had collapsed. The solution, therefore, was partly to redistribute wealth to the bottom so that ordinary Americans would be able to buy the products of U.S. factories and keep them running.[29]

Beginning with his famous "First 100 Days" in office in 1933, Roosevelt launched the alphabet soup of new agencies and federal acts known as the New Deal. In 1933, he created the Federal Emergency Relief Administration (FERA), which poured millions into federally sponsored poor relief for the first time. For the most part, in this "First New Deal," Roosevelt pushed through measures designed to stabilize the out-of-control economy, including the Banking Act of 1933, the Agricultural Adjustment Act, and the National Industrial Recovery Act (NIRA), which set up uniform wage codes across manufacturing sectors. Only with the so-called "Second New Deal" beginning in 1935 did Roosevelt create the modern welfare state and deliberately seek to transfer the nation's wealth downward through Social Security, Aid to Families with Dependent Children, unemployment insurance, and the Fair Labor Standards Act—which mandated a minimum wage and outlawed child labor.

The jewel in the New Deal crown of income redistribution was the National Labor Relations Act (NLRA), or Wagner Act, of 1935. The Wagner Act revolutionized workplace relations. Not only did it create the federal machinery in place ever since overseeing federally sanctioned union elections, but it forbade employers from interfering with their employees' efforts to organize unions and created the National Labor Relations Board (NLRB) to adjudicate newly defined "unfair labor practices" and punish those who committed them. For the first time in U.S. history, working people had federal protection of their civil liberties when they tried to organize unions, and a law that said their boss had to bargain with them or face a fine. The Wagner Act did not, however, apply to agricultural workers laboring in the fields or to domestic servants; neither did social security or unemployment insurance. Given the national demographics of employment, this meant that most African American and Mexican American wage workers, along with non–wage-earning women, were cut out of the New Deal's underconsumptionist loop.

In an upsurge from below that rivaled that of 1886, working people nonetheless rose up to seize the moment of opportunity. A group of progressive union leaders, long frustrated with the AFL's narrow craft union exclusiveness, split off from the AFL in 1935 to form a new national-level federation, the Congress of Industrial Organizations (CIO). The CIO's founders believed in industrial, rather than craft, unions, which would represent all workers at a given firm regardless of skill level, craft jurisdiction, race, or gender. By the end of 1937 new CIO-affiliated unions had organized millions of workers in labor's own alphabet soup of newly powerful international unions, including the United Auto Workers (UAW) with 400,000 members; the United Electrical Workers with 80,000; and the Steel Workers' Organizing Committee with 375,000. Especially after the UAW beat General Motors in the monumental Flint Sit-Down Strike of 1936–1937, the giants of corporate America swiftly, and astonishingly, surrendered to the CIO unions. Like its predecessor the Knights of Labor, the CIO sought to establish democratic control of the economy from below. The New Deal's Wagner Act created the window of opportunity for redistribution of wealth and power to the bottom. But working people themselves did the job, through union struggles full of risk and overflowing high spirits.[30]

In sharp contrast to the AFL, CIO-affiliated unions explicitly sought to organize workers across lines of ethnicity, race, and gender. The United Cannery, Agricultural, and Packinghouse Workers of America (UCAPAWA), for example, organized Chinese, Japanese, and Filipino cannery workers in Alaska; African American tobacco workers in North Carolina; and Chicano and Russian Jewish women in California fruit packing plants. But the CIO's gains were only partial. Most white workers still balked at joining with workers of color as complete equals. Most men still had a hard time thinking of female clerical and sales workers or domestic servants as fellow-workers, and the CIO left them out, for the most part. When the UAW in 1936 stormed the General Motors fort in the Flint sit-down strike, for example, it deliberately excluded the company's female clerical workers. The waitresses at the Rainbow Cafe in Cleveland who joined the Future Outlook League that same year knew that they, too, were still outside even the CIO's sphere.[31]

Roosevelt's second front for recovery was the international one. If the domestic solution was to find markets for the products of U.S. goods at home, the external solution was to ensure markets overseas.

"Enlightened self-interest dictates to each nation the need and the wisdom of a healthy expansion of its foreign trade," Roosevelt explained.[32] In 1934 he pushed through the Reciprocal Trade Act, the brainchild of his secretary of state, Cordell Hull, long known as an almost fanatical proponent of free trade. The Act granted the president unprecedented new powers to negotiate trade agreements on his or her own. It allowed for three-year treaties in which U.S. tariffs could be reduced by as much as 50 percent of their 1930 Smoot-Hawley levels, in individual agreements with foreign countries who, in turn, would agree to lower their own barriers. Any tariff break the United States extended to one particular country would, in turn, be extended to all the others.

This was the reciprocity idea of the nineteenth century finally realized on a grand scale, and a turning point in the nation's trade policy. The free traders finally won. The Reciprocal Trade Act, writes historian Walter LaFeber, was "supposed to resemble a giant wrecking ball knocking down tariff walls."[33] Wreck them it did. By 1939 twenty-one individual trade agreements had been clinched. In a new agreement with Brazil, for example, the United States slashed its tariffs on nuts, castor beans, and manganese and kept coffee and cacao tariff-free, while Brazil cut its tariffs on cars, radios, electrical batteries, cement, paint, fruit, and fish. By 1945 twenty-nine such treaties were in place, and U.S. tariffs had plunged by almost 75 percent.[34]

Powerful corporate and banking interests were behind this shift. Manufacturing corporations such as International Harvester and Zenith wanted to sell their U.S.-made products overseas without tariffs at the overseas end. Other corporations, such as United Fruit, wanted a free reign to invest directly in overseas operations. Powerful banks wanted to profit from loans both to foreign firms and to U.S. firms operating abroad. Ever since World War I had undercut Europe's imperial trading networks, these interests had wanted to dominate global trade under a U.S. flag. They particularly had their eye on Latin America, long considered—by the United States but not by Latin Americans—the exclusive turf of U.S. capitalists, in the name of a paternalistic domination that Roosevelt called the "Good Neighbor Policy." Powerful corporations, in sum, wanted to expand the U.S. economic empire. By the mid-thirties they had convinced Roosevelt that to do so would solve the Depression.[35]

As free traders, they naturally had no truck with Hearst and the

Buy American bloc. In a major speech on reciprocal trade agreements, Hull charged that Buy American advocates were really disguised pro-tariff interests. "There are some who exploit this slogan . . . by making it serve as a cloak for the promotion of special interests through the imposition and maintenance of unreasonable and embargo tariffs."[36]

Free-trade opponents of buying American argued, first, that it would lead to dangerous retaliation. The *New York Times*—which political scientist Thomas Ferguson refers to as "the free trade organ of international finance"—in December 1932, for example, approvingly reported a speech by Charles T. Riotte, executive secretary of the National Council of American Importers and Traders, in which Riotte argued that "if the 'buy-American' campaign . . . is permitted to attain serious proportions," a "campaign of retaliation" would result next to which the trade barriers following Smoot-Hawley "would appear mild."[37]

Opponents also argued that buying American would make it impossible for the European allies ever to pay off their debts. As C. M. Thomson wrote in to the *San Francisco Chronicle*, the rival paper to Hearst's *Examiner*, "Your 'Buy American' and 'No Cancellation of War Debts' seem quite contradictory. Will you please explain how foreign countries can pay us what they owe us if we will not take their goods in payment?"[38] *The Nation*, in a February 1933 article by Maxwell S. Stuart, seconded: "Foreigners can only purchase American products when they are obtainable at world prices and when they can secure the necessary American currency or its equivalent"—by selling to the United States.[39]

Buy American opponents especially delighted in mocking the logic of devolving geographic circles into which the movement did in fact devolve. Ohio state senator Marvin C. Harrison battled his state legislature's Buy American law "by proposing amendments that Ohio citizens should not trade with citizens of any other state; that residents of each county should not trade with residents of the other counties; and that the government be authorized to determine whether prosperity might not be restored permanently by restricting trade to township lines."[40] Senator Thomas P. Gore (no relation to Senator Albert Gore, Sr., or his son, the vice president), in a February 4, 1933, Senate debate over a law restricting employment on U.S. ships to U.S. citizens, proposed sarcastically,

Let's incorporate a provision that these "all American" seamen can breathe only American oxygen. They can take it along in American-made tanks. . . . Let's not stop there—we've got to go through with this. Let's provide that the ships can only ply waters emanating from American rivers. Let's be consistent.[41]

More seriously, opponents argued that the U.S. economy had long turned a corner in its volume of foreign trade and was irreversibly dependent on exports. "We are in the world market as sellers and we have much more to lose than gain by a policy of dog-eat-dog," a prominent accountant insisted in the *New York Times*.[42] Maxwell Stuart made the same point in his *Nation* piece: "Even a superficial glance is enough to disclose the fundamental fallacy in the 'Buy American' campaign. For more than fifty years the United States has maintained a 'favorable' balance of trade. Even in the darkest days of the depression there has a been a relatively substantial surplus of exports over imports."[43] Secretary of State Cordell Hull warned more explicitly in his speech on reciprocity: "A large number of vitally important branches of production in our country are geared to an output far in excess of our domestic requirements. These surpluses must be marketed abroad, if the industries producing them are not to stagnate."[44] It was too late for autarchy: the tide of imperial trade had long turned, and the nation was hooked on what it carried homeward.

The addiction was twofold: First, to sales of U.S. goods abroad. "Could California afford to lose its foreign markets for its products?" the *San Francisco Chronicle* asked. No. "We Californians have a lot of canned fruit, kerosene and gasoline, apples, dried fruit, raisins, barley, hops, redwood lumber and a host of other products which we depend on selling to people in other countries." Californians, the *Chronicle* concluded, "are not going to cut off their own right hand—even for the sake of a slogan."[45] Second, since the nineteenth century, U.S. firms had become addicted to raw materials that were only available overseas. *Business Week*, in a February 8, 1933, story entitled "Sure, Buy American!" estimated that "It is conservative to assume that one-tenth of us live directly upon export trade, and vastly more than that proportion make our living in industries—such as steel—that would collapse without imported crude commodities."[46] Charles T. Riotte, of the National Council of American Importers and Traders, in his speech quoted by the *New York Times*, listed "Silk, rubber, coffee, tea, cocoa, sugar, tin and manganese ore" as "only a few of the foreign raw materials upon which we are absolutely dependent."[47]

Finally, and not least, Buy American opponents went for the campaign's jugular: the jobs argument. Secretary of State Cordell Hull responded to AFL president William Green personally on this one. Green had written to Hull on July 31, 1934, quoting from a letter to Green from F. B. Gerhart of the United Match Workers—the same letter quoted earlier—in which Gerhart protested the importation of Japanese matches and asked for tariff protection. Tariffs wouldn't solve the match workers' problems, Hull wrote back a week later; they had caused them. "The old fallacy that imports of commodities displace the amount of American labor necessary to produce them most certainly has been divested of every shred of plausibility by the awful experience of American labor and the American people under the operation of our skyscraping trade barriers during recent years," Hull insisted.

> We must not lose sight of the fact that our export industries give employment no less important to American labor than do our industries which find themselves faced by competition with foreign-made products. If experience has taught us anything it is that when this nation seeks to stop up every crack and crevice in its trade walls so as to prohibit competitive importations, other countries in self defense or on retaliation impose embargoes against our surplus products.[48]

The addicts, in other words, created more jobs than their free-trade policies lost.[49]

The Buy American movement and Hull's free trade agenda were diametrically opposed: one looked inward to economic nationalism, to autarchy; the other looked outward to foreign trade, to empire. But like the nineteenth-century trade debate, in many ways both sides were, in the end, still similar. Like nineteenth-century sparring partners over trade policy, both Hearst and Hull still believed in a model of industrial capitalist development with the corporations in charge —however much the New Deal might impartially empower working people through trade unions. Both sides argued, as had Cleveland and

McKinley, that *their* approach would best avert revolution. After the Russian Revolution of 1917, three years of the collapse of U.S. capitalism, and the rise of German and Italian fascism on the horizon, such arguments carried an edge of real fear. Warren H. Atherton, commander of the California division of the American Legion, in his Buy American endorsement in the *San Francisco Examiner*, pointedly reminded Hearst's readers that "Every penny that goes out of our nation to purchase goods contributes to unemployment, uncertainty, and dissatisfaction in America."[50] Rosalie Harbey, regent of the Sequoia Chapter of the Daughters of the American Revolution, got his point. "Whatever will keep our workmen working and our people happy, should be the concern of every American. . . . I want to patronize home industry first."[51] Unhappy workmen might get dissatisfied, as Roosevelt, preaching for the opposite camp, well knew: "Foreign markets must be regained if America's producers are to rebuild a full and enduring domestic prosperity for our people. There is no other way if we would avoid painful economic dislocation, social readjustments, and unemployment."[52] "Social readjustments" was a polite term for revolution.

The other basis for consensus in the late nineteenth century had been empire. Here the Buy American proponents would appear to diverge. But if we move down the list of Hearst's daily list of "10 PROSPERITY POLICIES FOR AMERICAN PATRIOTS" past "Buy American" at the top, we find that point number two was "Encourage Pan-American reciprocity, consuming Pan-American raw materials and opening the markets of North and South America to our manufactured products, while providing work for our unemployed." Third was "Develop our merchant marine to serve our trade in times of peace and supplement our navy in time of war." Number five read: "Encourage our railroads to make transcontinental extensions and transcontinental steamship lines to connect our industry with world markets." Together, these were precisely the elements necessary for U.S. trade and military domination of Latin America. One critic concluded, "That is, we must always sell to foreigners, and never buy from them!" Like McKinley, Hearst wanted to have it all.[53]

A final and closer look at William Randolph Hearst's own affairs reveals a taste, in fact a vast moneyed enthusiasm for things foreign, which his critics at the time delighted in pointing out.[54] The paper on which he printed his Buy American exhortations was bought in Canada. In the 1933 newsreel in which he called on all patriots to buy American, he stood in front of the carved wooden doors of Hearst Castle, which he had imported from Europe. The castle itself was crammed with tapestries, furniture, suits of armor, and paintings Hearst had imported in a decades-long, bizarre obsession with literally buying up "ancient" European culture and reconstructing it on the central California coast. Hearst also owned another 65,000-acre estate in Northern California called Wyntoon, with its own castle and the alleged replica of an entire Bavarian village. He also owned his own real fourteenth-century castle, St. Donat's, in Glamorganshire, Wales, with 135 rooms and 1,300 acres of Welsh land to go with them. Hearst was also "one of the largest landowners in Mexico," with a 90,000-acre cattle ranch, a 350,000-acre chicle forest, 60,000 acres in Chihuahua, and a gold and silver mine. And he was one of the "principal owners" of the Cerro de Pasco copper and lead mine in Peru.[55] Hearst himself, in other words, had no problem buying foreign products and even foreign lands.

The very same Treasury and Post Office Appropriations Bill that contained the Buy American Act of 1933 also included funds for extending U.S. air mail service to Latin America, so the ever more powerful foreign traders could communicate with their dependents. In the fine print of the documents submitted as part of the debate lies a letter on behalf of the bill from C. V. Drew, representing the Cerro de Pasco Copper Corporation, partly owned by William Randolph Hearst: "We find that air mail not only expedites all important communications with our South American properties but affords the opportunity of being more explicit than possible with cables."[56] Hearst's private "economic train" was in truth an airplane, winging its way to profits in Latin America. Like Thomas Jefferson and George Washington, whose campaigns he echoed, Hearst exhorted the country to economic nationalism. But when it came to his own pocketbook and to the long-term future of corporate profits, his policies were something else altogether.

PEOPLE'S DIPLOMACY
The last word goes to a group of Americans Hearst included among his imaginary "Yellow Peril." Chinese Americans brought to the Buy

American question an unexpected twist, which takes us beyond the nation's borders—but not on Hearst's terms.

In a 1934 photograph entitled "Declaration of Protest," John Gutmann, a Jewish photographer who had just fled from Nazi Germany to the United States, captured the anonymous missives he found on a wall somewhere in San Francisco's Chinatown. In the photo's upper right-hand corner, a leaflet from the Young Men's China Club called on Americans to boycott goods "Made in Japan." In the photograph's center, over a swatch of enormous painted Chinese characters, someone had plastered a horizontal strip of paper: "BOYCOTT JAPANESE. BUY AMERICAN," it proclaimed.[57]

In 1931, after Japan invaded Manchuria in Northwest China, Chinese immigrants to the United States and their American-born children had launched an enormous campaign to boycott Japanese goods, through which they hoped to stop Japan's increasingly powerful military aggression. Then, in July 1937, Japan again invaded China, this time bombing Shanghai to pieces, and initiated full-scale war. Horrified, Chinese Americans merged their boycott campaign with fundraising for relief to China, in response. In New York City a newly formed General Relief Committee in six months raised a million dollars—in the middle of the Depression—in part through a compulsory system of monthly payments based on income level. Some activists organized spectacular street parades to publicize the boycott; others knocked on the doors of small businesses and tenement rooming houses to fill cans with money for ambulances; others persuaded longshoremen to refuse to ship scrap iron to Japan.[58]

The anti-Japanese boycott actually began in China, where it galvanized grassroots opposition to Japan. In Canton in 1932, for example, a Boycott Society led by student and labor groups seized several thousand bags of Japanese soybeans at the docks and threatened to destroy them. In Hong Kong that same year, one paper reported, "Japanese goods are only sold when their identity is difficult or unknown [sic]."[59] The boycott spread swiftly to Chinese emigrant communities throughout the world. When San Francisco's traditional benevolent associations, the Six Companies, called for a meeting to coordinate relief and boycott campaigns in 1937, they joined together three hundred communities in the United States, Mexico, and Central and South America.[60] Through these campaigns, Chinese who were dispersed throughout the world acted upon a global concept of economic nation: one that crossed national borders to coordinate individual and collective economic behavior on behalf of a desperate homeland.

In supporting the boycott, Chinese Americans were deeply concerned about the fate of their relatives still in China. Many also identified with a newly emergent Chinese nationalism in the face of Japanese attacks. But the boycott movement was also about their situation in the United States. Here is the final twist in our story: Chinese Americans in the 1930s believed that a stronger China would lead to greater equality *in the United States*. "'Had China been stronger,' it was often remarked in New York's Chinatown, 'we overseas [Chinese] would not be treated so badly in this country,'" historian Peter Kwong writes.[61] Renqiu Yu, in a study of the Chinese Hand Laundry Association of New York, similarly argues that Chinese in the United States joined relief and boycott efforts on behalf of China "in hopes that their contributions would help build a powerful China, and that a powerful China would in turn help elevate their own status in America," summarized by the association's slogan, "To Save China, to Save Ourselves."[62] Chinese Americans were aware that in 1905, after winning the Russo-Japanese War, Japan had been able to win concessions from the United States mandating better terms for Japanese immigrants. Kwong concludes: "Since the overseas Chinese assumed they would win respect only when their country did, for them patriotism became an indirect means of fighting for equal rights in the United States."[63] Chinese Americans' boycott of Japanese products, in other words, simultaneously expressed both a transnational sense of economic community and a desire to be fully accepted members of the United States.

Chinese Americans depicted their efforts as a "People's Diplomacy" through which ordinary people would reach out to non-Chinese Americans and affect foreign relations from the bottom up. Members of the Hand Laundry Alliance in New York, for example, printed up flyers asking their laundry customers to boycott Japanese goods; receptive customers in turn "made suggestions to the laundrymen on how to achieve more effective results."[64] Lorena How recalled that at the age of nine she would run with a group of friends into curio stores on Grant Avenue in San Francisco "and shout in our best English, 'Don't buy here ladies, this is a Japanese store.' " (The Japanese women proprietors had their own ideas about "People's Diplomacy": "they would chase us out with a large broom.")[65]

These overtures to non-Chinese Americans paid off. Especially after Japan's 1937 invasion of China, the boycott movement spread throughout the United States. Initially, support came from the Left, motivated in part by international Communist concern over Japanese imperialism. In October 1937, the American Committee Against War and Fascism and the Friends of China Committee, both connected with the Communist Party, sponsored a rally in New York at which fifteen thousand people showed up, thirteen thousand of them non-Chinese.[66] Soon liberals throughout the country endorsed the boycott. *The Nation* both officially endorsed it in a 1937 editorial and ran regular stories on its behalf.[67] The AFL, CIO, United Auto Workers, Kiwanis Club of Boston, Massachusetts State Grange, National Negro Congress, California League of Women Voters, and hundreds of other groups endorsed it. By early 1938 the boycott movement had become an international movement spreading far beyond the Chinese community, especially among religious and other groups concerned with peaceful solutions to the increasing threat of war.[68]

At the symbolic center of the U.S. movement was a refusal by women to wear silk stockings. Boycott proponents pointed out that the United States consumed 85 percent of Japan's raw silk exports, which, in turn, made up one-fifth to one-seventh of its total exports. Most of that silk went to stockings.[69] In an amazingly successful popular campaign, wearing cotton lisle stockings become a left-liberal status symbol. The press delighted in the opportunity the campaign offered for titillating stories. In January 1938, 652 leftist delegates from the country's more elite college campuses gathered at Vassar for a convention of the American Student Union. *Time* magazine reported that one young woman gathered with other students next to a bonfire in the snow, "kicked off her shoes, stripped the silk stockings off her legs and, standing bare-foot in the snow, hurled her stockings into the fire." *Time* loved the story:

> Other silk-clad girls followed suit, snatched the silk ties from male delegates. . . . they raced into the dormitories, returned with other armloads

of students' underthings. Around the fire danced the delegates chanting: *Make lisle the style, wear lisle for a while. If you wear cotton, Japan gets nottin.*[70]

Movies stars Loretta Young, Sylvia Sidney, and Frances Farmer swore off silk stockings.[71] Melvyn Douglas, Dashiell Hammett, Gale Sondergaard, Dorothy Parker, and Chinatown's own Anna May Wong organized a demonstration in Hollywood at which the six-thousand-person audience witnessed "a strip tease of silk stockings and silk undergarments disdainfully discarded and dropped into a red, white and blue wastebasket." The whole audience "joined . . . in a vociferous chant: 'Boycott Japan.'"[72]

A *Fortune* magazine poll in February 1938 found that 57.5 percent of all Americans favored the boycott.[73] In January 1938 six department store chains, including Woolworth's and S. H. Kress, announced they would no longer order Japanese goods.[74] The boycott had a serious economic impact. The Department of Commerce reported in the first six months of 1938 imports from Japan dropped 47 percent from the same period a year earlier.[75]

Through their boycott of Japanese products Chinese Americans expressed a transnational concept of economic nation that, like Pan-Africanism, evoked a people in diaspora united in support of a homeland far away. But, like the "Don't Buy Where You Can't Work" movement, it was also about breaking down walls of racism, fighting for equality, and bringing a fuller democracy to the domestic economy of the United States. The sign advocating "Buy American. Don't Buy Japanese" that John Gutmann caught in his photograph was, after all, printed in English. Its anonymous author was reaching out from a community contained by Hearst's racism to a broader American community and beyond, asking ordinary people to form their own "people's diplomacy" through a boycott of Japanese products. Far from being stereotypical "inscrutable Orientals," Chinese Americans were politically active Americans with their own ideas about foreign economic relations, seeking to explain their politics to, and be treated with dignity by, mainstream America.[76] Far from being indistinguishable "Asians," they drew stark lines between themselves and the Japanese.

Yet their boycott also landed right in Hearst's trap. If it taught non-Asian Americans to distinguish China from Japan and Chinese Americans from Japanese, at the same time it confirmed Hearst's earlier call to reject all products from Asia. Even as Chinese Americans sought to fight domestic racism, their boycott's popularity inadvertently drew on—and expanded—the very Yellow Peril hysteria they were fighting against.

WHAT GUTMANN KNEW

We opened our discussion of the Great Depression with Francis X. A. Eble, evoking George Washington and the birth of the economic nation and warning Congress of the specter of foreign trade. Eble, Hearst, and advocates of the Buy American movement had more in common with the Founding Fathers, it turns out, than they wanted to admit: like colonial merchants peddling moth-eaten clothes in the name of a people's nation, chemical and cement industry executives peddled their Made in America Club in the name of a unified, embattled America. But in the end, the Buy American advocates' rhetoric of economic nationalism was another smoke screen for elite profits.

The 1930s Buy American movement hinged on finger-pointing at "aliens," on an "Us versus Them" mentality in which loyal Americans huddled together to point outward. But attacks directed ostensibly outward kept turning inward, toward those inside the nation, until only white native-born citizens could be sure they were counted inside. African Americans knew the Buy American call was not for them; so did Chinese Americans. Both asked for a place in the economic nation or turned to their own concepts of economic nation. Yet those alternative nations were part and parcel of both groups' participation in an *American* nation. Indeed, both viewed their overlapping commitments as necessary struggles if they were to be full citizens in that overarching nation.

The Buy American movement of the 1930s, by directing its charges at foreigners, cleverly sought to divert Americans' frustration, fears, and anger away from corporate power or the structured inequalities of capitalism. Like the tariff debate of the 1880s, it was safe in a time of tremendous danger for the rich. The AFL took the bait and blamed "aliens." But most working people didn't. They chose the unsafe route: pointing the finger upward and organizing trade unions through which they sought democratic control of the economy. The CIO's millions of members used the Wagner Act's protection to restructure the negotiation of class power between working people and the corporations for the rest of the century. They even toppled a few corporate giants.

The giants were now themselves striding across the border to the South, grabbing up copper mines, banks, and plantations by the handful. They liked foreigners, especially the subservient kind, with whom they could be Good Neighbors in an expanded surge of paternalistic profits.

By 1939, though, other giants, some of them monsters, were starting to march across the globe, playing with ships and guns and gas ovens. Chinese Americans knew this well when they mobilized their boycott to stop Japan's military machine. John Gutmann, the photographer who captured their leaflets on the Chinatown wall, knew it all too well: a Jew, he had fled Germany as a refugee in 1933. Jewish Americans, along with Jews throughout the world, also knew. In the 1930s they built an international movement to boycott Nazi products that paralleled the Chinese boycott of Japanese products.[77]

Hearst's suspicious parochialism had no place in this new world of fascism, aggression, and genocide. The boycotts of Japanese and Nazi products and, in a different way, Roosevelt's triumphant free trade program all underscored how deeply embedded in the international economy were the American people in the 1930s, as the country hovered on the cusp of World War II and postwar domination of the global capitalist economy. The war would bring an unprecedented unity and collective purpose to the nation. But as a hundred thousand Japanese Americans were abruptly to learn, the newly unified wartime nation was still tainted with Hearst's legacy. James J. Shizuru, an American-born citizen, spent the first half of the war in an internment camp in Amache, Colorado, and the second half in the military intelligence language service of the United States Army. Fifty-five years later, he still boycotts the Hearst-owned *San Francisco Examiner.*[78]

CHAPTER 5

Making the World Safe for American Products

Imperial Free Trade in the American Century

As the "Golden Age" of U.S. prosperity waxed in the late 1950s, rumblings started growing about imports, job losses, and foreign competition, especially from Japan. By 1961 Larry Russell, a shop steward for the United Rubber Workers' union at the Firestone plant in Des Moines, Iowa, had been talking to his co-workers about the dangers of buying Japanese goods for quite a while. "I thought I should warn them it was a bunch of junk." Russell, a World War II Navy veteran and the son of Iowa farmers, had worked at the Firestone plant for about a dozen years and represented his union at the Polk County Labor Council in Des Moines. He also served as secretary of the council's Union Label Committee. In March 1961, he got the idea that his committee should convince the Des Moines labor council to mount a Buy American campaign. His fellow committee members, Henry Pontious from the autoworkers and Jim Titus from the plumbers, thought it was a great idea. They came up with four or five Buy American slogans. Jim's wife drew up some beautiful prototypes for Buy American bumper stickers the council could print up and distribute. In red, white, and blue printed on white, the 4- by 12-inch drawings looked great against a black backdrop, propped up on an easel when the committee presented its proposal at the council's meeting. The other delegates loved the idea. The council's president just thought one little formality was in order. Before they went ahead on their own, they decided to check with the national office of the AFL-CIO, which had merged in 1955. Off went a letter to Washington.[1]

On March 22 George Meany, president of the AFL-CIO, shot

back a personal reply to Russell. His answer was a resounding no. "I would hope that your Union Label Committee would not undertake such a campaign," he wrote.[2]

Why was Meany so opposed? Fifteen years earlier, AFL president William Green had enthusiastically endorsed Buy American campaigns; fifteen years later, the AFL-CIO would be spewing forth its own Buy American bumper stickers like there was no tomorrow. Meany himself explained in his 1961 letter to Russell:

> Millions of American workers are dependent for their livelihood on the sale overseas of the goods they produce. . . . The United States cannot hope to sell goods on the world market unless we are also willing to buy goods from other free nations.

In other words, "We must keep in our minds the necessity to find even more markets for American-made goods overseas." Equally important, he stressed, Cold War imperatives dictated a free trade position: "The free nations around the world will either trade with us, or, for lack of such trade, be forced to trade with the Soviet [sic] and its satellites. That would help the communist cause." Therefore, "a 'Buy American' campaign . . . would be to run contrary, not only to the policy of the AFL-CIO, but also against the best interests of American workers."[3]

Meany's reply captured exactly the AFL-CIO's position on trade issues at the peak of what *Life* publisher Henry Luce in 1941 dubbed the "American Century"—the period from World War II to the late 1960s when U.S. corporations enjoyed unprecedented dominance of the world's capitalist economies. In an about-face from the early Depression years, Buy American campaigns became unthinkable, because they would go against the orthodox grain of ever-freer trade. As Meany's letter explained, nationalist shopping was foolish, when the goal, instead, was to get the rest of the world to Buy American.

Meany and the AFL-CIO leadership had made a deal with the behemoth corporations that dictated U.S. foreign and economic policy at the war's end. They would join the corporations in an imperial consensus to dominate the world; they would embrace the corporation's free trade doctrines and march as cheerful soldiers in the Cold War. As they succumbed to the corporations' seduction, empire seemed to solve all their problems.

But, of course, it didn't. While the imperial deal seemed to solve

American working people's problems, it was no Golden Age for American workers. The deal was dependent, first of all, on U.S. corporate domination of the capitalist world, and especially on the exploitation of Third World peoples who, just like American workers, themselves wanted national sovereignty and economic democracy. While some industrial workers in the United States nonetheless benefited for a time from that domination, most working people at home were cut out of the deal. The inequalities and exclusions of the 1930s remained largely in place. Equally important for our story, the project of mutually assured prosperity, which seemed to solve so many problems, simultaneously contained the seeds of its own demise. Labor and the corporations were dancing together on thin ice. Soon the corporations would glide away, and American working people would be left to crash through—pushed in, in fact, by the same corporations.

The imperial free trade project of the American Century thus set the context for the crises of deindustrialization and unemployment of the 1970s, even as it trapped the AFL-CIO in an ideological and strategic mindset that would shape and limit its response to those same crises. Ironically, that mindset would also eventually produce the Buy American movement of the 1970s, when the AFL-CIO would come to think there was, indeed, no tomorrow and would plaintively wait for its partner to dance back.

FREE WORLD, FREE TRADE, FREE REIGN

To understand organized labor's embrace of the American Century and measure the new national consensus against Buy American campaigns in the 1950s and early 1960s, we need to begin with U.S. foreign relations in the postwar era.

The United States emerged from World II as the strongest economic power in the world. Germany and Japan lay in shambles; Western Europe and the Soviet Union were devastated; even Great Britain, the closest prewar rival, was left an economic disaster, its empire evaporating. The United States, meanwhile, escaped relatively unscathed. Its financial coffers were spilling over with wartime profits, and it owned half of the productive capacity of the entire world.[4]

Meanwhile, during the New Deal and especially World War II, the big corporations and the federal government had learned to cooperate tightly. In the quarter-century that followed the war they worked together hand-in-glove to carefully coordinate U.S. foreign, economic, and military policy to ensure that U.S. corporate profits would grow as never before. It was the fantasy world the corporations had been gunning for in the 1930s and well before. Now they were, indeed, at the top.

To stay on top, the U.S. corporations first had to beat back any alternatives to a U.S.-dominated capitalist economic system. The biggest threat, of course, was the Soviet Union. It was too big to wipe out; so instead the United States vowed "containment." By the end of the 1940s the United States had drawn a geographical and ideological line across the entire globe and had thoroughly militarized it. In so doing, U.S. policymakers set up two choices for the rest of the world: slide into godless Communism under Soviet bidding or enter the U.S. orbit under U.S. corporate tutelage.

This wasn't what most of the world's peoples had in mind. In postwar Western Europe, many governments were led by labor parties, social democrats, or even socialists, who preferred to eschew U.S. corporate control. They were interested in economic nationalism for their own people's benefit; open-minded about possible trading with the Soviet Union; and poised to nationalize private industry. The United States, by contrast, wanted to force open the vital European market and create a space for direct U.S. corporate investment. It wanted to make sure Europe didn't spiral away toward socialist or nationalist independence. Most immediately, Western Europe owed the United States $8 billion. Without dollars, it couldn't buy U.S. goods —and Europe was the single most important market for U.S. manufactured goods.

The Marshall Plan, or the European Recovery Act of 1947, was designed to solve those problems. The United States gave $17 billion to Europe over the following four years. Ostensibly, the purpose was humanitarian; but "there is no charity involved in this," Undersecretary of State Dean Acheson underscored. "It is simply common sense and good business." Congress, he insisted, had launched the Marshall Plan "chiefly as a matter of national self-interest."[5] The plan would give Europe its needed dollars while keeping it within the U.S.-controlled capitalist orbit. And it would guarantee markets for U.S. goods in a massive U.S. government–sponsored campaign ensuring that Europe bought American.

The final challenge was the Third World; and here the corporations fully cashed in on their Cold War ideological framework. The Third World mattered to U.S. corporations, first, because it contained crucial raw materials without which the engines of U.S. domestic manufacturing literally couldn't run. The nation's steel mills, for example, were overwhelmingly dependent on imported bauxite. U.S. policymakers needed to make sure no Third World countries turned to nationalism or socialism and cut off U.S. access to raw materials. Second, they wanted to make the Third World safe for U.S. corporate investments. Anticommunism gave the United States the pretext to intervene again and again in its self-proclaimed role as global policeman against alleged Soviet infiltration. If a Third World country balked at U.S. economic control, it was by definition in the throes of the Soviets.

The U.S.-dominated sphere—the "free world"—was thus locked in. Within that sphere, the corporations then institutionalized U.S. economic control. Before the war ended, at an international gathering in Bretton Woods, New Hampshire, in 1944, the United States created the International Monetary Fund (IMF), which codified global currencies at a stable exchange rate, pegged to the U.S. dollar. National currencies could only be exchanged for dollars, and dollars would be the medium for international exchange. Simultaneously, the United States founded the World Bank and contributed a third of the bank's $9.1 billion in funds, which were then lent to nations who played by U.S.-defined rules and denied to those who wouldn't. Together known as the Bretton Woods system, these arrangements ensured that for the next twenty-five years, financial transactions in the capitalist world would revolve around the U.S. economy, redounding to its benefit.[6]

U.S. trade policy needs to be understood in this broader context. With all their immense and growing productive capacity, U.S. manufacturing corporations needed open markets in which to sell their products without high tariffs or trade barriers. They needed to leap across national economic borders to buy those raw materials at bargain basement prices. Financiers, with all their money overflowing in the banks, needed places to invest without bars to foreign ownership. Given the weakness of the other capitalist industrial economies after the war, U.S. manufactured products could outcompete everyone else's. Free trade, therefore, was perfect for U.S. corporate goals. "Free trade is for the strong, protectionism is for the weak," and now the United States was not just strong but the strongest. Military policy opened the corporations' space; they were now "free" to enforce lower and lower trade barriers.

U.S. commitment to freer trade began with the first General Agreement on Tariffs and Trade (GATT) at Geneva in 1947, which initiated multilateral cuts in trade barriers. Using GATT and a regular series of renewals of the 1934 Reciprocal Trade Act throughout the 1940s and '50s, the United States steadily dropped its own tariff rates while forcing down tariffs and trade barriers throughout the capitalist world. "Trade liberalization," as it became known, climaxed with the Trade Expansion Act of 1962—which gave the president new independent powers to reduce tariffs and authorized across-the-board tariff reductions, not just item-by-item cuts. The Kennedy Round of GATT (1961–1967) cut the average tariff on manufactured goods worldwide by 35 percent; on vehicles and machinery by half. The percentage of U.S. trade, excluding oil and agriculture, on which tariffs were more than 15 percent plummeted from 63 percent to 15 percent.[7]

The system paid off splendidly for the U.S. corporations. By the late fifties the world bought American cars: the big three U.S. firms sold eleven and a half times as many cars as their three closest competitors.[8] The world bought American machine tools: one-third of all the machine tools produced in the world were made in the United States.[9] Meanwhile, foreign direct investment by U.S. corporations skyrocketed from $7 billion in 1938 to $32.8 billion in 1960 and then $82.8 billion by 1970.[10] The tentacles of U.S. corporate control reached into the interstices of every country outside the Soviet bloc. Coldly policing the "free world" against the forces of Soviet darkness, the American corporations bought up the world, and the world bought American.

IMPERIAL TEAMWORK
But why did Meany and the leaderships of the AFL and CIO sign onto the corporations' imperial agenda and leap so wholeheartedly into what might in retrospect look like a foolish deal with a devil who would later betray them? To answer that question, we need to begin

with labor's own postwar story and the particular form into which the labor movement evolved by the end of the 1940s. We need to return, again, to the line between "Them" and "Us."

The U.S. labor movement, too, emerged from the war stronger than ever. Both the conservative AFL and its progressive CIO rival grew enormously under union-shop agreements brokered during the war. The total number of union members leaped during the war from 10.5 million to 14.7 million. The CIO, especially, was no longer a fledgling but an acknowledged power broker in the U.S. corporate landscape. Like it or not, the corporations from now on had to deal with the collective representatives of millions of organized workers. But the challenge before the CIO, as historian David Brody has put it, was "the uses of power": what would it do with its new strength?[11]

In 1946, an enormous strike wave swept across the United States, as the war years' pent-up demand erupted. More workers went out on strike that year than in any other year in U.S. history before or since, a total of five million people in 4,630 strikes, including 800,000 steel workers, 225,000 autoworkers, and 174,000 workers in electrical manufacturing. But employer intransigence successfully limited labor's gains from the 1946 strikes. Most ominously, in 1947 a new Republican-controlled Congress passed the deliberately repressive Taft-Hartley amendment to the Wagner Act. Taft-Hartley's litany of anti-labor measures—bans on secondary boycotts, mass picketing, and the closed shop; presidential powers to intervene in strikes; excision of foremen from bargaining units, to name but a few—drastically constrained the tactics through which organized labor had won so much in the previous decade.[12]

Perhaps the most deadly part of Taft-Hartley was a requirement that all officials of unions who wanted access to the protective machinery of the Wagner Act had to sign affidavits swearing they were not, and never had been, members of the Communist Party. The loyalty oath requirement tore into the civil liberties of union activists, and it tore apart the CIO. Some CIO leaders refused on principle to sign the affidavits. But AFL officials jumped wholeheartedly onto the loyalty bandwagon; and by 1949 anticommunists in the CIO, too, had pivoted inward to attack any of their own constituents who refused to sign the oaths. Shooting off its own left foot, the CIO purged nine of its own international affiliates representing 900,000 union members, including the United Electrical Workers with 427,000; the Food and Tobacco Workers with 22,500; and the Mine, Mill, and Smelter Workers with 87,000.[13]

The Cold War was thus equally useful at home. In anticommunism the federal government not only had its pretext for power plays abroad but an ideological justification for police work in domestic class relations as well. By Cold War definition, dissent from the corporate agenda at home, like dissent from the corporate agenda abroad, was cast as a mark of Communism. The plan worked perfectly. Within three short years, labor's own McCarthyism had silenced not just the handful of Communist activists in the labor movement but, far more broadly, any dissenters from the corporate program.

With labor's left wing pushed out of the picture, the anticommunist inheritors of the CIO then brokered a deal with the big corporations in mass production. Known as the "postwar compact" or "labor-management accord," their agreement would stay roughly in place for the next quarter-century, symbolized by the 1950 five-year contract between the United Auto Workers and General Motors, known as the "Treaty of Detroit." "General Motors may have paid a billion for peace, but it got a bargain," *Fortune* magazine wrote of the contract. The UAW, on its side, got hefty wage increases, cost-of-living adjustments, paid vacations, holidays, pensions, health care, and an "annual improvement factor"—a percentage of profits from the company's productivity gains—all of which would continue to increase over the course of the 1950s and '60s. In exchange, the union traded away any input into long-term corporate planning and controls on productivity or the speedup. In other words, union workers got money benefits in exchange for giving up control of their firm's management and, most important, its future. Soon the UAW pattern echoed throughout the mass production sector, including steel, rubber, electrical manufacturing, mining, and metalworking.[14]

With the postwar compact the unions hitched their wagon to the star of U.S. corporate expansion overseas. "Labor is not fighting for a larger slice of the national pie," UAW president Walter Reuther actually insisted in 1946. "Labor is fighting for a larger pie."[15] The unions would help the corporations grow and grow and not ask too many questions. What was good for General Motors would now be good for the United Auto Workers and for the American people. "As long as the postwar boom continued and the economy grew, everyone could experience rising living standards without recourse to class conflict or social struggle," Kim Moody observes in a study of labor's postwar decline.[16] It was the nineteenth-century tariff debate all over again, only this time high productivity and imperial expansion, rather than the tariff, would make domestic redistribution of power and wealth unnecessary.

The Farm Equipment Workers' Union (FE), by contrast, argued in 1946 that "the only real method workers could employ to increase their living standards, and secure their future, was to fight for a larger *share* of the existing pie," historian Toni Gilpin writes. From the FE's point of view, the workers' "collective economic power should not be traded in for an illusory partnership with management. FE leaders were guided in their belief in one simple truth: for workers to get more, the corporations must get less." But in 1949, the CIO expelled the Farm Equipment Workers' Union, and within a few years the union had collapsed under combined assaults from the International Harvester corporation and the UAW. Any such alternative notions of the uses of power were successfully silenced.[17]

By the time the CIO and AFL merged in 1955, the two former rivals were so similar there was nothing left to fight about. Economist Richard Lester described the mid-fifties labor movement as a "sleepy monopoly."[18] The once-feisty CIO had stooped under the corporate wing that the AFL had never eschewed.

Logically, once committed to the bigger pie, the AFL, CIO, and then-merged AFL-CIO threw themselves wholeheartedly behind U.S. foreign policy. "Us" meant the Free World: labor and the corporations working together in a nationally based partnership to dominate the capitalist world. "Them" meant the Communists; and anyone who criticized "Us" was also by definition "Them." Initially, some elements in the CIO pursued an alternative model of internationalist labor solidarity, participating in the World Federation of Trade Unions (WFTU), which included representatives from Soviet-bloc countries as well as the U.S. bloc. But the WFTU fell by the wayside in the torrent of postwar anticommunism. By 1949 the CIO and the AFL had denounced it to form a rival, explicitly anticommunist body, the International Confederation of Free Trade Unions (ICFTU). During the late 1940s the AFL and CIO worked closely with Marshall Plan authorities to set up rival, anti-Left trade union blocs in Italy, France, and elsewhere in Europe. By the 1960s the AFL-CIO cooperated tightly with the CIA and State Department through a range of new bodies, including the Asian American Free Labor Institute, the African American Labor Institute, and the American Institute for Free Labor Development—on whose board of directors sat representatives from corporations such as United Fruit, the Anaconda Copper Company, and the Rockefeller interests. Their project: undermine democratic trade unions throughout the Third World and set up pro-U.S., rival, CIA-funded unions, all in the name of anticommunism.[19]

FREE TRADE UNIONISM

We can now understand Meany's wholehearted embrace of free trade. Long before their merger in 1955, both the AFL and CIO endorsed trade liberalization—the project of worldwide reduction of trade barriers—as essential to their dream of ever-expanding production. Stanley Ruttenberg, delivering the CIO's endorsement of trade liberalization in 1953, repeated U.S. foreign policy goals with parrot-like exactitude. First, he addressed the dollar gap: "We in the CIO realize the great need that countries abroad have for earning the necessary dollars they need with which to buy the many products they need in the United States." Second, he invoked the Cold War: "We also realize that trade by our allies enhances their ability to improve their standards of living and thus better resist Communist aggression." Third, he agreed with the need for raw materials. Finally—and perhaps most telling: "Workers in key industries, such as auto, steel, electrical machinery, and others, are dependent for their jobs upon exports."[20] The CIO's members, in other words, located overwhelmingly in the mass production sector, held an ineluctable economic stake in the U.S. export empire. The AFL's policy, for its part, was initially more restrained, torn between zealous anticommunism, on the one hand, and a few powerful affiliates who remained protectionist, as we shall see, on the other. But well before the AFL-CIO merger, the AFL jumped off its former tariff-neutrality fence to likewise endorse trade liberalization.[21]

By the time Kennedy was president, pushing through his Trade Expansion Act of 1962 and the Kennedy Round of GATT, AFL-CIO trade policy had congealed into wholehearted enthusiasm for trade liberalization. In 1961, the federation enunciated its policy in a 149-page report entitled *AFL-CIO Looks at Foreign Trade . . . A Policy for the Sixties*. The entire policy remained framed within the Cold War: "Our sister non-communist nations" desperately needed to export, it stressed; and "Our willingness to open our markets to their goods may influence both their chances for economic progress and their basic political decisions." U.S. self-interest, in the AFL-CIO's view, still coincided neatly with Cold War imperatives: "increased trade will also contribute to the requirements of our own economy both for goods we must obtain from abroad and markets for the products of our industries."[22]

The AFL-CIO's enthusiasm was not without caveats, however. In 1953, as a member of the Randall Commission on federal trade policy, United Steelworkers of America president David McDonald first raised the issue of trade adjustment assistance, or compensatory aid to industrial workers whose jobs had been displaced by imports. From then on, the AFL-CIO began attaching requests for trade adjustment assistance to its free trade endorsements.[23] The federation's landmark 1961 report highlighted requests for both trade adjustment assistance and international fair labor standards.[24]

During the 1950s and early 1960s individual international unions affiliated with the AFL-CIO also touted ever-freer trade. The International Brotherhood of Electrical Workers (IBEW), for example, in its monthly magazine in 1962 and again in 1964 explained to the union's members that "Exports are vital to the economy of the United States. They create jobs for American workers and profits for American businesses."[25] The editors meticulously calculated the net gain of exports over imports in the electrical manufacturing industry. In November 1958 they even ran a perky photograph spread called "Those Little Foreign Cars." "This influx of gas buggies from foreign lands is being welcomed heartily by thousands of discriminating Americans," they ensured.[26]

In retrospect, the self-confidence with which these unions greeted imports is stunning. "If I had the slightest feeling that increased trade, particularly imports, would be injurious to the American workingmen, I would not be here today supporting a policy of trade liberalization," United Steelworkers of America president David McDonald told Congress in 1955.[27] Monsignor Charles Owen

Rice, speaking twenty years later to the devastated steel town of Homestead, Pennsylvania, captured eloquently his community's former faith:

> We trusted in the smartness of our industrial leaders.
> We trusted in the great corporations.
> We trusted in money.
> We trusted in the power of steel.
> We couldn't imagine that there could ever be a day
>   that they'd be closing steel mills or that they
>   wouldn't need steel.[28]

It was an immense faith: a faith in the Communist devil, a faith in the U.S. corporations as infallible gods, and a faith in the mutually beneficial partnership between labor and capital. It was a national faith: nation-based corporations were joining with nation-based trade unions to arrange the world's affairs to their own benefit. And it was a deep faith, deep enough to wash over the fact that what was good for General Motors was not, in fact, good for the American people.

Meany's hostility to Buy American campaigns now makes sense: any political program smacking of economic nationalism would presumably shrink the Cold War pie.[29] Meany was, in fact, late onto the anti–Buy American bandwagon. National policymakers had already explicitly rejected the Buy American approach years before. The Buy American Act of 1933, it turns out, was never actually enforced until after World War II. Foreign competition was too weak during the Depression to necessitate its invocation; during World War II, the government suspended it. By the early fifties the Buy American Act was an awkward embarrassment, still on the books. In 1953, Frank E. Smith, Democratic congressman from Mississippi, introduced a bill repealing it. "It was the offspring of world-depression psychology," he wrote to the *New York Times*. "Today, quite incredibly, we have retained this anachronism."[30] In Smith's view, the Buy American Act was not only inflationary but sapped Europe's access to necessary dollars, while threatening U.S. access to raw materials.[31]

Smith's bill never passed, but other Buy American opponents soon triumphed. In April 1953, the U.S. government invoked the

Buy American Act to refuse a British bid on electrical generators and transformers for the Chief Joseph Dam in Washington State. As numerous critics immediately pointed out, doing so flew in the face of official policy commitments to rebuilding European trade. President Eisenhower, in response, issued an executive order on December 17, 1954, streamlining the Buy American Act's enforcement across departments and cutting down the threshold for accepting foreign bids from 25 percent to 6–10 percent below U.S. prices, low enough for foreign firms to leap over easily. Effectively, he disarmed the Buy American Act.[32]

Meany was not the only labor figure to reject buying American. Three days before he wrote his letter squashing Larry Russell's campaign, the United Auto Workers launched their own criticisms of buying American in a national radio broadcast from Detroit, repeated on seventeen other U.S. stations. "The mistaken peddlers of protectionism are selling a poison pill, coated with the saccharin of patriotism," warned Guy Nunn, UAW director of radio and TV. "Trade is, by definition, a two-way street," and on that street, he insisted, riches flowed back toward the United States. "We had a net balance [last year] in our favor of five billion dollars." Using the example of steel, Nunn argued that even what might look like import damage was in fact lucrative. Yes, the United States imported British steel, but it exported twice as much. An imported British car could even be made of U.S. steel. "To that extent, at least, the domestic purchaser of a British car has been 'buying American.'" But to advocate Buy American, Nunn insisted, was to join a "suicide cult" that meant protectionism, retaliation, and fewer exports.[33] Three years earlier, a UAW fact sheet on the import question had already cautioned union officials against Buy American sentiments: "When we decide not to buy a foreign-made product, at the same time, we also make a decision not to sell an American product in foreign markets."[34] Even the international union that would most vehemently attack imports twenty years later, in other words, in 1961 agreed with Meany: buy foreign goods and prosper.

INDUSTRIAL UNTOUCHABLES

But Larry Russell clearly didn't agree with Meany; neither did his Union Label Committee nor the other delegates to the Des Moines,

Iowa, Central Labor Council of the AFL-CIO. While Meany's free trade creed arched across the Cold War sky, plenty of folks on the ground still felt uneasy about or even hostile to imports, still felt something was amiss in the U.S. economy, still thought buying American was a good idea—or the UAW would not have had to protest so much.

Sylvia Porter, a nationally syndicated financial expert, raised the issue in her July 31, 1959, column: "The other evening I went to a stimulating but deeply disquieting dinner party," she began. For hours, she and her seat-mate had debated the "threat" of imported steel to the U.S. economy. Her head abuzz with the import question, "I came home and headed for a midnight snack." Moving aside a laundry basket that contained a new bathing suit, a new cap, and a silk robe, she put down on the kitchen table "a plate, a glass pitcher, a glass and an ash-tray—all purchased since June. . . . And suddenly my eyes saw something I hadn't seen before. Every product I had touched . . . had been an import." Then, "racing through the house to check what we had bought in the past six months[,] I got an ever greater shock." Over 60 percent were imports. Much to her horror, Porter had "gradually become a buyer of foreign products on a scale I hadn't dreamed of."

Sylvia Porter had experienced a prototypical Buy American panic attack. "Okay, what do we do about it?" she continued. Raise tariffs? "Hardly a satisfactory answer." Instead, she advocated, first, "modernization and efficiency of production" in the United States; second, "a powerful drive for new inventions and improved products"; and, last, "A realization by all of us that we are into an economic war for the markets of the world—including our own. I'm not proposing an aggressive 'Buy American' program, but I readily admit there'll be no more of that 60–40 ratio in purchases I make."[35]

If Porter, a highly respected financial expert, well within the mainstream of free-trade thinking (and the kind of woman who spent her dinner parties debating steel imports), had her doubts, far more critical of the free trade orthodoxy were the tens of thousands of working people who, in the postwar free trade deal, had been traded away. Trade liberalization meant an enormous *net* gain as exports exceeded imports. But some imports did continue to displace domestic production as part of the continuous process of "creative destruction" institutionalized in the capitalist economy.

The American Federation of Labor, in particular, always had its firm dissenters from the free trade faith. While the federation's commitment to U.S. trade policy at the national, official level waxed stronger over the course of the fifties, the number of international unions and sub-bodies that lobbied against trade liberalization also grew. In the late forties, the list included only glass and pottery workers, watch workers, and a few fishermen's unions. By the late fifties they were joined by the Textile Workers' Union of America, the United Mine Workers, the United Brotherhood of Carpenters and Joiners, bookbinders, hat makers, luggage and handbag makers, and an array of unions in the printing trades.[36] At AFL and then AFL-CIO conventions they spoke eloquently of the fate of the workers who had been traded away. E. L. Wheatley, for example, representing members of the Operative Potters' union who were losing their jobs from import competition, in 1959 retorted that it wasn't a simple matter of his members snatching up an equal job in a boom economy. "A lot of these ceramic plants operate back in the hinterlands, or back in the sticks, so to speak, and these men who have spent their entire lives in an industry and are up around an age of forty-five to sixty, have no other industry in the area to take up the slack." They weren't stupid, he said; they knew no one would hire them in Detroit or San Francisco.[37]

In the early 1950s members of the Display Fixture and Smoking Pipe Workers' Union submitted a brief to the United States Tariff Commission, pleading their similar plight. Their union had painstakingly organized five thousand or so workers who made briarwood pipes in the New York City area and finally gained them a contract guaranteeing paid vacations, life insurance, and health care, including free x-rays. Suddenly, the pipe workers charged, postwar competition from lower-wage pipe makers in Italy, France, and England had forced thirty shops to shut their doors, leaving fourteen hundred unemployed. "If this unreasonable and destructive type of competition . . . is not checked within the immediate future," the pipe makers warned, "it will surely devour and destroy the domestic pipe industry and thereby will also destroy the ability of American working men and working women to earn a livelihood."

Ninety-five percent of the pipe makers were over forty years old, "not at an age when changes can be made easily," the brief pointed

out. "They cannot, at such an age shift to another trade or occupation." U.S. trade policy was relegating them "to the status of industrial untouchables." They knew what was going on at the top:

> The union is fully cognizant of the fact that our present policy in Interna-
> tional foreign trade and commerce is not based on old theories of high
> and prohibitive tariff duties, protectionism and unreasonable restrictions
> on imports. We are fully aware of the International situation which
> makes it obligatory to sustain the economy of our allies.

But low-wage imports, the pipe makers insisted, amounted to unfair
competition and should be halted.[38]

By 1960 the big garment and textile unions had begun to advocate
protectionism loudly, although, like Porter, they stopped short of
advocating Buy American. Garment and textile industries, labor-
intensive with low capital investment costs, were relatively easy for
developing countries to establish. With lower wage bills and production costs than U.S. firms, foreign producers could sell on the U.S.
market at lower prices, if allowed in. In the late 1950s garment imports from Hong Kong and then Japan began to compete successfully
with U.S. garments on the domestic market. Outraged, the International Ladies' Garment Workers' Union called on the U.S. Tariff
Commission to impose a new formula: only imports that filled the
gap above domestic production, it argued, should be permitted access
to the U.S. market.[39]

Ongoing rumblings against imports produced occasional, if evidently rare, Buy American activities during the 1950s. In New York
City in 1955, the Union Label Trades Department of the Greater
New York Central Trades and Labor Council boasted an active "import committee" promoting the Buy American idea. In September,
the committee printed up a poster announcing "Buy Union—Buy
American" and sent it out to all its affiliated local unions.[40] The next
month the committee organized an anti-import demonstration in
New York City, "to bring the attention of the general public to facts
concerning the great influx of foreign-made goods produced by labor
with low income and poor working conditions, which has created
considerable hardship to a great many of our affiliated unions."[41]
Three years later, on September 4, 1958, ten thousand residents of
East Liverpool, Ohio, "lined the streets of the business district to wit-

ness" a "mammoth parade" opening "a campaign to curb the influx of foreign products into this country," reported the *Potters Herald*, published by the Operative Potters' union. Highlights included seven high school bands and "fire trucks from all departments in the area . . . sounding their sirens in support of the Buy American—Buy Union Label movement."[42]

The East Liverpool fire trucks and the New York demonstration were both coordinated through AFL and AFL-CIO activities promoting the union label. Most of the AFL-CIO label department's promotional literature in this period did not, though, mention Buy American or country of origin. It was more likely to stress labor-management cooperation, as did the department's annual "Union Label Industries" trade show. Beginning in 1938, the label department put on an extravaganza in a different city every year, celebrating pro-union manufacturers with displays demonstrating union-made products, and giving them away. At the 1960 show, for example, visitors could vie for canned hams, a typewriter, aprons, and a live calf ("To carry home the loot, the Retail Clerks will make available free shopping bags," promised a press release). "We visualize a repeat of the Sheep Shearing demonstration with the bo-peep theme," enticed the Amalgamated Meat Cutters in 1963, "this time using attractive young ladies in full costume as attendants."[43]

In 1961, as tensions over imports mounted, a small boomlet of Buy American activities spread across the country, contained largely within the labor movement—although we can include Sylvia Porter's 1959 attack as a sign of the same times. "Last Year's recession . . . has brought with it fresh pressures to 'Buy American,' to raise American import duties, to 'protect American jobs,'" the UAW's Guy Nunn granted in his March 1961 radio speech exalting trade liberalization (quoted earlier). "For the most part these pressures are professional. . . . They originate with particular industries or companies seeking special haven from competition." But "to a degree," he acknowledged, Buy American pressure "is a natural, if misguided, individual response to unemployment."[44]

What produced this ripple of Buy American sentiment? The steel strike of 1959 apparently prompted the first national discussions of rising imports—such as Sylvia Porter's dinner party chat. The UAW's Nunn attributed Buy American feelings to the recession that began in 1957, still deep enough in 1960 that Kennedy campaigned for president with the slogan "Get America Moving Again." America didn't move for a couple more years, heightening import anxieties. In 1962 the *Electrical Workers' Journal* reported that "Most of us are familiar with the popular bumper sticker which reads: 'Be American, Buy American—the Job You Save May be Your Own.' "[45] Some of those bumper stickers were generated by the New York Label Trades Department, the people who had produced the 1955 Buy American poster and demonstration. Union members and protectionist employers spotted them on bumpers and wrote in to the department for still more stickers, which they put on their own cars and shared with friends. Joseph Maraia, president of the L. P. Tile Company of Fairview, New Jersey, wrote the committee: "I think this campaign is a wonderful idea as it stimulates American people's thoughts on how foreign made merchandise is ruining American industry."[46] Sam Johnson, of Local 363 of the International Brotherhood of Electrical Workers in New City, New York, on March 22, 1961, wrote that his local was "organizing an educational promotion program regarding the 'Buy American' campaign," and asked for flyers, decals, stickers, and "all necessary literature."[47] That same month Larry Russell tried to launch his Buy American campaign in Des Moines, Iowa. That exact same day Meany wrote back stopping it.

YELLOW SUBMARINES

Import anxieties alone did not the Buy American boomlet make, however. Larry Russell himself, when asked why he had taken up the Buy American call in 1961, answered: "Remember this: I'm a World War Two veteran. That affects me. . . . I don't know as I was ready to forgive the Japs and start buying their stuff."[48] During the Great Depression, Buy American sentiments had been inseparable from Yellow Perilism. World War II only sharpened suspicions about invading Asians. These suspicions were still alive and well in 1961, when the exact same "foreigners" whom Americans had long blamed for domestic economic problems started selling again on the global marketplace.

We can trace a direct continuity between the 1930s and the 1960s, beginning with the war. AFL unionists up and down the West Coast joined the wartime assault against Japanese American citizens, casting them as genetically disloyal "aliens." Not only did both the AFL and the CIO countenance the incarceration of Japanese Americans, but as the government gradually began to release internees for work assignments in the Midwest and East, local AFL bodies escalated their protests against Japanese Americans. The members of Carpenters' Local No. 266 in Stockton, California, for example, in May 1943 "voted unanimously to protest the releasing of the Japanese" from the camps.[49] In December 1944, the Stanislaus County Central Labor Council in Modesto, California, "voted unanimously to protest the return of the Japanese to the State of California until after the War." The council dashed off a telegram to the state's two senators, warning that "Great trouble and strife are apt to occur if the Japanese are allowed to return"—to which strife they presumably planned to contribute.[50]

The Central Labor Council of Juneau, Alaska, went further: even after the war, its members wanted no Americans of Japanese descent in Alaska. "WHEREAS: We feel that Japan is the place for all Japanese," and "WHEREAS: There is no one person or persons who can segregate or distinguish one Japanese from another and there is no such thing as a loyal, American Jap and there never has and never will be," therefore "BE IT RESOLVED: That we, standing on our American rights, do hereby petition that there be no returning of any Japanese or anyone of Japanese ancestry to the Territory of Alaska for any reason whatsoever or for any period of time."[51]

Such wartime racial attitudes were by no means confined to the West. The Boston Joint Executive Board of the Hotel Employees and Restaurant Employees' Union, for example, in 1944 voted to "discourag[e] the employment of Japanese in the hotels of the City of Boston and questio[n] the loyalty to the United States of Japanese born in the United States." John J. Kearney, executive secretary of the union's Local 34 in Boston, in a speech disseminated nationwide that year, celebrated the decision with rhetoric that sounded like it came straight out of Lothrop Stoddard's *The Rising Tide of Color:* "more nations have been overcome through the infiltration of a foreign people than through actual warfare. . . . We have failed and neglected to grasp the significance of the growing population of Japanese on the Pacific slope of the U.S."

Kearney explicitly linked his own 1944 hostility toward Japanese Americans with prewar anti-Asian hostility among West Coast white workers. Since well before the war, he noted, the trade unions of California "have witnessed the destruction of their work standards and wage structures by the Japanese, and they have seen the scheming designs of the Japanese." Kearney also carefully specified that "No war hysteria has caused this condition, as it has been one of steady growth for years." He concluded by wrapping his selective denunciations of Japanese Americans within a multicultural cloak: "Our union was the first to admit negroes as members fifty years ago," he pointed out; its members represented "more than twenty-four nationalities." But Japanese Americans were different. Citizens or not, he wanted them out.[52]

Other voices did object loudly to the racial stigmatization of Japanese Americans, though their arguments were drowned out in the swamp of wartime racial hysteria. In June 1943, when the hotel and restaurant employees' union newsletter published an earlier article entitled "Japanese Menace to Catering Industry" and announced proudly a decision to refuse to cooperate with federal authorities who sought to place former internees in restaurant jobs, Honolulu Local #5 of the same union wrote back in horror: "Organized labor in some of parts of the United States . . . has temporarily fallen for the race-hating propaganda of the Hearsts and Martin Dies[es]," Arthur A. Rutledge, head of both the local and the Honolulu Central Labor Council, charged with disgust. "We in Hawaii must set our faces firmly against such a degeneration and backsliding from the ideal of the American Federation of Labor—an organization, we should remind ourselves, formed by the genius of an American who happened to be foreign-born and a Jew [Samuel Gompers]: *NO DISCRIMINATION BECAUSE OF RACE, COLOR, OR CREED.*" Rutledge refuted the charge that Japanese Americans were disloyal, and sang their praises as dedicated trade unionists. "It is nonsense to talk of the Japanese-Americans being a 'menace.' They can be a menace only to the extent that they get soured on unions by seeing the unions talk about democracy and freedom from discrimination, and then practice discrimination on them." Nonetheless, Rutledge granted,

> We do not want to give the impression that the Japanese Americans are a lot of union supermen. They have their share of chiseling "cockroach capitalists," "company men," phony foremen, pool hall bums, and Milquetoasts who faint when they hear the word "union." The point is, THEY ARE LIKE OTHER AMERICANS, some bad, most of them good; and the good ones make damn good union material.[53]

After the war anti-Japanese sentiments continued to fester, despite the fact that Japan was vanquished and was now a U.S. ally, under U.S. military control. Delegates to the AFL Union Label Council of New Jersey became suddenly alarmed in January 1946 at the prospect of a renewed "Yellow Peril" invasion of Japanese goods after the war. Delegate J. Ott of the Hudson County Allied Printing Trades Council warned: "Warehouses in this county stocked Japanese goods previous to Pearl Harbor, and some are now trying to get rid of these goods over the counter and if they are successful, we will find Jap made articles in all the stores." Delegate Powers of the jewelry workers jumped in, excitedly: "we could do a good job on this." Citing "the case of buyers being discouraged from buying Japanese articles in 1920 in California through threat of a boycott," he praised prewar anti-Asian agitation, just as Kearney had in Boston. Delegate Schade, from the Union County Central Labor Union, then volunteered that in Cleveland, labor activists had already forced the Rigby department store "to remove an exhibit of Japanese made goods through threat of exposing them." Delegate Wildstein then suggested the council escalate its campaign to a boycott of all foreign-made goods. But another delegate then "called attention to the fact that foreign countries can not buy from this country unless they sell goods here in exchange, that if we boycott all foreign-made goods, we will have no foreign market for our own goods."[54]

These men were savvy students of international economic relations. And they were careful to single out the Japanese as uniquely demonic. On January 18, 1946, the group sent a letter to all affiliates of AFL unions in the nation, urging "all AFL union members to boycott goods 'Made in Japan.'" Such articles, the letter explained, "were made with child and slave labor before Pearl Harbor and shipped to this country in exchange for scrap iron—pieces of which were shot in the backs of our boys on Guadalcanal and Iwo Jima. . . . Watch for them, and demand of the storekeeper that they be destroyed."[55]

Growing concern over imports and this special racial animus toward the Japanese converged dramatically in a 1955 standoff between the U.S. government, Japan, and the state of South Carolina over textile quotas. After World War II, the United States spent billions of dollars rebuilding the Japanese economy. Its goal was not only to position Japan as a capitalist ally in Asia, but also to make sure Japan didn't emerge too independent. Above all, it wanted to keep Japan from getting close to China, especially after Mao Zedong and the Communists came to power in 1949. As an AFL-CIO "fact sheet" explained in 1962, "To grow as a healthy, free economy Japan must expand trade. She would prefer to trade with U.S. [sic] and other free nations, but is aware of Red China's potential mass market for Japanese goods. Faced by discrimination from us and other free nations, she could be forced to turn to China trade."[56] For these strategic reasons, the United States encouraged the development of Japanese manufacturing, including the textile industry, in the later 1940s onward. By the mid-fifties, the Japanese textile industry was booming and needed overseas markets. The U.S. government, to help it out, in July 1955 lowered its quota on imported Japanese textiles.[57]

All hell broke loose in South Carolina. One of the strongest textile regions in the United States, it was home to powerful protectionists in the Democratic Party, who knew where their state's corporate interests lay. Local journalists immediately likened the trade concessions to Pearl Harbor. In March 1956 the South Carolina legislature passed a law requiring that any business that sold textiles originating in Japan had to post a sign in its window proclaiming "JAPANESE TEXTILES SOLD HERE." Lobbyists sped to Washington; discreet and not-so-discreet pressures were applied; and a rerun of the South Carolina tariff nullification crisis of 1832 loomed. In 1956 the Japanese government itself ended the crisis by volunteering to restore the quota on Japanese textiles.[58]

If those window signs sound familiar, they should. Between Hearst's "Yellow Peril" attacks on Japanese workers and goods in the 1930s, on one hand, and the Japan-bashing we will soon see erupt in the 1970s and '80s, on the other, snaked a continuous line of activism blaming Japan and Japanese Americans for U.S. economic ills and singling out Asian peoples as uniquely duplicitous in their economic behavior.

NO DEAL

To conclude our analysis of the American Century, we can pull back, finally, and look at the big picture. If thousands of industrial workers were traded away in the postwar deal between organized labor and the corporations, millions weren't part of the deal at all. For all their differences, George Meany and Larry Russell, as union members, held relatively privileged jobs and enjoyed the benefits of imperial cooperation with the corporations, if temporarily. But for most working people in the United States, the American Century was no such Golden Age.

The AFL and CIO continued to grow in the decade following World War II, but their merger in 1955 turned out to augur not expansion but stasis. Trade union membership in the United States peaked in the late fifties at around 33 percent of the labor force.[59] During the late 1950s and 1960s the complacent and happy AFL-CIO evinced little will to organize unorganized workers. President Meany himself actually asked: "Why should we worry about organizing groups of people who do not appear to want to be organized?"[60]

Trade unions represented only one sector of the labor force, overwhelmingly white men who worked for manufacturing firms. Outside this sphere most working people labored without union protection in an economy deeply segmented by gender and race. Labor force participation by women continued its long upward climb in these decades—from 27.9 percent in 1940 to 33.9 percent in 1950 and 42 percent in 1968.[61] But women workers stayed largely untouched by organized labor. Only 14 percent of female wage earners belonged to a union in 1960.[62] The unions remained entrapped in ancient stereotypes casting women as temporary workers, uninterested in trade unions. The labor movement had never shown much interest in clerical and service work, where most women labored. Without unions, women workers paid a steep price: their jobs were overwhelmingly dead end, part time, poorly paid, and without any of the pensions, vacations, or health benefits accruing to unionized workers.

The other line demarcating the postwar compact's circle was race. Only a small percentage of union members were people of color. Labor market segmentation did much of the work excluding them from the well-paid jobs covered by union contracts: Latinos, Native Americans, Asian Americans, and African Americans, like white women, were usually never hired for the jobs inside Meany's sphere in the first place. African Americans, well aware they were on the outside, in the late 1950s and early 1960s rose up with tremendous bravery and moral strength to claim basic U.S. civil rights denied them since Reconstruction. The exact same year the AFL and CIO merged, forty thousand residents of Montgomery, Alabama, started their pioneering thirteen-month boycott of the city's segregated buses.

The labor movement was itself part of the problem African Americans faced: During the 1950s and '60s lawyers for the National Association for the Advancement of Colored People filed suit after suit demonstrating the complicity of AFL-CIO unions in keeping African Americans out of union jobs.[63] As they had in the 1930s, white workers were still using trade unions to keep the privileges inside their circle reserved for whites. Here the Cold War did its work. The international unions purged from the CIO in 1949 had been among the strongest in the country fighting racism in employment. During the war they had melded civil rights activism with union activism to challenge white supremacy as never before. When the CIO kicked them out, the labor movement lost not only a significant percentage of its nonwhite members but also the will to reform its own racial politics or those of the nation.[64]

Throughout the American Century the federal government with increasing ferocity policed the larger circle around the nation's borders. The Immigration Act of 1924 was still in place, banning most immigrants from Asia and imposing strict quotas on other immigrants. During World War II, when big agricultural employers complained of labor shortages, the United States initiated the Bracero Program, through which it imported semi-indentured Mexican citizens, or *braceros,* on a temporary basis to work in the fields. Braceros weren't allowed to exercise civil rights in the United States or organize unions. Employers' abuses of braceros were legion. But the growers loved the program and convinced the government to extend it long past the war, until Congress finally abolished it in 1964.[65]

During this same period the federal government increasingly militarized the border with Mexico. Through national campaigns such as Operation Wetback in 1954, the Immigration and Naturalization Service initiated terrifying sweeps in search of undocumented workers, harassing both legal immigrants and people of Mexican descent who had been citizens for generations. Along the border electric fences and uniformed men with guns sprouted like weeds.[66] U.S. immigration policy during the American Century in effect inverted the nation's trade policy: As U.S. capital instituted freer and freer trade to

fly across borders overseas, it raised the gate for working people—
their own countries transformed by U.S.-based corporations—who
wanted to cross back the other way. Higher immigration gates, in
turn, just as they had in the 1930s, came as part of a larger package of
racial marking and suspicion. The citizenship of any "Mexican-
looking" person was still by definition open to challenge.

Mexican Americans, African Americans, white working-class
women, Japanese Americans—all were largely shut out of the American Century, although by the 1960s they were banging more and
more loudly on the door. "Them" and "Us" demarcated not just
Americans and Communists, but white male workers privy to the
boom versus everyone else. We can ask again: Whose economic nation?

CHICKENS, SOON TO COME HOME TO ROOST

Viewed from the top, the American Century seemed limitless in the
early 1960s. Books with titles like *The Perils of Prosperity* or *The
Affluent Society* packed bookstore shelves.[67] Blue skies seemed to smile
away at America. But not too far away on the horizon, a row of chickens on their way home to roost lined up in the sky, waiting patiently
for the decade's end. Precisely as the American Century climaxed, all
the forces were in motion that would produce the crises of the 1970s
and '80s—spawned by precisely the same forces that had produced
the boom.

The first challenge fluttered across the seas from Germany and Japan. The United States spent billions after the war reindustrializing
both nations, keeping them within the capitalist orbit. By 1960 it had
succeeded all too well. Both roared back as industrial powerhouses.
Western Europe and Japan now competed directly and successfully
against U.S. industrial products in steel, autos, machine tools, electrical manufacturing, and other industries, in the U.S. domestic market,
their own markets, and overseas. "Those little foreign cars" were
perky, indeed.[68]

One of the reasons Germany and Japan were so successful at developing new technologies and highly productive manufacturing processes was because they weren't spending money on their militaries.
Both were prohibited from doing so by the terms of the Allied victory at the end of World War II. The United States, meanwhile, spent

a higher and higher percentage of its GNP on its military every year. By 1968 military spending accounted for 9.2 percent of the U.S. Gross National Product, as opposed to 3.9 percent of Germany's and 0.8 percent of Japan's.[69] U.S. corporations—especially arms makers —enjoyed enormous economic advantages because of the nation's military dominance worldwide. But domestically, what might have gone into industrial development went into missile silos, radar, and fighter planes. Massive spending on the Vietnam war further warped the domestic economy.[70]

All that foreign direct investment, for which the military held open the gate, meant that U.S.-based corporations were opening up factories abroad right and left, in the Third World as well as in advanced capitalist countries. By 1966 U.S.-based corporations operating globally employed almost a third of their entire workforce overseas—a total of 3,324,321 non-Americans[71]—and had mutated into multinational corporations, the overseas products of which now started to compete with U.S.-made manufacturing. At the same time, funds that might have gone into building new plants in the United States or into modernizing existing domestic plants flowed overseas instead.[72] President George Baldanzi of the United Textile Workers, dissenting from the free trade faith at the 1961 AFL-CIO convention, presaged exactly the results of the capital outflow and trade expansion that Kennedy and Meany celebrated:

> When there are corporate interests . . . investing billions of dollars in the Common Market of Europe, that are establishing plants that are more modern than ours today, unless we get some safeguard against wholesale importation into this country, there is no guarantee that five years from now these same automated factories that are being built by American capital in many parts of the world that are utilizing slave labor, that they will not curtail operations in this country and dump all the cheap goods right back here in the United States.

The wage differential alone between the First and Third Worlds would drive the corporations abroad, he warned. "Don't feel that you are immune against this problem, because capital is a heartless beast. . . . It finds the level that is measured only by the dollar bill."[73]

Finally, the AFL-CIO was actively digging its own grave throughout the 1950s and '60s. Through its cooperation with the

State Department and the CIA, the federation helped undermine democratic trade unions in precisely the same Third World countries to which the corporations were moving their production facilities— Guatemala, for example. The corporations went there for the low wages. And wages there were low in part because the AFL-CIO, blinded by the Cold War star, helped keep them low by making sure their unions were pro-management and pro-United States. Why didn't they see what they were doing? They were thinking teamwork; they were thinking labor and management together making America strong; they were thinking any opposition to corporate goals means Communism. The lethargic monopoly of the AFL-CIO was asleep on its watch, drugged by the grand celebration of corporate benevolence and dreaming it was an equal partner.

FALLING IN PLACE

Asleep at the wheel of the AFL-CIO, George Meany didn't see that in 1961 all the elements of the crisis to come had settled into place. U.S. corporations were now thoroughly multinational, having planted their feet firmly abroad. The nation's military-centered economy sapped domestic economic development more thoroughly every year. Military intervention, meanwhile, kept Third World wages low. Most important, and ominously, the United States was no longer the only kid on the block.

By 1961 all the elements were in place as well that would shape the labor movement's response to the crisis. Labor leaders viewed themselves as partners with corporate managers, allied behind a corporate-led agenda of U.S. global domination. For the AFL-CIO leadership, domestic dissent from the pro-corporate program, whether within or outside the labor movement, equaled Communist infiltration. Union militancy was inappropriate and unnecessary.

For all their blinders, the AFL-CIO leaders were nonetheless right about one thing, though: There was indeed an Enemy Within. But it wasn't the Communists, and it wasn't the Japanese.[74]

Part Two

CHAPTER 6

So We'll Be Able to Make It in the U.S.A.

The ILGWU, the Union Label, and the Import Question

Suddenly, and dramatically, the crisis hit. Millions of the stable, well-paid union jobs in which so many American working people had believed evaporated overnight. During the mid-1970s through the early 1980s, U.S. manufacturers eliminated over 900,000 jobs every single year. Employment in steel alone plummeted 40 percent just between 1979 and 1984. In 1970, the United Auto Workers represented 1,502,000 people; fifteen years later, half a million of those men and women had lost their jobs. By the early 1980s unemployment rippled throughout the economy, devastating industrial communities and destroying much of the careful hope that working people had built in the postwar years. Twenty-five years too soon, the American Century came to an abrupt end.[1]

The corporations simply called off the postwar deal. Faced with serious international competition for the first time, U.S. corporations saw their profit rates start to fall in the 1960s. Searching for more lucrative investment pastures, they shut down domestic factories in the 1970s and '80s and fled overseas, where wages were cheaper and unions usually couldn't talk back. Or they pulled their money out of manufacturing altogether and sank it into health care, real estate, or insurance, where profits were higher, most jobs poorly paid, and unions weak. More overtly, they declared war on the labor movement.[2]

That economic drama produced the third, longest, and deepest wave of Buy American sentiment in U.S. history, as millions of

Americans, in a state of shocked panic, turned to popular economic nationalism. As it had in the 1930s, economic crisis fed popular beliefs that nationalist shopping could save jobs, rebuild the economy, and sustain healthy communities. As it had in the 1930s, Buy Americanism led to strange bedfellows. And just as it had in the 1930s, Buy Americanism descended into Asian-bashing as a scapegoat for corporate behavior.

We begin with the first set of players in the Buy American movement of the 1970s and '80s, organized labor, and examine the International Ladies' Garment Workers' Union (ILGWU) and then, in the following chapter, the United Automobile, Aerospace and Agricultural Implement Workers of America (UAW). Imports, both unions charged, were to blame for the nation's economic ills. Assiduously nationalist shopping could turn back foreign economic incursions at the border. As they promoted American products, the ILGWU and UAW nestled deeper and deeper into complex relationships with U.S. corporations. "Us" came to mean labor and management, teaming together to compete against "Them"—which meant foreign companies and foreign workers alike. But as every year passed, a contradiction at the heart of their strategy deepened: U.S. trade unions touted the products of U.S. corporations in a nationalist fever pitch precisely as those same corporations fled the nation's borders—or turned on working people within its borders.

With the case of the ILGWU we can see most clearly how organized labor's adherence to a Cold War mindset blinded it from responding effectively to the challenges of the 1970s and '80s. We can see the intimate relationships between union democracy and labor's strategic response to trade issues. Most fundamentally, we can trace clearly the increasing tension between nationalist solutions and global economic problems.

FASHIONS, U.S.A.

The ILGWU in the 1970s was in big trouble, and its trouble was only beginning. The union's leadership was well aware of two stark statistics. First, the ILGWU's membership was beginning a long free fall, from 457,517 in 1969 to 404,737 in 1973; to 308,056 by 1980; and a mere 146,506 in 1990.[3] Its plummet reflected both the decline of the U.S. apparel industry and the decreasing union sector within it. Second, apparel imports were skyrocketing. The numbers looked small at first: In the early 1960s, imports accounted for a tiny 2.5 percent of U.S. domestic sales. But by 1976, that number had shot up to 31 percent and would continue to climb in the 1980s until it hit 57.5 percent in 1987.[4]

The question was what to do. In response, the ILGWU leadership in the fall of 1971 revamped its entire strategic approach to attack imports. Reviving the AFL's Buy American call of the 1930s, only on a much larger scale, it fused trade unionism with nationalism and merged both with a new call to American shoppers for aid.

The ILGWU's import strategy was ultimately legislative. The plan was to persuade Congress and the president to impose federal import restrictions barring the entry of overseas apparel goods. In part, that meant intense lobbying, in collaboration with the ILGWU's counterparts at the Amalgamated Clothing and Textile Workers' Union (ACTWU), which represented workers in the men's clothing industry. They were joined by the AFL-CIO, which in 1971 turned a sudden about-face on the trade question. Responding to internal pressure from the ILGWU and other international unions, it endorsed protectionism wholeheartedly for the first time.[5]

In the fall of 1971 and in early 1972, the AFL-CIO, ILGWU, ACTWU, and other AFL-CIO affiliates threw themselves behind a congressional package of protectionist programs called the Foreign Trade and Investment Act of 1972, known popularly as Burke-Hartke. Burke-Hartke marked the highest point of trade union–sponsored protectionism in the twentieth century. It mandated elimination of tax incentives for U.S. corporations operating abroad, creation of a national commission to regulate and quantitatively restrict imports, passage of fierce anti-dumping regulations, expanded statistics on foreign trade, and, perhaps most radically, presidential powers to halt the flight of U.S. capital overseas.[6]

To ensure passage of Burke-Hartke and subsequent protectionist measures throughout the 1970s and '80s, the ILGWU leadership launched two interlocked national mobilizations that, according to plan, would together build pressure from below to pass such legislation. The first set of the union's anti-import foot soldiers would be the ILGWU's rank-and-file members. As ILGWU executive vice president Wilbur Daniels argued in a July 1971 memo to President Louis

Stulberg outlining the new program: "Our main objective must be legislative. . . . To achieve this legislative objective, we must operate at the Washington level, on a national basis and in local communities." Doing so, in turn, "means getting our members to take on active role, as well as other groups in the community."[7]

Throughout 1972 the ILGWU mobilized mass demonstrations by its members in support of Burke-Hartke. On November 17, for example, 450,000 union garment workers stopped work all over the country in protest against imports and in behalf of Burke-Hartke. In these protests, a set of uniform picket signs selected by the union's leadership not only argued that imports destroyed jobs in the United States but introduced the concept that shoppers, by buying American, could join in the struggle. Some slogans, such as "Stop Importing Unemployment—Limit Imports," straightforwardly called for import restrictions. But "Save American Jobs," when combined with "Buy American-Made Union Products," called out to consumers as well as legislators.[8]

The ILGWU's national leadership meticulously orchestrated these membership mobilizations from above, often in cooperation with the Amalgamated Clothing and Textile Workers' Union. An internal "Public Relations Projects" report, for example, specified lunch-hour visits by a "label coordinator" in each shop and a "personalized-computer-letter" signed by President Stulberg "to be sent to each member at their home reiterating the importance of maximum participation at every possible opportunity." Instructions to members for outreach in their communities explained exactly how to introduce the Buy American argument. Local activists should form a speakers' bureau and present

> an educational program aimed at the consumer in which we would disseminate the chilling statistics and facts to make them understand that tomorrow it may be their industry, their job and their family's security that is at stake. Therefore, it is in their best interest to support a Made in U.S.A. buying program.

Committees could also sponsor and publicize an essay context in the schools on "How Imports Hurt My Family and Me." The report ended with an extant ILGWU campaign in Philadelphia, where the local had visited members in their homes or worksites and presented each with a plastic shopping bag, sewing kit, or rain bonnet.[9]

The union's second army of foot soldiers in the anti-import war, according to plan, would be the American people. By bringing national loyalty to their shopping carts, they would stop the import influx. To reach consumers directly, the ILGWU leadership launched a new, anti-import campaign focused on its union label. More forcefully and successfully than the mobilization of its own members, the label campaign fused "Buy Union" with "Buy American."

The ILGWU had been promoting its union label extensively for over ten years, but those exhortations had almost never mentioned national origin. Heavy promotion of the ILGWU label dated back to 1959, when the union inserted a new clause into its contracts mandating that every garment produced in a union shop display a little ILGWU label sewn inside. In 1959 the union also launched a national advertising campaign that surpassed any previous union label promotion in U.S. history. Throughout the 1960s it continued vigorous label promotion.[10]

In this period the ILGWU aimed its label sights particularly at female shoppers. To entice them, the ILGWU produced and distributed a vast pamphlet literature offering up-to-the-minute fashion advice to the nation's women. During the 1960s its label department distributed over five million free pamphlets with such alluring titles as *The Long and Short of It—Dresses, That Is; How to Dress Your Little Girl;* or *Your Dream Wardrobe, and How to Make It Come True: A Fashion Guide to Young America,* which pictured a teenage girl chatting on the phone, hair in a pony tail, legs attired in fashionable slim-cut pants. On the cover of another a leaping UCLA cheerleader, holding up the ILGWU union label, introduced *College Wardrobe: A Guide to the Right Clothes for Where You Are Going.* All promised to keep American women at the cutting edge of fashion while guaranteeing the economic security of those who sewed their clothes.[11]

As part of this program the union produced a modish semi-annual film called "Fashions, U.S.A." Its distribution was quite extensive—the film's spring 1962 edition, for example, was screened in 235 cities. Each season's film opened amidst swirling upbeat orchestral arrangements. "Hello, I'm Eleanor Lambert," welcomed a svelte blonde woman, in her pearls and suit looking every inch like Kim Novak in Alfred Hitchcock's *Vertigo.* "I chose the fashions you're about to see. It's part of the Consumer Service Department of the International Ladies' Garment Workers' Union Label Department." She introduced its director, Min Matheson, less glamorous but nonetheless trimly suited, who explained that her department had two purposes: to keep American women and girls up-to-date and to "help the American woman recognize the contribution made to fashion, and in fact the whole American way of life, by the 450,000 people who work to produce our beautiful, fashionable and well-made clothes." Thank you, said Lambert graciously. "And now, let's look at the news in day-time fashion. Here's a preview of what you'll see wherever well-dressed women gather. . . ."[12]

Despite all this activity, though, the ILGWU union label of the 1960s had yet to burst into televised song; and most important for our story here, it did not yet include the "Made in the U.S.A." appendage. The actual label only stated the union's name, with at times the slogan "This label is a symbol of decency, fair labor standards and the American way of life."[13]

Then, in 1971 and '72, the ILGWU leadership, as part of its new anti-import strategy, revamped and modernized all its label promotional materials. Arguments for the label shifted from female fashionability to national economic viability. From 1971 onward, "Made in the U.S.A." stood out prominently on every union label and every ILGWU advertisement. Now the ILGWU put its energies full tilt behind fusing "Buy Union" with "Buy American." New ads read, for example:

> This label stands for:
> - The creativity of American design.
> - The skill of American workmanship.
> - The importance of American jobs.
>
> Look for our label when you shop.[14]

The union did everything it could to wrap its union label in a nationalist flag, associating itself with all the icons it could think of from mainstream American popular culture, beginning with the World Series. "Baseball. The Great Un-American Game," an ILGWU newspaper advertisement proclaimed during the 1972 World Series, for example. "While the American flag is being raised for the opening of the World Series, think of *this*. Most of the baseballs we use in America aren't made in America any more." Nor were the gloves American-made. "They're being 'dumped' here as part of a flood of low-wage foreign goods." The solution? Buy American: "When Americans don't buy what other Americans make, Americans lose their jobs." And look for the union label—"The job you save may be your own." In 1974, the ILGWU sponsored a series of nationwide radio broadcasts during the World Series featuring actress Shelley Winters. John Denaro, director of the union's label department, gushed in a press release: "Universally known Shelley Winters promoting our 'MADE IN U.S.A.' theme in so completely an American scene as the World Series is bound to make millions of people conscious of the importance to them of the ILGWU label . . . as a job saver in our industry."[15]

Shelley Winters had her charms, but the real hit was the singing ILGWU television chorus. It first appeared on November 11, 1975, and within months its tune had burned into the public conscience. A single, clear female voice began, "Look for the union label, when you are buying a coat, dress, or blouse." In joined a few other voices; the camera pulled back to show four or five other singers, mostly women. "Remember somewhere, our union's sewing, our wages going to feed the kids and run the house." By the second verse the camera revealed two dozen men and women, white, black, Asian, Latino, their chorus swelling. "We work hard, but who's complaining. But through the I.L.G. we're paying our way." By the end the viewer was singing along: "So always look for the union label. It says we're able to make it in the U.S.A."[16]

Sometimes an African American couple in their thirties explained, before the song, that the ILGWU helped them get ahead. Sometimes an older white woman explained that the ILGWU made her feel secure as a senior citizen. In another version a plain-talking white man in a bolo tie, and with just a hint of a Texas or Arkansas accent, explained, "There used to be more of us in the International Ladies' Garment Workers' Union, but a lot of our jobs disappeared because a lot of the clothes Americans are buying for women and kids are being made in foreign places. And when our jobs go," he continued, "we can't support our families or pay our taxes or buy the things other Americans make. Think of that when your label says import instead of union."[17]

The dignified ILGWU chorus with its catchy tune and impeccable appeal was so popular that it spawned parodies on television programs for years thereafter. A comedy sketch featuring Donny Osmond on his short-lived *Donny and Marie* show in the late seventies, for example, showed a handful of tired, dirty Confederate soldiers splayed along a fence. Donny, in uniform, lamented to his mates that since Northerners and Southerners were both wearing rags, it was becoming harder and harder for him to distinguish Confederates from Yankees. I'll show you how to tell who's a Yankee, his mate replied, stepping up into song and dance with Donny and his comrades: "Watch for that union label, if you are telling the North from the South."[18]

Carol Burnett spoofed the swelling chorus; so did *Saturday Night Live*, in what seems safe to call the most unique Buy American ad of all American history. Lorraine Newman started out deeply serious, in close up, just like the man in the bolo tie. "Every time you buy pot from Mexico or Colombia, you're putting an American out of work. We here at the American dope growers' union support ourselves by growing marijuana in American soil. We've had a pretty hard time on our own," she explained, sounding word for word like the earnest ILGWU members, "but with the union we can lead decent lives and stay off welfare. That's *my* union, and that's what our union label stands for." The woman proudly held up a plastic bag with the "American Dope Growers" logo upon it. In chimed the chorus, including Gilda Radner: "So look for the union label, when you are buying a joint, lid, or pound. . . . it says we deal for the U.S. of A."[19]

Saturday Night Live's ability to parody the ILGWU merely illustrated how popular and pervasive the union's call to look for the union-made, American-made label had become—and how successfully the ILGWU leadership had fused the two in the national political imagination. By the late seventies millions of American shoppers believed not only that foreign imports were destroying the jobs of innocent American workers (who could also belt out a snappy tune) but that they themselves could save those same jobs if only they "looked for the union label"—and looked for the "Made in the U.S.A." label just as carefully. Country of origin now symbolized domestic employment and domestic class relations alike.

YELLOW APPAREL

When it launched its modernized, anti-import label campaign in the early seventies, the ILGWU added a third element to its fusion of nationalism with trade unionism, this one less innocent than baseball gloves. Drawing on the pre–World War II tradition of Yellow Perilism lying latent in the nation's racial memory, it chose to play the race card.

In early August 1972 the ILGWU plastered a full-page poster across the New York City subway system, which simply pictured a huge American flag, underneath which bold letters proclaimed "MADE IN JAPAN." Smaller text below asked, "Has your job been exported to Japan yet? . . . If not, it soon will be unless you buy the products of American workers who buy from you." Another version of the text warned, "Every year, Americans salute more and more American flags that weren't made in America. Flags that bear the stars and stripes and little tags reading Made in Japan or Taiwan or Hong Kong." American industries were shutting down as "foreign goods flood the market." Evoking the American Revolution, the text warned: "Chances are if Betsy Ross . . . were alive today, she'd be standing in line for her unemployment check." The solution? Look for the ILGWU union label. "This label stands for the creativity of American design, the skill of American workmanship, the importance of American jobs."[20]

That subway poster elicited an immediate storm of protests against its racial politics. Within days the union's mailbox was filling with carefully measured but firm requests to withdraw the advertisement immediately. On August 11, a group called Asian Americans for Action submitted the poster to Eleanor Holmes Norton, then commissioner of the New York City Commission on Human Rights, and asked the commission to "take action regarding this ad."[21] On the 22nd it joined the Japanese American United Church, the Asian Coalition, the United Asians Community Center, and the Japanese American Association in a meeting with John Denaro, head of the ILGWU's Union Label Department, to request that the poster be "discarded immediately."[22] After the ILGWU refused to do so, on August 25, a hundred protesters picketed on the sidewalk in front of the union's national office, wearing sandwich boards displaying the advertisement. Eight Asian American organizations endorsed the pickets, including the Princeton Asian American Student Organization and the New York chapter of the Japanese American Citizens' League, joined by an array of other groups such as the Third World People's Coalition and the Center for United Labor Action.[23]

Public attacks on the union's poster mounted. By the end of September both a *Wall Street Journal* editorial and a letter published in the *New York Times* had condemned the union; community groups had presented petitions with hundreds of signatures; and Japanese-language and Japanese American newspapers, radios, and television shows in New York and up and down the West Coast had all condemned the ad.[24]

The critics agreed that the ILGWU's "Made in Japan" poster drew on and fostered the historic sentiments against Asian Americans that had produced prewar Yellow Peril hysteria and its offspring, World War II internment. Joan Shigekawa, an American citizen who had spent part of her childhood in the internment camps, wrote ILGWU president Stulberg that she was "shocked to see a subway placard sponsored by the ILGWU which called forth racial hostility against the Japanese."[25] She reminded him that "the roots of racism have strong economic underpinnings and that they go back for a long time and have yielded a bitter harvest." Asian Americans for Action, in its letter to the Human Rights Commission, argued: "Those of us Japanese-Americans who lived through the internment camps of the '40's have no intention of once again in the '70's being made the scapegoats of the ruthless quarrels between industrial powers in Japan and the United States."[26] Stanley K. Abe, an organizer with the Westside Community Mental Health Center of San Francisco, specifically linked the ad with AFL attacks on Asian Americans during the Great Depression: "Many people within the various Asian communities cannot help but feel threatened by the thrust of the ILGWU media campaign because it has ominous similarities to the anti-Japanese campaigns by organized labor during the late 1930s."[27]

Anti-Asian attacks in both the 1930s and the 1970s, they charged, fed upon the racist idea that biology was destiny, that Asians and Asian Americans were a monolithic, indistinguishable mass. "It was only 30 years ago that 110,000 of us—two-thirds American citizens—were herded into American concentration camps during World War II because we 'looked like the enemy,' " reminded Glenn Omatsu, assistant editor of a Japanese American newspaper in San Francisco. The *Wall Street Journal,* in an editorial entitled "Reviving the 'Yellow Peril' " condemning the ad, observed that "throughout the Korean and Vietnam wars . . . there were gratifyingly few attempts to revive the familiar anti-Oriental shibboleths," and that Americans of Asian descent were increasingly accepted in mainstream U.S. society. But recently, it reported, economic tensions with Japan had produced an alarming increase in racism against Asian Americans. "The word 'Jap'—a racial slur every bit as deplorable as the much more familiar slurs known to every Archie Bunker fan—increasingly crops up in newspaper headlines."[28] The poster did indeed elicit immediate harassment on the street. One woman spat out, "You dirty Jap" at a Japanese American girl sitting under one of the ILGWU's subway ads.[29]

Critics pointed out that the poster singled out Japan and Asians while never mentioning other sources of imports. "It has not escaped notice that there is no similar public complaint against the import of popular French and Italian fabrics," Bruce Biossat observed in a nationally syndicated newspaper column.[30] Jimmy G. S. Ong, of Asian-Americans for Affirmative Action in Berkeley, wrote to the ILGWU: "White Europe took lots of jobs away from the United States. Why did not the ILGWU have a hate ad against the whites from the European countries?"[31]

The critics concluded that the ILGWU was scapegoating Japan rather than identifying the real problems confronting the American economy. "To reduce complicated international economic issues to the simple level of a campaign against the working class people of other countries is sloganeering unworthy of your Union," argued Joan Shigekawa.[32] Michio Kaku, a Princeton physicist, agreed: "American businesses are firing workers in this country and setting up businesses elsewhere to rip off the American people . . . this is something [the] I.L.G.W.U. has not pointed out," he told the *New York Times*.[33] "Unemployment is not made in Japan; it's made in America."

A final, moving letter arrived from Genora Johnson Dollinger, the leader of the Women's Emergency Brigade of the Flint, Michigan, sit-down strike of 1937 (and the star of the 1978 documentary film about the brigade, *With Babies and Banners*). "As one of the original organizers of the U.A.W. . . . and one who has felt close to your International Union and its history," she began a handwritten note,

> I respectfully urge you to seriously consider your "Made in Japan" ad— in the light of how many other people are reading it. Since moving out here a few years ago I have learned from my Japanese ancestry friends of the genuine horror they went through in the days of World War II. The scars remain in the older generation and the younger ones are the first to fight organized discrimination of any kind.

American runaway shops were proliferating abroad, Dollinger pointed out. "Why not go after the American corporations and put the blame where it belongs?" The ILGWU, she concluded, "is too great a name in labor history to have associated with such confusing propaganda."[34]

But the ILGWU also got positive letters from people who saw the subway poster and loved it. "This morning I noticed your beautiful ad depicting our American flag," enthused Marie A. Connelly of Jackson Heights, New York. "I thought it was wonderful . . . and I hope a great many more people abide with what it states."[35] Rodney E. Armstrong, of New York City, wrote in: "I would like to have five or so of your recently distributed posters showing the American Flag and a headline 'Made in Japan.' I would like to display them and show them to my friends."[36]

In response to the barrage of criticism, the ILGWU was stubbornly unrepentant. Informing ILGWU president Stulberg of an early call to the union's office asking that the ad be withdrawn, Executive Vice President Wilbur Daniels reported that "I gave her no assurance that any action would be taken."[37] Interviewed at the October 25th demonstration, Gus Tyler, assistant president, told the *New York Times,* "The last thing we expected was that anyone would charge us with racist implications. . . . It's unbelievable."[38] Throughout the fall the union would neither admit guilt, retract the poster, nor apologize. It did concede somewhat in a letter to the *Wall Street Journal:* "May we . . . join with you in warning against the use of present economic difficulties to harass people of the Oriental descent in the U.S. [sic]." The union tried to suddenly cast itself as a defender of Asians in the United States: "ironically, among the victims of unregulated imports are Oriental-Americans."[39] The ILGWU's standard response letter to complaints during the controversy was a bit more pugnacious, couched in the hostile charm of the guilty. It recounted the union's difficult struggle with burgeoning sweatshops and pointed out the union's diverse membership, which hailed "from every ethnic sector of our community." The ILGWU, it insisted, had no intention of allowing either "the loss of jobs and earnings to sweatshop competition" or "the loss of their human rights to bigots."[40]

The closest the ILGWU came to making an apology was a new advertisement it ran in the *New York Times Magazine* on Christmas

Eve, 1972. The full-page ad simply portrayed four lines of large Chinese characters, with an English translation in deliberately tiny letters below: "We address one another as brother and sister." The accompanying text read: "We speak to each other in many languages because we are a union of many different people. But whatever the language, we address one another as brother and sister. This is in the tradition of American unions where people, who have come together to work for a better life, see one another as members of one family." The ad wasn't exactly a retraction. But neither was it coincidental that it looked exactly like the "Made in Japan" ad and sang a very different tune, this time in Chinese. Thereafter, ILGWU advertisements, when they disparaged imports, were careful to list an array of countries—including European ones—from whence they issued.[41]

With its "Made in Japan" campaign, the ILGWU decided to play with Asian-bashing fire and got its fingers burned. In the two decades to come the racism it fed would spread like wildfire. And just as in the 1930s, putting out that fire would prove difficult indeed.

THE UNION'S TARIFF

Much of the "look for the union label" advertisement's appeal came from its authenticity: the singers were actual ILGWU members, presenting their case to the American people. The last line of the song punned on both the "Made in the U.S.A." theme, and their struggles: "So we'll be able to make it in the U.S.A." However authentic, though, those sincere choral members were not directing their own union's show. The ILGWU's leadership, which arranged the advertisements, was increasingly distant from the rank-and-file garment workers on whose behalf they labored. Precisely as they ran those TV ads, the leaders developed another element of their anti-import program that, however well-intentioned, edged them further and further away from the union's membership and brought them into an increasingly dubious alliance with apparel manufacturers.[42]

By the 1970s and '80s, the ILGWU's membership, even as it declined, had undergone a fundamental demographic transformation. During the union's classic glory days of the 1920s and '30s, its membership had been overwhelmingly Jewish, with a significant and increasing Italian immigrant and African American constituency. By the 1950s they had been augmented by large numbers of Puerto Ricans. After 1965, though—when the federal government lifted its restrictions on immigration from Latin America and Asia—tens of thousands of immigrants from China, Taiwan, Hong Kong, Korea, Mexico, and Central America found work in the garment industry. By the time the ILGWU launched its TV programs, most workers in the garment industry were Chinese or Latin American immigrant women.[43]

The union's top and middle-level leaders, though, remained caught in a fifty-year time warp. They were almost entirely Jewish and Italian men from the community that had originally built the union in the first two decades of the century. During the 1950s and '60s, "The traditional white leadership of the ILGWU was unwilling to accept blacks and Puerto Ricans as equal partners in an interracial union, to share control of the organization with nonwhites, or to permit them to participate in the power that derived from such institutional authority," writes Herbert Hill, former attorney for the National Association for the Advancement of Colored People (NAACP).[44] In 1972, twenty-two of twenty-four members of the union's General Executive Board, plus its president and first vice president, were still Jewish or Italian. Throughout the 1970s and 1980s, all but one were men—in a union that had been 80 percent female for more than fifty years and a majority female since its inception. And the one woman was the only African American.[45] The union did not include any Asian Americans until after its 1995 merger with the Amalgamated Clothing and Textile Workers' Union, and then only one.

By the 1970s the union's leadership had become an engine that ran of itself, with little interaction with the members and a culture of its own that had been established by the 1940s and remained largely unchanged since. Jeff Hermanson, former organizing director, describes "a tremendous gap between the leadership and the workers." The men who ran the ILGWU literally could not speak to the members of their union. They came to work every day and rode to the top floors of a building towering far above the shops, just blocks away, in which rank-and-file ILGWU members labored. Although the ILGWU's leaders sincerely believed they were working, hard, on behalf of the members, they also thought they knew what was best and didn't ask the members' opinions.[46] "The ILGWU made little effort to establish its presence on the factory floor," observes Peter Kwong in a study of New York's Chinatown.[47]

The ILGWU's import mobilizations in the 1970s and early '80s reflected this internal culture. As we have seen, meticulous instructions to local union committees told members what exactly to do, from the top down. We can get a feel for the hierarchical coordination of these mobilizations from Nick Aiello, who organized anti-import demonstrations as a business agent for the Amalgamated Clothing Workers in New Haven, Connecticut, throughout the 1970s and '80s in cooperation with the ILGWU. Aiello, an Italian-American who speaks with pugnacious enthusiasm, burned then and now with a passionate loyalty to the union label and American-made products, combined with a gut-level hostility to Japan. "I may buy something made in England, something made in Britain, [but] Japan—why should I support that?" he announces. "I didn't attack them; they attacked Pearl Harbor." Aiello recalls his role in the anti-import mobilizations: "They would come up with a directive . . . that this is what we have to do. . . . And so, what I did when I get my directive, I call my chair people together . . . from each plant, sit down with them," in a meeting. " 'This is what we're going to do.' 'Fine.' 'Okay, you, you, you . . . get your people ready.' Buses will be in front of your factory. Each of you stewards make sure those people are on that bus." The buses would arrive at the New Haven Green, the demonstrators would hoist their picket signs and march about, Aiello would give a speech, cameras would flash, and all would trot back onto their respective buses. "I WAS THERE!" insists Aiello. "I didn't let the girls or the women do it alone." These were "popular" Buy American, anti-import demonstrations, to be sure; but their centralized control from above—tinged with a not-so-subtle paternalism—offers a sharp contrast to mobilizations still to come in the United Auto Workers.[48]

The union's divide between top and bottom made possible a set of agreements between the ILGWU's uppermost leadership and unionized garment manufacturers that, in turn, widened the union's internal gap even further—so far as to make the membership almost irrelevant.

The story is convoluted and shrouded in technicalities. From the 1920s onward, ILGWU contracts had specified that if a unionized manufacturer subcontracted any of its production to a nonunion shop, the manufacturer would have to pay "liquidated damages" to the union, at a rate prorated to the sales price of nonunion goods. The union's goal was punitive: in theory, the amount of liquidated damages would be high enough to provide manufacturers with a disincentive to subcontract to a nonunion shop. The idea was that the union would then go after all the remaining nonunion shops, organize them, and establish control over the whole industry.[49]

Then, in the early 1970s, imports arrived, and the picture changed. The ILGWU launched its anti-import legislative campaign, handed its members picket signs, and launched its TV ads. It also noticed that unionized domestic manufacturers, their eyes on cheaper overseas labor, were themselves starting to subcontract part of their production abroad. So, around 1975, the ILGWU inserted a new provision into its contracts establishing a higher rate of liquidated damages for nonunion overseas production than for domestic. The idea, again, was punitive. The union hoped to provide a disincentive for the manufacturers to import.[50]

But at the same time the system was lucrative for the ILGWU, since many manufacturers chose to pay the fine on imports while retaining part of their work in union shops. Liquidated damage payments shot up from $700,000–800,000 a year in the early 1970s to $4,442,055 by 1981. The union argued that it was spending the money to protect the domestic apparel industry and organize those shops that stayed in the United States. In October 1976, President Chick Chaiken announced that the ILGWU planned to expend its hefty liquidated damages funds on the "look for the union label" television advertisements, which by the decade's end were costing $2 million a year. U.S. garment manufacturers operating overseas thus footed the bill for the TV ads' earnest plea that American shoppers eschew imports.[51]

That wasn't all. During the 1980s, the union's membership continued to plummet, which meant that the ILGWU's dues income dropped accordingly, from $18 million a year in 1983 to $12–14 million in the late '80s. At the same time the union's income from liquidated damages steadily climbed, to an impressive $10,358,701 by 1988. Meanwhile, the price of running the union label ads on prime time TV had risen sharply. In 1981 Chaiken decided the "look for the union label" ads were just too expensive and dropped them. By that point many of the union's regional affiliates—known as "joint boards," in particular subsectors of the industry—started running budget deficits. With the label campaign out of the picture, the ILGWU leadership started spending the liquidated damages money not on fighting imports but on general operating expenses to subsidize the affiliates and run the national office in New York.[52]

By the late 1980s and early 1990s, the union's power in the industry had shrunk considerably, and with it, the union's ability to extract liquidated damages from most domestic employers. It was chasing fewer and fewer dollars from fewer and fewer manufacturers and was willing to cut deals with those firms that kept at least part of their production in U.S., unionized plants. The formula for damage payments ratcheted ever-downward, as the ILGWU followed a policy one former official calls "appeasement." Liz Claiborne, for example, paid 70 percent of the amount it owed the union in 1990, but only 36 percent in 1993.[53]

The crucial—and most controversial—turning point came in the late 1980s or early '90s when the ILGWU's rate of liquidated damages sank below the level at which it was punitive and prevented a shift overseas, and became merely a payoff. For a given manufacturer, it became cheaper to subcontract large amounts of work overseas and just pay the union for the right to do so. Michael Babcock, president of the Leslie Fay Companies, which had paid the ILGWU $4 million in the previous five years, charged in 1994 that liquidated damages no longer had a deterrent function, "because even with the added expense, it is still cheaper for companies to import or use non-union shops than to use high-priced unionized manufacturing facilities." For the garment manufacturers who kept some production domestic and union, liquidated damages payments became a routine budget item. "While we don't like liquidated damages," explained Robert Karp, general counsel of Liz Claiborne, "we consider it a cost of doing business." Industry insiders came to call liquidated damages "the union's tariff."[54]

Defending liquidated damages in 1998, Jay Mazur, president of the ILGWU from 1986 onward, insisted, "Monies collected for liquidated damages are used to organize workers, defend union members, promote the union label, and fight sweatshops."[55] But if the ILGWU was able to pay for all those functions with liquidated damages funds, it paid its own price. The problem, in part, was that the system cut the union's actual members out of the loop. A unionized firm could move work overseas, lay off or never hire domestic union members, and the union would still collect the money. The deal was cut between the leadership and the manufacturers. Jeff Hermanson, the ILGWU's organizing director from 1990 to 1998, observes, "the union from the 1940s on depended more on its relationship with employers than on the relationship with workers." By the early 1990s the ILGWU's income from liquidated damages came almost to match its income from members' dues. Both paled next to its income from real estate and securities investments.[56]

The ILGWU's glorious "Look for the Union Label" advertisements attacking imports and calling on American shoppers to Buy American, then, were funded by some of the very apparel firms who were moving production offshore in order to get away from paying for union wages, benefits, and working conditions. The ads might forefront the union's rank and file, but the ILGWU leadership was more engaged in cutting complex deals with the smaller and smaller circle of manufacturers that would deal with the union at all, than with empowering garment workers to fight for themselves. The game, though, couldn't last—and everyone on the inside knew it.

COLD WAR, WARM CHAIRS

As Mazur's statement makes clear, in responding to imports and to its own membership decline, the ILGWU always intended to pursue a final strategic element: organizing nonunion shops in the United States. But its organizing efforts throughout the 1970s and '80s proved largely fruitless. Explaining why brings us back to the ILGWU's internal culture but also to the structural transformation of the apparel industry itself, which created an enormous organizing challenge for the ILGWU. Unfortunately, the union's leadership had tied its own hands in the 1950s and couldn't untie them in the 1970s and '80s to meet that challenge.

The ILGWU's attacks on the "import threat" set up a stark contrast: On the one side were domestic employers, domestic workers, and unionized shops. On the other side were "imports," made by "foreign" workers in nonunion shops owned by "foreigners." But the actual development of the industry in the 1960s was much more complicated, and so, in turn, was the organizing question.

First, as the liquidated damages question suggests, U.S.-based, unionized companies were jumping over each other in the 1970s to themselves produce goods overseas. Much of this production was made possible because of a revision of federal import policy in 1963. Item 807 of the U.S. Tariff code, inserted that year, allowed U.S. apparel firms to cut garments in the United States, send the fabric to Mexico or the Caribbean to be sewn at cheap wages, and re-import the finished garments back into the United States but only pay import duties on the value added overseas—that is, on the workers' wages. Item 807 opened the trade gate for U.S.-based firms to flock to the greener, duty-free, and lower-waged pastures of the Dominican Republic, Haiti, Barbados, Jamaica, and Mexico. Between 1983 and 1987 garment imports under the program swelled from $416 million to $1.12 billion. In 1984, there were four apparel plants working for U.S. firms in Jamaica, for example; in 1987, there were seventy, employing twenty thousand people sewing in such all-American labels as Jockey, Levi Strauss, Ocean Pacific, and Hanes.[57]

U.S.-based firms soon expanded further to subcontract garment production overseas outside the geographic sphere of Item 807. Liz Claiborne, for example, started making jeans in Hong Kong. Like 807-protected overseas production, much of this work was subcontracted by U.S.-based firms that retained a significant—if shrinking—domestic, unionized component of their production. In the late '80s and especially in the 1990s these older, established manufacturers were themselves outclassed by a new group of competitors: domestic mega-retailers such as Target, K-Mart, and Wal-Mart, who skipped over the manufacturers altogether to directly contract foreign production themselves.[58]

Federal trade policy deliberately encouraged the shift of the domestic apparel industry abroad. Even the classically threatening "flood of imports" produced by "foreigners" that arrived on the U.S. market in the 1970s and '80s entered because the U.S. government decided to open the floodgate for its own strategic geopolitical reasons.

As we have seen, Cold War objectives underlay the thrust toward trade liberalization in the 1950s and '60s, as U.S. strategists deployed free trade strategically to keep other nations within a U.S.-dominated capitalist sphere. The same objectives continued to drive trade policy during the 1970s and '80s and led policymakers to trade away the domestic apparel industry for strategic reasons. In 1987 Bruce Smart, U.S. Undersecretary of Commerce for International Trade, explained the Cold War formula underlying U.S. trade policy in India, China, and Indonesia, for example: "If we are to shut them out [of the U.S. apparel market] and prevent them from moving forward, we clearly tilt their attitudes toward our adversaries and away from the trend that now exists in which they are tilting toward us."[59] Economist Richard Rothstein concluded in a 1989 study of the apparel industry, "Behind the lack of enthusiasm for restriction of apparel imports lies a desire to curry favor with apparel exporting nations for foreign policy reasons completely extraneous to textile and apparel trade."[60]

The cast of apparel-exporting nations the United States wooed changed over time, but the objectives stayed the same. From the 1950s onward, the United States sought to lure Japan, Hong Kong, and Taiwan away from alliances with the Communist government of mainland China and used quotas on apparel as part of the bait. During the 1960s, '70s, and '80s, the United States used Item 807 and then the Caribbean Basin Initiative to quell left alternatives in Mexico, the Caribbean, and Central America, and to keep all three within a U.S. economic and political orbit. Then, in the 1990s, as China emerged as a powerhouse exporting nation, the United States—in contrast to European nations—opened its trade doors to Chinese garments as part of a long-term strategic hope of simultaneously courting, taming, and profiting from China. In every case, the U.S. government deliberately traded away the domestic garment industry.[61]

The domestic apparel industry did not, however, disappear altogether. In a final development—and structural challenge to the ILGWU—U.S.-based apparel manufacturers, in addition to going overseas, started opening up more and more nonunion sweatshops within the United States itself, especially after the Reagan administration in the 1980s gutted longstanding regulations against industrial homework. In Los Angeles, for example, apparel employment—most of it nonunion, much of it under sweatshop conditions--grew from 60,000 in 1972 to 120,000 by 1989.[62]

In its strategic approach during the 1970s, '80s, and early '90s, the ILGWU leadership was trying to grapple with this vast transformation of the garment industry. But it never rose to the challenge of its most basic job of organizing the domestic nonunion sector. The ILGWU's membership plummeted not just because domestic jobs went overseas, but also because the union failed to keep the domestic sector unionized.

Why? Primary responsibility lies with the garment manufacturers, who fired workers who talked about joining unions, who threatened to shut down if workers voted one in, and who did everything they could to create a hostile climate for union organizing. During the 1980s and '90s federal officials, moreover, gutted enforcement of basic legal protections for union organizing. But the ILGWU, too, bears responsibility. At the local level, and even at the union's top, hundreds of creative and dedicated union activists gave years of their lives to organizing garment workers in this period. In the shops, thousands of garment workers risked their livelihoods on dangerous organizing campaigns in the face of hostile employers. They were well aware of the benefits of union representation and wanted them. But at the union's top, the will to support organizing just wasn't there. The ILGWU's topmost leadership was frozen in its chairs, unwilling to spend the money necessary to fund organizing campaigns properly. One level beneath them, a second tier of complacent chair-warmers at the regional level who controlled actual organizing campaigns was often hostile to younger agitators seeking to organize using innovative, dynamic methods.[63] Maria Soldatenko, in a 1992 study of Latinas and garment labor in Los Angeles, found that "the ILGWU wanted a 'quick fix.'" "They did not want to invest the time and money to organize Latinas in Los Angeles." She concluded: "Latinas are excluded from positions of power, leadership, and decision making even though it is clear that their skills and leadership would prove invaluable to any union drive."[64]

By the 1980s the ILGWU's leadership started losing interest in garment workers altogether. "It was a constant struggle to keep people focused on the industry," recalls Jeff Hermanson, who served as organizing director of the New York metropolitan region from 1986 to 1990 and then national organizing director from 1990 to 1998. Like other international unions whose membership was eroding during this period, the ILGWU started sniffing around for other groups of workers who might be easier to organize than garment workers. During the late 1980s and early 1990s the ILGWU mounted organizing campaigns among PepsiCola drivers in Pennsylvania, light manufacturing workers in Chicago, and nursing home workers in Florida. Some officials started talking about shifting the ILGWU out of the apparel industry altogether.[65]

The picture was not a complete disaster—the union did fight, and win, a number of defensive struggles to keep union shops union. It organized about one thousand new workers a year during the 1980s and early '90s. But overall, the ILGWU's organizing record was grim. Yet because dues from members only represented one portion of its annual income, the union could keep functioning nonetheless—at least for a time.[66]

The ILGWU's failure to organize, however, was as much about overseas nonunion labor as it was about the domestic front. We should not fall into the union's own trap of viewing the organizing question as an entirely domestic one. As garment industry jobs moved overseas, the ILGWU failed to follow them. During the 1930s and '40s garment manufacturers had moved their jobs from New York City to Pennsylvania and New Jersey to get away from the union. The ILGWU followed and organized those shops. During the 1960s, '70s, and '80s the companies again moved, to the U.S. South and to Los Angeles; and the ILGWU at least tried, if with only minimal effort, to follow. But when the companies made their third move to exploit foreign workers, the union stopped short at the border. Workers on the other side were suddenly Asian foreigners willing to work for cheap wages and a threat to jobs that belonged to Americans. Even if they worked for the very same apparel manufacturers as did domestic union workers, even if they were even more exploited than U.S. workers, once they were on the other side of the border they were the enemy and their products were malicious imports that were to blame for U.S. workers' plight.[67]

Here the ILGWU's Cold War chickens came thumping down to roost. The union's leadership couldn't make that leap over the border because it was trapped in its Cold War ideological cage. During the entire second half of the twentieth century, the ILGWU's top leaders were at the forefront of U.S. labor support for Cold War–driven foreign policy. In part through their participation in a group called Social Democrats, U.S.A.—in which ILGWU president Chick Chaiken was deeply involved—ILGWU leaders were instrumental in shaping AFL-CIO foreign policy, which included support for the U.S. invasion of Guatemala in 1954, the war in Vietnam, and intervention in El Salvador during the 1970s and '80s.[68]

As the government traded away much of the domestic apparel industry, the ILGWU leadership's adherence to its Cold War agenda boxed the union in, strategically. ILGWU lobbyists lobbied against Item 807 and the Caribbean Basin Initiative, but only halfheartedly. They didn't like it when a U.S. company closed a plant and moved to El Salvador because wages were cheaper there, but through the American Institute for Free Labor Development (AIFLD) they had actively worked for decades to undermine left-wing or militant unions that had been trying to improve working conditions in that very same country. They might attack "imports" coming in from Hong Kong, Taiwan, or Japan, but they couldn't attack the anticommunist agenda that admitted such imports in order to lure all three nations away from cooperation with China—which Chaiken and others high up in the ILGWU leadership referred to as "Red" China long after the phrase had passed out of mainstream conversation.[69]

Cold Warriorism tied the union's hands at home as well. The ILGWU's anticommunist leadership was deeply suspicious of and hostile to domestic radicalism, including trade unionists who questioned AFL-CIO support for U.S. intervention in El Salvador during the 1980s. But many of the most energetic organizers who might have lent vision and creativity to the ILGWU's organizing efforts were leftists—and therefore unwelcome in the union.

During the 1970s and early '80s the ILGWU leadership had set up a stark contrast between domestic union jobs and foreign sweatshop labor. But the industry itself was by no means so simple to demarcate, since U.S.-based companies—including unionized ones—both fled overseas and forced domestic working conditions downward at home. "Foreign" workers might work for those very same companies whose flight overseas had been paid for by the U.S. government. The ILGWU played the nationalist card in public, asking Americans to spurn imports and protect those within. But in private it supported Cold War policies that helped U.S. companies play the working people of the First and Third Worlds against each other. Nationalism and the legacy of anticommunism had blinded them to the class politics of corporate-led globalization.

AMERICA: A UNION OF ALL NATIONS

The ILGWU's anti-import, anti-foreign approach created a final contradiction: between the union's nationalist approach to the jobs question and the international origins of its members. In this case, though, the contradiction proved inescapable, and its resolution opened the way for the ILGWU to begin to map a new path through the garment industry and the global economy.

On the one hand, the union's Buy American campaign invoked an implicit "Us," Americans, versus "Them"—foreigners. Just as had similar campaigns in the 1930s, the campaign called for a circling of the nation's economic wagons, inscribing a border of national identity inside which all-American dollars would circulate. The Buy American call assumed a concrete economic, political, and geographical border and reinforced nationalism to enhance the fate of those within.

Yet both the union and its members simultaneously transcended national borders. Its name, after all, was the *International* Ladies' Garment Workers' Union; and by the 1980s a majority of its members were foreign-born. In their union activism, as at home, they spoke many languages other than English. Immigrant ILGWU members at a 1972 demonstration in New York City, for example, carried signs with anti-import slogans printed in Chinese and Spanish as well as English.[70] As the union's Buy American, anti-import campaign wore on, the tension between the union's nationalist slogans and its international membership mounted to almost absurd proportions. We can glimpse it in a 1983 New York City "Rollback Imports" demonstration, in which ILGWU members marched in national costumes and sashes representing "Chile," "China," "Nicaragua," and dozens of other nations, while waving little American flags. At the front of the procession, their banner proclaimed proudly: "AMERICA. A UNION OF ALL NATIONS. I.L.G.W.U."[71]

The "international" part of the ILGWU's name, as with many other unions, meant, in practice, the United States plus Canada. The Canadian part posed thorny challenges to the "Buy American" program. *Justice,* the union's magazine for its members, inadvertently captured the problem in 1983 when it excitedly reported a new slogan, "Think of the union label as a little American flag in your clothes," then continued: "The union is studying ways to extend such programs to Puerto Rico and Canada." During the 1960s, Canadian locals of the ILGWU managed a separate label program promoting Canadian-made ILGWU garments, with a different label that read "Canada E'tiquette Syndicale Union Label" around the ILGWU logo, with "CLC" (Canadian Labor Congress) appended after "AFL-CIO." "The Union Label is *as Canadian as a Prairie wheat field*," one pamphlet read. "Its presence on a garment tells you it was produced in a Union shop by Canadian workers enjoying Canadian wage and working standards." The ILGWU label sewn on in the United States, by contrast, omitted the "CLC" (and, needless to say, substituted baseball gloves for prairie wheat fields).[72] After the anti-import campaign began in the 1970s, the ILGWU organized anti-import demonstrations in Canada, but they didn't include the Buy American slogan, though parallel U.S. demonstrations did. Canadian products in the United States were foreign products, to be sure; but the union didn't count them among the "import threat"—in part because the workers who made them received relatively high wages, comparable to those in the United States, and in part because those workers were union sisters and brothers.[73]

By the 1980s these tensions between nationalism and internationalism were sharpening. Increasingly, the ILGWU leadership celebrated the international origins of its members, forging what we might call a "multiculturalist nationalism." During a 1983 ILGWU march in New York, for example, *Justice* reported, "Both the English and Chinese-languages [sic] choruses, conducted by Malcolm Dodds and Kong Tung Wong, respectively, sang from separate floats. . . . Colonial, Dixieland, and glockenspiel bands also played, as did the band from the New York Chinese School."[74] A 1987 photograph in *Justice* entitled "Dance 'Made in the U.S.A.'" pictured four women, arms outstretched on a lawn. "Seen here in their 'Made in America' T-shirts (donated by the ILGWU's Northeast Department) are members of the Tokunaga Dance Ko of New York City," the caption read. The dancers, it reported, planned to wear the shirts on an imminent tour of Japan. "Their program, 'Made in America,' is printed to look like a garment ticket, and describes their performance, which exhibits a variety of American culture," including "American Indian dance steps and modern dance performed to American jazz."[75]

Yet the ILGWU continued to press forward with its anti-import campaign—to the point where ILGWU members were asked to demonstrate against workers in the very countries from which they had just emigrated and where family members might still labor. "One can imagine how difficult it is for Chinese women to demonstrate against imports made by Chinese women in Hong Kong, Taiwan, and the People's Republic—where many have only recently come from," noted Peter Kwong.[76]

Gradually, pressure built from within the union to rethink its focus on imports. The "Made in Japan" poster affair had served as an early warning that defining foreign imports as the sole problem carried dangerous racial overtones. By the 1980s, the mid-level staff of the ILGWU started to include a smattering of Asian Americans and Latinos, who began to both express their own reservations about some of the international's policies and serve as a conduit for member input from below. Staff members at ILGWU Local 23-25 in New York City, for example, developed coalitions with community groups in Chinatown in order to build support for a strike by Chinese workers against Chinese employers. When, in the midst of their campaign, the leadership chose to picket the Chinese embassy in New York in protest against imports, staff members suggested that doing so would hinder their efforts to win over the Chinese immigrant community, and the planned demonstration was dropped.[77]

May Ying Chen was one of these new staffers. A Chinese American active in Asian American politics, Chen came on board ILGWU Local 23-25 in 1984. In 1988 she and several other Asian American activists in the New York City labor movement met at a Cornell University-sponsored class on Asian American labor history. They soon founded the Asian Labor Committee, which started raising concerns specific to Asian workers in the labor movement, such as workplace discrimination against Asians and rising anti-Asian violence, and working for a stronger presence of Asian Americans in the labor movement's leadership. The ILGWU was one of the beneficiaries of their work.[78]

During the 1980s the divergence between the union's increasingly Latina and Chinese immigrant membership and its European American male leadership became increasingly challenged from below. John Laslett and Mary Tyler, in a 1988 study of the ILGWU in Los Angeles, found tensions "between the older generation of Anglo leaders, who ran the union at the top, and some of the younger, militant Latino leaders."[79] By the late 1980s dissidents throughout the country were grumbling about the ILGWU's entrenched leadership, especially its failure to adequately support organizing and adapt to the cultures of its members.[80]

These pressures from below, combined with the accession of Jay Mazur from the heavily immigrant Local 23-25 to the ILGWU presidency in 1986, helped make the ILGWU the most progressive union in the country on immigration policy. Since its inception, the union's members had always been overwhelmingly immigrant. By the late 1970s the ILGWU's immigrant members were increasingly undocumented. Although statistics for ILGWU members are not available, around a third of all apparel workers in New York City lacked legal status; in Los Angeles—the other main center of the industry—"almost the entire workforce." While the ILGWU had always been pro-immigrant, in 1975 it spoke out in support of the rights of undocumented workers as well as of legal immigrants for the first time. "If you don't defend the rights of immigrants, you undermine the rights of *all* workers," underscored ILGWU immigration project director Muzzaffar Chisti. "Once inside the country, the rights of undocumented workers should be the same as everyone else's." ILGWU representatives not only testified at government hearings on behalf of undocumented workers from 1979 onward, but challenged the constitutionality of raids by the Immigration and Naturalization Service (INS). By the 1980s the ILGWU's Immigration Project provided a range of legal services to its members, such as advice on naturalization and citizenship, help in bringing in family members, or assistance for members seeking political asylum. The project served between 1,100 and 1,200 members a year.[81]

Meanwhile, it became increasingly clear at the ILGWU's top that the union's legislative approach on the import question was failing. Fifteen years of national political mobilizations and high-powered lobbying had failed to pass a single protectionist measure. Congress repeatedly passed measures protecting the apparel industry during the late 1970s and early 1980s, but presidential vetoes overrode them all. Protection of the domestic garment industry was steadily being traded away; and with Reagan's ascendancy in 1980 free traders reigned more triumphant than ever. After a final defeat in 1984, the

ILGWU decided it was futile to focus on federal import restrictions and backed off.

In 1986, ILGWU president Sol "Chick" Chaiken retired; Jay Mazur, from the New York immigrant Local 23-25 took his place, and the icebergs finally started to break free. In his speeches, Mazur started making it clear that the ILGWU was not interested in attacking foreign workers but in establishing international solidarity. Rather than continue futile attempts to stop imports, the union shifted to advocating international fair labor standards, institutionalized in trade agreements. Rather than asking that working people eschew the products of foreign workers, the union started meeting with delegations from apparel workers overseas. Painstakingly, often through direct worker-to-worker visits or staff exchanges, the ILGWU started building international solidarity from the bottom up.[82] The union's internal problems did not evaporate—liquidated damage payments continued to flow in under Mazur's watch, and no great advances took place on the organizing front in the late 1980s or early '90s. But Mazur was not the Cold Warrior his predecessor had been; he brought a new generation of advisers to the union's top; and he opened the door for an entirely new strategic approach for the union.

WE ADDRESS ONE ANOTHER AS BROTHER AND SISTER

Buying American, as a political strategy for organized labor, rested on the concept of an economic nation that stopped at the nation's political and geographical borders. It assumed that money spent on a dress "Made in the U.S.A." would stay inside the country and be reinvested in hiring more Americans to make more dresses for good union wages. But by the 1970s and '80s, neither the workers who made the dress nor the profits it produced stopped at the border. An "American" company name might grace its label, but the seamstress who made it might be working in Malaysia, Mexico, or Taiwan. Or she might be Malaysian, Mexican, or Chinese but residing in Los Angeles, sewing away at subminimum wages in a hot storefront. If she worked in Los Angeles, she might have a sister just over the border in Mexico, sewing for the same company at still lower wages. The profits from that dress might fly anywhere in the world, seeking the highest rate of return with no thought for the nationality of the worker.

The ILGWU's "Buy American" call had always depended on the equation of American jobs with good jobs. Now the equation broke down: buying American might just mean buying the product of a domestic sweatshop. The tidy equation of "Fashions U.S.A." was shattered. Eleanor Lambert and Min Matheson, the two lovely ladies explaining the latest styles on their couch in the union's 1962 film, would have had a hard time thirty years later spending their fashion dollars on union-, U.S.-made garments on the cutting edge. For them, Fashions U.S.A. meant a smart little jacket for the fall season, purchased with respect for the woman who made it. But for the garment industry, Fashions U.S.A. only meant a corporate shell based nominally in the United States, as the manufacturers went global, like a heat-seeking missile flying at the speed of international capital toward the lowest wages anywhere on earth.

The ILGWU, frozen in the Cold War, at first turned to economic nationalism—with a brief foray into explicit Asian-bashing—in response. Its leaders were more comfortable negotiating dubious collaborations with garment employers than with listening to and empowering rank-and-file garment workers and fighting to organize garment shops, whether in the United States or beyond its borders. But by the 1990s the ILGWU was finally in pursuit of garment employers over those same borders. In December 1972, when it had apologized in the *New York Times Magazine* for its "Made in Japan" poster, the ILGWU had insisted in Chinese that "We Address One Another as Brother and Sister." Two decades later, that slogan finally began to take concrete form.

CHAPTER 7

Demons in the Parking Lot

Autoworkers and the "Japanese Threat"

The scene was like something out of a Batman cartoon. The first man lifted the sledgehammer, planted his feet wide apart, sighted over his left shoulder, and THWACK! sank it deep into the car with a grunt of pleasure. The crowd roared. The next man paid his dollar, swaggered up to the car, hefted the sledgehammer back and forth from one hand to the other, and suddenly WHAM! swung it into the car's front corner, taking off its headlamp. OOH! AAH! went the crowd. Next in line was a woman. Grinning at the crowd, she picked up the sledgehammer like she'd been using one all her life, and WHACK! sent it through the car's windshield. The crowd went crazy.[1]

The object of their aggression was a Toyota, its assailants members of the United Auto Workers at a union picnic in the 1980s. If the ILGWU's "look for the union label" song burned itself into the memories of millions of TV watchers in the 1970s, even more emblematic of Buy American campaigns by the 1980s was the image of an unemployed auto worker in Detroit smashing a Japanese car. Autoworkers' hostility to Japanese imports captured the public imagination in the 1980s and early '90s, carrying the Buy American idea to the forefront of popular culture. Like the ILGWU's, the autoworkers' Buy American campaign was intricately embedded in relationships between the union's leadership and its rank-and-file, and between the union and employers. But there was one big difference: the UAW's Buy American movement didn't, in large part, begin at the union's top: it surged up from the bottom.

The autoworkers' union turned out to be no more able than the ILGWU to read the global handwriting on the wall. Meanwhile, the

AFL-CIO's feet, we shall see, seemed encased in cement. As trade union membership nationwide sank from a third of all nonagricultural workers in 1953 to less than one in five by 1984, the federation responded with a flurry of inactivity. Like the UAW, it seemed caught in a time warp from the 1950s.

But not everyone in the labor movement embraced nationalism, by any means. Throughout the period critics within the UAW and AFL-CIO, as in the ILGWU, continued to propose alternative solutions to the crisis. Outside the federation the United Electrical Workers articulated a diametrically different understanding of "Us" and "Them." Much later, when the AFL-CIO and the American people came to discover the full implications of economic globalization, their arguments would suddenly make sense.

HUNGRY? EAT YOUR IMPORT

UAW members had been the classic beneficiaries of the American Century and the postwar compact between labor and the corporations. Protected by union contracts, they had enjoyed high wages, excellent health benefits, pensions, and what seemed to be job security. They were proud people: proud to be autoworkers, proud to be UAW members, proud to be Americans. Suddenly, in the late 1970s and early 1980s the bottom fell out of their world. Between 1978 and 1981 alone, automobile employment plummeted from 760,000 to 490,000. Individual autoworkers, even if their plants hadn't just shut down, lay awake at night wondering who would be next, trying to figure out how they would feed their families when their turn came. They saw what had already happened to their friends and neighbors. They were searching for a solution.[2]

Beginning in the late 1970s, well after the ILGWU's first "Made in the U.S.A." ads first appeared, UAW members, either on their own initiative or with the help of local and regional-level union staffers, decided to promote American-made products to save themselves and their communities. They invented Buy American slogans, printed up bumper stickers, and plastered them on their cars. They arranged for Toyota bashings at union picnics; they hand-lettered picket signs; they designed T-shirts; they painted billboards.

"The only way to put America back to work is for people to quit buying foreign-made cars," Frank Podwoiski of Detroit UAW Local

182 argued in a typical letter to the UAW's magazine, *Solidarity.*[3] At the UAW's 1977 International Convention an older man, with a reso-lute and slightly grim look on his face, held up a handmade sign at his table reading: "WE BUY WHAT WE BUILD AND WANT TO BUILD WHAT WE BUY."[4] His sign summed up the basic logic: buying American would reinforce a prosperous national circuit be-tween producers and consumers, who would ensure their own jobs and those of their fellow working Americans by nationalist shopping, as expressed in the bumper sticker "BUY AMERICAN: THE JOB YOU SAVE MAY BE YOUR OWN." These appeals melded in-dividual self-interest with a sincere compassion for other American working people at economic risk. "Above all *Buy American* and *Boy-cott* the union busters," appealed UAW member Claudette Pippins in the UAW Local 598 *Eye Opener.* "You'll be helping workers less for-tunate than you to have a happy holiday season."[5]

Of course, for autoworkers, buying American meant in particular not buying a foreign car. Almost as famous as the Toyota bashings in this period was the legendary sign that one day appeared in the parking lot of Solidarity House, the UAW's national headquarters in Detroit. "UAW PARKING RESERVED FOR U.S. AND CANADIAN VEHICLES ONLY. PLEASE PARK IMPORTS ELSEWHERE."[6] Soon parking lots at union halls and auto plants throughout the country sprouted similar warnings. Visitors who in-nocently arrived in Japanese cars were told they weren't welcome or to park elsewhere.

Hostility to Japanese cars quickly spilled over into more generic fury at Japan. Outside the Linden, New Jersey, General Motors plant, an autoworker set fire to a Japanese flag while a thousand people wav-ing American flags cheered wildly and loudspeakers blared Bruce Springsteen singing "Born in the U.S.A." "They're crucifying our auto industry," Bob Freeman, a member of UAW Local 595, told a reporter at the scene.[7] Often, these protests invoked Pearl Harbor and World War II. When Ford employees organized a picket line at a Toy-ota dealer's in the Detroit area, they printed in big letters on their sign, "WE DID IT IN '45. WE CAN DO IT AGAIN IN '92!! BEAT THE JAPANESE DEFICIT!!"[8] In Florida, a man named Robert McKesson printed up anti-Japan bumper stickers and T-shirts that pictured an airplane dropping radios, televisions, and cars onto the

United States, with "Pearl Harbor II" emblazoned across them. McKesson estimated he sold twenty thousand of his products in one year, with the largest number going to union autoworkers, steelworkers, and electrical workers.[9] A war was under way, these union members believed. When General Motors in 1991 announced it was going to close twenty-one plants, the UAW shop committee at its Willow Run plant in Michigan responded with an anti-Japan leaflet:

> A call to arms for all Americans to declare war on Japanese products and all non American made products! When Japan bombed Pearl Harbor— we went to war! . . . And when Japan threatens the security of American jobs we must go to war again—with a complete boycott of all products not made in America![10]

Hostility to Japan, in many of these activities, in turn spilled over into hostility to all Asian nations. "It makes me boil inside to discover after I've bought something that it's been made in South Korea or some other place," Mary E. Daniel of Richwood, Ohio, wrote in *Solidarity*.[11] Roger Gotthardt, editor of Local 696's newsletter, *Union Eyes,* told how, out shopping one day in a department store, his son showed him a hat that read: " 'MADE BY AN AMERICAN, WORN BY AN AMERICAN, PAID FOR BY AN AMERICAN.' I liked the hat and was going to buy it when I looked at the tag inside to see what state it was made in. It said MADE IN CHINA!!!!!"[12]

All too often autoworkers' arguments in favor of Buy American employed stereotypical images and language that stretched far back into U.S. history. In 1978, hand-drawn cartoons that read "We Have to Beat the Japs" suddenly appeared all over the Clark Street Cadillac plant in Detroit, picturing caricatured Japanese workers with slanty eyes and tricky smiles.[13] Along with the term "Jap," the idea of evil "foreigners" reappeared. Roger Gotthardt, upon discovering the "Made in China" label in his hat, concluded: "You know, it makes you feel really good, to know it takes a foreigner to tell Americans how good it feels to be an AMERICAN."[14] Other stories about imports revived classic Yellow Peril images of "floods" of Asians "invading" American shores. In visual imagery straight out of the Hearst press, the May 1981 cover of *Solidarity,* the UAW's official magazine, was headlined "THE TRACTOR INVASION" and portrayed a fleet of tractors bearing Japanese flags, climbing up out of the sea onto the West Coast of the United States.[15] Other references were more subtle. Harold A. Massey, in the *Local 685 News* from Kokomo, Indiana, warned: "Before it is too late, we must do our part to stop the flow of imports from taking our livelihood from us by Buying American"—again, evoking fears dating back to early in the century that Asians were about to engulf the United States.[16]

Racial stereotyping made it possible, in turn, for some autoworkers to blame all Asians for auto unemployment, including Americans of Asian descent. In autoworker communities, day-to-day harassment of Asian Americans escalated. The most famous case was the 1982 murder of Vincent Chin. Late on the night of June 19, 1982, two white autoworkers, Ronald Ebens and Michael Nitz, one of them recently laid off, were hanging out in a Detroit strip joint. "You little motherfucker, you're the reason we don't have jobs," Ebens spat at Vincent Chin, a Chinese American resident of Detroit visiting the bar to celebrate his upcoming wedding. When Chin came over and confronted Ebens, a fight broke out. Ebens and Nitz followed Chin out of the bar, found him at a diner, chased him down the street, and beat him with baseball bats until he was dead.[17] In the Chin murder, the autoworkers' Buy American logic played itself out to its most dangerous point: Buy American equaled don't buy imports, equaled don't buy Japanese, equaled don't buy Asian, equaled blame all Asians, equaled blame Asian Americans, equaled bash them, just like a Toyota.

When General Motors or Ford or Chrysler laid off American autoworkers, Buy American sentiment thus focused their resultant anger: Japan was to blame—or even all people of Asian descent. But not all Buy American advocates descended into Japan-bashing; and Vincent Chin's murder was only the most brutal end of a usually less violent, if nonetheless insidious spectrum of hostility to Asian Americans. Even autoworkers' anger at "foreigners" could be toned down to a more subtle nationalist lack of interest in the fate of workers in other countries. "I think 'Buy American' because you'll keep somebody working," explained Dan Roche, a front-end aligner at Ford's Wayne Assembly plant in Detroit, in a 1986 interview. "It's not that you hate somebody else in another country; but hey, we have to make our own [automobiles], and they should make their own. It's up to their government to help their people." Here Roche, like economic nationalists in the 1930s, melded his support for buying American products with an implicit argument for autarchy—and an indifference to foreign workers' situation.[18]

But buying American as a solution also focused working people's anger on their fellow Americans. If the American people could solve the problem by buying American, therefore Americans who did not buy American were to blame as well as Asians. "There will always be automobiles, but they may be made somewhere else," Roche told his interviewer. "If people in this country let that happen, they are as much to blame as anybody. We've lost the feeling of nationalism." UAW members unleashed some of their strongest ire at other Americans who bought imports. "The American people now have something to be proud of, they helped put 29,000 people out of work!!" Roger Gotthardt, the man with the made-in-China hat, raged.[19] The guilty included unemployed working people—even fellow UAW members. "I . . . have a gripe about these people buying foreign cars," spat out E. J. "Red" Blade, of Local 12 in Toledo, Ohio. "They are standing in line at the welfare and unemployment offices. Why don't they go to Japan and Germany and stand in line over there for those benefits?"[20] Sandra Dennis, secretary of the United Union Label Committee of UAW Region 1-C, let go with the same palpable anger: "Our own Union Brothers and Sisters are buying these products. Maybe they should find a job in one of our competitors foreign countries car assembly plants and try to live on their wages [sic]."[21] All these examples illustrate the extent to which UAW members were watching their fellow-workers' purchases for country of origin, vigilantly try to enforce buying American in their own daily lives.

It is difficult to assess the overall pattern of Buy American activities among rank-and-file UAW members. Buy American slogans and activities cropped up all over the country, although they seem to have been strongest in the upper Midwest, the historic center of automobile employment where UAW loyalties were strongest and where entire communities were most often devastated by auto layoffs in the 1980s. Buy American activities seem to have been somewhat more popular among white UAW members than among African American or Latino members. But African Americans also expressed loyal Buy American sentiments; for example, Claudette Pippins, the woman cited earlier who spoke with compassion of buying American in order to help one's fellow Americans at Christmas time, was African American.

Men evidently organized the Toyota bashings and most relished participating in them; but women—both UAW members and the wives of members—picked up those sledgehammers, too, and shared men's anger at Asian imports. "Whenever I go to a department store, I just boil, because everything seems to be made in Japan, Hong Kong, Taiwan, Philippines, Korea, etc., etc.," wrote Marty Dodson, the wife of a laid-off Ford employee from Local 1111 in Indianapolis.[22] Lois Piazza, married to Sam Piazza, president of Local 398, issued a Buy American call in the *Sparkler,* his local's newsletter, aimed specifically at women: "Women: It's Up to Us to Save American Industry!" She began by invoking common sayings such as "Behind every successful man is a woman supporting him," or "The hand that rocks the cradle rules the world," then drew on the World War II theme with a women's twist.

> I'm told that during World War II, the women took over and ran the factories. With the backing of the women, the war was won! Okay ladies, if our country is to survive, we must pull together again, as our mothers, grandmothers and great-grandmothers did. . . . We're in a different kind of war today. We are becoming a nation of imports!
>
> The next time you pick up a product to buy, check to see if it's made in the U.S.A. If it's not, think of this: is it worth putting my neighbor or someone in my family out of work for.

Piazza concluded: "HOW'S THAT FOR A WOMAN'S VIEW-POINT!"[23]

While men were organizing Toyota bashings, women organized their own public spectacles in support of American products. In April 1987, the Women's Committee of Local 651 put on its Second Annual Union and American Made Fashion Show. Here we can trace a direct link between the ILGWU's Made in the U.S.A. campaigns in the 1970s and the UAW activism that followed. "The idea to hold this even came to us late in 1985 as the Women's Committee pondered the plight of textile and garment workers," explained Theresa Mullen, the committee's chair. "The Women's Committee can relate to the problems these workers face, as we see our own automotive production drastically affected by Japanese and other imports." The women's answer was to buy American in "*all* of our industries in this Country" [emphasis in original]. Their fashion show featured "two beautiful cakes . . . one in the shape of an American flag and another in the shape of the UAW seal." The accompanying photo spread showed an equal number of African American and white models from the union local, parading up and down a runway in evening wear, fur coats, men's suits, casual outfits, and gym wear.[24]

While Buy American sentiments and activities appear to have been both widespread and quite popular, it is important to note that buying American was just one of many solutions to automobile industry layoffs that rank-and-file members advocated in the 1970s, '80s, and early '90s. Letter-writers to *Solidarity,* for example, proposed everything from controlling corporate salaries to lowering environmental standards to nationalizing Chrysler. A very few explicitly criticized the Buy American approach. Carl E. Nilson of Local 1005 in Parma, Ohio, wrote: " 'Buy American' is a N.A.M. (National Association of Manufacturers) shuck! Those foreign cars are (almost) all made by good union men who are citizens of free countries, friendly to the U.S.A." Union members weren't to blame. The problem, rather, was "a U.S. government that allows 9% unemployment and double-digit inflation to keep the slush-fund type of businessman fat at the expense of our paychecks." Nilson concluded: "Buy American is just a variation on the tired old bosses' line of 'you workers fight each other for jobs.' "[25]

Fred Wulkan of Boston District 65 in November 1982 wrote in "to explain why I, like many members of my local, think this is not a good slogan for the UAW."

> The thrust behind "Buy American" is to blame consumers—mostly working-class Americans like ourselves—for the problems in the auto industry. It's saying that if only consumers did the right thing, then we would have our jobs back. . . . Not only is this alienating many people who should be our allies, but it also places responsibility in the wrong place.

Instead, Wulkan argued, "it's the auto companies who didn't listen to the UAW when we said to build fuel-efficient cars years ago. It's GM and Ford and Chrysler who are shipping our jobs overseas." The "international corporate system" had produced a "worldwide over-capacity in the auto industry." Individual shopping habits couldn't change any of that, wrote Wulkan. "Say we did all buy 'American.' Would that stop GM from importing hundreds of thousands of components," subcontracting to nonunion shops, or using robots to replace union workers? "No."[26]

TEAM DREAMS

The passion, energy, and anger animating rank-and-file Buy American activities were all their own. But the UAW's top leadership nonetheless set the context in which they chose their Buy American approach. As UAW members groped for a way to empower themselves and their communities, they did so in relationship to a strategic vacuum at the top of their international union. The UAW leadership, faced with a crisis for which it was in no way prepared, reacted with everything but militancy, setting the context for Buy Americanism, it turns out, as much by omission as by commission.

Official support for buying American did issue from Solidarity House, the UAW's national headquarters in Detroit. As early as 1975, President Leonard Woodcock approved the printing of fifty thousand bumper stickers with the slogan "Get U.S. Moving. Buy an American Car," which he chose from a list of eleven possible slogans (including "Do It in an American Car").[27] In October 1980, the UAW launched what the *Washington Post* called an "An Arsenal of Buy-American Car Ads." One described the plight of Bill Cunningham, "who lost his job recently because someone somewhere in the U.S. bought a foreign car." Another started off, "Every ship bringing foreign-made cars to America carries a hidden cargo. Unemployment."[28] The union's goal here, though, was less to salvage jobs through nationalist shopping than to pressure the Federal Trade Commission to impose curbs on auto imports.

Nonetheless, Solidarity House continued to crank out Buy American slogans. In 1981, the UAW headquarters sent out caps reading "Buy American" to all local unions with more than fifteen hundred members; printed up six thousand bumper stickers to give out to rank-and-file visitors to Black Lake, the union's resort center in Michigan; and ensured that every officer, every regional office, and the lobby of Solidarity House were well-stocked with bumper stickers.[29] Three UAW-produced bumper stickers appeared on the wall above the anti-import sign in the Solidarity House parking lot: "Buy American," "Unemployment: Made in Japan," and "Hungry? Eat a Foreign Car."[30] All of them issued forth with either the implicit or explicit approval of President Douglas Fraser (1976–1983), who himself went on a 1982 national "whistle stop" tour of U.S. airports exhorting U.S. car buyers to Buy American, "flanked by union members wearing 'Buy American' sandwich boards and handing out leaflets and buttons."[31]

Key figures at the UAW's top were aware that in promoting "Buy American," they were potentially contributing to anti-Asian racism. On March 18, 1982, Lee Price, the union's Research Department staff member responsible for trade issues, circulated a confidential memo cautioning the UAW's top leadership about its response to the imports question. "I would like to suggest that all our orientation sessions *explicitly* address a potentially explosive issue: racist remarks," Price began. UAW leaders "would not say such things ourselves, but we must assume that a few of those who will ultimately be called on to represent the UAW could possibly say them if not cautioned." He acknowledged that "We cannot avoid mentioning Japan," given the structure of the global automobile industry. "But we need not mention race, physical features, ethnic slurs, or World War II." Price suggested that UAW spokespersons focus on the behavior of both U.S. and Japanese automakers and "teach people to pre-empt the charge of racist motives by using *compliments to make our case*" [emphases in original]. Otherwise, the UAW might easily be tainted as racist, he cautioned. Its opponents "will be watching every statement on behalf of the UAW for a slip. We should make every effort not to blow it by letting the UAW become associated with racism in the minds of Congress, the media, and ultimately the public." In sum, "Racist remarks are not only inappropriate but will greatly detract from our efforts to get Congressional support."[32]

In these and other efforts, national-level UAW staff members mixed instrumental concern over political damage control with a sincere concern about racism. Doug Fraser evidently designed his speeches consciously to avoid racial references and was evidently reluctant to take on the import question because of its racial implications. Throughout the 1980s the editors of *Solidarity* deliberately tried to deflect anti-Asian racism by running stories on solidarity with Japanese trade unionists.[33]

Nonetheless, the leadership, knowing full well it was potentially contributing to racism, still chose to attack Japan. To understand why, we need to pull back a bit and examine the UAW's leadership, its positions, and its politics by the early 1980s.

While the ILGWU was shuddering from its import shock during the 1970s, the UAW leadership was still riding high. Throughout the decade it remained self-confident, even cocky, and continued to exact gains from the Big Three auto companies. In its 1976 contract with Ford, for example, the UAW gained a new paid holiday, a 3 percent wage increase, and the extension of vision care to additional family members.[34] Longtime president Walter Reuther, still in his prime, died in a plane crash on his way to the UAW's resort at Black Lake, Michigan, in 1970. The UAW's new leadership, under Leonard Woodcock (1970–1977) and then Douglas Fraser, briefly extended Reuther's liberal vision, setting high hopes on Jimmy Carter's 1976 Democratic election to the presidency.[35]

By 1978 it was clear, though, that the corporations had something new and ugly in mind, and Carter would prove no savior. A frustrated Doug Fraser, in a rare moment of oppositional fervor, announced, "I believe leaders of the business community, with few exceptions, have chosen to wage a one-sided class war in this war . . . against working people, the unemployed, the minorities, the very young and the very old, and even many in the middle class." The postwar deal, in sum, was off: "The leaders of industry, commerce and finance in the United States have broken the fragile, unwritten compact previously existing during a period of growth and progress."[36] Fraser called it exactly: the postwar compact was indeed over.

For the UAW, it ended abruptly in the fall of 1979 with the Chrysler bailout. All through the late 1960s and especially the 1970s, as U.S. companies' share of the domestic auto market dropped—to 71 percent by 1981—the Big Three had continued to churn out gas guzzlers for the top end of the market. The oil price shock of 1973–1974 increased demand for small, fuel-efficient cars, but the U.S. companies paid little mind. Their share of the world auto market, meanwhile, plummeted from 61 percent in 1960 to 37 percent by 1980. The world no longer bought American.

By the end of the 1970s the Chrysler Corporation, in particular, was in big trouble. In 1979 Chrysler claimed it was about to go bankrupt. In stepped the nation's big banks, who arranged a megadeal in which they underwrote a congressionally approved package of $750 million in loans. There was one little catch to their offer: the UAW would have to open its contract with Chrysler and make vast concessions. A flurry of negotiations ensued, and by the time the dust had settled into a final bailout package, the UAW had given up twenty paid holidays a year, $1.15 an hour per worker (leaving Chrysler workers $3.00 an hour below Ford and GM), cost-of-living increases, pension increases, and already-negotiated raises. All told, the UAW's concessions added up to a billion dollars in autoworkers' hard-earned money.[37]

The day after the deal was announced, the phone at Solidarity House was ringing off the wall. It was Ford calling; it was General Motors. Me, too, they chimed in. Within six months the UAW had opened its contracts with Ford and GM and granted them the same concessions it had Chrysler. Soon, phones rang at other union halls all over the nation. Not only companies who were at economic risk, like Chrysler, demanded and got concessions, but soon profitable companies, too—including Texaco, Caterpillar, United Parcel Service, and Kroger—got their unions to open contracts and give back. By 1984–1985 some of the most profitable corporations in the country, such as Greyhound, United States Steel, and Phelps Dodge, had asked for and obtained concessions. Then the less-profitable came back for a second round. Within five short years the downward spiral had not only torn apart the package of ascending benefits the UAW had negotiated since World War II, but had shattered long-established pattern bargaining in steel, meatpacking, trucking, and grocery sales, in which wages and working conditions had been standardized nationwide. The percentage of union contracts with cost-of-living (COLA) clauses dropped from 68 percent in 1979 to 31 percent in 1986. The postwar deal was, indeed, off.[38]

The UAW leadership agreed to the auto companies' demands with stunning alacrity. At first, their main response was merely to say yes and answer the next phone call. By 1981, though, the union's top leaders had recovered enough to launch a congressional initiative mandating domestic content in automobiles, effecting an about-face from free tradism to protectionism ten years after the AFL-CIO's. "International trade in automotive products today bears no resemblance to the textbook world of 'free trade,'" UAW president Doug Fraser explained.[39] Known officially as the Fair Practices in Automotive Products Act, the UAW's bill mandated that by 1985, all vehicles sold in volumes of 100,000 to 150,000 annually had to be manufactured with a 25 percent U.S. domestic content. Following an ascending scale, the required domestic content grew until it reached 90 percent for sales over 500,000 a year. In essence, the UAW was saying that any company that wanted to sell cars in the United States would have to build a good part of them within its borders. The nation needed an industrial policy, it stressed. Unlike Brazil, Germany, Italy, South Korea, all of whom maintained strict controls on imports and imposed domestic content constraints, the United States was allowing an import free-for-all.[40]

In 1982 and '83 the UAW's top leadership launched an all-out national mobilization in support of the measure, which in many ways paralleled the ILGWU's earlier anti-import legislative mobilizations. In both the 1982 and 1983 congressional sessions, the measure passed in the House of Representatives but failed in the Senate.

Domestic content as a tactic built on many of the premises behind Buy American campaigns: it assumed a national economic circuit of funds from consumers to producers that, if closed, would produce prosperity for working people. "It will allow consumers to invest in the American economy regardless of which cars they decide to buy" and thus will "help millions of American workers keep their jobs," as one lobbyist explained.[41] But in important ways, domestic content marked a departure for the UAW leadership. UAW leaders, in the campaign, pivoted somewhat to criticize both foreign and U.S.-based firms for failing to invest in U.S. workers. Yet their criticisms remained only small peeps of protest, and the leaders continued to tip the balance of their analysis toward blaming Japan. "Content legislation not only will address the savaging of the American economy by the Japanese," declared Fraser when he launched the campaign. "It will also confront the exporting of American jobs and capital by General Motors and Ford." Note how, in Fraser's words, General Motors and Ford were "exporting," while Japan was "savaging."[42]

The leadership's foray into criticizing U.S. corporate behavior proved a brief and singular one. After 1983 the UAW leadership's main, and only, response to the crisis was to advocate labor-management cooperation. Donald Ephlin, UAW vice president, summed up the union's approach in a January 1981 speech at the University of Michigan. "Troubled times bring people together, and I think we can cooperate in ways that were unthinkable a few years ago."[43] Ephlin and other high-ranking UAW staffers had actually been thinking the unthinkable since the early 1970s. During that decade, the Big Three U.S. auto companies—General Motors, in particular—had started studying their Japanese rivals' management techniques. By the early 1980s, in an effort to raise their own productivity on the shop floor, the U.S. companies began to import "jointness" or the "team concept" into U.S. auto manufacturing.[44]

Under these systems, management reorganized the production process into labor-management "teams," in which line workers were encouraged to contribute suggestions about how best to structure production. Management's invitation to workplace democracy and input from below was a welcome one, but superficial and ultimately treacherous: the corporations were not planning to relinquish control over long-term investment or strategic planning. "Teamwork," meanwhile, encouraged individual workers to help management automate or speed up their own jobs ("design your own pink slip," as critics put it) and to turn in their less productive or enthusiastic co-workers—all in the name of greater productivity. It deliberately encouraged individual identification with the company rather than collective loyalty to one's fellow workers or union.

For the corporate managers who embraced the idea, support for "jointness" began with the assumption that the problem with the U.S. economy was competitiveness. U.S. companies needed to be able to compete better on a world market. Only by increasing productivity—output per person-hour—could they compete. To do so, workers and management needed to cooperate tightly as a "team." Once again, what was good for General Motors was good for American working people. Only now, General Motors was having trouble competing, so the team had to consolidate its ranks and pull together. Team GM meant Team U.S.A.

By the mid-eighties, it meant Team UAW as well. The UAW officially endorsed the team concept in its 1987 contracts with Gen-

eral Motors and Ford. By March 1988 the idea was institutionalized in
six Chrysler plants, seventeen GM plants, and two Ford plants, plus
the Japanese-owned plants with and without UAW contracts.[45] "The
challenges in the marketplace from both foreign and domestic competitors . . . require a fundamental change," read new language in the
UAW-GM 1984 contract, for example. "This change can only occur
by . . . fostering a spirit of cooperation and mutual dedication."[46]
With almost no discussion with the union's membership, the UAW
leadership imposed team concept structures on local unions throughout the country. The apotheosis of UAW support for teamwork was
the General Motors Saturn plant in Spring Hill, Tennessee, which
produced its first car in 1990 amidst a great deal of hoopla about a new
ethos of teamwork and cooperation, and a new structure of production. "Jointness" offered a veneer of workplace democracy and respect for autoworkers' intelligence and creativity—which autoworkers craved. But underneath that veneer, it committed all autoworkers
to working faster and faster, for less and less, so that "we" could compete.[47] In essence, the UAW leadership was committing rank-and-
file autoworkers to a new system of institutionalized speedup.

INSTITUTIONALIZED PARANOIA

But Solidarity House did not the UAW make. While the top leadership nestled tighter and tighter into its alliance with management, in
the same years many UAW members were finding their own, more
militant and oppositional, ways to address the crisis. Jerry Tucker, a
UAW activist in St. Louis, quickly emerged as the leader of one set of
alternatives. A powerful and compelling speaker and strategist, in
1981 and 1982 Tucker led a successful struggle by five hundred members of UAW Local 282 who made auto parts at the Moog Electronics
plant in St. Louis. Moog, like companies throughout the country, had
demanded sweeping concessions, including a $3.00 an hour wage cut.
Rather than strike in protest, the workers deliberately let their union
contract expire, rendering its no-strike clause and constraints on employee behavior inoperative. Then they initiated an "in-plant strategy," also known as "running the plant backwards." Meticulously
and ever so cleverly the Moog workers followed every official company rule imaginable, slowing down production until management
couldn't stand it any more and gave in. After a six-month struggle, the

union not only defeated Moog's wage cut but won a 36 percent wage increase over the next three years.

Tucker emerged a hero. He had proven that concessionary demands could be beaten back. Then, on a much larger scale, in 1984 he helped six thousand UAW members working for LTV-Vought, an aerospace defense contractor in Grand Prairie, Texas, repeat the same feat. Together, the Moog and LTV campaigns not only revived older tactics such as the slowdown; they also "created an atmosphere involving the rank and file in collective action on the job," *Labor Notes* editor Kim Moody observes.[48]

A second alternative movement emerged in Los Angeles. In three short years, between 1980 and 1982, U.S. auto companies had closed five of their six auto plants in California. By 1982 the only one left was the General Motors plant in Van Nuys, in the San Fernando Valley. Over 50 percent of the plant's workers were Latino, and 15 percent African American. When GM announced it would close the Van Nuys plant, members of Local 645 spearheaded a community campaign to "Save GM Van Nuys." Building a creative alliance of Latino organizations, ministers, the Rainbow Coalition, and many other community groups, they took their campaign to government officials, organized mass public meetings, and threatened to organize a boycott of General Motors throughout Southern California. Although the plant eventually closed, they did keep it open for several additional years.[49]

By mid-decade critical voices within the UAW, going crazy with frustration after five years of concessions and few signs of resistance at the top, coalesced into an overt dissident movement known as the New Directions Caucus. It started in UAW Region 5, which embraced Missouri, Arkansas, Louisiana, Kansas, and the Southwest. Local leaders started questioning the UAW national leadership's willingness to grant concessions. In 1986 Jerry Tucker ran for Region 5 director against the incumbent and, in a complex voting system, lost by a fraction of a vote. In a rerun, he won and served a brief partial term, only to lose again the next year. But the New Directions Caucus only grew, nationally, until it counted 10 percent of the delegates at the UAW's 1989 national convention, a larger number than it sounds, since a significant percentage of the voting delegates owed their jobs to the top leadership.

The caucus focused on two big issues: first, concessions. "To End the Decade of Decline Our 1990 Bargaining Agenda Must Change," its leaflets proclaimed. Rather than say yes to the corporations, the caucus argued that the union should fight to "reduce worktime with no loss of pay to create jobs and promote real job security"; fight outsourcing by the companies—that is, subcontracting of union work to non-union parts plants; "end mandatory overtime while members are laid off"; and organize new members. It could do so only through a second, equally important struggle: as caucus members put it, "For a Democratic UAW." Internal democracy was essential to any rank-and-file led, successful union, New Directions activists argued. "We must . . . confront the reality of an undemocratic 'one-party' International leadership at a time when we desperately need pluralism, accountability and a democratic debate on the direction of our union."[50] The Preamble to the New Directions Constitution declared: "Our union must defend workers from corporate attacks. Only a strong democratic union can coordinate this struggle to regain past concessions, and prepare the membership to resist future exploitation."[51]

Not surprisingly, the UAW leadership at Solidarity House was deeply threatened by New Directions, by Jerry Tucker, and, indeed, by any alternative strategy that went against the official grain of teamwork with the corporations. Tucker tells a revealing story that captures the UAW's internal leadership dynamics exactly. While he was briefly on the UAW Executive Board as Region 5 director, the subject of nine thousand GM workers on indefinite layoff in Flint, Michigan, came up. In his report, then vice president Donald Ephlin mentioned that the average work week in Flint was forty-eight hours a week. Tucker pointed out the contradiction—why were some members working so much overtime while others were laid off? It was as if he had never said a word. Tucker kept pushing the point: why was the union helping speed up workers, and encouraging mandatory overtime, while other autoworkers were laid off? "This is not what a union is all about," he insisted. Finally, Ephlin turned to him and said, "Jerry, you just don't get it! It's our job to make these companies lean and mean." ("No, Don, I just don't get it," replied Tucker.)[52]

Tucker tells a second, even more revealing story. At the climax of the LTV struggle in Texas, Ray Majerus, UAW secretary-treasurer, and Ken Worley, Region 5 director, worked out a secret deal with LTV's management to settle the conflict by giving up the union's COLA clause, acquiescing to the two-tier wage system, and gutting health care. They assumed Tucker would go along. Tucker, though, refused and went ahead with the in-plant strategy that successfully eliminated all those concessions. Thereafter, Tucker was *persona non grata* within the UAW's upper leadership. "Within a couple of weeks, they were attacking me," Tucker recalls. According to Tucker, Majerus arranged a little lunch. After the small talk, he told Tucker, "You understand you're embarrassing our international executive board. Here we are making . . . major concessions to the world's largest corporations. . . . Here you are down here proving it doesn't have to be that way. That's a problem. You understand we're not going to put up with that."

Nor would the leadership embrace the Van Nuys struggle in Los Angeles. In 1984 the editors of *Solidarity,* the union's magazine, drew up a big spread celebrating the campaign to keep GM Van Nuys open. The story was in page proofs, about to go to press, when word came down from the leadership at the top to kill it. They didn't want the rank-and-file to know about the Van Nuys struggle, even though stories covering it had already run in the *Wall Street Journal, Los Angeles Times,* and throughout the mainstream press.[53]

Why was the leadership so threatened? To answer that, we have to look even closer at the union's top leaders. The men who led the UAW by the early 1980s were far removed from the union's militant CIO origins. These were men who, for decades, had successfully maneuvered their way up through the union's vast bureaucratic ranks. One former staff member describes Owen Bieber, UAW president from 1983 onward, and his fellow officers as "the epitome of bureaucratic inbreeding."[54] Bieber and his allies were trained to negotiate ever-plumper contracts in cushy hotel rooms. For three decades they had viewed themselves as corporate partners. When the mass layoffs of 1979–1982 and the Chrysler bailout swept down like an avalanche, they were paralyzed. Like deer in the auto companies' headlights, they were totally unprepared to handle the situation. "They were clueless," recalls *Labor Notes* editor Kim Moody. "They had no experience, . . . no analysis of the changes of the period" with which to make sense of the situation.[55]

Ever since Walter Reuther had consolidated his power in the 1940s, the UAW had been run by one-party rule. The group in control at the union's top, known as the "Administration Caucus," would brook no challenges to its authority. But as UAW membership plummeted in the 1980s, as Tucker's successes mounted, and as the New Directions Caucus increasingly questioned the leadership's ability to lead, the UAW's top leaders ensconced in Solidarity House reacted with "institutionalized paranoia," in the words of Jeff Stansbury, an editor of *Solidarity* at the time. "They were just mightily scared. Every little dissent that arose . . . scared the hell out of them."[56]

Not without reason, these leaders were terrified that rank-and-file UAW members, if unleashed in militant struggles against the corporations, would turn against them, too. Since the 1950s' postwar contract the UAW, like so many other international unions, had structured itself around containing rank-and-file militancy—both to ensure stable contracts with the employers and to ensure stable jobs for union bureaucrats at the top. Now the whole system threatened to crack wide open. To keep it in place, the leaders desperately needed to make it look like they were doing something to meet the crisis. Pushing for labor-management cooperation—"helping GM get lean and mean"—gave them the appearance of positive action. But it wasn't enough for the rank and file.

This is where the Buy American question fits in. As the avalanche of layoffs crashed through autoworkers' lives, the leadership offered nothing but more cooperation, more teamwork with the corporations. Rank-and-file UAW members got more and more frustrated, more and more angry. They needed something to do with their anger. Buying American gave them something to do. Attacking Japan, Asians, and Asian Americans gave them someone to hate. "The general overtone of import-bashing racist reaction may have emerged essentially from the ranks in the local union leadership," Jerry Tucker observes. "But the union's national leadership, in addition to sitting mute when that happened and therefore allowing that kind of racist response, really didn't have any answer other than their version of jointness."[57] The UAW's top leadership, in other words, created the vacuum that Japan bashing then filled. Kim Moody argues even more firmly that the UAW leadership, by forcing concessions down the members' throats, itself created their anger.[58] Jeff Stansbury, the for-

mer *Solidarity* editor, suggests that the leadership knew exactly what
it was doing: it knew the grassroots Buy American movement served
as a safety valve for rank-and-file militancy.[59] Rather than attack the
corporations or the leadership, union members could swing sledgehammers at Toyotas.

What could the leadership have done differently? Throughout
the 1980s UAW activists suggested numerous alternatives, in addition
to those implemented in Los Angeles, Texas, and Missouri. The Big
Three auto companies had plenty of capital to invest in new plants,
new projects, they point out; the UAW could have bargained for re-
investment, rather than fight a hostile Reagan administration over
domestic content legislation. It could have refused the downward spiral of concessions. Many critics—such as Jane Slaughter in her 1983
book, *Concessions, and How to Beat Them*—argued that concessions
didn't save jobs; they only devastated working people's standard of living and working conditions.[60] Slaughter and other critics argued that
the UAW could have put funds into new organizing, thus raising
standards at the nonunion parts plants to which the companies increasingly subcontracted their work. It could have gone overseas, to
cooperate with progressive unions in Mexico and other countries to
which the Big Three moved production.

But all these approaches would have required a more complex
definition of the nature of the problem, because imports alone did
not produce the UAW's crisis. Entirely on their own, to increase their
profits, the U.S. companies automated their plants, increased the pace
of work, and subcontracted to domestic nonunion firms, and then
laid off tens of thousands of autoworkers. GM shut down its Van Nuys
plant, for example, not because the plant couldn't compete with the
Japanese, but because all three auto firms had decided to consolidate
their production in the Midwest.[61]

As the UAW leadership chanted "teamwork" in the name of U.S.
competitiveness and the rank-and-file chanted "Buy American," the
Big Three auto companies were, in fact, fleeing overseas as fast as they
could. They directly invested in the exact foreign auto corporations
with whom they were ostensibly competing. By the end of the 1980s
Ford owned 25 percent of Mazda; Chrysler owned 24 percent of Mitsubishi.[62] They moved their own production overseas, both to reach
foreign markets—as other countries imposed their own domestic

content regulations—and to assemble vehicles for import back into the United States. In 1991 the Big Three automakers built almost 600,000 cars and trucks in Mexico, of which they imported 275,000 back into the United States.[63] Between 1982 and 1987 General Motors garnered one-fourth of all its profits overseas. "The goal in the very near term is to have 50 percent of our capacity outside of North America," explained a GM spokesman by 1997. A year later GM chairman John F. Smith, Jr., announced that GM planned to invest heavily in China, becoming, he promised, a Chinese company, "not a U.S. company in China."[64]

For the auto industry, any national "Us" was rapidly disintegrating. A 1992 cover story in *Business Week,* on the flight of U.S. auto plants to Mexico, captured the new distinctions nicely, if inadvertently: "With a savings of up to $1,000 a car, the new partnership between First and Third World neighbors could get the U.S. auto industry back into the race with Japan." The "U.S. auto industry," in that sentence, was neatly separable from any actual workers laboring in the United States.[65]

Japanese auto firms, meanwhile, were playing the exact same game. During the 1980s Toyota, Honda, and Nissan all started building factories, known as "transplants," in the United States. The first, and most symbolic, was the New United Motors Manufacturing, Inc., or NUMMI plant in Fremont, California, a joint operation owned by General Motors and Toyota. Most of these plants opened nonunion, but at the NUMMI plant and the Mazda plant in Flat Rock, Ohio, the UAW did broker union contracts.[66]

Just as it had in the garment industry, the equation underlying "Buy American" in the auto industry had long been shattered. A car bearing the name of an all-American company like Ford could be manufactured in Mexico by Mexican workers. A car bearing a "foreign" name like Honda could be made in Ohio by American workers. The Honda could even bear the UAW union label—while the Ford from Mexico did not. The corporations, in sum, went international. They simply walked away from American workers, walked away from the UAW. Or they pivoted inward to attack the living and working standards of U.S. workers by demanding outrageous concessions or by subcontracting to small parts plants in the United States, where wages were far below UAW standards.

But the UAW went nationalist. The leadership stayed the course of partnership, institutionalized since in the 1950s. Hey, they insisted, we're a national team! Still blinded by their Cold War deal, they were terrified of criticizing the corporations, terrified of rank-and-file militancy, terrified of the internal democracy that would be necessary if the autoworkers were to stop their downward spiral. Ultimately, they were terrified of class politics. Instead, they stuck to the "we" of economic nationalism in thrall to the corporations. But what was good for General Motors wasn't, in fact, good for the autoworkers.

Gary Huck and Mike Konopacki published a classic cartoon in 1985 that captured the contradiction between the UAW's approach and General Motors' response. It showed a forlorn, barefoot man under a palm tree, standing on a tiny island in the shape of the United States, holding up a picket sign reading "Buy American." Nearby, a caricatured cigar-smoking boss floated away on a raft of logs marked "Runaway U.S. Industry." Waving at the first man, he called out "Bye, American!!"[67]

JURASSIC PARK

The UAW and ILGWU's turn to Buy Americanism was replicated throughout the U.S. labor movement in the 1970s and '80s, if in milder form, as a quick look at the broader picture makes clear.

Right on the heels of the Chrysler bailout, in 1981 Ronald Reagan assumed the U.S. presidency, and one of the first things he did was to declare war on the labor movement. When, on August 3, 1981, members of the Professional Air Traffic Controllers' Organization (PATCO)—who had just endorsed Reagan in the election—went out on strike to protest job stress and inadequate management, Reagan announced on television a mere four hours later that all ten thousand members were fired, permanently, and proceeded to permanently blacklist and replace them. His action was unprecedented, his message clear: he would do everything in his power to bust the labor movement.[68]

The corporations joined right in. They not only demanded all the concessions we have seen but changed their attitude toward unions to one of aggressive hostility. They hired expensive anti-union law firms. They fired workers who tried to organize: by 1986 the rate at which workers were fired for organizing unions had quadrupled from 1960 levels. They ignored the strictures of the National Labor Relations Act: rather than observe the law, they just paid heavy fines. If workers did succeed in voting in a union, managers dilly-dallied in negotiations for years, trying to avoid signing a contract until they could initiate a decertification election. During the 1980s unions lost half of all representative elections; but even when they did win, they only obtained a contract half the time. Reagan, for his part, stacked the National Labor Relations Board with pro-management judges. The effect of all this on the labor movement was immediate and devastating. Strikes dropped from 381 in 1970 to 235 in 1980, and to 54 by 1985. Total union membership in the private sector fell from 37.5 percent in 1953 to 19 percent by 1982 and 12.1 percent by 1994.[69]

The AFL-CIO's response was largely to roll over and play dead. The metaphors employed by commentators to describe the AFL-CIO at the time, and well into the early 1990s, either portrayed the federation as moribund—as in "dead in the water"—or as an agglomeration of "dinosaurs." Activists referred to the AFL-CIO's convention at Bal Harbour, Florida, as "Jurassic Park." Under the lackluster leadership of president Lane Kirkland, the AFL-CIO seemed unable to respond at all. In 1985 it finally came out with a study entitled "The Changing Situation of Workers and Their Unions"; but after chronicling labor's demise, the document's main recommendation was only that the federation provide financial services to nonmembers.[70] The AFL-CIO made no substantial commitment to organizing new members, found no public voice to denounce the corporations, and remained firmly wedded to the Democratic Party.

AFL-CIO leaders did lobby strenuously on behalf of protectionist legislation throughout the period. As early as 1972 the federation coordinated the congressional campaign for Burke-Hartke; and throughout the 1970s and '80s its lobbyists worked with affiliated international unions on behalf of import restrictions and other trade legislation, all of which failed. But as the corporations fled overseas, the federation, like the ILGWU and UAW, couldn't break out of its Cold War framework. Its International Department continued to accept millions of dollars from the U.S. State Department each year, to train and advise right-wing unionists in the Third World, and to undermine democratic trade unions. In 1987, for example, the AFL-

CIO's American Institute for Free Labor Development alone took in over $14 million in government funds. Year in, year out, domestic visitors to the AFL-CIO's George Meany Center in Silver Spring, Maryland, could rub elbows in the cafeteria line with CIA-funded trade unionists from overseas, on training junkets in the United States, courtesy of the AFL-CIO. The federation just couldn't make the leap to global solidarity with militant workers throughout the world, who were struggling with the very same corporations that were simultaneously attacking U.S. workers. True solidarity stopped at the U.S. border.[71]

For the AFL-CIO, as for the UAW and ILGWU, imports were the menace, not U.S. corporate policies. And with the import menace came, once again, racialized imagery evoking the Yellow Peril. The federation's Industrial Union Department issued a special imports issue in 1977, replete with attacks on Asia and including a stereotyped—if modernized—drawing of a Chinese worker in a straw hat, fishing for televisions and radios. Another drawing was captioned, "Tens of thousands of jobs and job opportunities in the color TV industry have been lost directly because of the flood of color TV sets from abroad, mainly from Japan."[72] Once again, a "flood" from Japan was to blame—not the flight of U.S. corporations abroad, or corporate hostility to organizing within the United States—and the illustration showed an enormous wave of TV sets, marked with Japanese characters, crashing down upon three American workers.

The AFL-CIO did help issue labor's Buy American call, but even here it displayed a characteristic lack of energy. Buy American promotion belonged on the turf of the Union Label and Service Trades Department, an independent unit within the AFL-CIO, which controlled its own finances and program and consisted of an administrative assistant and two officials in a corner office of AFL-CIO headquarters in Washington, D.C. In 1981, the Label Department decided to add "Buy American" to all its materials promoting the union label. "The destructive problem with imports has led us to equate 'union-made' with 'Made in the U.S.A,'" Earl McDavid, secretary-treasurer of the department, explained. The department printed red-white-and-blue posters featuring the Statue of Liberty, proclaiming "AMERICAN IS BEAUTIFUL. Buy American . . . and Look for the Union Label." It designed graphics, such as one with a grinning

Uncle Sam pointing at the reader, commanding, "I Want You to Buy Union-Made in the U.S.A.!" which were picked up by local union newspapers throughout the country. It printed bumper stickers reading "BUY UNION—SAVE AMERICA"; and, last but not least, handed out plastic bags at its annual Union Industries show, bedecked with stars and stripes and the slogan "Save Jobs . . . Buy American."[73]

Local unions throughout the country launched Buy American activities as well, entirely on their own initiatives. In 1985 unions in Pittsburgh, Pennsylvania, decided to organize the city's first Labor Day parade in years with the theme "Put America Back to Work: Buy American-Made Products." On one especially popular float, a beefy American steelworker smashed a Japanese car full of stereotyped Asians with buck teeth.[74] In Birmingham, Alabama, in 1983, the Central Labor Council organized a Buy American parade and rally at which a "focal point . . . was the chance for the participants to vent their frustrations on the two (2) Toyota cars which were destroyed with sledge hammers," an AFL-CIO Label Department staff member reported. The first car "was drawn through the streets behind a wrecker and smashed en route." Rally-goers paid for the chance to hit the other. The crowd, the observer admitted, got somewhat "unruly" and started vandalizing foreign cars alongside the march's route.[75]

Parking lot signs proliferated. In Gainesville, Florida, Local 1205 of the International Brotherhood of Electrical Workers (IBEW) put up letters announcing "Buy American" under the big plastic sign in front of their union hall. Across the lawn, a painted wooden sign read "Parking for American Made Vehicles ONLY."[76] As the Birmingham rally illustrates, these activities all too often echoed the alarmist anti-Japan rhetoric characteristic of much Buy Americanism. A visitor to the Missoula, Montana, AFL-CIO Labor Temple in 1991 could pick up bumper stickers reading "Say No to Tokyo! Buy American"; "Buy American, Not Japanese" (with a slash across a Japanese flag); and "Don't Give Jobs to Japan. My Future Depends on It," picturing a little white baby.[77]

One lone voice in the trade union crowd, however, sang a completely different tune. The United Electrical, Radio, and Machine Workers of America (UE), one of the unions purged by the CIO in 1949, had always remained outside the AFL-CIO's Cold War consensus. During the 1980s and early '90s the UE rejected the Buy American approach altogether. "While it is understandable that many U.S. workers advocate a 'Buy America' policy, it will not succeed in ending oppression of foreign workers or protecting our jobs," argued a resolution delegates passed at the union's 1990 convention. "By viewing foreign workers as an enemy to be beaten in a dog-eat-dog competition, U.S. workers will only be playing into the hands of the multinationals that seek to drive wages and working conditions down to the lowest common denominator."[78] Chris Townshend, the UE's Political Action Director in Washington, D.C., in 1996 described Buy American campaigns as a "foolish diversion." "You get into this messy kind of minutia," he said, deciding whether a German-made product is taboo or not, for example, when it's union-made "and probably made under better wages and conditions than its counterpart here that's not union. . . . Is that the way to go about actually building the labor movement or is it mobilizing politically to force our will on the bosses to stop them from moving these plants overseas?" Townshend also argued that Buy American campaigns place labor in a dangerous position of promoting employers: "Each and every one of your Buy American, Buy Union programs becomes . . . another way to lay down with the boss. . . . The boss is happy to be able to have your seal of approval put on their behaviors."[79]

In contrast to the UAW, the UE rejected labor-management cooperation and "jointness" from the 1980s onward. "Under a smoke screen of the need to remain 'competitive', these schemes are merely the latest attempts by corporate America to increase profits by speed-up and job cuts, to attack real unions, and stop workers from joining unions," a Policy Resolution passed at the 1995 UE convention declared. "Workers can decide very little on their own because the bosses set the boundaries of what can be discussed. Ultimate power and decision-making always rests with management."[80]

From the UE's viewpoint, the real problem was corporate restructuring, capital flight, and the relentless drive for profits. "The conglomerates and multinationals, with no ties to any community or in many cases to any country, shift capital at will, like a giant game of monopoly, without regard for the consequences," argued a 1980 resolution. As early as the 1960s, as U.S. jobs in electrical manufacturing began to evaporate, the UE, in response, proposed a thirty-five-hour work week, controls on capital flight, and an end to federal tax laws that subsidize U.S. corporate production overseas. For the "Buy American" slogan, the UE substituted: "Foreign Competition: Made in the U.S.A."[81]

DEMONS IN THE PARKING LOT

Members and leaders alike of the trade union movement were trying to find a way to address the enormous corporate earthquake shaking down the American working class in the 1980s and '90s. The challenge before them was enormous; and for millions, economic nationalism, and Buying American in particular, made a great deal of intuitive economic sense. If they could keep Toyotas out of the union's parking lot, maybe they could keep out the demons at their backdoor, clawing for more concessions, more unemployment, and more subservience to the corporations' hungry demands.

But by pointing the finger at imports, the unions once again built a wall between themselves and solidarity with working people on the other side of the U.S. border. "Foreigners" became the enemy, and foreigner bashing slid rapidly into racist attacks against all Asian peoples and their products. Pointing the finger outward, they missed the Enemy Within: the monster of corporate profit-mongering, chewing up and spitting out American working people. That monster, though, wasn't even satisfied with wrenching down the standards of living of American working people in the 1980s and 1990s. It chewed and spat out working people all over the globe. Increasingly, the enemy within was prowling wherever it chose.

CHAPTER 8

This Label Means Bigger Profits
Corporate-Sponsored Buy American Campaigns

In 1992 a deliberately disturbing television commercial appeared on national television throughout the United States, very slickly produced, and very creepy. In the opening image a standing woman hugged a sweater close to her chest, chilled. A dog appeared, barking upward as trash blew by. Then the camera captured a dozen grim people standing by a dock or warehouse, frozen. Passively, their arms dangling at their sides, the people stared up at an enormous back-lit crate being lowered down toward them by an unseen crane. Letters stamped on the crate read "IMPORTED." The mood was *Close Encounters of the Third Kind.* Alien ships were loading alien goods in mysterious crates. "Over half a million people" have already lost their jobs in the U.S. clothing industry, a male voice intoned. "And the worst part is, we're doing this to ourselves, because we're buying so many imports." Buy American, it commanded, "and we won't have to throw in the towel."[1]

It was sort of a dark side version of the ILGWU's happy chorus, with passive workers paralyzed by the specter of crates full of imports loaded by invisible alien forces. (We are left imagining a giant green praying mantis from another planet operating the cranes.) The expensive feel of the advertisement and its appearance on prime time right before the Christmas shopping season suggests, though, that there was a lot more money behind the Buy American movement of the 1970s, '80s, and early '90s than could be mustered by a few declining trade unions—and that the labor movement was not the only group of Americans to blame the nation's economic ills on a contest between "aliens" and the shopping habits of American working people.

The advertisement was produced, it turns out, by an organization called Crafted With Pride in U.S.A., which itself was funded largely by corporations from the U.S. textile and apparel industry. Throughout the 1980s and early 1990 these and other corporations jumped on the Buy American bandwagon as a marketing device for their products, extending the idea of nationalist shopping far beyond the reach of the labor movement and its sympathizers. Not only the textile and apparel industry, but major corporations such as Wal-Mart and New Balance, built their marketing strategies in this period around the Buy American call. As had so many before, Wal-Mart, New Balance, and Crafted With Pride structured their campaigns around an assumed economic nation, in which a "we," embracing both corporate strategists and the American people, promoted common interests by together shopping the American way. Once again, corporations could lead the national team onward and upward, if only the American people would buy the products they touted as "Made in the U.S.A."

But when we pull back the curtain on their promotions, the plot, as usual, thickens. Just like William Randolph Hearst and his friend from the chemical industry Mr. Eble during the 1930s, the corporations promoting Buy American in the 1980s and '90s turn out to have had visions of the economic nation that could leave working people and their notions of economic democracy in the dust, and that had a lot more to do with keeping their profit rates up than with keeping well-paying, secure jobs in the United States. And just as with Hearst and Eble, behind the curtain of Wal-Mart and New Balance's Buy American promotions lurked a few surprises. Like the stereotyped capitalist with the cigar in Huck and Konopacki's cartoon of the desert island, they were waving "Bye! American"—while they paid advertising agencies a lot of real money to hawk "Buy American."

ANOTHER LITTLE LABEL

At first the Crafted With Pride in U.S.A. Council, which produced that ominous ad, seems rather straightforward. It was founded in April 1984 by a coalition of fabric distributors, cotton growers, makers of home furnishings and, especially, manufacturers of synthetic fibers and domestically produced fabrics and garments (hence the bad pun lurking in the ad: "so we won't have to throw in the towel"). They funded the council to the tune of $40 million for its first three years. In 1987 the American Textile Manufacturers Institute (ATMI), the main body representing textile manufacturers, refunded the next three years for $45 million. Originally, the council counted 115 members. Soon it grew to 300, including companies outside the textile-fiber-apparel complex, such as Wal-Mart and Georgia Power —whose largest customer, not coincidentally, was the state's textile industry.[2]

These textile firms were concerned about their industry's economic future. By the 1980s the U.S. textile industry, along with the apparel industry, was facing serious competition from overseas firms for both its domestic and foreign markets. Between 1980 and 1985 combined imports of fabric, garments, and yarn were growing at a rate of 17 percent a year, while annual imports of apparels and textiles doubled to $2 billion. U.S.-based textile firms closed 250 mills between 1980 and 1985 as their share of the domestic market, long assured, seemed to be slipping out of their fingers.[3] Promoting American-made textiles offered a way to stem the flow.

Some affiliates outside the textile industry were dragged into Crafted With Pride by a bit of serious arm-squeezing, however. At the same moment that the textile firms launched Crafted With Pride, the Coca-Cola corporation—based, along with Wal-Mart and the textile industry, in the Southeast—decided to launch a new line of "all-American" clothing with the Coca-Cola label. Certain Southern textile firms found out that Coca-Cola's clothes were in fact produced in Hong Kong and Macao, and they were incensed; one even threatened to pull all Coke products out of its plant lunchrooms. At an August 1985 meeting with textile executives, Coca-Cola repented, promised to work with its subcontractor to produce the garments at home, and suddenly coughed up a $5 million contribution to Crafted With Pride.[4]

Crafted With Pride's goal was to increase the domestic market share of U.S.-made apparel and textile goods. Its stated mission was to "convince consumers, retailers, and apparel manufacturers of the value of purchasing and promoting U.S.-made products."[5] To do so, the council focused on national-market television advertising. Its first advertisements, launched in 1986, were much more upbeat than the one with which we opened, that depicted the frozen people along the dock. They featured movie stars and celebrities such as Bob Hope,

Wonder Woman, Billie Dee Williams, Linda Evans, Don Johnson, and even O. J. Simpson proclaiming their faith in American products while a cheerful model pranced through clothing racks explaining the value of U.S. goods. These ads were relatively simple in their message, relying on sheer celebrity endorsement of American-made products to win over the audience.[6]

In 1991 Crafted With Pride launched a second series of television advertisements, this time deliberately less cheery. The dock scene was just one of these new ads. Another featured a long line of equally paralyzed Americans shuffling across a bare plain into the limitless distance, eventually arriving at an unemployment office. "More than the entire population of Cincinnati, more than all the men and women in the Marine Corps, more than four times the number of unemployed autoworkers," the ominous voice droned. "Since 1980 over half a million Americans who make clothing and home fashions have lost their jobs because we don't realize the impact of buying imported goods."[7] A third ad, shot with oblique camera angles, opened with a little boy asking his mommy, who walks back and forth across a hall at the back of the scene, "Why do we have to move?" "Because your father lost his job." "Was he fired?" "No. They closed his plant." "Why?" "Because a lot of people are buying clothes made in other countries, not ours." Robert Swift, executive director of Crafted With Pride, acknowledged at the time the deliberate shift in tone of these new advertisements: "In the 1980s, there was a happier mood in America. . . . Now the mood is more protective."[8] All three new advertisements essentially sought to frighten the American people into buying American, while encouraging them to blame themselves for layoffs.[9]

The council's other main activity was to distribute a product tag that it copyrighted and that is still a familiar sight on domestically produced textiles and other products. Featuring a red-and-blue star on a white background, it read: "Crafted With Pride in U.S.A." A promotional pamphlet containing copies of the label, designed for industry usage, promised openly: "This label means bigger profits."[10] Throughout the late 1980s and early 1990s Robert Swift, Crafted With Pride's director, also operated a clipping service of materials on trade issues he deemed relevant and wrote regular editorials and letters to editors on trade questions on behalf of the council.[11]

A simple enough story, then, of a marketing plan organized by an industry seeking to preserve its share of the domestic market. Crafted With Pride's full origins, though, are a bit more complicated.

When Ronald Reagan came into office in 1981, he carried with him a triumphant Republican commitment to free trade, reinforced by a deep orthodoxy in mainstream economic thought against protectionism. All of a sudden the textile corporations, long effectively protected, were on shaky protectionist ground, forced to counter the official free trade line—just as overseas manufacturers eyed the U.S. market. Domestic textile manufacturers' Republican allies in the Reagan administration agreed to continue protection nonetheless. But they insisted that the textile industry would have to do its share to prove it could compete in a free-trade, free-market economic world. There would be no more free rides.

In response, the industry organized three interlocked initiatives to prove itself. The first was Crafted With Pride in U.S.A.'s advertising campaign. The second was known as Quick Response, an initiative under the auspices of Crafted With Pride as well as other industry bodies, such as the American Textile Manufacturers Institute. Quick Response was essentially a restructuring of the delivery process. Textile and fiber producers modernized and sped up the procedures through which they responded to market demands at the retailers' end. These producers felt that Quick Response was necessary in part because power in the industry was shifting from manufacturers to retailers. As retailers merged into larger and larger conglomerate giants in the 1980s, they both restructured the nature of retailing into megastores such as Wal-Mart and used their newfound mastery of vast retailing markets to turn around and make demands on the manufacturers. To satisfy the newly hungry retailers, the textile, fiber, and apparel manufacturers cut back dramatically on lead times for manufacturing, guaranteed faster replenishment of popular products, streamlined their information flows, and invested in new technologies that were more flexible. Their goal was to reduce the overstock left at the retailers' end, on which the retailers would lose money in markdowns.[12]

As part of its Quick Response program and overall strategy of luring in large retailers, Crafted With Pride from 1987 through the early 1990s became an official sponsor of the Miss America Pageant. In

1990, for example, the council's newsletter reported that "designer Julie Duroche . . . created 51, one-of-a-kind, U.S.-made gowns in fiery red for each contestant."[13] Debbye Turner won that year ("The poised veterinary student captivated the audience and judges with a lively marimba medley"[14]). After reviewing her wardrobe for the season, she announced: "The U.S.-made fashions are perfect to keep me looking my best during my busy schedule. I can't wait to try them on."[15] Crafted With Pride set up an interlocked program in which Miss America spent her year visiting department stores across the country, touting displays of American-made goods set up by Crafted With Pride and chatting on the radio about the Made in the U.S.A. textile and apparel label. When Miss America appeared on WUSA-TV in Washington, D.C., for example, it rolled right off her tongue that "the fiber, textile, and apparel sector accounts for 10% of the U.S. manufacturing force."[16] In 1992, Carolyn Suzanne Sapp (who "captivated the judges and audience with her show-stopping rendition of 'Ain't Misbehavin'' and her articulate remarks on parental involvement in education") wore only U.S.-manufactured clothing throughout her reign.[17]

The third initiative was known as the Fiber, Fabric, and Apparel Coalition on Trade, or FFACT. Under its auspices the industry undertook more traditional lobbying activities in Washington, D.C. Echoing the ILGWU's 1971 "Made in Japan" subway poster, its promotional materials pictured an American flag with the corner turned up and a little label reading "Imported," with the slogan "GIVE AMERICA A FIGHTING CHANCE. STOP UNFAIR IMPORTS."[18] The textile corporations could play the race card, too.

PAY ATTENTION TO THE MAN BEHIND THE CURTAIN

Before she started on her national tour promoting American products, though, Miss America Debbye Turner went on a little trip to South Carolina where, according to Crafted With Pride's newsletter, "she learned firsthand about state-of-the-art U.S. textile manufacturing technology during tours of weaving plants and finishing plants."[19] It wasn't just chance that she paid that visit: someone very important lived in South Carolina, in a "modest brick house" in Spartanburg.[20] For all the array of industrial alliances Crafted With Pride represented, it nevertheless turns out to have been a one-man show, and the one man lived in that brick house.

A visit to the council's headquarters offers another clue. Crafted With Pride in U.S.A. resides in the Milliken Building, a nine-story edifice resting on a prime block of Sixth Avenue between 39th and 40th streets in midtown Manhattan. After an introduction to a receptionist ensconced behind a thick glass wall, the visitor is shown up to a spacious expanse of prime office space upstairs, donated by the man whose company owns the skyscraper: Roger Milliken of Spartanburg, South Carolina.[21]

Roger Milliken (not to be confused with Michael Milken, the "king of junk bonds") is one of the most powerful people in the United States. He is also one of the most secretive, almost obsessed with privacy. One textile industry expert quipped that Roger Milliken "makes a clam seem like an open mouth."[22] "You've crossed the line," he growled in response to most questions about his company from a *Forbes* reporter in a 1989 interview.[23] Colleagues and journalists speak of Milliken as immensely charming when he wants to be—capable, for example, of persuading Sam Walton of Wal-Mart or, say, Coca-Cola, of contributing large sums of money to Crafted With Pride.[24]

His money comes from textiles. In its 1990 list of billionaires, *Fortune* listed Roger Milliken and his brother Gerrish Milliken as being worth $1.2 billion, largely because of their ownership of 34 percent of Milliken & Co., one of the biggest textile companies in the United States. The brothers also own 41 percent of Mercantile Stores, Inc., which in 1981 included eighty-four department stores across the country. Milliken & Co. is one of the great mysteries of the U.S. corporate world. It is privately held by the Milliken family and managed with Roger's legendary secrecy. According to *Business Week,* "no one outside the company—and very few inside—knows what Milliken & Co.'s earnings look like."[25] *Forbes* estimated in 1989 that, "if sold today," it would be worth $3 billion.[26]

Roger's grandfather, Seth Milliken, founded the company in 1865 as a dry goods jobbing operation in Portland, Maine. Selling fabrics for textile mills, Milliken knew exactly which mills were at financial risk, and as shaky ones were about to topple he snatched them up at bargain prices. During the Great Depression, as the industry got even shakier, his son Gerrish Milliken, Sr. (Roger's father), continued the same practice, until Deering, Milliken & Co. (as it was then known) had become a major player in Southern textiles. By 1989

the firm owned over sixty plants, including ten in the area of Spartanburg, South Carolina. By 1996 the company generated over a billion dollars in sales a year and employed 14,300 people. While its
products are diverse, the company has focused on synthetic yarns and
fabrics, such as a patented synthetic knit fabric Milliken unveiled in
the late 1960s called "Visa." Milliken & Co. manufactures the fabric
for Avis, Hertz, McDonald's, and Burger King, while another of its
lines had captured 40 percent of the market for acetate fabric used in
coat and casket linings. Milliken & Co. is largely debt-free. The cash
it generates is invested right back into the company for the most part,
funding purchases of the most advanced technologies Milliken can
get his hands on. According to *Business Week,* Milliken "has been
known to place a big order for new machinery simply to tie up the
manufacturers' capacity and delay delivery to rival textile producers."[27]

Roger Milliken is also a deeply political man. Like William Randolph Hearst before him, he is so rich that he can be somewhat icono-
clastic, following his own political inclinations wherever they take
him—although they always take him in a direction that will protect
the domestic textile industry. *Forbes* magazine actually entitled a 1989
story "Can Roger Milliken Emulate William Randolph Hearst?"
(The parallel drawn was on a different front, however: whether the
aging Milliken could control his own posthumous succession in his
company.) *Forbes* calls Milliken "the conservative's conservative."[28]
He was one of the founders of the Heritage Foundation, the preemi-
nent conservative think tank of the 1980s and 1990s. He was one of
the biggest backers of Barry Goldwater's 1964 candidacy for the U.S.
presidency and has been a major financial and political backer of successful Republicans ever since. According to Jim Edwards, the governor of South Carolina from 1975 to 1979, "Richard Nixon would
not have been president and Ronald Reagan would not have been
president were it not for Roger Milliken," (and Jim Edwards might
not have been governor, we might speculate).[29] Between 1985 and
1993 Milliken donated $345,000 to GOPAC, Newt Gingrich's Re-
publican fundraising engine, of which Milliken was also a founder.
In exchange, Gingrich took a break from his usually militant free-
trade position to briefly support import protection for the textile industry.[30]

By 1992, though, as the battle over the North American Free Trade Agreement (NAFTA) climaxed, Gingrich retreated to free tradism. Milliken, frustrated, started looking around for a new protectionist partner. First he backed Ross Perot in 1992. Then he settled on Pat Buchanan. "Pat Buchanan has my unqualified support," Milliken declared during Buchanan's 1996 bid for the presidency. "It is about time someone stood for the American working man and woman. Their goals must become our nation's."[31] Buchanan's own goals included banning abortion, abolishing affirmative action, condemning homosexuality, instituting school prayer, and expanding military force along the border with Mexico. In February 1995, Milliken hosted a fundraiser for Buchanan that garnered $46,500. Milliken himself donated the maximum legally allowed to Buchanan's campaign, as did numerous people with addresses in Spartanburg, South Carolina, election records show.[32]

Milliken also found more creative ways to fund Buchanan. In the years between his 1992 and 1996 presidential campaigns, Buchanan headed a tax-exempt organization called American Cause. It inhabited the same building as the Buchanan campaign, organized conferences that headlined Buchanan, and drew up a list of contributors that it rented to the Buchanan campaign. Roger Milliken contributed a cool $2.1 million to American Cause's lobbying wing, which agitated vigorously against the General Agreement on Trade and Tariffs (GATT). Milliken went on to serve as a member of Buchanan's five-member inner circle of advisers during the campaign.[33]

Inside his company, Milliken is known as something of a "benevolent dictator" who runs the company with a tight rein—all the while talking teamwork.[34] "We are all together in a giant Noah's ark," Milliken declared in 1985, regarding the import challenge.[35] But in the case of Milliken & Co., Mr. Milliken is Noah, bossing the ark. His company exudes one of the deepest commitments to "jointness" and "total quality management" in the world. "Every member of our company is an associate and not an employee," Milliken announced in 1989. "Whether we work in a manufacturing plant or an office. Whether we are a member of management or not. In Milliken it is a team effort."[36] By 1988 Milliken had reorganized his plants into 1,600 "Corrective Action Teams," 200 "Supplier Action Teams," and 500 "Customer Action Teams," involving "process improvement specialists." In 1989 he won the Malcolm Baldridge Award from the U.S. Department of Commerce for his team-concept management systems and their success in increasing productivity.[37]

But when it came to his ark, this Noah got to decide who got onto the boat and who was pushed overboard. In 1967, *Business Week* reports, "suddenly deciding that the company was saddled with excessive overhead, he fired 600 middle-management personnel without warning."[38] In his own 1989 report on the company's "Pursuit of Excellence" teamwork program Milliken boasted that "the approach has resulted in nearly 700 fewer management positions and has improved both morale and product quality within the company."[39] Nor were nonmanagement "associates" necessarily safe from layoffs. In 1990, Milliken & Co. closed its Robbins, North Carolina, textile plant, which had employed 235 workers. In 1994 it shut plants in Lockhart and Spartanburg, South Carolina. In 1995 the company shut down its New Prospect Plant in Spartanburg.[40]

As one might have guessed by this point, there are absolutely no unions on Roger Milliken's ark. Milliken is known as one of the most powerful anti-union businessmen in postwar U.S. history. His reputation comes largely from the Darlington case, a famous case in U.S. labor law. On September 6, 1956, workers at the Darlington, South Carolina, textile plant owned by Milliken (then Deering-Milliken), voted 256 to 248 to join the Textile Workers' Union of America (TWUA) (which would later merge with the Amalgamated Clothing Workers' union to become the Amalgamated Clothing and Textile Workers' Union of America [ACTWU]). Milliken had threatened earlier that if the employees voted for a union, he would shut the plant; and true to his promise, the very next day after the election he announced the mill would close—although the company had just spent $400,000 in the previous nine months to modernize it. Milliken was making a deliberate point to all his employees: Join a union, and your plant will shut down, forever.[41]

The Darlington workers, though, backed by the textile workers' union, charged that Milliken, with his deliberate threats and shutdown, had committed an outrageous unfair labor practice. After six long years the National Labor Relations Board (NLRB) ruled in their favor. Deering-Milliken, it concluded, owed the workers their back pay for all the subsequent years and had to restore their jobs.

Milliken, though, wouldn't back down and appealed the case to the Supreme Court, which, in 1965, again ruled against him, using the case to set a major labor-law precedent: an employer could not shut down a factory to keep a union out. But Milliken still wouldn't quit and tied the Darlington case up in the courts for the next fifteen years. Finally, in 1980, he settled, agreeing to pay $5 million in back pay. By that time, though, 126 of the original 553 workers were dead. Summarizing the case in *The Nation,* David Corn describes it as "The longest-contested case in the history of the N.L.R.B. . . . a monument to Milliken's passionate hatred of unions." Irrespective of the $5 million settlement, Milliken's strategy worked. For all his rhetoric of employee input and teamwork, Milliken's empire remains 100 percent union-free to this day.[42]

SLEEPING WITH THE ENEMY?

All the more astonishing, therefore, is the fact that both the International Ladies' Garment Workers' Union (ILGWU) and the Amalgamated Clothing and Textile Workers' Union (ACTWU) were full-fledged supporters of Milliken's Crafted With Pride in U.S.A. from its inception in 1984. Both unions donated funds to Crafted With Pride; both sent high-ranking staff members to its monthly meetings in New York for years; both knocked on the doors of Congress alongside Milliken and his allies on behalf of import restrictions.[43]

In September 1983, the ILGWU's magazine, *Justice,* ran a full-page spread with the Crafted With Pride logo displayed prominently. The story opened: "As a prominent member of the American Fiber, Textile, Apparel Coalition, created to promote pride in American-made goods, the ILGWU took part in the coalition's launching of its 'Crafted with Pride in the U.S.A.' campaign in late July." The article went on to celebrate union president Sol Chaiken's participation in a "kick-off" rally in Washington, D.C., including "a luncheon gathering moderated by Senator Strom Thurmond (R-S.C.)" The presidents of both the American Apparel Management Association (AAMA) and the American Textile Manufacturers Institute (ATMI) also shared a few words. "From the nation's capital, the campaign fanned out to communities heavily dependent upon the manufacture of textiles and apparel: Greenville, North Carolina, Allentown, Pennsylvania," and, of course . . . Spartanburg, South Carolina. At the Allentown rally, Ike Gordon of ILGWU Local 111 "remarked that the ILGWU has always stressed the 'Buy American' theme, and expressed hope that retailers would cooperate now, too, by identifying articles of clothing made in this country."[44]

Why did the ILGWU and ACTWU enter into such a pact with their otherwise bitterest enemy? "It's the only industry in the United States where the unions and the workers work together since the early sixties on a combined import policy," notes Art Gundersheim, formerly ACTWU director of international affairs and its liaison with Crafted With Pride for over ten years (the ILGWU's delegate was Herman Starobin, research director). Both unions knew exactly who they were dealing with—it was ACTWU, after, that had fought the Darlington case. "Every other union used to say 'You guys are crazy. How do you possibly deal with this on one side and then hate him on the other?'" recalls Gundersheim. "And I say, 'We don't have a choice.'"[45] Both unions were seeking congressional protection from imports; so was Roger Milliken and much of the textile industry. Both unions had framed their strategic approach around economic nationalism and the Buy American call; so had Roger Milliken. All were looking for allies. Susan Cowell, staff director and a vice president of UNITE!, recalls, "They [the unions] were very consciously getting in bed with the enemy. This was the way that together they could win."[46]

It was also the logical outcome of economic nationalism: nation trumped class; and once it did, even the most noisome of partnerships was acceptable and viable, if distasteful. While, on the shop floor, the ILGWU and ACTWU largely eschewed the labor–management cooperation schemes that the United Auto Workers so wholeheartedly endorsed, both, in essence, embraced the basic concept of teamwork with corporate managers when it came to trade policy. Again, what was good for GM was good for the American worker. It was the postwar compact all over again, only remade in the globalized economy. Again, labor and management were pulling together as a team to compete in the global marketplace against workers abroad.

By the late 1980s, though, the ILGWU was finally beginning to wake up from its dream of nationalist partnership, as we have seen— in part because the apparel industry was already walking away. By 1990 the textile industry, too, was beginning to trot overseas. Many of the larger textile manufacturers, such as Burlington and Guilford, with dollar signs in their eyes started coveting foreign production as their domestic market slipped. In January 1992 two prominent textile manufacturers, Springs Industries, Inc., and Greenwood Mills, announced they were pulling out of Crafted With Pride. The climax came over NAFTA: as Milliken jumped from Gingrich to Perot to Buchanan, searching for a nationalist opponent to NAFTA, the executive committee of the American Textile Manufacturers Institute (ATMI) endorsed NAFTA. Milliken was only one of a very few textile executives who opposed the trade agreement. For the vast majority, the shift was logical: If the textile corporations were to move overseas, they would need free trade to grease the wheels.[47]

After 1992, Milliken was left home alone with Pat Buchanan. Milliken stayed the course through the mid-1990s, still a protectionist. But that didn't stop him from opening his own plants abroad. In 1995, Milliken and Co. bought a textile plant in Japan that manufactured the fabric for the inside of cars. By 1994 he owned eight plants in Denmark, Belgium, France, and the United Kingdom, employing 1,048 people.[48]

SUPERSTORES, SUPERPATRIOTS, SUPERPROFITS

Standing by Roger Milliken's side at the 1985 press conference at which he announced that Coca-Cola would be donating $5 million to Crafted With Pride stood another Southern corporate leader: Sam Walton. Walton was one of the people whose support Milliken enlisted for Crafted With Pride. In mid-1985, the founder and chief executive officer of Wal-Mart unleashed the second national-level, corporate-sponsored Buy American initiative of the 1980s and used it to help accumulate some of the highest profits of the late twentieth century. Like Milliken, Walton cast himself as the superpatriot friend of American working people. And like Milliken, he was a billionaire.[49]

Wal-Mart leaped into the Buy American fray in March 1985, when it launched a program called "Bring It Home to the USA." It promised to stock American-made goods as much as possible, display them in special exhibits, and develop links to U.S. producers to encourage U.S. manufacturing. Walton began the campaign by publicizing a letter to three thousand Wal-Mart vendors, in which he declared that "The nation's trade deficit is a serious problem. I strongly believe the future of Wal-Mart, U.S. manufacturing, and our nation depends on our ability to correct this problem."[50] He promised to work closely with domestic producers, encouraging their sales to Wal-Mart. "Our goal . . . is to strengthen the partnership between retailers and manufacturers to develop increased competition, in price and quality, between American-made goods and imported items," Wal-Mart president David Glass told the press. "The result will be more jobs created or retained and the retention of American dollars that otherwise would be spent offshore."[51] Here Glass evoked the Buy American dollar circuit: Wal-Mart was promising to capture dollars within the national boundaries and keep them from leaking out overseas, sapping the nation's economic health.[52]

Wal-Mart's marketing goal was to use the Buy American call to attract patriotic Americans into its stores. By shopping at Wal-Mart, they would be saving jobs and contributing to the nation's economic vitality. In each of its hundreds of stores throughout the country, Wal-Mart hung giant signs that declared "All American Savings" and "Wal-Mart: Keeping America Working and Strong." The company's marketing strategists designed red, white, and blue streamers that stretched from each store's high ceiling down to special tables promoting American products. As shoppers flowed down the store's main aisle, they passed under an enormous American flag to find American-made goods in specially designated sections. Soon the store was crowing about the success of its program in saving the nation's jobs. In press releases and its annual reports, it claimed that by 1992 it had created forty-one thousand jobs and kept $6 billion within the country that would otherwise have gone abroad.[53] Business analysts, meanwhile, hailed Wal-Mart's Buy American campaign as a resounding success.

Certainly, the Wal-Mart corporation was thriving and would continue to boom into the 1990s. By the early 1980s its skyrocketing success was legendary. In 1990 it passed up both Sears and K-Mart to become the largest retailer in the United States. The next year it counted 1,683 Wal-Mart stores in the United States, plus 198 Sam's Clubs (a version of Wal-Mart) and four supercenters. Wal-Mart kept growing and growing and growing. Three years later it counted 1,953 Wal-Mart stores, 419 Sam's Clubs, and 68 supercenters. The company produced colossal profits. Between 1975 and 1985, its profits swelled an average of 37 percent every year. 1992 sales topped $54 billion; by 1996 they had nearly doubled to $105 billion, producing a $3.1 billion profit.[54]

The man behind this particular curtain, Sam Walton, founded Wal-Mart in 1962 near Bentonville, Arkansas, where its headquarters still reside. Walton built his Wal-Mart chain on the concept of "everyday low prices." The idea was to advertise the store's low prices, stock goods in huge amounts, and pressure producers to keep prices down. The formula paid off spectacularly for Walton. In 1985 *Forbes* listed him as the richest person in the United States, worth $2.8 billion. Five years after his death, members of his family still counted as numbers nine, ten, eleven, twelve, and thirteen on the *Forbes* list of the four hundred richest Americans, ranging from Jim C. Walton (number 9) with $6.5 million, to S. Robson (number 13) with only $6.3 million. In 1998 the family's combined fortune placed them as the second richest in the world, between Bill Gates and the Sultan of Brunei.[55]

SAM'S SCAM

But three days before Christmas 1992, *Dateline NBC* broke a big story on Wal-Mart. It charged that underneath those huge Made in the U.S.A. signs, in the special section reserved for American-made products, lurked the products of child labor imported from Bangladesh. Brian Ross, a reporter for NBC, had pretended he was an American apparel buyer and sneaked a video camera into a Bangladeshi factory allegedly making men's shirts for one of Wal-Mart's private labels, Jeans Wear. "What we saw were three floors of children . . . some as young as nine and ten . . . making clothes for Wal-Mart," who said they made between $12 and $20 a month, Ross reported. *Dateline NBC* then secretly brought a camera into a Wal-Mart store in the United States and filmed jackets made by Bangladeshi children appearing under its "Made in the U.S.A." signs. NBC found the same jackets under the same display in eleven Wal-Marts in Georgia and Florida.[56]

Wal-Mart moved immediately into damage control mode. David Glass, who succeeded Sam Walton as CEO, told NBC that he had "sent someone to Bangladesh and found no evidence of child labor in the factories making Wal-Mart merchandise." When NBC's reporter pushed Glass harder, he snapped back, "You and I might perhaps define children differently." The manager of the factory in Bangladesh claimed that "the workers just look young because they are malnourished adults."[57] By January 4, though, Wal-Mart had discreetly admitted that a "mistake" had been made in a single store when the jackets had been placed under the display. "We admit that mistake and extend apologies to any customers we offended."[58]

Within two days of the *Dateline NBC* story dozens of nearly identical advertisements suddenly appeared in newspapers in Oklahoma, Wisconsin, Massachusetts, and Arkansas reading: "We Support Wal-Mart's *Buy American* Program." Suppliers of goods to Wal-Mart, not the company itself, paid for the ads, including General Electric Lighting, Poulan Weed Eater, and Remington. Small as well as large vendors to Wal-Mart anted up for these advertisements. The Riverside Paper Company of Appleton, Wisconsin, and Shade Computer Forms of Green Bay, Wisconsin, for example, spent $1,300 to pay for an advertisement in the *Green Bay Press-Gazette* defending Wal-Mart. Both Wal-Mart and the suppliers insisted the ads had been placed "without any prompting from Wal-Mart Stores, Inc." But their immediate and identical appearances were beyond coincidence.[59]

The suppliers' eagerness to pole-vault when Wal-Mart merely said jump illustrates the enormous clout Wal-Mart and other mass retailers had achieved in relation to domestic producers by the late 1980s. As its giant stores multiplied, Wal-Mart controlled a larger and larger share of domestic purchasing for retail goods and could, as a result, increasingly call the tune for its suppliers. Many individual vendors became financially dependent on Wal-Mart, which became their single biggest customer. Wal-Mart's Buy American program only deepened these relationships, as Wal-Mart intervened in domestic producers' management structures, production processes, and price structures in the name of obtaining "efficient" American products. The Gitano Group, Inc., for example, which manufactured discount clothes, shifted its production to 10–20 percent U.S.-made at Wal-Mart's behest. Soon Gitano was selling a third of everything it made to Wal-Mart. But then Wal-Mart decided Gitano was mismanaged and cut way back on its orders to the company. Gitano went bankrupt, and goodbye went all the American jobs that had been created. Similarly, Wal-Mart courted Rubbermaid and began stocking Rubbermaid products throughout its stores until the chain counted for 15 percent of Rubbermaid's revenues. But when the price of raw materials for rubber goods went up, Wal-Mart wouldn't let Rubbermaid raise its prices and started stocking its rivals' goods. Down went Rubbermaid, which in 1995 announced it would close down nine factories and lay off 9 percent of its workers.[60]

Wal-Mart's power to shape the world of domestic production has since then extended far beyond rubber dish drains. In September 1996, Wal-Mart announced it would ban from all its 2,300 stores the latest album by Grammy-award-winning pop singer Sheryl Crow, costing her producers an estimated $400,000 in sales. Wal-Mart claimed it barred Crow and other artists because of violent and sexually explicit content. But Sheryl Crow's album, quite to the contrary, contained a lyric explicitly condemning violence and not coincidentally targeting Wal-Mart: "Watch our children as they kill each other with a gun they bought at Wal-Mart discount stores." In other instances, record executives successfully convinced their artists to change lyrics or even their names under pressure from Wal-Mart.[61]

The gap between Wal-Mart's Buy American tune and its actual behavior widened every passing day. Wal-Mart is perhaps most famous for its devastating impact on small businesses and local communities. Wal-Mart described itself in 1994 as a "community-oriented corporate citizen,"[62] but the company "has emerged as the main threat to Main Street, U.S.A.," notes Albert Norman in *The Nation*.[63] Wal-Mart's basic pattern has been to choose a rural site on the outskirts of a town or small city, where land is cheaper and taxes can be avoided. Typically, it opens a new "big box" store with an immense range of goods purchased at volume discounts from suppliers, and sells them at prices below cost for the first year. Then, after shoppers are accustomed to patronizing Wal-Mart and believe it offers the best prices, it inches prices up.

Meanwhile the Wal-Mart store's business grows by siphoning off sales from small businesses in the town's older commercial center. A study by Kenneth Stone of the impact of Wal-Mart on Iowa communities found that nearby stores lost an average of 53.6 percent of their sales in the first year after a Wal-Mart opened up.[64] In the classic pattern, as their sales drop, the older stores go under, and the city center

is left a ghost town. Crime rates rise, while the city's tax base—with
sales dollars slipping off to Wal-Mart outside of town—plummets.
The ripple effects are disastrous to these communities. As small businesses go under, local newspapers, for example, lose their advertising base, since a Wal-Mart store typically doesn't advertise much after
it has become successful. According to a University of Massachusetts study, "one dollar spent in a locally-owned business has four to
five times the economic spin-off of one dollar spent in a Wal-Mart
store."[65] The Wal-Mart dollar goes back to corporate headquarters in
Bentonville, Arkansas, to be used as the Wal-Mart directors see fit.[66]

Of course, Wal-Mart does create new jobs for Wal-Mart employees. In 1992, with 365,000 employees, Wal-Mart was in fact one of
the biggest employers in the United States—with more workers than
Ford, Chrysler, and General Motors combined. Like Roger Milliken, Sam Walton spoke of all his employees as "associates." "By 'associates' we mean those employees out in the stores and in the distribution centers and on the trucks who generally earn an hourly wage for
all their hard work," explained Walton in his autobiography. "Our relationship with the associates is a partnership in the truest sense."[67]
Sam Walton was big on the team spirit, routinely starting off staff
meetings with a rousing Wal-Mart cheer: "Give me a W, Give me an
A . . ."[68] But just as with Milliken & Company, he was outspokenly
anti-union. "I have always believed strongly that we don't need
unions at Wal-Mart. . . . They only care about jobs if they are *union*
jobs, many of which, frankly, have priced themselves out of the market either with unrealistic wages or total inflexibility."[69]

So far, Wal-Mart has succeeded in keeping its stores almost 100
percent union-free. In 1994, when it bought 122 Woolco stores in
Canada, it refused to buy 7 of the chain's stores that were unionized.
As a result, a thousand unionized workers in those stores were fired.
Wal-Mart then lowered wages at the stores it did buy. Only one Wal-
Mart store, in Windsor, Ontario, has union representation. Although
the union lost the election, the Ontario Labour Relations Board
ruled that Wal-Mart's behavior during the campaign was so hostile
that the union should be certified anyway. Wal-Mart's " 'subtle but
extremely effective threat' to employees' jobs," it found, "made the
result of a representation election meaningless."[70] In other contexts
Wal-Mart has harassed pro-union employees. In 1994, a clerk at a

New Hampshire Wal-Mart, for example, won a $15,000 settlement from the store after it fired her for trying to organize a union.[71] Wal-Mart store employees remain poorly paid with few benefits. An article in *The Ecologist* reports that "Wal-Mart rarely pays its workers more than the minimum wage." On average a full-time Wal-Mart employee earns $12,000 year, even including income from an employee profit-sharing plan much touted by Wal-Mart. Most Wal-Mart "associates" only work part-time and thus do not receive health benefits or pensions. Wal-Mart has been found to violate even the most basic of workplace regulations. In October 1997, a small item on page one of the *Wall Street Journal* reported that Wal-Mart had agreed to pay $325,000 in back pay to 933 Connecticut employees, night stockers at the store whom Wal-Mart had refused to allow to leave during their meal breaks. "Wal-Mart now lets the workers leave for lunch and will be 'moving into compliance' with other similar state laws," the *Journal* reported. Wal-Mart, in other words, talked quite a line about saving and creating good American jobs with its "Bring It Home to the USA" slogan. But its own employees didn't themselves bring much home—if they were allowed to leave the store at all.[72]

By the early 1990s the gap between Wal-Mart's announced super-patriotism and its drive for superprofits had widened into a vast chasm. All the time Wal-Mart was preaching "Buy American," it was not only evidently buying imports for its stores hand over fist but, along with other mass retailers, was itself evolving into a major contractor for overseas production. The Bangladeshi garment factory captured on *Dateline NBC* was just the tip of a vast iceberg of Wal-Mart-sponsored imports. "Some of the company's biggest private brands—over which it has the most control—come from overseas," noted Jeffrey Fielder of the AFL-CIO Food and Allied Services department. He cited ceiling fans and shoes from China and hand tools from Taiwan.[73] In 1992 the AFL-CIO found 314 different Wal-Mart products that had been made in China on sale in U.S. stores.[74] Sam Walton himself acknowledged in his Buy American program's second year that Wal-Mart was only buying American if the products available were of the same price and quality as comparable imports.[75]

Discount Store News, an industry publication, presents an even more complicated picture. Wal-Mart, it reports, was able to brag about Buying American and all the products it had shifted from imported to domestically produced because it started out with a higher percentage of imported goods than other discount stores in the first place. "What Wal-Mart has done is decrease its percentage of foreign-made goods more than any other major chain. But that is a direct result of its primary focus on offshore production; it simply had a larger base to cut back from than did its competition."[76] Industry analysts point out that until 1989, Wal-Mart's annual report included tabulations of the jobs its Buy American program had retained and created, but after that, it dropped the section, suggesting the numbers would not add up in Wal-Mart's favor any more.[77] *Chain Store Age Executive* quoted an anonymous retailer: "Walton is doing what everybody else is doing, that is continuing to buy the best values wherever they come from, whether it's from Japan, Korea, Brazil, Mexico and not from the U.S. . . . If Sam Walton bought American, he would not be competitive and his stores would be losing money. And he's not doing that."[78]

Wal-Mart has an explanation. According to David Glass, Sam Walton's successor at the helm, Wal-Mart's demand is so huge, it's too big for U.S. factories to supply.[79] William Treece of the Coalition of Missouri Shoe Workers, protesting in 1992 against Wal-Mart's continuing importation of "millions and millions of shoes," put forward a different analysis: "Sam Walton and Wal-Mart said for years they would buy American whenever they can, but we in the Missouri footwear industry know this is nothing more than Sam's Shoe Scam."[80]

The company that chanted "Bring It Home to the USA" was in fact bringing its profit dollars home to Bentonville, Arkansas, and then reinvesting them overseas, not just in production but, increasingly, in new Wal-Mart stores abroad. In March 1994 Wal-Mart bought its 122 Woolco stores in Canada. In late 1992, it bought a 50 percent interest in Cifra, a Mexican discounter, and by the end of 1996 had opened 41 stores in Mexico, including a 244,000 square foot "Supercenter" in Mexico City. By the mid-1990s Wal-Mart was launching or planning to open vast chains of stores in Brazil, Argentina, China, and Indonesia as well. Bob L. Martin, in charge of Wal-Mart's international operations, in August 1997 described the Latin American market as a luscious profitable fruit waiting passively for Wal-Mart: "There is low-hanging fruit hanging all over the place," he observed. "The market is ripe and wide open for us."[81] In 1996, Wal-

Mart estimated its annual overseas sales at between $5 and $6 billion and planned to at least double that figure by 2001. *Forbes* anticipated that the percentage of Wal-Mart's sales coming from overseas would shoot up from 4 percent in 1996 to 18 percent by 2001.[82]

All the while that Wal-Mart continued to feed economic nationalist sentiments in the United States with its "Made in the U.S.A." program, the company was playing the same game in the other countries to which it was fleeing. When it opened its Canadian stores after buying Woolco, Wal-Mart ran a campaign celebrating its all-Canadian character, with full-page advertisements insisting, "Wal-Mart is a Canadian company, managed by Canadians and staffed with Canadian Associates."[83] In 1994 its annual report announced, without any sense of contradiction, that Wal-Mart had launched a "Buy Mexican" program, "paralleling our well-established 'Buy American' program."[84]

Wal-Mart, in other words, has had no problem with manipulating nationalism in at least three countries simultaneously. Its superpatriotism only extends as far as the bottom line. Wherever profits are to be found, there goes Wal-Mart, whether making jackets in Bangladesh or tools in Taiwan, or selling jackets and tools in Argentina and Indonesia. Wal-Mart's headquarters remain on U.S. soil; it still makes most of its profits at home; and it is still one of the biggest employers in the United States. But when Wal-Mart does "Bring It Home to the U.S.A.," it brings home minimum-wage jobs without benefits, in which workers can even be forbidden to leave the store during their lunch breaks. Or else it fosters precarious manufacturing jobs in which suppliers are forced to drive down their labor costs and prices to satisfy an ever-voracious and fickle buyer. Unions have no place in Wal-Mart's America. This might be "Team U.S.A.," where everyone's an "associate," but as with Milliken & Company, the profit motive sets the team rules, and the "folks" at the top of the corporation decide who plays.

BALANCING ACTS

Consider, finally, the case of the New Balance shoe company, the third most prominent corporate sponsor of Buy American campaigns in the 1980s and '90s. Caught bragging that its shoes were made in the U.S.A. when they were not, New Balance, unlike Wal-Mart, fought back at its accusers and, rather than play by the new global rules, tried to change the rules altogether.

In February 1992, New Balance, a relatively small athletic shoe producer based in Boston, Massachusetts, decided to try to pull ahead of monster competitors like Nike and Reebok by riding the Buy American train. Just as President George Bush returned home from a visit to Japan to discuss touchy trade issues, the company ran a series of newspaper ads in the *New York Times* and major papers all over the country, announcing that its shoes were made in the U.S.A. "Mr. President: Here's one American-made vehicle that has no problem competing in Japan," taunted the first ad, which claimed that New Balance shoes appeared on over a million Japanese feet.[85] A second series boasted that New Balance "is the only company that makes a full line of athletic shoes here in America."[86]

Jim Davis, founder and CEO of New Balance, told *USA Today,* "It's the in thing today; it's an American-made product."[87] Paul Hefferman, New Balance's vice president for marketing, spoke baldly about the company's opportunism: "You don't often get an emotional hot button to push. We have one, and we're going to push it."[88] New Balance pushed it all the way to the bank. The company's sales leaped 20 percent after the ads ran and another 25 percent in 1994. "Being one of the nation's last domestic sneaker makers has turned into a marketing boon," observed *U.S. News and World Report.*[89]

The only problem with New Balance's brilliant nationalist campaign was that it was based on lies. On September 20, 1994, nineteen months after the campaign began, the Federal Trade Commission (FTC) charged New Balance with falsely claiming that its shoes were made in the U.S.A. According to the FTC, New Balance's ads implied that all its shoes were entirely made in the U.S.A., when a third of its shoes actually came from overseas; and of the shoes made in the United States, more than half the components were imported. Moreover, it wasn't true that "hundreds of thousands" of U.S.-made New Balance shoes had made it to Japan; the number was more like ten thousand pairs.[90]

Oops. In response, New Balance admitted it had overstated its Japanese sales. But it stood its ground on the American-made question. "We do make shoes here . . . Our competitors don't," insisted Kathy Shepherd, the company's public relations specialist.[91] In interviews, Shepherd and New Balance CEO Jim Davis conceded that only 70 percent of the shoes it sold domestically were made in the U.S.A. Of those, they admitted, only between 70 and 75 percent of the components were American-made. The soles, they said, just couldn't be made in the U.S.A. at a reasonable price and had to be imported from Taiwan and China. Sometimes the company brought in pre-sewn uppers, too.[92]

A reporter for the Providence, Rhode Island, *Business News,* pushing the issue, got Davis to admit to a lot more. New Balance had four factories in the United States, Davis told him—two in Massachusetts, two in Maine—employing "over 700" people. Davis also identified a New Balance factory in Britain, producing for the European market. As for other overseas production, "We don't have any other factories but we do subcontract some product in the Far East. We have licensees and joint ventures around the world." Pressed, Davis estimated that "we probably employ about 1,500. If you include the joint ventures— I never thought about it—could be 2,500 to 3,000." He had "never thought about it"?[93] It seems stunningly implausible that the smart and savvy businessman who founded and built New Balance had never even counted the number of his employees. Once counted, his own estimates reveal that of approximately 2,750 total New Balance workers, only 700 worked in the United States.

Davis wasn't stupid, just very cagey, and very, very angry about the FTC messing with his all-American marketing scheme. Immediately, he announced that he would fight back. "This is ludicrous. . . . We've done everything we can to manufacture here, and if some bureaucrat who has never met a payroll wants to sit back and say we can't put 'Made in the U.S.A.' on our shoes, we're gonna fight it."[94] Davis turned around, mobilized a lot of allies, and demanded that the FTC revamp its definition of "Made in the U.S.A." The FTC's standard, dating from administrative decisions over the past fifty years, defined an American product as "all or virtually all made in the U.S.A." That concept was completely dated, Davis charged, and impossible to achieve in the new global economy. Therefore, the FTC should lower its standard to 50 percent made in the U.S.A. so that loyal domestic manufacturers could save U.S. jobs but still compete in a globalized marketplace. In the next two years Davis spent over a million dollars fighting both his own company's case and for a general revision of the standard.[95]

In the process of that fight, Davis, the champion of domestic jobs, increasingly bared his stripes. In June 1995 he told the *Providence Business News* that he planned to invest $25 million in new U.S. factories—but only if the FTC rules changed. In October 1997 he told Tom Brokaw on *Dateline NBC* that he would hesitate before opening another U.S. plant under the old rules. "That sounds like a threat," responded Brokaw. "No, it's not a threat. It's survival," Davis retorted.[96]

Another exchange, this one in *Footwear News,* was even more revealing. "Would you like to see more [athletic footwear] firms manufacturing here?" asked the reporter. "No," replied Davis. "Why not?" "We think (being domestic) is a real competitive advantage." The reporter then asked, "As you look ahead, how do you see the state of manufacturing in the U.S.?" Davis answered, "Excellent. . . . People are realizing you have to have an industrial base in the country." It's an astonishing exchange: Davis was essentially saying he only wanted to make shoes in the United States as long he was the sole manufacturer in the nation; otherwise, Bye American! Then he turned around and declaimed how badly the country needed manufacturing jobs.[97]

Davis, like Roger Milliken and Sam Walton before him, pitched his campaign on behalf "the guy on the factory floor," for whom his patriotic benevolence was intended. Like Milliken and Walton, he referred to his factory workers as "teams" and advertised that his factories were assembly-line free. Like Milliken's and Walton's, though, they were also union-free. When workers at New Balance's Allston, Massachusetts, plant started a campaign to bring in the ILGWU in 1992, for example, leaflets in Spanish, English, and Portuguese popped up on the factory's bulletin boards, warning the employees that after another union had organized plants in the area, two-thirds of the plants had closed. Jim Davis gave a "captive audience" speech to the workers, casting the union as a scheming interloper that would cause plant shutdowns. Meanwhile, he spent a million dollars fighting the FTC over the right to move half his production overseas and still claim his shoes were made in the U.S.A.[98]

Jim Davis hit a nerve in the corporate community. Allies rushed in. He wasn't the only one eager for an opportunity to benefit from the Buy American call while simultaneously reaping the profits of overseas production. Days before New Balance's trial was scheduled to open before the FTC, the commission announced that it was postponing the case and that it would open up its definition of "Made in the U.S.A." for possible revision. "A number of comments came in suggesting that the FTC take a fresh look," Jodie Bernstein, head of the FTC's Bureau of Consumer Production, told the press. "The way goods are manufactured and sold is far different than 50 years ago." The agency, she said, needed to "to 'strike a balance' between 'the recognition that our policies must keep up with changes in the global economy' and the need to 'ensure that consumers are not deceived,'" the *Los Angeles Times* reported. Accordingly, the FTC asked for public comment on the appropriate definition of "Made in the U.S.A."[99]

As part of that process, the commission invited representatives from industry, labor, and consumer groups to a two-day workshop in Washington, D.C., on May 26 and 27, 1996. Present at that workshop was almost the entire cast of characters of the Buy American movement of the 1980s and '90s, including the United Auto Workers, the AFL-CIO Union Label Trades Department, and, of course, Crafted With Pride in U.S.A. on the one side, and New Balance, with allies such as the 3M Corporation (Minnesota Mining & Manufacturing), Motorola, Whirlpool, and the Footwear Industries of America, lined up on the other side.[100]

New Balance and its allies argued that given the realities of globalized production, the standard for "Made in the U.S.A." should be revised downward to 50 percent domestically produced. "It's not a practical standard in the global economy we are in," Gail T. Cumins of the American Association of Importers and Exporters argued.[101] U.S.-based manufacturers could only compete if they made part of their products overseas. Without a mixed label, manufacturers would have no incentive to produce in the United States. Mitchell J. Cooper of the Rubber and Plastic Footwear Manufacturers Association put it baldly: "by having a standard that's virtually impossible to achieve with FTC's position, they are denied the competitive advantage of a 'Made in U.S.A.' label."[102] And without that label, there would be no incentive to produce in the United States at all. "To apply the 'virtually all' [standard] would in fact encourage us to close U.S. companies," threatened 3M's representative, "because there is no reason that exists, minus that, to have a U.S. company."[103] In sum, only by claiming their products were American-made, when they were only half American-made, could U.S. corporations save American jobs.

Steve Beckman from the United Auto Workers, for the other side, read the handwriting on the wall: If the FTC lowered its standard, "the most likely result would be a very significant diminution of the U.S. content." Which, in turn, would undermine U.S. jobs. "If letting them use it is going to allow companies that are currently at 95 percent to go down to 30 percent, which is what a lot of people seem to be interested in, that's not going to create jobs in the United States. That's not going to add value to the U.S. economy. It's going to reduce it."[104]

Individual letter-writers who responded to the FTC's call for public comment were outraged at the idea of lowering the standard. "What the heck is going on?" demanded Patricia Stamm of Fenton, Michigan, who identified herself as "an angry Union member and consumer." "This ruling change would be terrible. I want to know where the product is made when I buy it and not be tricked. . . . What is the matter with you people????"[105] Dr. Herbert W. Samenfeld of Aurora, Colorado, agreed: "I do not wish to be hoodwinked into buying foreign made goods."[106] Harold Tuchel, an industrial electrician in Waterloo, Iowa, agreed and shared his insights into the whole FTC input process: "The reason I have furnished these comments to the FTC is that such comment sessions usually are skewed by multinationals and big business. The Made in USA label is not to promote either . . . but a guide to consumers to buy American products."[107] The individual respondents' position was overwhelming, their tone blunt, their argument simple: Anything less than 100 percent would be deception. Period.

The Federal Trade Commission, caught between a rock of popular input and a hard corporate sell, at first tried to stake out a position in the middle—in effect, partially granting the corporations' demands. In May 1997 it announced that it planned to revise the "Made in the U.S.A." standard downward to 75 percent. In response, the National Consumers' League; the National Council of Senior Citizens; Ralph Nader's group, Citizen Action; the AFL-CIO; two dozen international unions; a small group of domestic manufacturers; and an array of agricultural groups came together to form the Made in U.S.A. Coalition. Mobilizing a formidable lobbying apparatus—aided by a newborn fear in Congress that year of organized labor's voting power—they soon emerged victorious. On December 1, 1997, the FTC announced it was dropping all efforts to revise its standard downward. The "all or virtually all" standard would stay put.[108]

Jim Davis saw it coming and caved. On September 6, 1996, New Balance settled with the FTC and agreed to stop claiming that its shoes were American-made when they were made overseas. "We were not deliberately misleading the public," Kathy Shepherd, New Balance's public relations director, backtracked. "Our intention was never to make people think all our shoes are made in the U.S., because some of them aren't."[109]

PREYING FOR GAIN

Crafted With Pride's dockside television advertisement, bought and paid for by Roger Milliken, represented the dark side of the Buy American movement indeed: it turns out that up there, operating the crane, loading the crates marked "imports," weren't some mysterious alien green praying mantises but instead Milliken, Sam Walton, and Jim Davis, preying on the American people's sense of nationhood and fears about the economic future. They had those people on the dock right where they wanted them, paralyzed, helpless, watching passively as the powers above them moved the levers silently into the night.

Wal-Mart and the textile corporations claimed that their campaigns would save jobs, but they were taking their profits from domestic sales and often investing them overseas. The whole logic of saving jobs by buying American was dependent upon the concept of a partnership between U.S. workers and corporate allies. But the corporate side of the team—like the auto and apparel industries—was itself fleeing overseas. Even when these corporations stayed home with their money, they were hostile to organized labor.

But that Crafted With Pride dockside scene was only a fiction, after all, a fantasy America conjured up by Roger Milliken. The real American people weren't so passive. Even if they had been persuaded by Sam Walton to patriotically flock into his store, Americans had their own ideas about how to get by and who was operating the cranes. And in the 1990s those ideas were changing fast.

CHAPTER 9

Nationalism from the Bottom Up
Popular Buy American Movements

Economic relations between the United States and Japan reached a nadir in January 1992 with two diplomatic faux pas. On January 8th, President George Bush took a famous trip to Japan, where he hoped to persuade the Japanese government to allow greater entry of U.S. products and thus help balance the growing trade deficit between the two countries. Unfortunately for Bush, the trip became famous not because of any trade concessions he muscled through but because in the middle of a state dinner, the esteemed U.S. president lost his lunch into his lap. Although the U.S. press was discreet in its coverage (film footage was unavailable in the United States), the incident only heightened public attention to Bush's failed mission and fed anxieties over U.S.–Japan trade tensions.[1]

Thirteen days later an equally unfortunate remark issued from the mouth of the speaker of Japan's lower house, Yoshio Sakurauchi: "U.S. workers are too lazy," he charged. "They want high pay without working." Sakurauchi, as had Bush, quickly apologized. But the damage had been done. Americans were outraged.[2]

Before Bush could arrive home, the two incidents had converged to produce a feeding frenzy of economic nationalism and Japan-bashing. In those first three months of 1992 the Buy American movement reached a popular climax. Stories on the Buy American question leaped onto the front page of daily newspapers throughout the country; letters to editors advocating nationalist shopping swelled op-ed pages; independent groups promoting American products proliferated, along with threats to bomb Tokyo. Legislators introduced a raft of new laws mandating the government procurement of U.S.

products. Expanding far beyond the control of either the labor movement or the big corporate campaigns, the Buy American movement
became truly popular—and in the process revealed its ugliest racial
underside.

But even as it reached its greatest strength, the Buy American
movement shattered on the realities of globalization. The U.S. economy had long passed the global point of no return, becoming so inte-
grated into the international economy that an "American product"
had become as elusive as a good union job. Soon, even the most virulent nationalists couldn't find American products to buy or sort out
where to draw the economic border. Even Crafted With Pride figured out something was up when its own expensive polls started to
reveal that, despite massive public approval for the concept, "Buy
American" wasn't quite playing right in Peoria.

BUMPER STICKER ECONOMICS

By early 1992, as the movement climaxed, it played itself out to its
logical extremes, echoing with eerie similarity the Buy American
movement of the Great Depression.

Unemployment rates had been high for over a decade. Layoffs
continued to ripple through industrial communities. For most working people economic insecurity was beginning to feel like a permanent condition. It was clear that the good old days of the 1950s and
'60s were long gone and not coming back. A 1990–1991 recession
only deepened working people's gloom and sense of insecurity.[3]
Then, in 1991, the Gulf War convulsed the country. On the one
hand, the war reinforced popular anxieties about the United States'
declining military and economic role in a "New World Order"
following the collapse of the Soviet bloc. On the other hand, it focused domestic economic anxieties abroad, offering a militaristic, nationalist answer to the country's ills. Individuals, particularly white
working-class men, could reassure themselves that despite their own
plummeting economic fates, their tough nation could assert itself
militarily.

The militarist solution in turn fueled the kind of angry, nationalist, anti-foreigner mood behind Buy Americanism. After the war
wound down, a lot of Americans were left just as economically inse-
cure as ever, all dressed up for combat with an enemy abroad but with

nowhere to go. Sakurauchi's remark in January 1992 and Bush's return from Japan, after he failed to whip the trading enemy, were like throwing lighter fluid onto a fire that had been seething for twenty years.

"In the middle ten days of January . . . 'Buy American' sentiment reached a fever pitch," the *San Francisco Chronicle* reported.[4] Ann Landers described an "avalanche" of "unpredictably passionate" letters on the Buy American question.[5] William Lynott, founder of the Buy America Foundation, reported that the Buy American enthusiasm was "phenomenal." Even Lynott, the truest of true believers, admitted in 1992 that the movement "borders on being rabid."[6] On February 3 *Newsweek* jokingly called it "the ultimate in bumper sticker economics."[7]

But the people who carefully affixed bumper stickers to their cars and trucks were quite serious. Popular Buy American advocates were trying to formulate a grassroots economic theory that would both explain the nation's ills and empower individuals like themselves to do something to solve them. As Joseph R. Banister wrote in to the *San Jose Mercury-News,* "The question is, what can the individual citizen do now and in the future to turn this recession around[?]"[8] For Banister, the answer was that individuals should Buy American—as it was for A. N. Pasquini, who wrote to the Albany, New York, *Times Union*: "We don't need tariff laws to get all these lost jobs back for our people. All we need to do is simply stop buying foreign made goods."[9] Commenting on the Buy American phenomenon in January 1992, David Stewart, a professor of marketing and consumer behavior at the University of Southern California, observed: "We don't often see the relationship between our own behavior and what's happening in the economy. . . . All the national economy is, is the outcome of all the individual actions we take."[10] Buying American, in other words, gave people a sense of democratic control over an economy well out of their control. The *New Yorker* picked up on this appeal in a May 11, 1992, cartoon: In it, a car salesman insisted to a concerned, well-off couple, "But we're not just talking about buying a car—we're talking about confronting this country's trade deficit with Japan."[11]

If the strategy were to work, though, the couple had to buy the American car and also make quite sure that other Americans bought one, too—otherwise, they had just sacrificed themselves for nothing.

Exactly as trade union advocates had in the early 1990s, popular Buy Americanists were quick to circle downward and inward to blame fellow American shoppers. "The real culprits who have caused the loss of the American-built market share and the resulting layoffs are not the Japanese imports but those who buy them," editorialized the *St. Louis Post-Dispatch*.[12] And once again, Buy American advocates were also quick to blame the unemployed themselves: "I am also disturbed at the American people for letting it happen to themselves by buying (foreign cars), and other foreign-made goods like there was no tomorrow," Edward Cooksley wrote in from Largo, Florida, to the *St. Petersburg Times*. "The next time the owner of a (foreign car) asks why his son or daughter cannot find a good job, the answer will be staring him right in the face when he goes out to the garage."[13]

Throughout the country the groundswell of economic nationalism also spawned new, independent organizations promoting the Buy American idea. Although they varied, the basic function of these groups was to direct people toward American-made products, usually by producing and distributing a guidebook for shoppers. Flag Labelling All Goods and Services (F.L.A.G.S.) of Rapid City, South Dakota, for example, compiled and distributed *A Buyers' Guide to American Products*.[14] Some of these outfits appear to have been designed to create jobs for the entrepreneurs who dreamed them up (lending new meaning to the slogan "the job you save may be your own"), although their promotions were motivated by sincere nationalist impulses as well. American Pride, Inc., of Fairhope, Alabama, issued the *Made in the U.S.A. Product News*, which informed readers of Buy American activities nationwide, and also sold "Buy American" golf caps, T-shirts, and tote bags along with an audio cassette by Steve Vaus, featuring cuts such as "We Must Take America Back."[15]

In other cases the founders of these organizations were true believers in buying American, motivated not by profits but by a deep faith that by helping people Buy American, they were helping save their country. Phyllis Manrod of Rockford, Illinois, for example, in 1992 founded a free phone service called BUY USA, which advised shoppers about where to find American-made goods. She got some donations but mostly funded the operation with her own money and time, helped out by neighbors and friends who volunteered hundreds of hours answering phones.[16]

All too often, a certain indignant obsessiveness came to characterize these organizations. Their grassroots constituents, in particular, betrayed both an unveiled anger at Asia and an obsessive eschewal of all things foreign, as if a war were on and a poisonous gas of imports was oozing into the nation's homes. The tone is clearest in the quarterly newsletter of the Buy America Foundation. Founded in November 1991 by William Lynott, a retired Sears executive, the important-sounding "foundation" mostly consisted of Lynott operating by himself out of his home in the suburbs of Philadelphia. His main activity was to produce a quarterly newsletter promoting American products. Each issue featured a "Buy American Hall of Fame," congratulating American-made manufacturers for their domestic products, followed by awards of laudatory "Orchids" (to Steven Spielberg, for example, for replacing the Toyota Land Cruisers in the novel version of *Jurassic Park* with Ford Explorers in the film) and condemnatory "Onions" (to the Boy Scouts for ordering uniforms "made in a foreign country").[17] Other pages featured letters from individuals offering shopping tips or asking for help finding a particular product from a domestic source ("I have been looking for years for a jog suit (wind suit) that is not imported and have had no luck").[18]

For all the helpfulness readers expressed to each other in finding domestic goods, their general tone was one of seething anger, directed especially at all-American icons, such as the Boy Scouts, that failed to Buy American. "I visited Tombstone, Arizona and walked into American Legion Post #24. They were selling lapel pins in the shape of a tombstone, price: $3.00," wrote in P. V. of Freeland, Pennsylvania. "I bought one. When I got home, I looked at the back. You guessed it—Made in Taiwan. I felt like smashing it with a hammer."[19] The anger in these readers' reactions is palpable. "D. E. B." of Freedom, New Hampshire, announced proudly: "Recently, we received a gift from the issuers of our Visa card: a hand-held calculator made in China. . . . I hope Visa heard the loud thud as my calculator hit the trash."[20] "M. S." of Barrington, New Jersey, boasted that "I send Eddie Bauer catalogs back to the C.E.O. with imported items circled. I send 'free gifts' back to Readers' Digest because they are made in China."[21] Some even described themselves as obsessed: "We must fight to keep our economic sovereignty as a nation," wrote M. K. D. of Tarrytown, New York. "My wife and I are obsessive about buying

American products, from paper clips to automobiles."[22] It's as if these correspondents had appointed themselves Buy American police, policing themselves, each other, and the nation in their shopping habits. In the process they constructed a sense of shared political community but also reinforced a sense of righteous fury at those who didn't share their obsession.

The Buy America Foundation's correspondents, like the authors of letters to newspaper editors, constructed a Buy American movement leached of class politics, ever-silent regarding support for the labor movement. Phyllis Manrod of BUY USA, for example, when asked if her phone service listed union-made products, replied curtly, "I don't care as long it's made here."[23] Bill Lynott's newsletter did not suggest looking for the union label and did not promote trade union–sponsored Buy American activities, although it did note them on at least one occasion.[24] The Made in the USA Foundation was the one exception that, in its own silence, proves the rule. Founded by Joel Joseph in 1989, the foundation was another one-person entrepreneurial operation, the main function of which was to produce a regularly revised guidebook, *Made in the USA*. Unlike all the other organizations, though, the Made in the USA Foundation received direct trade union funding from its inception. The United Auto Workers (UAW) donated the original $5,000 that launched it, and in 1996 Joseph received the equivalent of $25,000 in free rent in downtown Washington, D.C., courtesy of the Communication Workers of America (CWA). For all those union dollars, though, the Made in the USA Foundation's guidebook to American-made products in its first five editions never printed a word identifying which products also carried a union label. In 1996 it finally started listing union-made as well as U.S.-made goods. But even then, Joseph points out, some of its readers utilized the book to identify union-made products to *avoid*.[25]

The unions might have seen it coming. When the ILGWU, UAW, and other trade unions chose to promote Buy American in the 1970s and '80s, they consciously chose a path of partnership with employers, one that preached teamwork and common interests. Corporations such as New Balance, Wal-Mart, and Milliken & Company, as we have seen, quickly signed up for that deal but just as quickly banned unions from their all-American teams. In their own way, the

Buy American organizations were preaching teamwork, too, only this time from the bottom up. In their popular version of the Buy American team, individualized consumers would dedicate themselves to assiduously seeking out the products of any company with an American name—whatever the firm's union status, however it treated its employees. In doing so, they played right into the hands of the corporations. Indeed, the corporations saw right away what a deal they were getting: New Balance donated $5,000 to Phyllis Manrod's BUY USA, while the Ford Motor Company, New Balance, and Anheiser-Busch all made hefty contributions to Joseph's Made in the USA Foundation. It should come as no surprise that when readers bought the foundation's *Made in the USA* guide, it wouldn't help them look for the union label.[26]

THE BATTLE FOR THE PURSE STRINGS

Throughout the 1970s, 1980s, and early 1990s Buy American advocates also tried to push forward on the legislative front, hoping to institutionalize buying American by mandating government purchase of American products. By the early 1990s they had won an impressive array of state and local battles. But precisely as the popular commitment to buying American that lay behind these laws peaked, it wasn't the economic nationalists but the free traders who rose up and suddenly won the war.

At the federal level, the Buy American Act of 1933 remained on the books, requiring federal agencies to purchase American goods whenever the price was the same or within 6 percent of any foreign alternative. During the late 1970s congressional pressure to expand the act mounted. Finally, in 1988, Congress passed an amendment to the Buy American Act, tightening its restrictions on foreign bids for defense spending. Foreign bids for defense expenditures would now have to be 50 percent cheaper than U.S. bids in order to be selected. At the same time, legislative and executive attention focused on the enforcement question. To what extent were federal agencies actually observing the act? Support for buying American reached tokenistic heights. In 1985 Congress passed a law that declared the week beginning October 1 "National Buy American Week," in light of the nation's trade deficit, "calling upon the people of the United States to observe such week with appropriate ceremonies and activities" (left unspecified). More concretely, in 1994 Congress passed the American Automobile Labeling Act, which required labels specifying country of origin on all cars sold in United States. Buy American laws, if difficult to pass given the overwhelming commitment in Congress to free trade, were also difficult for members to vote against. As one congressional aide put it, "No one wants to be accused of not supporting Buy American."[27]

The self-appointed chief proponent of Buy American legislation throughout this period was an offbeat congressman named James Traficant, a Democrat from Youngstown, Ohio. Traficant, of Italian and Slovak-Hungarian descent, is known for his unpredictable political opinions, which drive both congressional Democrats and Republicans crazy, and for a passionate commitment to buying American. He likes to talk about trade issues by using sports metaphors—describing the United States as a handicapped horse, for example, or himself as an "old quarterback" who "keeps score" and has the smarts to see the big picture of the economic game. Almost yearly since his initial election in 1984, Traficant has introduced new Buy American legislation. In 1987 alone he proposed a measure allowing tax breaks for purchasers of U.S.-made automobiles, another giving tax breaks for U.S. firms that buy American, and a third banning Japanese bids on U.S. government contracts for ten years. In 1994 he proposed that Congress censure the Ohio state lottery for buying plastic key rings from Taiwan.[28] All of Mr. Traficant's measures failed.

More successful were efforts to pass local- and especially state-level laws mandating government purchase of American-made goods. Several states already had Buy American laws on the books dating from 1933. Beginning in 1967 states started to pass a new wave of Buy American laws, especially in the period from 1978 through 1981, until thirty-five states had some form of Buy American legislation in 1990. The pressure for these measures was less popular than it seemed. Much of the lobbying came from the steel industry or from the auto- and steelworkers' unions, and most of the laws were industry-specific, in contrast to the federal legislation. Of eighteen laws passed in 1981, for example, eight mandated only the purchase of U.S.-made steel.[29]

Just as they had during the Great Depression, these state- and local-level Buy American campaigns devolved in the 1980s into movements to promote the purchase of state- or locally produced goods, revealing again the movement's inward-turning logic. In a classic formulation, when the Orlando, Florida, city council decided to award a contract outside the county, a local citizen objected that "Taxpayer money should . . . be spent in Orange County."[30] Advertisers invented "Made in Montana" labels, mounted "Made in Santa Cruz" campaigns, and exhorted shoppers to "Buy Chicago." A second round of guidebooks cropped up, helping shoppers keep their dollars inside these smaller and smaller circles—such as a "Made in Alaska" guidebook that Bill Lynott recommended in his *Buy America Newsletter*. Many of these campaigns were mounted by local merchants who saw an immediate opportunity to profit by pushing their own products. But for shoppers, "buy local" campaigns also reflected a democratic impulse to keep funds circulating inside a regional orbit where consumers could keep an eye on their money and ensure that it worked to sustain good, local jobs. By the 1990s environmentalists also began to advocate "buy local," pointing out the wasteful fuel and transportation costs of moving food and other commodities long distances for no good reason.[31]

Only once, in Los Angeles in 1992, did legislators ask for a popular referendum from voters on the Buy American question. In December 1991, the city of Los Angeles accepted a bid from the Sumitomo Corporation of Japan to produce streetcars for a new transit system, rejecting a competing bid from an American firm, the Morrison-Knudsen Corporation of Idaho, in part because the company lacked experience. Popular anger erupted immediately. On January 22, 1992 —fourteen days after Bush lost his lunch in Japan—the City Council voted 11–0 to overturn the bid. "We can invest in ourselves or sell ourselves out," announced the leader of the anti-Japanese pack, councilman Zev Yaroslavsky.[32] On February 5 the council decided to put a "Buy American" city charter amendment before the voters. On June 2 the measure, which required the city to give preference to American goods, passed with a 55.2 percent "Yes" vote.[33]

A victory for the Buy American forces? Yes. But the public debate around the Los Angeles measure simultaneously flushed opponents of buying American out of the political woodwork. Critics immediately leaped up to counter that the measure was dangerously protectionist. It would cause severe economic damage to both Los Angeles and the nation. "As a major world port and trading center, Los Angeles cannot afford to turn inward and protectionist," the *Los Angeles Times* editorialized in repeated opposition.[34] It marshaled all the litany of anti-Buy American arguments in play since the modern movement first emerged in the 1930s: "The 'Buy American' movement is dangerous. . . . It is the municipal equivalent of national trade protectionism."[35] Protectionism, in turn, was dangerous because it undermined U.S. exports: "We all need to keep in mind that over the years the American economy has benefited mightily from foreign sales of its products." Barriers to exports "in the long run would be self-defeating."[36]

As fast as Buy American advocates could throw their measures on the books in the early 1990s, the free trade orthodoxy was closing in on them. In large part, as the *Los Angeles Times*'s opposition suggests, self-interested export sectors lay behind free traders who suddenly rose up to argue that protectionism would damage sales abroad. Along these lines, the *St. Louis Post-Dispatch,* for example, protested that the Buy American Act and similar laws "can indirectly cost us jobs in some of our most competitive, high-technology industries."[37] The *New York Times,* as it had throughout the century, functioned as the premier free-trade organ, defending the trade liberalization heights from the Buy American heathens. In part, it did so directly through editorials, mustering, for example, the classic foreign-exchange argument: "If Americans buy fewer Japanese, German or British cars, then the Japanese, Germans and British will earn fewer dollars with which to buy American soybeans. Or American computers, airplanes, pharmaceuticals and chemicals and graduate school educations." The *Times* suggested that "matters of external trade" be left "to officials who know the difference between facile xenophobia and hard-won foreign earnings."[38] More subtly, it covered the grassroots Buy American phenomenon with ostensibly objective reportage that masked clever opposing arguments. "Does 'Buy American' Mean Buying Trouble?" asked a page-one headline on January 27, 1992. Inside, headlines queried: "Is 'Buy American' a Direction for Recovery, or Does It Signal Tunnel Vision? Will Short-Term Revenge Yield Long-Term Regrets?" The *Times* left no doubt as to the answer to all three questions.[39]

Not all Americans, by any means, were convinced that they

should Buy American, and many independently came to oppose buying American, as letters to editors made clear. Most often, their arguments centered on the question of quality. "I'm one of those who still gets chills and a lump in my throat when our flag goes by," began Kenneth Stanley in a letter to the *Buffalo News.* "So in 1993 I switched to Chrysler. The results: . . . multiple problems and, worst of all, refusal to live up to the warranty. . . . Quick, tell me again why I should buy American?"[40] Often these opponents pulled back from an immediate disgust with the quality of American products to a larger analysis of industrial problems in the United States. K. S. Risk from Rockville, Maryland, wrote to the *Washington Post,* for example, "The only incentive a manufacturer has to improve his product is saleability [sic]. If we are willing to purchase an inferior American car, then there is less incentive for the manufacturer to spend time or money on improvement. I too want to help America. I am contributing my little push by buying a Honda."[41]

On one level these popular arguments were distinct from the strategically oriented arguments marshaled by the big metropolitan papers in service to a free-trade agenda. They usually focused only on the quality question and merely expressed an unwillingness to sacrifice oneself economically for the good of backward companies. On another level, though, they reinforced the free-trade framework by implicitly endorsing an open, unregulated market in which firms—and nations—competed, and the most efficient survived. Individual shoppers, in this line of thought, should encourage the healthy functioning of the free market and its corollary, free trade, by choosing the highest-quality, most cost-effective products. As a result the inefficient would drop by the wayside and the individual consumer, in theory, would prosper.

The same implicit arguments emerged in the "avalanche" of mail Ann Landers received on the Buy American question in 1992 and 1993. Ann herself unleashed the controversy by innocently suggesting that the United States needed to export as well as import and that buying American might therefore not be the best idea. She got a lot of irate mail from Buy American loyalists ("If I were in a position to buy the most expensive foreign luxury car, I would still stay with a Ford").[42] But she also got a lot of letters expressing disgust with low American quality. Best was a letter from "Pat in Connecticut Who

Has Had It with American Junk": "When I can drive my American-made car home without calling the motor club to come and get it started, put on American-made clothes without having the seams split, don American-made shoes without tears in the lining and heels that run down after two weeks . . . and pick up an American-made pen that doesn't leak all over my blouse pocket, *then* I will have the right to demand that my congressman do something about the unfair balance of trade."[43] Pat in Connecticut here constructed a sort of reverse import panic-attack story in opposition to buying American. But Pat also returned responsibility for trade relations to individual consumers. In focusing her argument on quality issues, she implicitly blamed U.S. corporations for inefficiency—thus circling back to the free-trade position.[44]

However outnumbered in Ann Landers's column, these popular opponents to buying American had Congress, the U.S. president, and, at least for the time, history on their side. Twenty-two months after Bush's trip to Japan, seventeen months after the Los Angeles election, in November 1993 the free-trade forces triumphed decisively with the passage of the North American Free Trade Agreement (NAFTA). NAFTA abrogated all trade restrictions between the United States, Canada, and Mexico, creating one big economic trading union of the three nations on January 1, 1994. Petty state-level Buy America laws were nothing in the face of this immense steamroller creating an open playing field for the corporations, which would now be freer than ever to play the working people of all three countries off against each other, picking and choosing their playsites depending upon where labor was cheapest, unions nonexistent, and environmental restrictions weakest. NAFTA was the triumphant outcome of the long twentieth century of ascendant free trade.

Yet NAFTA also reflected something newly dangerous. The post–World War II era of free trade had been predicated upon U.S.-based corporations operating multinationally. The corporations had extended their tentacles overseas but had also brought home a certain amount of bacon to U.S. working people and kept many of the plum jobs at home. By the late 1980s, though, the biggest of these corporations had become *trans*national, with a boot solidly planted in dozens of countries and only a corporate shell in their original homeland. The imperial element of free trade wasn't gone: NAFTA reinforced the power of U.S.-based corporations to intervene freely in the economies of Canada and Mexico. But NAFTA also signaled the transnational corporations' power to pay homage to the people of no nation, not even those of the United States. This was victorious free trade, as before, but with a new trick. The unity of national corporations and the nation's people had been sundered.[45]

A year later Congress approved the Uruguay Round of the General Agreement on Tariffs and Trade (GATT) and moved free trade onto an even higher, more global plane. Slipping through Congress in 1994 with little of the controversy surrounding NAFTA's passage, GATT replicated NAFTA on an international scale. Nations signing on to it agreed to abolish all tariffs and barriers to trade, creating a single international trading pool in which the corporations could swim about freely. To enforce the new freedoms, GATT created a new international body, the World Trade Organization (WTO), charged with adjudicating disputes and punishing any signatory found to have impeded the corporate flow.

Most important for our story, with little press coverage GATT handed the Buy American opponents their greatest victory: in one fell swoop, GATT banned all signatory nations from enforcing government procurement laws giving favor to domestic products, with the exception of defense spending. It thus obliterated all the local, state, and federal Buy American laws passed from 1933 onward. In the new GATT regime, they were proclaimed barriers to free trade.[46] The legislative contest between the economic nationalists and the free traders was, for the time at least, settled.

BIGOTS CRAWLING OUT FROM UNDER ROCKS

The internal logic of the Buy American movement played itself out, finally, in the field of race. As the movement peaked in the early 1990s, it produced an orgy of anti-Asian racism, in which the long-lived monster of Yellow Perilism rose up once again and splattered itself across the nation's landscape. Some elements of organized labor had played a role in waking up the beast in the 1970s and '80s, as we have seen. But most of the racism embedded in the Buy American movement did not emerge from trade unions at all but, rather, from simmering popular resentments against any form of Asian economic competition, combined with a century-old eagerness to portray Asian peoples as inherently racially dangerous. As one magazine reflected, " 'Buy American' campaigns may have given bigots an excuse to crawl out from under their rocks."[47]

As early as 1971 Representative James Mann introduced into the *Congressional Record* a ballad entitled "The Import Blues," by one of his South Carolina constituents: "I got the import blues . . . and I got 'em bad," it began; "I'm a cotton mill man . . . and my heart is sad." Charming enough, but not the Buy American pitch that followed:

> Buying Jap-made goods so sleazy to see
> Is a darn fool thing for you and me
> And I'm fightin' back because I won't run
> From the slant-eyed people of the Risin' Sun.[48]

Much of this hostility to Japan, like that expressed by rank-and-file autoworkers noted earlier, focused on reviving World War II. An April 1991 letter circulating in Fairfax, Virginia, from a group called Americans for Fair Play, for example, exhorted: "Now, some five decades after 'the day that will live in infamy' the Japanese are attempting to do economically what they could not do militarily—conquer America! . . . *we must pledge our time, our sacred honor, and our fortunes to defeat a totally brutal economic competitor.*"[49] These ideas were not just held by easily dismissed fringe elements. They grew out of still-vibrant memories of World War II, heightened by the mainstream press. On November 1, 1991—two months before Bush's trip to Japan—the *San Jose Mercury-News* headlined a page-one story, "Pearl Harbor Grudges Linger," and reported that almost a quarter of Americans "continue to bear a grudge" for Pearl Harbor and 60 percent "still insist it was right to drop atomic bombs on Japan."[50] The leap from World War II resentments to anti-import sentiments was a short one. A 1972 Phoenix, Arizona, Chevrolet advertisement read, for example: "Remember Pearl Harbor, when they tried to take your country from you. They are back with cheap imports to take your jobs, pensions and social security."[51]

Many who attacked Japan for its economic activities moved quickly from depicting an "economic war" to advocating real war, often by recommending that the United States drop new atomic bombs on Japan. On the anniversary of Pearl Harbor in December 1991, entrepreneurs in El Dorado, Arizona, offered for sale a "revenge" T-shirt, depicting a mushroom cloud and reading "MADE IN AMERICA. TESTED IN JAPAN."[52] That slogan showed up on shirts and mugs all over the country or mutated into even uglier forms. At a gun show in San Mateo, California, in March 1992, a vendor wore a shirt depicting the red circle of the Japan flag, with a screw inserting itself and the slogan underneath, "Next Time use a Bigger Bomb."[53] Overt racists now found it acceptable, even lucrative, to unleash the baldest of bigotry in public. A January 16, 1992, advertisement for Crawford Buick GMC Trucks in El Paso, Texas, read:

> OFFICIAL NOTICE TO JAPANESE CAR & TRUCK DEALERS; FROM GENERAL T. CRAWFORD; RE IMMINENT OUTBREAK OF HOSTILITIES; Y'all have until Wednesday, January 29th at high-noon to cease and desist the practice of selling Japanese Cars and Trucks in El Paso County, U.S.A. FAILURE TO HEED THIS WARNING WILL RESULT IN A DECLARATION OF WAR. . . . We Will gain the inevitable triumph—General T. Crawford. AT CRAWFORD BUICK GMC TRUCKS, WE DON'T SPEAK JAPANESE.[54]

Racial stereotyping of Japanese and other Asian people was inseparable from this popular upsurge of Japan bashing. Asked in January 1992 what he thought about buying American, Monsanto employee Russ Kuttenkuler objected to the "kind of sneaky tactics" Japan employed to obtain markets. "They are very cunning," he warned.[55] Kuttenkuler didn't just happen to use those words randomly. He was drawing on the classic stereotype of Japanese people as being inherently sneaky, clever, untrustworthy, and inscrutable. Buy American advocates projected all these racial stereotypes onto economic behavior. "I'm getting sick and tired of these Japs trying to take this country over," exploded James Bucher, chair of the Imperial County, California, Board of Supervisors, right after the anniversary of Pearl Harbor. "They'll do it one way or the other. Through their sneak attacks or through their dollars."[56] References to "slanty eyes" proliferated—as in the "import blues" song quoted earlier.[57] The racial epithet "Jap" passed back into accepted public parlance and reappeared in graffiti.[58]

According to many Buy American advocates, Japan was plotting to take over the United States economically and about to succeed. Sensationalized reports in the late 1980s and early 1990s rang regular alarms over Japanese capital investments in the United States. Mitsubishi's 1989 purchase of Rockefeller Center in New York was a particular favorite.[59] On January 24, 1992, the *San Jose Mercury-News* featured two banner headlines at the top of its first page. One announced: " 'Buy American' Feeling Beginning to Percolate." The other, not coincidentally, proclaimed: "Japanese group offers to buy Seattle Mariners."[60] This genre focused, as did Lynott's correspondents, on all-American icons such as baseball or the ice rink at Rockefeller Center, reinforcing the notion that the Enemy was deep within and going for our most precious cultural resources.

The height of this genre, and perhaps the most influential single work promoting it, was Michael Crichton's novel *Rising Sun*. Crichton hit the top of the best-seller list in 1992 with this sensationalized drama of Japanese capital plotting to take over the city of Los Angeles and ultimately the entire United States. The message of his book was not subtle. In one typical passage Crichton had a senator confide: "You know, we have to be careful. We are at war with Japan. . . . Loose lips sink ships." Another character adds, "And remember Pearl Harbor." The senator drops his tone to a whisper. "You know, I have colleagues who say sooner or later we're going to have to drop another bomb. . . . But I don't feel that way." Smiling, he adds: "Usually." At another point the senator warns, "As our economic power fades, we are vulnerable to a new kind of invasion."[61] This language sounded like it came out of Lothrop Stoddard's 1920 *The Rising Tide of Race.* Crichton, lest his book be dismissed as unscholarly trash fiction, appended an afterword in his own voice in which he warned, "the Japanese have invented a new kind of trade—adversarial trade, trade like war, trade intended to wipe out the competition," and included a bibliography of nonfiction sources on Japan's economic growth and its alleged threat to U.S. economic power.[62]

Prominent critics who were quoted liberally in the paperback edition approved of and reinforced Crichton's point. "Where Crichton really excels [is] the detailing of the many ways in which Japan has penetrated America, and the very real dangers this poses," the *Chicago Sun-Times* applauded. "The Japanese make no bones that to them business is war, and that a part of the war is conducted by neutralizing public opinion." *Publishers Weekly* seconded: "[This] entertaining, well-researched thriller cannot be easily dismissed as Japan-bashing because it raises important questions about that country's adversarial trade strategy and our inadequate response to it."[63]

As the approving critical response to Crichton's novel suggests, Japan bashing, racial stereotyping of all Asians, and the interweaving of both with Buy American advocacy wormed their way to the center of the American cultural and political mainstream. For example, on October 5, 1988, U.S. Representative James Traficant, the Buy American zealot, warned on the floor of Congress: "Our soldiers won the war, but Congress is letting Japan win the peace. . . . The day will come when America's cash crops will not be soybeans and wheat and corn: they will be rice, and we will have a rice paddy on the East Lawn of the White House."[64] In an interview six years later he acknowledged that the remark had gotten him into hot water but then twice volunteered the exact same remark freely and sincerely at a later point in the interview.[65] In 1982, Representative John D. Dingell (D-Michigan) told his congressional colleagues in the Democratic Environmental Caucus that the chief foreign competition in the automobile industry came from "the little yellow people." An "embarrassed silence" followed, the *New York Times* reported. "Several members said: 'What?' " Dingell reiterated: "The little yellow people . . . You know, Honda."[66]

Almost ritualistically, Buy American advocates prefaced their Japan-bashing or racist remarks with the assurance that they were not Japan bashing or racist. On February 2, 1992, the *Washington Post* interviewed two St. Louis barbers who had just promised a one-dollar discount to any customer who drove up in an American-made car. "We are not Japan bashing," they explained. "We are just America pushing."[67] Reviewing Crichton's *Rising Sun* on page one of the *New York Times Book Review,* Robert Nathan insisted that "Despite the book's provocative tone, Mr. Crichton is no xenophobe, no fool, no ranting bigot. The questions he poses are of great consequence in the debate about America's condition at the end of the American century."[68] Bill Lynott opened a 1993 pamphlet advertising his Buy America Foundation by distancing himself from the person "On the extreme right . . . who waves the American flag and shouts things like, 'Remember Pearl Harbor.' " Such ideas were "dangerous" and "extremist," he underscored.[69] Lynott thus set himself up as the reasonable, rational Buy American advocate, by contrast. But three years later he reported with outrage in his newsletter: "*An unfortunate sight:* Hollywood actor Martin Sheen on TV, abjectly apologizing to the Japanese people for America's use of the atomic bomb in World War II."[70]

Exactly as it had in all earlier periods of resurgent hostility to Japan, the Buy American movement spurred on racism that equated Japanese Americans with Japanese-based capital and indiscriminately blamed all Americans of Asian descent for U.S. economic troubles. We can see this at play in California, where a customer yelled, "Buy American!" at a group of Japanese American diners[71] and where vandals wrote "Go back to Asia" on the walls of a Japanese American community center.[72] From the early 1970s and increasingly into the 1990s, Asian Americans were once again viewed as not Americans, eternally not assimilable and dangerous by reason of alleged race. In West Los Angeles in 1991, a Girl Scout troop composed largely of girls of Japanese descent sat outside a market selling cookies, just like tens of thousands of other American girls around the country. People passing by these girls, though, called them "Japs," and one shopper told them, "I only buy from American girls."[73] "I'm being asked 'What are you,'" Mas Fukui, an aide to a Los Angeles County Supervisor, reported at the end of February 1992. "When I say I'm an American, they say 'You know what I mean.' That has not surfaced since the '40s."[74] At the end of February 1992 at the University of California, Berkeley, the Cal Bears beat the Clemson, South Carolina, football team in the Citrus Bowl. Just as U.C. Berkeley chancellor Chang-Lin Tien, of Chinese descent, walked up to the podium to address a post-game rally, a group of Clemson loyalists began to chant: "Buy American! Buy American!"[75]

Exactly as it had in the 1930s, the popular Buy American movement of the 1980s and '90s pivoted inward to attack the citizenship status of all Asian Americans. In applying racial concepts to Japanese economic actions, Buy American advocates drew a racial line around the border of economic America and cast Asian Americans outside that border. Any Asian-looking people masquerading as Americans were only an ages-old Fifth Column of devious, untrustworthy aliens—the racial enemy within.

The racial politics of the 1970s–1990s Buy American movement were even more complicated, however. For African Americans, the question was as complex as it had been in the 1930s. This time around, many African Americans appear to have enthusiastically endorsed buying American. Their support focused on the pervasive racism in Japan toward African Americans. Economist Julianne Malveaux, for example, in September 1990 opened her syndicated column, "Here they go again. Once a year the Japanese government lets loose with a racial slur. Once a year African American people get angry and get to hollering." Malveaux concluded that "From where I sit the response to Japanese slurs needs to be a well-focused selective buying campaign. . . . Not only should we boycott, but we need to ask others who oppose Japanese racism to do the same thing. . . . The Japanese can take their Sonys and shove them!"[76] When Sakurauchi issued his "lazy Americans" remarks in January 1992, many African Americans understood it as yet another racist attack on black Americans in particular. Benjamin L. Hooks, then executive director of the National Association for the Advancement of Colored People (NAACP), called on African Americans to Buy American in protest. "We don't hate anybody," he insisted, when asked if the NAACP were Japanbashing. "But we want to take care of our own."[77] As they had in the 1930s, African Americans were interpreting the Buy American call with a twist: they had specific reasons to be more critical of Japan than did other Americans. And they knew that lines of racism within the United States made it imperative they "take care of their own."

As the overall Buy American movement climaxed, it fused with a new, ugly hostility to immigrants, once again replicating the Buy American logic of the early 1930s. Once again the progression of Buy American arguments began with mild enough slogans, such as "Products Made by Americans for Americans."[78] But next came the equation of "Americans" or "American workers" with "American citizens." In a retort to Ann Landers, "Annemarie in Philadelphia" wrote, for example: "Do us all a favor, Ann. Tell your readers to check the tags on their clothing and refuse to buy anything not made by our fellow citizens."[79] At that point immigrant bashing started to kick in. "These days, companies and politicians are encouraging us to buy American products. Well, why don't these companies hire Americans," a correspondent wrote in to columnist Jeffrey Zaslow in the *Chicago Sun-Times* on March 11, 1992. "I see a lot of foreign people taking Americans' jobs. . . . This is unfair. Americans should hire Americans."[80] In September of that same year Dick Seymour of Baltimore, Maryland, wrote in to the *Automotive News:* "How come General Motors didn't 'Buy American' when it chose its new vice president for purchasing? Instead, it named a Spaniard."[81]

"American made," in this context, could slip over into "American owned," a sly signal that the owner wasn't an immigrant. In the southern United States the marquees of motels sprouted signs in the 1980s and '90s proclaiming, "American Owned and Operated"—a not-so-subtle stab at motels owned by local immigrants from India and Pakistan. Passing through Nashville, Tennessee, in 1989, one tired cross-country traveler discovered it was almost impossible to find a motel room that night because a Baptist convention had filled up all the available space. Finally, a sympathetic motel operator conceded that another motel down the road was in fact available. "But it isn't American-owned," she confided.[82]

These were not idle, innocent sentiments. By 1995, with help from the political ambitions of California governor Pete Wilson, they had helped produce the tidal wave of anti-immigrant hostility that led to the passage of California ballot Measure 187, which mandated that undocumented immigrants be cut off from the state's educational, health, and social services and which triggered anti-immigrant measures throughout the country.

In the 1930s, Buy American advocates had argued that buying a foreign product was the same thing as hiring a "foreigner." In the 1990s, Buy American sentiment did not as overtly slide over into immigrant-bashing. But the arguments behind buying American—inscribing smaller and smaller national circles, marking them with race, and arming the barriers—converged neatly with resurgent calls to militarize the borders against invading immigrants. Once again, the nationalist advocates of buying American missed the big picture: At the exact same time, corporate capital was going ever more global and tearing down national economic borders to capital mobility right and left. Just as the corporate free traders triumphed with NAFTA in 1992 and GATT in 1994, Buy American advocates and their anti-immigrant allies raised higher the border for labor mobility with California's Measure 187 in 1995. Corporate executives could almost be seen laughing. As they flitted about the globe in their corporate jets, they could look down at each nation's workers, increasingly trapped within nation-state borders.

But plenty of people were wary of the Buy American movement's racism, just as plenty of Californians had voted against Measure 187.

Japanese Americans themselves were not passive victims and protested vigorously against the new racist resurgence, beginning with their objections, noted earlier, to the ILGWU's 1972 "Made in Japan" subway ad. In late 1991 the Japanese American Citizens League (JACL) collected examples of racist incidents and language into a pamphlet entitled *Comments from Across the United States That Engage in or Contribute to Japan Bashing*.[83] " 'Buy American' campaigns have created a xenophobic atmosphere in which racial animosity is being directed solely at one country, and one country alone: Japan," the JACL charged in another leaflet linking Buy American campaigns with attacks on Asian Americans. "The rhetoric and scapegoating must stop."[84] In 1988 a group of Asian-Americans produced the film *Who Killed Vincent Chin?* about the Detroit Chinese American man murdered by autoworkers, and distributed it on college campuses throughout the country, precisely to combat resurgent hostility to Asian Americans.[85]

Criticism of the racism embedded in Buy American campaigns was by no means limited to Asian Americans. We can find immediate evidence of the power of disapproving public opinion in so many Buy American advocates' need to preface their Japan-bashing or racist remarks with an insistence they weren't Japan bashing or racist. Some of the critics were free traders conveniently discovering an anti-racist cloak, but most were not. When "M. D." wrote to *Chicago Sun-Times* columnist Jeffrey Zaslow advocating "hire American," Zaslow replied: "Who do you define as an American? Someone whose ancestors came over on the Mayflower? Who's a foreigner? Someone who arrived in this country after you did?" He noted the hostility toward the potential sale of the Seattle Mariners to Japanese investors and concluded: "I am very troubled by the rising 'Buy American' rage."[86] For all the praise for Crichton's *Rising Sun*, most reviewers were quick to criticize it. The reviewer in the *Nation*, for example, mockingly suggested that the cover for the book when it came out in paperback might feature "a caricature of World War II–era Prime Minister Tojo skulking off into Rockefeller Center with Doris Day over one shoulder."[87] We can note that when Representative James Dingell blurted out his "little yellow people" remark to his congressional colleagues, he was met with "an embarrassed silence."[88]

Some of the strongest criticisms of the racism in Buy American came from the labor movement. *Labor Notes* of Detroit, Michigan, for example, a progressive magazine from the left wing of the labor movement, in June 1992 put out a special issue on Japanese workers and the Japan question, entitled "Are These Our Enemies . . . or Our Friends?", which roundly criticized the racial politics of Buy Americanism. "Condemning Japan is a misdirection of our anger. When we blame 'the Japanese,' we forget what our own bosses are up to," cautioned staff member Jane Slaughter. She drew a strict distinction between Japanese corporations, who pioneered many of the "team concept" ideas imported by U.S. corporate managers, and Japanese working people, who faced the same struggles as American workers.[89]

One of the most articulate criticisms of the movement's racism came from Kevin Starr, state librarian of California and the author of numerous classic books on the history of the state. On June 14, 1992, just after the passage of the Buy American charter amendment in Los Angeles (Measure G), Starr published an opinion piece in the *Los Angeles Times* condemning the measure. In it, he marched straight back through California's anti-Asian history: "As in 1913 Japan-bashing reasserts itself as the cutting edge of Los Angeles public life," Starr charged, referring to the state's 1913 anti-alien land law. "And now the city of Los Angeles has inscribed another Alien Land Law in its Charter, as if to say to the world: 'In your face!' . . . Los Angeles is a xenophobic, protectionist enclave." Three years before the passage of Proposition 187 Starr foresaw that "the principle of exclusion, which is at the core of Proposition G, will reproduce itself, exclusion upon exclusion." Starr concluded that Los Angeles was "a city that has returned to the constrictions, the fears and hatred, of its older identity. Only now, the oligarchs have Ph.D.s, wear jeans and listen to public radio, and the Folks are a strange amalgam of xenophobic whites and people of color who have been persuaded to pull up the ladder against their own kind."[90]

Starr called it exactly: from the anti-Chinese movement of the 1870s and '80s through the exclusionary movements of the 1910s and '20s, from the Buy American movement of the 1930s through World War II internment and beyond, anti-Asian racism snaked through both California's history and the nation's, lashing out the instant economic competition from Japan became viable in the 1970s. At root was not just the deep-seated notion that all Asian peoples were racially

"other" and eternally foreign but the racialization of economic relations. Many Americans believed that Asian economic viability and
competition with the United States were simply racially inappropriate. As David Abney points out in a history of Japan bashing, the
post–World War II U.S. military reconstruction of Japan only reinforced the notion that the Japanese people should be ever-
subservient, ever-grateful to the Great White United States Father.[91]
If the Japanese dared pursue their own economic goals, they were
sneaky, cunning aliens, deserving of atomic bombs. The Buy American movement of the 1970s, '80s, and '90s was inseparable from this
heritage: it both fed on the legacy of anti-Asian racism and itself nur-
tured it. Buying American promised to rescue the American nation.
But as before, in the process it pushed millions of nonwhite, noncitizen Americans outside of the nation's lifeboats, often violently. It
feasted on nationalism; but in reply to the question Whose nation? to
all too many Americans, it answered, Not yours.

DISCOVERY NOTIONS, OR, CATS OUT OF BAGS

Yet just as the Buy American movement reached its racist depths and
popular heights, its adherents made two interrelated discoveries,
which together signaled that the movement's days were numbered.

The first revelation we can call the Discovery of Globalization. In
late January and early February 1992, as Japan bashing climaxed,
newspapers and magazines all over the country dispatched reporters
to write Buy American stories. But when the stories came back, they
almost all reported the same discovery: there was no such thing as an
American product. The headlines were almost identical: " 'Buy
American': It's the Backlash Battle Cry, But It's Easier Said Than
Done"; " 'Buy American' Push Has Problem—What's American?";
" 'Buy American' Is Not Easy as Foreign, Domestic Brands Intermin-
gle." Over the course of 1992, '93, '94, and the remainder of the de-
cade, news stories reiterated the increasing impossibility of buying
American, in a new, updated version of the import panic attack story:
Ms. Consumer rushed out to Buy American and discovered she
couldn't.[92]

To begin with, many products bearing the names of American-
owned companies were actually made abroad. "I commend you if
you join the Buy American movement because of national pride or

patriotism," warned Julius Ballanco in *Contractor* magazine. "But be careful, because that American-brand product actually might not be American."[93] The little town of Greece, New York, in a much-publicized incident, discovered globalization the hard way. It was looking for a new hydraulic excavator to keep its creeks cleaned out. In mid-January 1992, the town board voted to reject a bid from Komatsu and instead chose a John Deere model that cost $15,000 more. But within a week they found out that Komatsu was actually part of a U.S.-Japan joint venture, that the company's headquarters lay in Lincolnshire, Illinois, and that the Komatsu excavator was made in the good old U.S. of A. Meanwhile, the John Deere was part of a joint venture with Hitachi, and although its engine was made in Iowa, the excavator itself was made in Japan.[94]

Others discovered that a product ostensibly made by a U.S.-based company might in fact be composed of ingredients from dozens of nations. Howard Mack, a sixty-eight-year-old retired General Motors worker, put it best in an interview at a Buy American rally in Atlanta: "We want to buy American, but we can't tell what was made here. . . . It's kind of like scrambled eggs. You never see them get unscrambled."[95] On April 13, 1994, the *San Francisco Chronicle*'s ever-popular Question Man asked: "Do You Think It's Important to Buy American-Made Goods?" "Yes, we should make an effort," replied Jo Dziubek, "but since a global economy is the order of the day, it might be difficult to do. For example, component parts of a product may be made in a foreign country, but the final product may be assembled in the U.S."[96] Jo Dziubek figured it out: the eggs were already scrambled.

Newspapers and magazines themselves became agents explaining the process of globalization through charts and graphs as well as interviews. The *San Jose Mercury-News,* for example, ran three successive graphics, the first of which, on October 6, 1991, featured a full-color diagram of a Ford Crown Victoria, showing that its fuel tank came from Mexico, its shock absorbers from Japan, its electronic engine control from Spain, and its front spindle from Britain. On January 1, 1992, a new chart asked, "Can you buy American?" and listed the national origin of the two models *Consumer Reports* had rated highest in each of five categories, such as color TVs. Most were made overseas. Finally, on May 8, 1992, asking, "Confused over content?" the *Mercury-News* printed an index of domestic content that informed the reader "How American, how foreign" were twenty-nine popular cars, ranging from the virtuous Ford Taurus (with a score of 100) to the lowly Nissan 300ZX (scoring 8).[97]

Just as they had during the nonimportation campaigns of the American Revolution, Buy American advocates also discovered that there was a whole lot of cheating going on. Bill Lynott's newsletter was packed full of irate nationalists delineating their repeated betrayals by firms that simply lied and said their products were made in the U.S.A. when they weren't. In July 1994, *Consumer Reports* ran a rather sobering one-page spread featuring blatant liars, including an advertisement for a can of Hormel corned beef prominently marked "product of Brazil," with a "Made in the U.S.A. It Matters!" logo at the bottom; an advertisement for a scale model of a "Harley-Davidson, Born in the U.S.A." that had been made overseas; and, most preposterously, a clothing tag printed with two American flags and two messages: "Keeping Americans Working" and "Made in Thailand."[98]

Ordinary people also started pointing out the hypocrisy of corporate Buy American campaigns. Lee Iacocca, the Chrysler chairman, was a particular object of popular ire when he started touting Buy American in the early 1990s. "What gets me most in Iacocca's message is the hypocrisy of the campaign," fumed Dick Marlowe in the *Orlando Sentinel*. "Chrysler has long since gone international but would like for the rest of us to buy American."[99] Others saw right through Crafted With Pride's advertisements. Laura Luburich, an office manager in Chicago, told a reporter as early as 1986: "I think those ads are ludicrous when they feature people like Don Johnson of 'Miami Vice.' Everything he wears on that show is made in Italy by Giorgio Armani."[100] She didn't buy American.

The final, and most problematic, discovery was that foreign-owned firms were manufacturing automobiles and other products on American soil and hiring American workers by the tens of thousands to make them. As George F. Murphy of New Milford pointed out in a letter to the Bergen City, New Jersey, *Record* on November 21, 1991, "many of these 'foreign' cars are assembled here in the United States by American workers."[101] Overseas companies were themselves quick to toot this horn. Toyota, for example, ran a Camry advertisement announcing, "The Best Car Built in America Just Got Better," and a Tacoma advertisement insisting, "Talk about home town heroes; every Tacoma is made right here in Fremont, California."[102] In case shoppers missed the all-American point, Honda announced that its sedan was "manufactured in America since 1982" and lined it up visually with a baseball, a pair of cowboy boots, and a hamburger.[103]

The Japanese transplants on U.S. soil created a thorny problem for Buy American advocates. Some embraced their issue. *Consumer Guide,* in its *Best American Cars 1992,* for example, listed both Toyotas and Hondas that had been made in the U.S.A. Others refused. The strongest resistance emerged at U.S.-owned automobile plants and UAW union halls, where parking lot signs still banned "imports" and welcomed "American cars." In the parking lot closest to the Ford assembly plant in Wayne, Michigan, for example, a Ford Festiva made in Korea was welcome, but a Mazda Navajo, wasn't—even though that Navajo was made by UAW members in Kentucky. At other sites UAW members continued to harass visitors who arrived in Japanese-named cars made by UAW members in U.S. plants. On January 25, 1992, UAW members even mounted a Buy American protest at a Mazda assembly plant near Detroit, in which the workers were their fellow union members.[104]

The loyalists were fighting a frustrating and losing battle. The task of buying American had become either impossible or too difficult to undertake, and people knew it. Buy American purists were left sputtering, the ambivalent left uninspired, and the critics smugly victorious.

Around the same time—1993 and 1994—Crafted With Pride made the second discovery. Since the 1980s a fleet of survey-takers had queried samples of Americans about the Buy American question. But the closer they got, the more puzzling it looked, until, by the mid-nineties, it became clear that there was trouble in Buy American paradise.

When Crafted With Pride first decided to launch its program, it assessed all the available survey data on Americans' interest in buying American. "All our research results indicated that consumers were ready, willing, and predisposed to buy 'Made in U.S.A.' products," Robert Swift, its executive director, concluded.[105] One 1984 consumer survey, for example, found that 60 percent of Americans "no-

ticed carefully" the country of origin of their purchases and thought
it was important to Buy American.[106] After the Buy American boost-
erism of the late 1980s and early '90s, surveys showed that Americans'
desire to Buy American had shot way up in response, particularly during the first quarter of 1992.[107]

Together, these surveys give us our broadest look at popular support for buying American. Not surprisingly, enthusiasm was strongest
in the Midwest and Northeast—where industrial layoffs had been
most brutal—and weakest in the West. It increased with age. The one
study that gauged ethnic differentials reported that 58 percent of African Americans bought American, as opposed to 42 percent of "His-
panics." Least enthusiastic—again, not surprisingly—were Asian
Americans, only 24 percent of whom said they bought American.
(The report did not present any other groups.) Surveys also showed
that women were more likely than men to want to Buy American.[108]

In most respects these patterns correlate with support for the Buy
American organizations. The correspondents in Bill Lynott's *Buy
America Newsletter* were largely from the East, South, or Midwest; few
came from the West; none of them signed with Asian or Spanish sur-
names. Gender was unclear because Lynott converted all first names
to initials. Joel Joseph, head of the Made in the USA Foundation,
claimed fifty thousand members in his organization by the mid-1990s
and estimated that 60 percent of them were male and most were
white. The typical enthusiast, he said, was a white male World War II
veteran—men such as Larry Russell, the Des Moines, Iowa, rubber
worker who in 1961 wrote to George Meany advocating Buy American. Overall, the evidence suggests that men were more likely to
write letters to the editor, join organizations, and protest in public
against imports. Women could be even more dedicated Buy Americanists, but they showed their support through a quieter, more private
manner in their daily lives as assiduously nationalist shoppers—such
as the person who wrote in to Bill Lynott seeking help in finding an
American-made jogging suit.[109]

After 1991, though, Crafted With Pride discovered that something was very wrong. The surveys revealed an immense gap between
respondents' desire to Buy American and their actual shopping habits.
In part, it was a problem with survey methods. Asked if they cared
about Buying American, respondents said sure, having just been reminded by the question to care. More important, though, people

tended to insist they bought American even if they didn't. "There is a big gap between how people respond to a survey and what they are actually buying off the shelves," Harry Bernard, a retail consultant in San Francisco, told *Adweek*.[110] The Buy American uproar of early 1992 caused a brief upward blip in purchases of American cars, in particular, in the first quarter of 1992. But it was only a blip.[111] "Everyone has been stunned about the astounding lack of success the whole campaign had," observed one Crafted With Pride council member.[112]

Here we arrive at the final punch line: the main effect of all the millions of dollars and grassroots energy expended on Buy American promotions was only to make shoppers feel guilty as they bought more and more imports. *Advertising Age* concluded: "Consumers are increasingly saying they will 'Buy American' but feel guilty because they don't necessarily act with their pocketbook."[113] Or, as *Forbes* put it, summarizing an August 1992 poll: "They still buy the goods they consider the best value for their money; if the goods aren't American, more consumers just feel more guilt."[114] The Buy American movement, in sum, mainly caused American shoppers' guilt quotient to go up. Bradford Fay, research director at the Roper Operation, a polling group, concluded: "The overall preference for American-made products is really a mile wide and an inch deep."[115]

Much of the problem lay with the old twin specters of price and quality. As Leo J. Shapiro, head of a Chicago research firm, observed, "The spirit is there to buy American, but the value isn't always."[116] People wanted to Buy American if the price and quality were the same as with imports. But they usually weren't. To Buy American as much as one wanted required concrete financial outlays, which shoppers were unwilling to fork over. "The notion that patriotism transcends self-interest is absolutely nuts," observed Laurel Cutler, a marketing executive, especially regarding expensive purchases like cars.[117] To buy American when the domestic product was more expensive was the same thing as sending off a cash donation to the retailer or producer in the name of saving U.S. jobs. Shoppers just didn't choose to do so.[118]

Millions of Americans had lost their jobs and seen their wages fall, their family's income shrink, and their communities devastated. Throughout the 1980s and 1990s the poor got poorer and the middle strata of working people sank lower and lower economically. In order to reverse all those dynamics, these exact same people wanted to Buy

American. But that was the catch. Precisely because they had lost their jobs and had seen their wages and family incomes shrink, they could less and less afford to pay extra to Buy American. The Buy American movement thus contained a glaring and inescapable internal contradiction: The very same people who flocked to Wal-Mart in search of lower prices and bulk commodities were least able to afford to be picky about country of origin. "I can't afford to be patriotic in that way," explained Virginia O'Brien, a fifty-year-old mother of six on Chicago's South Side.[119] Thomas Tashjian, an analyst for First Manhattan Co., in 1993 confirmed: "Basically, to the lower- and moderate-end shopper, value-pricing is a lot more important than patriotism."[120]

Housewares magazine reported that two types of stores led the way in import purchases. The first was composed of mass retailers like Wal-Mart or Costco, which catered to Americans such as Virginia O'Brien, who were at the bottom of the economic ladder.[121] The second group of stores, though, was made up of "upscale retailers." While the poor got poorer, the rich were getting richer, and with wealthy shoppers, quality and international cachet were everything. For them, cultural prestige rested on owning the correct fashionable objects, as often as not imported. "Price is not the number one issue," a buyer for Bloomingdale's reported. Well-off customers "insist on having the finest Japanese porcelain, Italian ceramics and German electronics."[122] The U.S. economy was spinning off two groups: rich and poor. And, for quite different reasons, neither bought American.

The final reason people didn't Buy American, though, was that it was no longer possible to do so. The structures of production and distribution had become so global that even the most nationalist shoppers couldn't Buy American. Bill Lynott's newsletter was littered with frustrated reports of unfound jogging suits or Boy Scout uniforms made only in Taiwan. Quality and price aside, in multiple categories—VCRs, hydraulic excavators, lapel pins in the shape of a tombstone—American products didn't exist.

The cat, in sum, was out of the bag. The American people had discovered globalization and, like willful sheep, had strayed far away from the path Roger Milliken had laid for them. Milliken himself knew it. As early as 1989 his Crafted With Pride Council admitted publicly that its program wasn't working. By 1994 Milliken, upon discovering that people just wouldn't do his bidding, lost interest in the operation and turned his energies to Patrick Buchanan's presidential campaign instead.[123]

HIGH NOON IN THE GARDEN OF GOOD AND EVIL

The third week of January 1992 marked high noon for the Buy American movement. The idea of purchasing American-made products as a strategy for national salvation reached its greatest heights of popular legitimacy and, as it did so, played out its internal logic to its furthest extremes. What in earlier contexts had merely been teamwork between organized labor and the corporations, in the popular movement slid downward into a near-total silence about labor's role. Nationalism trumped class analysis altogether. The question became not whether a given key chain or jogging suit or Boy Scout uniform had been made under sweatshop conditions enforced by union-busting millionaires, but whether it had been made in the U.S.A. Popular Buy American advocates promised, nonetheless, to protect and to serve the American people; but the inward-looking protection of "us" against threatening "foreigners" spiraled downward into a narrower and narrower clubbishness. What began innocently at the border of Orange County, Florida, or the State of Alaska ended less innocently at an economic border drawn by race or citizenship.

Just as the movement reached its greatest heights, though, it hit the iceberg of globalization, and the iceberg won. In 1993 and '94 corporate advocates of free trade and their allies in the federal government marched right over the Buy American movement to pass NAFTA and then GATT in rapid succession. Buy American advocates could preach nationalist shopping all they wanted, but the big players were changing the rules right in front of their eyes to make it easier and easier for the corporations to transcend nation-states altogether.

Or so they thought. In 1992, the year President George Bush lost his lunch, something else was lost, too: the American people's innocence about the global economy. When they rushed out to Buy American and discovered they couldn't, they also discovered that the eggs were scrambled, that economic integration made their Buy American strategy unworkable. The question remained: What would they do with their new knowledge?

Conclusion
Up from Nationalism

In late June 1992, in the middle of the United Auto Workers' triennial Bargaining Convention in San Diego, California, sociologist Harley Shaiken approached UAW regional director Bob King and asked if he could take a few of the union's delegates on a tour of the *maquiladoras,* or manufacturing plants, in Tijuana, just over the Mexican border fifteen miles away. The NAFTA fight was looming on the horizon, and Shaiken thought rank-and-file UAW members might be interested in seeing working conditions in Mexico. He expected maybe 30 or 40 people would sign up, at best. "The first surprise was the numbers," Shaiken recalls. Over 350 delegates signed up—for a tour that started at 5:30 in the morning. "There was that level of interest."

Addressing the group in the Holiday Inn before the tour left, Shaiken gave a brief talk on what the members were likely to see, "emphasizing that we often view this as losing American jobs, but really the framework ought to be that workers in Mexico were looking for a decent life, and what they were striving for was the very same thing that the people in this room were concerned with and willing to fight for." The delegates then filed onto eight Greyhound-sized buses outside. They were a diverse lot, reflecting the UAW's most active membership by 1992: about a third African American, 20 percent Latino, a few Asians, and the rest white; about a third were women. Most were in their forties and fifties, serious union activists who had served for years as shop stewards or union committee members. All of them were rank-and-file autoworkers, largely from the Detroit region. As the buses caravanned down the Interstate in the early morning light, there was a good feeling among the people on board—a lot of joking, camaraderie, back-patting; the generous good-feeling of a day off. "But there wasn't any real connection to what was about to happen thirty miles down the road," Shaiken recalls.

As soon as the buses passed into Mexico, they drove through the Otay Mesa Industrial Park, one of the oldest industrial parks in Tijuana, where many of the larger *maquiladoras* were located. "People were looking with real interest at an industrial park that could as easily be in Dearborn, Michigan, as in Tijuana, Mexico. That was the first thing that *really* got people's attention." Pressured for time—the delegates had to be back in San Diego by 2:00 P.M.—the buses then drove out through a large swath of Tijuana to one of the new squatter settlements on the outskirts of the city, "La Florida," where many of the *maquiladoras'* workers lived in shacks made of packing crates, scraps of wood, and bits of tin. Shaiken had arranged for a few community leaders to speak to the visitors in a soccer field at the edge of La Florida. The UAW members were supposed to get off the bus, meet with the activists, then get back on the buses and go home.

What happened next was "fundamentally different from what we had planned," Shaiken remembers with amazement. The minute the buses pulled into the soccer field and opened their doors, all 350 UAW members immediately fanned out across the field. Many of them wearing the shiny green baseball jackets of UAW Region IA, they passed into the narrow streets of the surrounding neighborhoods and disappeared. Within minutes—even though only a few spoke Spanish—they had established "this extraordinary human contact" with the residents, asking about their jobs, their houses, their kids; and they were soon invited into people's homes. "The intensity of the human connection in the houses I saw was just extraordinary," Shaiken recalls. "These UAW workers spoke to *maquiladora* workers and their families and didn't view this as a different setting, but had a deep feeling, 'There but for the grace of God go I.'" In one house, the visitors were talking with a woman with six or seven children and asked why the children weren't going to school. The woman replied that she had no money to buy shoes. At that point many of the five or six UAW members inside were crying, and they immediately emptied their wallets and gave the woman whatever money they had with them. "You know, I grew up in a very poor rural town in Alabama," one UAW member later told Shaiken; "but what I saw in Alabama was nothing compared to what I saw here." It gradually dawned on the delegates, moreover, that these *maquiladora* workers, living in incredible poverty, were among the most productive workers in the entire world.

Eventually, the trip's organizers rounded up the delegates and got them back on the buses, and they headed back north toward the border. On the way back, the mood was utterly different. The tone was subdued, quiet; people were talking about what they had seen, what it meant, what the lives of their counterparts in Mexico were like. A number of people, both men and women, were quietly crying. By the time they had reached San Diego, UAW members on all eight buses had spontaneously taken up a collection, and together, they raised $1,500. "You couldn't measure the impact by the minutes and hours," Shaiken recalls, still astonished six years later. "Some told me that day, some told me in Detroit six months later, some told me two years later, that it had been among the most moving experiences of their entire lives."[1]

These were the very same autoworkers who, ten years earlier, might have picked up a sledgehammer and bashed it into the windshield of a Toyota. By 1992, they had begun to discover not just globalization but international labor solidarity, and to understand workers in other countries not as alien "foreigners" but as fellow workers sharing the same aspirations, facing the same challenges, and often employed by the very same companies. Rank-and-file autoworkers were beginning to learn about the working conditions U.S. corporations maintained outside the nation's borders and to wonder what the corporations had in mind next for U.S. workers. They began to grasp the broad scheme of capital mobility, free trade, and the global "race to the bottom" across national boundaries. They had begun to pivot, in sum, away from the anti-import nationalism of the Buy American approach and toward alternative avenues to the empowerment of working people in relation to global capital.

THE DISCOVERY OF TRANSNATIONAL SOLIDARITY

What happened to those individual UAW delegates in Tijuana was not a fluke. Thousands of other workers from unions as diverse as the Communications Workers of America (CWA), the Teamsters, and the garment workers established worker-to-worker ties across borders in the late 1980s and 1990s. Gradually, leaders of their national-level unions were re-thinking their approach to international relations and talking about global solidarity. Strategists at the Machinists', garment workers', and other unions began to emphasize concrete links with their counterparts in other countries. The early example of the United Electrical Workers' cross-border work with Mexico's independent union, the Frente Auténtico de Trabajaradores (FAT), loomed large.[2]

The United Mine Workers of America (UMWA) made a concrete commitment to solidarity with its counterparts overseas, with impressive results. In 1983, the Exxon Corporation had closed a four-year-old, $50 million coal mine in West Virginia represented by the UMWA and invested instead in a new mine in El Cerrejón, Colombia, which quickly became the largest coal-exporting mine in the world. Colombian workers successfully organized the mine, but when they tried to strike for better wages and conditions the military intervened in 1986 and '88. In 1990, the United Mine Workers decided to get involved. As then president Richard Trumka argued,

> Our goal is to strengthen unions in low-wage countries so they are strong enough to fight for decent wages and working conditions to raise their standard of living up to our level. If we don't, the multinational corporations will attempt to lower our standards to the lowest international common denominator.[3]

In 1990 the UMWA invited the president of the Colombian miners' union, SINTERCOR, on a solidarity visit to the United States. During the next four years it initiated a letter-writing campaign to corporate officials, traveled to Colombia during SINTERCOR's negotiations with Exxon, set up cross-border union training, and filed a petition under the Generalized System of Preferences, a U.S. tariff system, charging EXXON with violating "internationally recognized worker rights." The UMWA joined with the Metalworkers' International Federation to apply diplomatic pressure throughout the world. In 1992, the Colombian miners won a 29 percent wage increase and another 23 percent for the next year, plus a 50 percent increase in housing expenditures. Two years later they got 24 percent and 20 percent raises for the two subsequent years—all without striking. For mine workers, international solidarity paid off immediately.[4]

The struggle against NAFTA in 1993 proved the most important turning point in the development of new approaches in the U.S. labor movement. As ratification of the trade agreement loomed, U.S. union officials started realizing the stakes involved in trade policy and began lobbying hard against NAFTA. In the process they started talking to each other across union lines; began working more closely with Canadian and Mexican unions; and formed new alliances with environmental groups like the Sierra Club. In the course of the battle a new consciousness and a new set of cooperative relationships emerged.[5]

Then, in 1995, the AFL-CIO finally kicked out the dinosaurs at its top (or at least most of them). As union membership continued to plummet in the early 1990s, more far-seeing national union leaders finally pressured lackluster president Lane Kirkland to resign in 1995. His chief henchman, Secretary-Treasurer Thomas Donohue, then assumed the helm temporarily. Later that year, in the first contested election since 1896, John Sweeney, president of the Service Employees' International Union (SEIU), beat out Donohue. Sweeney initiated a new regime at the AFL-CIO. While the jury remains out on his administration's effectiveness and the extent to which it represents a new departure, Sweeney initiated three vast improvements at the federation. First, he committed millions of dollars to organizing new members, appointing creative and experienced staffers who quickly re-energized the organizing department with such new initiatives as the Organizing Institute (training new, high-powered union organizers) and Union Summer (offering young people internships in which to experience the labor movement firsthand).[6]

Second, the AFL-CIO reversed its international policy. Sweeney appointed Barbara Shailor of the International Association of Machinists, an experienced strategist in transnational solidarity, to be director of the AFL-CIO's international affairs. More reluctantly, in 1997 the federation's executive board decided to shut down its federally funded overseas operations, including the American Institute for Free Labor Development (AIFLD) and the Asian American Free Labor Institute (AAFLI) and form a new American Center for International Solidarity. The link with CIA-sponsored unions was at last severed; real international solidarity could henceforth begin to take its place.[7]

Finally, the AFL-CIO started to break away, if meekly, from its lock-step relationship with the Democratic Party. The first rupture came with the 1993 NAFTA battle, when the AFL-CIO proved willing, at last, to oppose President Clinton. Clinton won that round; but in late 1997 the AFL-CIO was able to stop congressional ratification of special authority for the president to negotiate "fast track" trade agreements. In all these departures, the AFL-CIO was finally waking up from its dream of nationalist partnership and beginning to develop a new politics of opposition.

Meanwhile, in the mid-1990s, other independent activists mounted a series of effective campaigns that brought issues of workers and globalization to center stage in the media. The National Labor Committee in Support of Workers' Human Rights in Central America, in particular, hit headline pay dirt with the Kathie Lee Gifford case. In 1996, Gifford, a nationally syndicated talk-show host, announced she was attaching her name to a new line of clothes marketed through Wal-Mart. She said she would affix a label on each dress or shirt proclaiming that "a portion of proceeds from the sale of this garment will be donated to various children's charities." Activists from the National Labor Committee soon revealed, though, that Kathie Lee's garments were produced by thirteen-year-old girls working for thirteen cents an hour in Honduran sweatshops. Gifford tearfully defended herself on her TV show and swore up and down that she just didn't know and would never let it happen again. But days later the committee further revealed that only blocks away from Gifford's New York City studio, immigrant workers were laboring at subminimum wages to produce still more Kathie Lee signature garments. Not surprisingly, Kathie Lee thereafter enlisted herself in the cause of abolishing sweatshops.[8]

The National Labor Committee has formed a close working partnership with UNITE!, the garment workers' union into which ACTWU and the ILGWU merged in 1995. They have mounted new public-awareness campaigns pressuring corporations like Nike, the GAP, and Walt Disney to adopt "codes of conduct," in which they agree to keep wages and working conditions above sweatshop levels wherever they subcontract their work.[9]

Together, these campaigns have helped shift the axis of public debate away from nationalist attacks on foreign workers and toward a more class-based challenge to transnational corporations (or national celebrities) as they profit off the exploitation of both foreign and domestic working people.

NEITHER A FREE TRADER NOR A NATIONALIST BE

But all these efforts to construct international working-class solidarity are foolish, mainstream economic orthodoxy tells us. On television, in the daily newspaper, in radio interviews, discussions of trade issues glorify the unregulated "free market economy" and speak of free trade as if it were a scientific truth proven in a physics laboratory by objective men in white coats. Only by removing all barriers to investment and letting the capitalists do whatever they want, mainstream analysts argue, can we have jobs, homes, food, prosperity.

But far from reflecting "natural laws" of economic relations, "free trade" is merely a historically constructed theory that has been devised to legitimate the goals of corporate interests and the elite Americans who profit from them. In the nineteenth century, as we have seen, politicians pushed the idea of free trade to advance capitalist interests in the export sector. These advocates sought low tariffs at home in order to sell their products abroad without trade restraints at the other end. By the 1930s, as the American industrial empire emerged the strongest in the world, its enthusiasts promoted everfreer trade because U.S. corporations could win handily at that game. Under the rules of unrestricted trade, most U.S. products could beat out their competitors and U.S. corporations could get all the raw materials they wanted at cheap prices. After World War II, trade liberalization provided further access to the raw materials and overseas markets that U.S. corporate interests craved. More recently, in the new era of NAFTA and GATT, U.S.-based corporations have pushed free trade in order to liberate themselves from the boundaries and regulations of nation-states altogether. In all these periods, the "freedom" of free trade has meant, in effect, corporate liberty to call the shots of international economic relations in whatever manner has best suited their profit rates at a given moment.

The only alternative, we are told, is virulent protectionism. But neither should we fall into that trap. Economic nationalism poses equal dangers for working people. The answer is not to put up higher and higher walls against the products of other working people overseas, as if their goods carried an economic disease capable of rotting away the national economic health. Economic nationalism and Buy American campaigns cut U.S. working people off from solidarity with the rest of the world's workers. They set up U.S. workers as part of a nationalist team allied with U.S. corporations, ostensibly pulling together within the high national walls of protectionism. That model of national partnership blinds us to the machinations of corporate team members within the nation's walls, as they develop increasingly clever strategies to keep profits high and to lower U.S. workers' standard of living. Buy American campaigns blind us to corporate capital's willingness to simultaneously play the nationalist card at home and flee overseas with its investment dollars. Country of origin becomes a surrogate for a developed class politics at home—and in foreign economic relations.

Throughout the twentieth century, the Buy American call has come as part of a package deal with anti-Asian racism, and it would be naive to expect that the two are now separable. In the 1930s and the 1990s alike, the racial politics of Buy Americanism have also been fused with immigrant-bashing. Products and workers from Canada and Europe have been welcomed; while those from Latin America and Asia, especially, have been suspect. The Buy American legacy reinforces, moreover, the concept of Asian Americans as eternal foreigners and casts over a third of the world's people as sneaky, dangerous, inappropriate trading partners.

In the 1930s, and again in the period from 1970 to the early 1990s, Japan took first place in the Yellow Peril contest. As we enter the new century, though, and China emerges as a powerful nation both economically and militarily, it is rivaling Japan in the national racial imagination. "As a nation we can handle only one Asian bogeyman at a time," observes historian John Dower, "and these days Japan is down and China is up as the country with the greatest potential and the greatest potential menace."[10] We can only speculate whether the sleeping giant of Yellow Perilism is dead, or if it is just taking a little nap, only to wake up roaring.

If the giant of racist economic nationalism does wake up, Pat Buchanan will no doubt be shouting into its ear. After years of attacking feminism and affirmative action, and endorsing anti-homosexual ideas, the religious Right, and other ultraconservative values, Buchanan has repackaged himself in the last years of the 1990s as the friend of the working man, tilting against the global corporate enemy. Yet he remains tight with textile mogul Roger Milliken, silent about the labor movement, and hostile to immigrant workers. That way danger lies: Buchanan offers us the ultimate specter of economic nationalism's dangerous logic.[11]

The alternative to economic nationalism is not, as Buchanan would have it, a return to an idealized Golden Age of the 1950s, in which the United States ruled the world and all working families allegedly prospered. The problem with that dream, as we have seen, is that millions of working people didn't prosper, racism flourished, and the United States did try to rule the world, with disastrous results. Through the nuclear arms race, gunboat diplomacy, and decades of CIA adventurism, it successfully repressed much of the rest of the globe in order to bring wealth home to the United States. The world's peoples are no more interested in subservience and repression today than they were in the 1950s and '60s. They have the same aspirations to democracy and national sovereignty as do people in the United States, and we need to reject models of foreign relations based on military or economic domination, however lucrative.

ECONOMIC DEMOCRACY BEGINS AT HOME

If there is no going back, how, then, do we go forward? There are no easy answers. But we can imagine at least six elements of a new approach to foreign economic relations. At their core, they boil down to a new conceptualization of the line between "Them" and "Us" and a new understanding of the meaning of the economic nation.

First, as already discussed, we need to construct concrete alliances of international labor solidarity that carry real clout. Second, we can fight to embed international labor standards in trade agreements. Many union activists have argued that we can turn around and use the new era of international trade agreements in working people's favor, by demanding that minimum standards for labor rights and working conditions be part of any international agreement. NAFTA, for example, does include weak "side agreements" delineating labor standards, inserted at the last minute as a meager concession to organized labor. We can fight to make those standards real.[12]

Third, with all the historical dangers of protectionism carefully in mind, we can try to imagine trade policy that includes some barriers to trade, based on the conditions under which goods have been produced. We don't want to fall into the corporate trap of advocating completely free trade. But in employing some tariffs, quotas, or other

trade barriers, we always need to keep in mind: whom are we protecting? Corporate profits in a particular industry? Or the long-term
interests of working people, all over the globe, and their empowerment?[13]

Fourth, we need to fight racism and understand race relations as
part and parcel of trade relations and immigration policy. As California's ballot propositions eliminating social and educational services
for undocumented workers and their children (Proposition 187),
eliminating affirmative action (Proposition 209), and banning bilin-
gual education (Proposition 227) have made clear, issues of labor mobility, domestic class relations, and the border with Mexico have become once again intertwined with the politics of racial hostility and
scapegoating. We cannot construct a new class politics of trade and
foreign economic policy without simultaneously addressing the politics of race at home.

We also need to start talking about controls on capital mobility.
For all the nasty proposals floating about that propose to control labor
mobility across national borders through immigration restriction, we
have heard little about barriers to capital mobility. Why should corporations be free to profit from workers in a given community and
then flee to wherever they can make an even higher profit rate? How
about barring them from leaving in the first place? Or, by imposing
legal limits on the allowable rate of profit, why not remove the basic
incentive to move many investments in the first place? These proposals are not as far-fetched as they might sound. In 1972, the AFL-CIO's
Burke-Hartke measure in Congress included traditional protectionist
measures but also controls on capital mobility. Ultimately, we can't
solve the trade question without questioning—and challenging—
the logic of capitalism. As long as we let the primacy of profits and the
structure of corporate ownership of the workplace reign supreme,
corporate managers and bankers will always have to obey the logic
of competition that pits worker against worker—both within the
United States and across national borders—in order to keep profits up
and satisfy Wall Street.

Finally, and most fundamentally, we need to talk more about economic democracy. Whose economic nation is this, anyway? What
kind of nation do we want to construct—and for whom? When those
carpenters, shoemakers, merchants, and silversmiths climbed onto

the *Dartmouth,* the *Beaver,* and the *Eleanor* in Boston Harbor in 1773 and broke open those chests of British tea, they acted upon a grass-roots democratic impulse to control their country's economic affairs from below. In the process they gave birth to a new nation-state, built, in theory, upon democratic control of economic affairs. Ever since the Boston Tea Party and the nonimportation movement of the American Revolution of which it was part, the Buy American movement has been sustained by such individual Americans seeking, through their private shopping choices, to exercise democratic control over their nation's economy.

We need to celebrate the Buy American movement's basic democratic ideal but look to alternative modes to achieve it. U.S. history is full of creative and suggestive alternatives, only a few of which we have explored here: the moral economy sustained during the Revolution by price controllers, slaves, and seamen; the vision of a cooperative economy and trade relations put forth by the Knights of Labor; the transnational communities of Chinese and African Americans, building bridges abroad in order to fight racism at home. We need, ultimately, to link democracy and foreign relations. Only when we take seriously true democratic control of the economy from below can we move beyond a misguided national chauvinism and start building relations of economic equality, at home and abroad.

NOTES

Preface

1. For examples of the genre, see T. J. Edwards, "Have Yourself a Made-in-U.S.A. Christmas," *San Jose Mercury-News*, December 22, 1994; *New Haven Register*, December 20, 1991; Russell Baker, "Did Paul Revere Ride Through Korea?" *Santa Cruz Sentinel*, January 4, 1995; *Chicago Tribune*, June 29, 1987.

2. For an accessible overview of the debates, see Eyal Press, "The Free Trade Faith—Can We Trust the Economists?" *Lingua Franca*, Vol. 7, No. 10 (December–January 1998).

3. For examples of the search for a progressive, alternative politics of trade, see Jeremy Brecher and Tim Costello, *Global Village or Global Pillage: Economic Restructuring from the Bottom Up* (Boston: South End Press, 1994); Tim Lang and Colin Hines, *The New Protectionism: Protecting the Future Against Free Trade* (New York: The New Press, 1993); Jerry Mander and Edward Goldsmith, eds., *The Case Against the Global Economy and for a Turn Toward the Local* (San Francisco: Sierra Club Books, 1996); Kim Moody, *Workers in a Lean World: Unions in the International Economy* (London: Verso, 1997); John Cavanagh, John Gershman, Karen Baker, and Gretchen Helmke, eds., *Trading Freedom: How Free Trade Affects Our Lives, Work, and Environment* (San Francisco: Institute for Food and Development Policy, 1992); John Cavanagh, Lance Compa, Allen Ebert, Bill Goold, Kathy Selvaggio, and Tim Shorrock, *Trade's Hidden Costs: Worker Rights in a Changing World Economy* (Washington, DC: International Labor Rights Education and Research Fund, 1988); Mark Levinson, "Economists and Sweatshops," *Dissent* (Fall 1997): 11–13; John Cavanagh and Robin Broad, "Global Reach: Workers Fight the Multinationals," *The Nation*, Vol. 262, No. 11 (March 18, 1996): 21–25.

1. Whose Economic Nation?

1. Quoted in Benjamin Woods Labaree, *The Boston Tea Party* (New York: Oxford University Press, 1964), p. 134.

2. Quoted in Labaree, *The Boston Tea Party*, p. 133.

3. Labaree, *The Boston Tea Party*, pp. 126–145.

4. Quoted in Alfred F. Young, "George Robert Twelves Hewes (1742–1840): A Boston Shoemaker and the Memory of the American Revolution," in Herbert G. Gutman and Donald H. Bell, eds., *The New England Working Class and the New Labor History* (Urbana: University of Illinois Press, 1987), p. 27.

5. Quote is from Arthur M. Schlesinger [Sr.], *The Colonial Merchants and the American Revolution, 1763–1776* (New York: Frederick Ungar Publishing Co., 1957), p. 167; Labaree, *The Boston Tea Party;* Young, "George Robert Twelves Hewes."

6. Labaree, *The Boston Tea Party*, pp. 141–145.

7. Quoted in Young, "George Robert Twelves Hewes," p. 27.

8. Quoted in Labaree, *The Boston Tea Party*, p. 145.

9. The phrase "Whose Nation?" is

Linda Colley's; I am indebted to her analysis of the class politics of economic nationalism in "Whose Nation? Class and National Consciousness in Britain 1750–1830," *Past and Present*, No. 113 (November 1986): 97–117.

10. Quoted in Morey Rothberg, "John Franklin Jameson and the Creation of *The American Revolution Considered as a Social Movement*," in Ronald Hoffman and Peter J. Albert, eds., *The Transforming Hand of Revolution: Reconsidering the American Revolution as a Social Movement* (Charlottesville: University Press of Virginia, 1995), pp. 19–20.

11. Schlesinger, *Colonial Merchants*, pp. 63–64, 91–156; Virginia Nonimportation Resolutions, 1770, in Julian P. Boyd, ed., *The Papers of Thomas Jefferson*, Vol. 1, 1760–1776 (Princeton, NJ: Princeton University Press, 1950), p. 44. For the sequence of the agreements, see Schlesinger, *Colonial Merchants;* Charles McLean Andrews, *The Boston Merchants and the Non-Importation Movement* (New York: Russell & Russell, 1968, repr. of 1916).

12. Schlesinger, *Colonial Merchants*, pp. 182, 198.

13. The most thorough treatment of the nonimportation movement remains Schlesinger, *Colonial Merchants*; see also Andrews, *The Boston Merchants and the Non-Importation Movement;* for the cultural meanings of nonimportation rituals, see Ann Fairfax Withington, *Toward a More Perfect Union: Virtue and the Formation of American Republics* (New York: Oxford University Press, 1991). For a more recent interpretation casting the nonimportation movement in terms of consumer behavior and summarizing the literature, see Terrence H. Witkowski, "Colonial Consumers in Revolt: Buyer Values and Behavior During the Nonimportation Movement, 1764–1776," *Journal of Consumer Research*, Vol. 16 (September 1989): 216–226.

14. "The Association," October 20,

1774, in Samuel Eliot Morison, *Sources and Documents Illustrating the American Revolution, 1764–1788, and the Formation of the Federal Constitution* (Oxford, England: Clarendon Press, 1923), pp. 122–125. See also Schlesinger, *Colonial Merchants*.

15. On popular resistance giving birth to transcolonial political institutions, see, especially, Pauline Maier, *From Resistance to Revolution: Colonial Radicals and the Development of American Opposition to Britain, 1765–1776* (New York: Random House, 1972).

16. "The Association."

17. Morison, *Sources and Documents*, p. 124.

18. Schlesinger, *Colonial Merchants*, p. 498.

19. Quoted in Schlesinger, *Colonial Merchants*, p. 189. For crowd action and the Revolution, see Maier, *From Resistance to Revolution;* Dirk Hoerder, *Crowd Action in Revolutionary Massachusetts, 1765–1780* (New York: Academic Press, 1977); Jesse Lemisch, "Jack Tar in the Streets: Merchant Seamen in the Politics of Revolutionary America," *William and Mary Quarterly*, 3rd Ser., Vol. 25, No. 3 (July 1968): 371–407.

20. Quoted in Schlesinger, *Colonial Merchants*, pp. 481–482.

21. Quoted in Dirk Hoerder, *Crowd Action in Revolutionary Massachusetts, 1765–1780* (New York: Academic Press, 1977), p. 206.

22. Quoted in T. H. Breen, " 'Baubles of Britain': The American and Consumer Revolutions of the Eighteenth Century," *Past & Present*, No. 119 (May 1968): 103.

23. Quoted in Maier, *From Resistance to Revolution*, pp. 126–127.

24. "The Association," quoted in Morison, *Sources and Documents*, p. 124.

25. Schlesinger, *Colonial Merchants*, p. 107; "Virginia Nonimportation Agreement," June 22, 1770, in *Papers of Thomas Jefferson*, pp. 43–44.

26. Quoted in Mary Beth Norton,

Liberty's Daughters: The Revolutionary Experience of American Women, 1750–1800 (Boston: Little, Brown and Company, 1980), p. 159.

27. Quoted in Laurel Thatcher Ulrich, "'Daughters of Liberty': Religious Women in Revolutionary New England," in Ronald Hoffman and Peter J. Albert, eds., *Women in the Age of the American Revolution* (Charlottesville, VA: University Press of Virginia, 1989), p. 225. On giving up luxuries and imports, see Edmund S. Morgan, "The Puritan Ethic and the American Revolution," in *The Challenge of the American Revolution* (New York: W. W. Norton, 1976), pp. 88–138; Breen, "'Baubles of Britain,'" pp. 73–104; Schlesinger, *Colonial Merchants.*

28. Quoted in Edmund S. Morgan and Helen M. Morgan, *The Stamp Act Crisis: Prologue to Revolution* (Chapel Hill: University of North Carolina Press, 1953), p. 27.

29. Andrews, *The Boston Merchants,* p. 37.

30. Quoted in Breen, "'Baubles of Britain,'" p. 103.

31. Quoted in Joan Hoff Wilson, "The Illusion of Change: Women and the American Revolution," in *The American Revolution: Explorations in the History of American Radicalism,* ed. Alfred F. Young (DeKalb, IL: Northern Illinois University Press, 1976), p. 398.

32. Quote: Norton, *Liberty's Daughters,* p. 169. On the spinning bees, see Norton, *Liberty's Daughters,* pp. 157–169; Hoff Wilson, "The Illusion of Change," pp. 397–398; Ulrich, "'Daughters of Liberty,'" pp. 214–227.

33. Quoted in Norton, *Liberty's Daughters,* p. 167.

34. Quoted in Ulrich, "'Daughters of Liberty,'" p. 218.

35. Schlesinger, *Colonial Merchants,* p. 77.

36. Ibid.

37. Schlesinger, *Colonial Merchants,* p. 492.

38. See also Hoff Wilson, "The Illusion of Change," pp. 395, 421.

39. Gary B. Nash, "The Failure of Female Factory Labor in Colonial Boston," *Labor History,* Vol. 20, No. 2 (Spring 1979): 165–188.

40. Schlesinger, *Colonial Merchants,* p. 123.

41. Eric Foner, *Tom Paine and Revolutionary America* (London and New York: Oxford University Press, 1976); James H. Hutson, "An Investigation of the Inarticulate: Philadelphia's White Oaks," *William and Mary Quarterly,* 3rd Ser., Vol. 28, No. 1 (January 1971): 22–23; Maier, *From Resistance to Revolution,* p. 119.

42. Maier, *From Resistance to Revolution,* pp. 118–119.

43. Andrews, *Boston Merchants,* p. 23.

44. Andrews, *Boston Merchants,* p. 26.

45. Schlesinger, *Colonial Merchants,* pp. 135, 197, 210; Marc Egnal and Joseph A. Ernst, "An Economic Interpretation of the American Revolution," *William and Mary Quarterly,* 3rd Ser., Vol. 29, No. 1 (January 1972): 3–32; for a different interpretation, see Thomas M. Doerflinger, "Philadelphia Merchants and the Logic of Moderation, 1760–1775," *William and Mary Quarterly,* 3rd Ser., Vol. 40, No. 2 (April 1983): 197–226.

46. Quoted in Egnal and Ernst, "An Economic Interpretation," p. 21.

47. Quoted in Schlesinger, *Colonial Merchants,* p. 210n.

48. Schlesinger, *Colonial Merchants,* p. 248.

49. Breen, "'Baubles of Britain'"; Morgan, "The Puritan Ethic and the American Revolution"; Barbara Clark Smith, "Food Rioters and the American Revolution," *William and Mary Quarterly,* Vol. 51, No. 1 (January 1994): 3–38; Hoff Wilson, "The Illusion of Change," p. 397.

50. Barbara Clark Smith, "Social Visions of the American Resistance Movement," in Ronald Hoffman and Peter J. Albert, eds., *The Transforming Hand of Revolution: Reconsidering the*

American Revolution as a Social Movement (Charlottesville, VA: University Press of Virginia, 1996); Smith, "Food Rioters"; Breen, "Baubles of Britain"; Morgan, "The Puritan Ethic"; Andrews, *The Boston Merchants*, p. 47, argues that the movement against extravagance began before anti-importation.

51. Quoted in Rhys Isaac, *The Transformation of Virginia, 1740–1790* (Chapel Hill, NC: University of North Carolina Press, 1982), p. 251.

52. Quoted in Morgan, "The Puritan Ethic," p. 98.

53. Edward Countryman, *The American Revolution* (New York: Hill & Wang, 1985), p. 87.

54. Schlesinger, *Colonial Merchants,* p. 92.

55. Quoted in Smith, "Social Visions," p. 44.

56. Quoted in Maier, *From Resistance to Revolution,* p. 128.

57. L. H. Butterfield, ed., *Adams Family Correspondence*, Vol. 2, June 1776–March 1778 (Cambridge, MA: Harvard University Press, 1963), pp. 295, 305.

58. Quoted in Smith, "Food Rioters," p. 8.

59. Quoted in Foner, *Tom Paine,* p. 166.

60. Smith, "Food Rioters," p. 14.

61. Smith, "Social Visions," p. 31.

62. Smith, "Social Visions," p. 32.

63. Smith, "Food Rioters," pp. 8–9, for Fishkill story; estimate of seven thousand men is from Smith, "Social Visions," p. 39; for gender composition, see Smith, "Food Rioters."

64. Quoted in Smith, "Food Rioters," p. 7.

65. Quoted in Hoerder, *Crowd Action in Revolutionary Massachusetts,* p. 238.

66. Andrews, *Boston Merchants,* p. 35.

67. Quoted in Elizabeth Cometti, "Women in the American Revolution," *New England Quarterly,* Vol. 20 (1947): 336.

68. Quoted in Cometti, "Women in the American Revolution," pp. 336–337.

69. Quoted in Willard Sterne Randall, *Thomas Jefferson: A Life* (New York: Henry Holt, 1993), pp. 170–171.

70. Quoted in Douglas Southall Freeman, *George Washington: A Biography,* Vol. 3: *Planter and Patriot* (New York: Charles Scribner's Sons, 1951), p. 229.

71. Schlesinger, *Colonial Merchants,* p. 168. The evanescent "crowd" got the last word. On October 28, a dozen people "of Some Considerable Rank," including a merchant, a tailor, and other members of the Sons of Liberty, attacked Mein in Boston, joined later by a thousand-person strong mob that had already formed to tar and feather another suspect. Mein fled with a shovel wound. His newspapers soon lost subscriptions, his bookselling business plummeted, and dirt covered the door of his printing office. Anonymous leaflets appeared, likening Mein to the devil and banishing him "To some dark Corner of the World . . . / Where the bright Sun no pleasant Beams can shed,/ And spend thy Life in Horror and Despair." In November another mob attacked Mein, who wounded a soldier and finally left for England. Maier, *From Resistance to Revolution,* p. 127; Andrews, *Boston Merchants,* pp. 69–72 and 72n; Schlesinger, *Colonial Merchants,* pp. 159–178.

72. Schlesinger, *Colonial Merchants,* p. 529.

73. My analysis of seamen and their politics is dependent upon Marcus Rediker, *Between the Devil and the Deep Blue Sea: Merchant Seamen, Pirates, and the Anglo-American Maritime World, 1700–1750* (Cambridge, England, and New York: Cambridge University Press, 1987); Peter Linebaugh and Marcus Rediker, "The Many-Headed Hydra: Sailors, Slaves, and the Atlantic Working Class in the Eighteenth Century," in *Crossing Cultures: Essays in the Displacement of Western Civilization,* ed. Daniel Segal (Tucson: University of Arizona Press, 1992), pp. 105–141; Marcus Rediker, "A Motley Crew of Rebels: Sailors, Slaves, and the Coming

of the American Revolution," in Hoff-
man and Albert, *The Transforming Hand of
Revolution,* pp. 155−198; and Lemisch,
"Jack Tar in the Streets."

74. Lemisch, "Jack Tar in the Streets,"
p. 383.

75. Quoted in Rediker, "A Motley
Crew of Rebels," p. 169.

76. Rediker, "A Motley Crew of
Rebels," p. 161; Lemisch, "Jack Tar in the
Streets."

77. Quoted in Rediker, "A Motley
Crew of Rebels," p. 155.

78. Quoted in Rediker, "A Motley
Crew of Rebels," pp. 187−188.

79. Rediker, "A Motley Crew of
Rebels," p. 170.

80. Lemisch, "Jack Tar in the Streets,"
pp. 397−399.

81. Quoted in Lemisch, "Jack Tar in
the Streets," p. 390.

82. Linebaugh and Rediker, "The
Many-Headed Hydra"; Rediker, *Between
the Devil and the Deep Blue Sea.*

83. Benjamin Quarles, "The Revolutionary War as a Black Declaration of
Independence," in *Slavery and Freedom in
the Age of the American Revolution,* ed. Ira
Berlin and Ronald Hoffman (Charlottesville, VA: University Press of Virginia,
1983), p. 285.

84. Phillis Wheatley to the Rev. Sam-
son Occom, February 11, 1774, quoted in
*Am I Not a Man and a Brother: The Anti-
slavery Crusade of Revolutionary America,
1688−1788,* ed. Roger Bruns (New York:
Chelsea House, 1977), pp. 307−308.

85. James W. Loewen, *Lies My Teacher
Told Me: Everything Your American History
Textbook Got Wrong* (New York: Simon &
Schuster, 1995), p. 146.

86. Quoted in Norton, *Liberty's
Daughters,* p. 164.

87. Ibid.

88. Quoted in Freeman, *George Washington,* Vol. 3, p. 243.

89. Boyd, *Papers of Thomas Jefferson,*
Vol. 1, p. 44.

90. Morison, *Sources and Documents,* p.
123.

91. W. E. B. Du Bois, *The Suppression of
the African Slave-Trade to the United States
of America 1638−1870* (New York and London: Longmans, Green & Co., 1896), pp.
41−42.

92. Petition of Prince Hall and Other
Blacks, January 13, 177, in Bruns, *Am I
Not a Man and a Brother,* pp. 428−429.

93. Petition of New Hampshire Slaves,
November 12, 1779, in Bruns, *Am I Not a
Man and a Brother,* p. 453.

94. Quoted in Peter H. Wood, "'The
Dream Deferred': Black Freedom Strug-
gles on the Eve of White Independence,"
in *Resistance: Studies in African, Caribbean,
and Afro-American History,* ed. Gary Y.
Okihiro, (Amherst, MA: University of
Massachusetts Press, 1986), p. 176. On
slaves' hopes and strategies during the
Revolutionary period, see Wood;
Quarles, "The Revolutionary War as a
Black Declaration of Independence";
Billy G. Smith, "Runaway Slaves in the
Mid-Atlantic Region during the Revolutionary Era," in Hoffman and Albert, *The
Transforming Hand of Revolution,* pp. 199−
230; Jeffrey J. Crow, "Slave Rebellious-
ness and Social Conflict in North Caro-
lina, 1775 to 1802," *William and Mary
Quarterly,* 3rd Ser., Vol. 47, No. 1 (January
1980): 79−102; Sylvia R. Frey, *Water from
the Rock: Black Resistance in a Revolution-
ary Age* (Princeton, NJ: Princeton Uni-
versity Press, 1991), pp. 81−107; Gary B.
Nash, *Forging Freedom: The Formation of
Philadelphia's Black Community, 1720−1840*
(Cambridge, MA: Harvard University
Press, 1988), pp. 38−65; Ira Berlin, "The
Revolution in Black Life," in Young, *The
American Revolution,* pp. 349−382.

95. Wood, "'The Dream Deferred,'"
p. 177.

96. Wood, "'The Dream Deferred,'"
p. 178; Nash, *Forging Freedom,* p. 45.

97. Fritz Hirschfeld, *George Washington
and Slavery: A Documentary Portrayal*
(Columbia, MO: University of Missouri
Press, 1997), pp. 22−25.

98. Wood, "'The Dream Deferred,'"
pp. 178−179.

99. Schlesinger, *Colonial Merchants,* p. 235; Henry Laurens to John Laurens, August 14, 1776, in Bruns, *Am I Not a Man and a Brother,* p. 427; Wood, " 'The Dream Deferred,' " p. 179; David Duncan Wallace, *The Life of Henry Laurens* (New York: Russell & Russell, 1915, repr. 1967), p. 235.

100. Gary Nash, *Race and Revolution* (Madison, WI: Madison House, 1990), p. 60.

101. Hirschfeld, *George Washington and Slavery,* pp. 24–29, 112–117; Loewens, *Lies My Teacher Told Me,* pp. 146–147.

102. Quoted in Merrill Jensen, *The New Nation: A History of the United States During the Confederation, 1781–1789* (New York, NY: Knopf, 1950), p. 426.

103. Quoted in Michael Parenti, *Democracy for the Few,* 6th Ed. (New York: St. Martin's Press, 1995), p. 53.

104. Quoted in Edmund S. Morgan and Helen Morgan, *The Birth of the Republic, 1763–89,* Rev. Ed. (Chicago: University of Chicago, 1956, 1977), pp. 147–148.

105. Morgan, "Puritan Ethic," p. 136.

106. Morgan, "Puritan Ethic," p. 137.

107. Quoted in William Appleman Williams, *The Contours of American History* (Cleveland: The World Publishing Co., 1961), p. 112.

108. Quoted in Williams, *Contours of American History,* p. 143.

2. The Class Politics of the Tariff

1. Sidney Ratner, *The Tariff in American History* (New York: Van Nostrand, 1972), p. iii.

2. Kathleen Brady, *Ida Tarbell: Portrait of a Muckraker* (New York: Seaview/Putnam, 1984), p. 186.

3. Alexander Hamilton, "Report on the Subject of Manufactures," December 5, 1791, in *The Papers of Alexander Hamilton,* ed. Harold C. Syrett (New York: Columbia University Press, 1961–1987), pp. 230–340.

4. Jonathan Hughes, *American Economic History,* 3rd Ed. (New York: Harper Collins, 1990), pp. 53, 384.

5. The classic general histories of the tariff remain Ratner, *The Tariff in American History;* Frank Taussig, *The Tariff History of the United States* (New York: G. P. Putnam's Sons, 1892, and several subsequent editions); and Edward Stanwood, *American Tariff Controversies in the Nineteenth Century,* 2 Vols. (New York: Russell & Russell, 1903). For more recent and analytical studies, see Judith Goldstein, *Ideas, Interests, and American Trade Policy* (Ithaca, NY: Cornell University Press, 1993); Jonathan J. Pincus, *Pressure Groups and Politics in Antebellum Tariffs* (New York: Columbia University Press, 1977); Tom E. Terrill, *The Tariff, Politics, and American Foreign Policy, 1874–1901* (Westport, CT: Greenwood Press, 1973); David A. Lake, *Power, Protection, and Free Trade: International Sources of U.S. Commercial Strategy, 1887–1939* (Ithaca, NY: Cornell University Press, 1988); Alfred E. Eckes, Jr., *Opening America's Market: U.S. Foreign Trade Policy Since 1776* (Chapel Hill, NC: University of North Carolina Press, 1995).

6. Robert V. Remini, *Henry Clay: Statesman for the Union* (New York: W. W. Norton, 1991), pp. 1–3, 21.

7. Remini, *Henry Clay,* pp. 3, 5, 22, 498, n. 5; Maurice G. Baxter, *Henry Clay and the American System* (Lexington: University Press of Kentucky, 1995), hemp quote, p. 5.

8. Quoted in Stanwood, *American Tariff Controversies,* Vol. 1, p. 212.

9. Quoted in Robert Reich, *The Work of Nations: Preparing Ourselves for 21st Century Capitalism* (New York: Knopf, 1992), p. 21.

10. Ibid.

11. Quoted in Goldstein, *Ideas, Interests, and American Trade Policy,* p. 71.

12. Quoted in Baxter, *Henry Clay and the American System,* p. 27.

13. W. Elliot Brownlee, *Dynamics of Ascent: A History of the American Economy,*

2nd Ed. (Chicago: Dorsey Press, 1988), p. 355.

14. H. Wayne Morgan, *William McKinley and His America* (New York: Syracuse University Press, 1963); Matthew Josephson, *The Politicos, 1865–1896* (New York: Harcourt, Brace & World, 1938), p. 328.

15. William McKinley, Speech on the Mills Tariff Bill, May 18, 1888, in Ratner, *The Tariff in American History*, p. 127.

16. McKinley, Speech on the Mills Tariff Bill, in Ratner, *The Tariff in American History*, p. 128.

17. Quoted in Nell Irvin Painter, *Standing at Armageddon: The United States 1877–1919* (New York: W. W. Norton, 1987), pp. 79–80.

18. McKinley, Speech on the Mills Tariff Bill, in Ratner, *The Tariff in American History*, p. 128.

19. Ibid.

20. Adam Smith, *An Inquiry into the Nature and Causes of the Wealth of Nations* (Oxford, England: Clarendon Press, 1976).

21. Piero Sraffa, *The Works and Correspondence of David Ricardo*; Vol. 1: *On the Principles of Political Economy and Taxation* (Cambridge, England: Cambridge University Press, 1962), pp. 128–149.

22. Josephson, *The Politicos*, pp. 363–364.

23. Allan Nevins, *Grover Cleveland: A Study in Courage* (New York: Dodd, Mead & Co., 1962).

24. Grover Cleveland, Message to Congress, December 6, 1887, in Ratner, *The Tariff in American History*, p. 119.

25. Cleveland, Message to Congress, December 6, 1887, in Ratner, *The Tariff in American History*, pp. 122–123; on the 1888 debate, see Joanne Reitano, *The Tariff Question in the Gilded Age: The Great Debate of 1888* (University Park, PA: Pennsylvania State University Press, 1994).

26. Quoted in Ratner, *The Tariff in American History*, p. 124.

27. Ida Tarbell, *The History of the Standard Oil Company*, 2 Vols. (New York:

Macmillan, 1904); David M. Chalmers, "Ida Minerva Tarbell," in *Notable American Women, 1607–1950: A Biographical Dictionary*, Vol. 3 (Cambridge, MA.: Harvard University Press, 1971), pp. 428–429; Brady, *Ida Tarbell*.

28. Ida Tarbell, *All in the Day's Work: An Autobiography* (New York: Macmillan, 1939) pp. 267, 268; Ida M. Tarbell, *The Tariff in Our Times* (New York: Macmillan, 1911).

29. Tarbell, *The Tariff in Our Times*, p. 352.

30. Tarbell, *The Tariff in Our Times*, p. 335.

31. Tarbell, *The Tariff in Our Times*, p. 262.

32. Tarbell, *The Tariff in Our Times*, pp. 331–361 (quotes, 338, 335).

33. Quoted in William Appleman Williams, *The Contours of American History* (Cleveland and New York: World Publishing Co., 1961), p. 230.

34. Williams, *Contours of American History*, p. 231.

35. James L. Huston, "A Political Response to Industrialism: The Republican Embrace of Protectionist Labor Doctrines," *Journal of American History*, Vol. 70, No. 1 (June 1983): 44–46.

36. Josephson, *The Politicos*, pp. 330, 402.

37. Josephson, *The Politicos*, pp. 363–364.

38. William Appleman Williams, *The Tragedy of American Diplomacy*, Revised and Expanded Edition (New York: Delta, 1962), p. 27.

39. Walter LaFeber, *The Cambridge History of American Foreign Relations*, Vol. 2: *The American Search for Opportunity, 1865–1913* (Cambridge, England, and New York: Cambridge University Press, 1993), pp. 26–27.

40. LaFeber, *The American Search for Opportunity*, p. 133.

41. Conversation by the author with Arthur MacEwan, August 1996.

42. Stanwood, *American Tariff Controversies in the Nineteenth Century*, Vol. 2, pp.

135–138; Terrill, *The Tariff, Politics, and American Foreign Policy*, pp. 74–89.

43. LaFeber, *The American Search for Opportunity*, p. 1.

44. LaFeber, *The American Search for Opportunity*, p. 26.

45. McKinley, Speech on the Mills Tariff Bill, in Ratner, *The Tariff in American History*, p. 128.

46. Cleveland, Message to Congress, in Ratner, *The Tariff in American History*, p. 124.

47. U.S. Congress, Senate Committee on Education and Labor, *Report of the Committee of the Senate Upon the Relations Between Labor and Capital, and Testimony Taken by the Committee*, 4 Vols. (Washington, DC: Government Printing Office, 1885).

48. Terrill, *The Tariff, Politics, and American Foreign Policy*, p. 32.

49. Huston, "A Political Response to Industrialism," p. 50.

50. Williams, *The Contours of American History*, p. 363.

51. Huston, "A Political Response to Industrialism," p. 54.

52. Tarbell, *All in the Day's Work*, p. 278.

53. Donald G. Sofchalk, "John Jarrett," in Gary Fink, ed., *Biographical Dictionary of American Labor* (Westport, CT: Greenwood Press, 1984), pp. 315–316.

54. Senate Committee on Education and Labor, *Report of the Committee*, Vol. 1, p. 1122.

55. Senate Committee on Education and Labor, *Report of the Committee*, Vol. 1, p. 1127.

56. Senate Committee on Education and Labor, *Report of the Committee*, Vol. 1, p. 1137.

57. Senate Committee on Education and Labor, *Report of the Committee*, Vol. 1, p. 1157.

58. Senate Committee on Education and Labor, *Report of the Committee*, Vol. 1, p. 1127.

59. Senate Committee on Education and Labor, *Report of the Committee*, Vol. 1, p. 1139.

60. Sofchalk, "John Jarrett," pp. 315–316. For Jarrett's views, see also John Jarrett, "The Story of the Iron Workers," in George E. McNeil, *The Labor Movement: The Problem of To-Day* (New York: M. W. Hazen Co., 1887), pp. 268–311.

61. David Bensman, *The Practice of Solidarity: American Hat Finishers in the Nineteenth Century* (Urbana, IL: University of Illinois Press, 1985), pp. 58–59, 113–114; Mary Blewett, forthcoming study of New England textile workers in the nineteenth century (University of Massachusetts Press, 2000).

62. Stuart B. Kaufman, ed., *The Samuel Gompers Papers*, Vol. 1: *The Making of a Union Leader, 1850–86* (Urbana, IL: University of Illinois Press, 1986), pp. 241–242.

63. *Journal of United Labor*, October 25, 1884, p. 821. My thanks to David Montgomery for the reference.

64. On the Knights of Labor, see Susan Levine, *Labor's True Woman: Carpet Weavers, Industrialization, and Labor Reform in the Gilded Age* (Philadelphia: Temple University Press, 1984); Richard Oestreicher, *Solidarity and Fragmentation: Working People and Class Consciousness in Detroit, 1875–1900* (Urbana, IL: University of Illinois Press, 1986); Leon Fink, *Workingman's Democracy: The Knights of Labor and American Politics* (Urbana, IL: University of Illinois Press, 1983); Peter J. Rachleff, *Black Labor in the South: Richmond, Virginia, 1865–1890* (Philadelphia: Temple University Press, 1984); Gregory S. Kealey and Bryan D. Palmer, *Dreaming of What Might Be: The Knights of Labor in Ontario, 1880–1900* (New York: Cambridge University Press, 1982); Robert E. Weir, *Beyond Labor's Veil: The Culture of the Knights of Labor* (University Park: University of Pennsylvania Press, 1996).

65. *Journal of the Knights of Labor* (formerly *Journal of United Labor*), April 10, May 15, 1890.

66. *Journal of the Knights of Labor,* December 23, 1890.

67. *Journal of the Knights of Labor,* May 29, August 14, 1890.

68. Arthur Burgoyne, *The Homestead Strike of 1892* (Pittsburgh: University of Pittsburgh Press, 1979, repr. 1893); David P. Demarest, Jr., *"The River Ran Red": Homestead 1892* (Pittsburgh: University of Pittsburgh Press, 1992); Paul Krause, *The Battle for Homestead 1880–1892* (Pittsburgh: University of Pittsburgh Press, 1992).

69. Quoted in Demarest, *"The River Ran Red,"* p. 113.

70. Cartoons reprinted in Demarest, *"The River Ran Red,"* pp. 59, 104.

71. Demarest, *"The River Ran Red,"* pp. 59, 104.

72. Alexander Saxton, *The Indispensable Enemy: Labor and the Anti-Chinese Movement in California* (Berkeley: University of California Press, 1971).

73. Herbert G. Gutman and Ira Berlin, "Class Composition and the Development of the American Working Class, 1840–1890," in Herbert G. Gutman, *Power & Culture: Essays on the American Working Class,* ed. Ira Berlin (New York: Pantheon, 1987), pp. 380–394 (quote, p. 385).

74. Karl Marx, "Speech on the Question of Free Trade," Brussels, February 1848, in Karl Marx and Friedrich Engels, *Collected Works,* Vol. 6 (New York: International Publishers), p. 463.

3. Circling the Wagons

1. United States Congress, Senate Committee on Interstate Commerce, Hearings on the "Buy American" Act, S. 1720 and an Amendment, June 7, 12, and 13, 1939 (Washington: United States Government Printing Office, 1939), pp. 84, 96.

2. Senate Committee on Interstate Commerce, "Buy American" Act Hearing, pp. 84–89.

3. Senate Committee on Interstate Commerce, "Buy American" Act Hearing, p. 85.

4. Senate Committee on Interstate Commerce, "Buy American" Act Hearing, pp. 83, 84, 88, 92, 98.

5. Robert S. McElvaine, *The Great Depression: America, 1929–1941* (New York: Times Books, 1984), pp. 66–67, 74–90; American Social History Project, *Who Built America? Working People and the Nation's Economy, Politics, Culture and Society,* Vol. 2: *From the Gilded Age to the Present* (New York: Pantheon, 1992); Irving Bernstein, *The Lean Years: A History of the American Worker, 1920–1933* (Boston: Houghton Mifflin, 1960), pp. 247–311.

6. Bernstein, *The Lean Years,* p. 257; McElvaine, *The Great Depression,* p. 257; Caroline Bird, *The Invisible Scar* (New York: David McKay, 1966); Broadus Mitchell, *Depression Decade: From New Era Through New Deal,* Vol. 9: *The Economic History of the United States* (New York: Holt, Rinehart, Winston, 1961), pp. 82–119.

7. W. A. Swanberg, *Citizen Hearst: A Biography of William Randolph Hearst* (New York: Charles Scribner's Sons, 1961); Ferdinand Lundberg, *Imperial Hearst: A Social Biography* (New York: Equinox Cooperative Press, 1936); Oliver Carlson and Ernest Sutherland Bates, *Hearst: Lord of San Simeon* (New York: Viking, 1936); Rodney P. Carlisle, *Hearst and the New Deal: The Progressive as Reactionary* (New York: Garland, 1979); *National Cyclopedia of American Biography,* Vol. 39 (New York: James T. White Co., 1954), p. 8.

8. Swanberg, *Citizen Hearst;* Lundberg, *Imperial Hearst;* Carlisle, *Hearst and the New Deal;* Carlson and Bates, *Hearst; National Cyclopedia of American Biography.*

9. Swanberg, *Citizen Hearst,* p. 237.

10. "Children Enlist to Aid 'Buy American,'" February 1, 1933, Hearst Metrotone News Service, in University of California, Los Angeles, Film Archive. See also "'Buy American' to Help Pros-

perity, Says W. R. Hearst," January 14, 1933.

11. On Hearst and the debt question, see *San Francisco Examiner* (hereafter *SFE*), November 19, December 2, 5, 6, 9, 20, 1932; January 7, 1933.

12. *SFE,* December 7, 29, December 30, 1932.

13. *SFE,* December 27, 1932.

14. *SFE,* January 1, 1933.

15. *SFE,* December 29, 1932.

16. *SFE,* December 30, 1932.

17. *SFE,* January 7, 1933.

18. *SFE,* January 7, 1933.

19. *SFE,* February 6, 1933.

20. *New York Times* (hereafter *NYT*), January 23, 29 (Paris quote), April 16, May 22, 1933; *Literary Digest,* January 7, 1933.

21. Akira Iriye, *The Cambridge History of American Foreign Relations,* Vol. 3, *The Globalizing of America, 1913–1945* (Cambridge, England, and New York, 1993), pp. 64–65, 88–91, 120–121; Walter LaFeber, *The American Age: United States Foreign Policy at Home and Abroad Since 1750* (New York and London: W. W. Norton, 1989), pp. 324–326; Carlisle, *Hearst and the New Deal,* p. 47.

22. Stephen Constantine, "The Buy British Campaign of 1931," *Journal of Advertising History,* Vol. 10, No. 1 (1981): 44–59; *NYT,* February 26, December 24, 1933; Ian M. Drummond, *British Economic Policy and the Empire, 1919–1939* (London: George Allen and Unwin, Ltd., 1972), pp. 36–37, 66–67.

23. *NYT,* February 2, 1933.

24. *NYT,* March 28, 1933.

25. *NYT,* October 31, 1933.

26. *SFE,* December 30, 1932; January 4, 1933.

27. Isaac F. Marcosson, "Britain's Purse Strings," *Saturday Evening Post* (November 18, 1933): 16–17, 96–97.

28. Foreign Commerce Department, Chamber of Commerce of the United States, " 'Buy National' Movements in Relation to Domestic and Foreign Trade,"

(Washington, DC: Chamber of Commerce of the United States, 1933), pp. 3–4, Accession 1960, Chamber of Commerce of the United States Records, Series II, Publications, Box 14, Hagley Museum and Library, Wilmington, Delaware.

29. *NYT,* October 5, 1932; see also *NYT,* February 8, 1933; *Pittsburgh Courier,* February 18, 1933; and *Cleveland Plain Dealer,* April 12, 1933, for awareness of Britain's campaign.

30. James Goodwin Hodgson, *Economic Nationalism* (New York: H. W. Wilson, 1933), p. 3; Iriye, *Cambridge History,* pp. 99–100.

31. Hodgson, *Economic Nationalism,* p. 9.

32. Hodgson, *Economic Nationalism,* p. 122.

33. For a sympathetic treatment of economic nationalism and Smoot-Hawley that differs from my own, see Alfred E. Eckes, Jr., *Opening America's Market: U.S. Foreign Trade Policy Since 1776* (Chapel Hill: University of North Carolina, 1995).

34. *NYT,* April 16, 1935.

35. Quote: *Cleveland Plain Dealer,* March 2, 1933; see also January 4, February 7, 8, March 21, 22, 23, 31, April 12, 1933; *SFE,* December 30, 1932, January 1, 6, 21, 1933.

36. *SFE,* January 2, 1933.

37. C. K. Alexander, Edwin M. Fitch, and Haldor R. Mohat, *The Truth About "BUY AMERICAN"* (Madison, WI: Research Associates, 1933), p. 4. See also *NYT,* February 7, 1933.

38. *Richmond* (publication of the Richmond Chamber of Commerce), Vol. 7, No. 5 (November 1920): 1, 3; Vol. 7, No. 7 (January 1921): 1; Vol. 8, No. 4 (October 1921): 2, 10; Vol. 8, No. 5 (November 1921): 10, 16; in the Virginia Historical Society. I am grateful to Barbara Bair for sharing this material with me.

39. *NYT,* May 11, 1933.

40. *NYT,* March 25, May 11, 1933.

41. *NYT,* March 5, 1933.

42. Alexander, et al., *The Truth About "BUY AMERICAN,"* p. 1; see also *SFE,* January 4, 1933, for Buy California.

43. Donna E. Goehle, "The Buy American Act: Is It Irrelevant in a World of Multinational Corporations?," *Columbia Journal of World Business,* Vol. 24, No. 4 (Winter 1989): 10–11; Morton Pomeranz, "Toward a New International Order in Government Procurement," *Law and Policy in International Business,* Vol. 11, No. 4 (1979): 130–133; Rene De La Pedraja, *A Historical Dictionary of the U.S. Merchant Marine and Shipping Industry Since the Introduction of Steam* (Westport, CT: Greenwood Press, 1994), pp. 18–09, 286–287; *SFE,* December 31, 1932; *NYT,* June 12, 1927, and February 6, 1932; "Government Procurement of American Goods," Hearing of the House Committee on Interstate and Foreign Commerce, April 26 and 27, 1928 (Washington, DC: Government Printing Office, 1928); "Transportation of Coal—Department Letter," Published Hearing, February 5, 1907, 59th Congress (1906–1907), Collation, pp. 451–461 (Congressional Information Service Document No. H46–0.68).

44. *Washington Post,* February 5, 1933.

45. Goehle, "The Buy American Act," pp. 10–11; Pomeranz, "Toward a New International Order in Government Procurement," pp. 130–133; *Congressional Record,* Senate, January 31, 1933 (73rd Congress) (Washington, DC: Government Printing Office, 1933), pp. 2985–2986; January 24, 1933, pp. 2356–2359; February 2, 1933, pp. 3171–3177; *NYT,* January 11, 17, 19, 20, February 3, 4, 1933; *Washington Post,* February 5, 1933.

46. "Government Procurement of American Goods," pp. 12–13.

47. "Government Procurement of American Goods," pp. 12–13.

48. *Congressional Record,* U.S. Senate, February 2, 1933, p. 3175.

49. *NYT,* November 12, 1933 (quote); August 9, 1936; Albert Nelson Marquis, *Who's Who in America,* Vol. 19 (1936–1937) (Chicago: The A. N. Marquis Co., 1936), p. 739.

50. Quote: *NYT,* April 5, 1936. On the Made in America Club: *NYT,* April 5, August 9, 1936; February 21, July 4, November 11, 1937; *New York American,* October 7, 1935; Francis X. A. Eble to Francis P. Garvan, March 15, 1934, in Francis Garvan Collection, Box 26, Folder 4, University of Wyoming Archives, Laramie, Wyoming; Eble to Garvan, September 13, 1935, December 19, 1935, October 8, 1936, all in Box 12, Folder 4; "Made in America Club, Inc., Statement of Cash Receipts and Disbursements, January 15, 1936," Box 12, Folder 4; Francis P. Garvan to William Randolph Hearst, January 7, 1935, Box 12, Folder 4. I am grateful to Thomas Ferguson for generously sharing this material with me. See Thomas Ferguson, "Industrial Conflict and the Coming of the New Deal: The Triumph of Multinational Liberalism in America," in Steve Fraser and Gary Gerstle, eds., *The Rise and Fall of the New Deal Order, 1930–1980* (Princeton, NJ: Princeton University Press, 1989), pp. 3–31.

51. Eble to Garvan, September 13, 1935.

52. Garvan to Hearst, January 7, 1935.

53. Quote: Selig Perlman, *A Theory of the Labor Movement* (New York: Macmillan, 1928), p. 232; Bernstein, *The Lean Years;* David Montgomery, *The Fall of the House of Labor: The Workplace, the State, and American Labor Activism, 1865–1925* (New York: Cambridge University Press, 1987); Dana Frank, *Purchasing Power: Consumer Organizing, Gender, and the Seattle Labor Movement, 1919–1929* (New York: Cambridge University Press, 1994).

54. Bernstein, *The Lean Years,* pp. 334–357.

55. Charles William Vear, "Organized Labor and the Tariff," Ph.D. Diss.,

Fletcher School of Law and Diplomacy, 1955, pp. 1–90.

56. F. B. Gebhart to William Green, July 30, 1934, AFL-CIO Legislative Department Records, Box D1/A/27, Folder 1/27/38, George Meany Archives, Silver Spring, Maryland.

57. "Resolution No. 10, Eastern Conference Board of the United Cement Workers of the Eastern District, to the National Council of United Cement Workers," n.d. [1937], AFL-CIO Legislative Dept., Box D1/A/27, Folder 1/17/41; Ira Weimer to William Green, n.d. [1932], AFL-CIO Legislative Dept. Records, Box D1/A/27, Folder 1/27/41.

58. Testimony of Frederick Donohoe, "Government Procurement of American Goods," p. 14.

59. *SFE,* January 1, 5, 1933.

60. *NYT,* July 7, 1938.

61. *American Federationist,* Vol. 44, No. 12 (December 1937): 1365.

62. *American Federationist,* Vol. 45, No. 12 (December 1938): 1341.

63. *American Federationist,* Vol. 47, Pt. 2, No. 2 (August 1940): 23.

64. *American Federationist,* Vol. 48, No. 5 (May 1941): 20. See also Vol. 45, No. 9 (September 1938): 983; Vol. 46, No. 9 (September 1939): 985; *NYT,* April 15, 1935.

65. Frank, *Purchasing Power,* pp. 209–210.

66. *American Federationist,* Vol. 37, No. 5 (May 1930): 581–582.

67. *SFE,* January 5, 1933.

68. *SFE,* December 28, 1933.

69. Ibid.

70. *SFE,* January 2, 1933.

71. *SFE,* December 29, 1932.

72. *SFE,* December 29, 1932.

73. *SFE,* January 3, 1933.

74. *SFE,* January 1, 1933.

75. *SFE,* December 31, 1932.

76. *SFE,* January 1, 1933.

77. "Government Purchase of American Goods," p. 14.

78. *SFE,* January 1, 1933.

79. *SFE,* January 4, 1933.

80. *SFE,* February 23, 1933.

81. Senate Committee on Interstate Commerce, Hearings on the "Buy American" Act, 1939, pp. 106, 120.

82. John Higham, *Strangers in the Land: Patterns of American Nativism* (New York, NY: Athaneum, 1963); William Preston, Jr., *Aliens and Dissenters: Federal Suppression of Radicals, 1903–1933* (Cambridge, MA: Harvard University Press, 1963); Kenneth Jackson, *The Ku Klux Klan in the City, 1915–1930* (New York: Oxford, 1967), p. 236; Kathleen Blee, *Women of the Klan: Racism and Gender in the 1920s* (Berkeley: University of California Press, 1991).

83. Quoted in Roger Daniels, *The Politics of Prejudice: The Anti-Japanese Movement in California and the Struggle for Japanese Exclusion* (Berkeley: University of California Press, 1962), p. 70.

84. *San Francisco Chronicle,* August 26, 1907.

85. *San Francisco Chronicle,* August 26, 1907. For the Yellow Peril and Hearst's role, see Roger Daniels, *The Politics of Prejudice;* see also Gary Y. Okihiro, *Cane Fires: The Anti-Japanese Movement in Hawaii, 1865–1945* (Philadelphia: Temple University Press, 1991).

86. Daniels, *The Politics of Prejudice,* p. 78.

87. On Washington, Frank, *Purchasing Power,* p. 171; on California, Daniels, *The Politics of Prejudice,* pp. 46–64.

88. Quoted in Daniels, *The Politics of Prejudice,* p. 97.

89. Lothrop Stoddard, *The Rising Tide of Color Against White World-Supremacy* (New York: Charles Scribner's Sons, 1920); Daniels, *The Politics of Prejudice,* p. 68.

90. Stoddard, *The Rising Tide of Color,* pp. vi, 297–298.

91. *SFE,* December 18, 1932.

92. *Washington Post,* February 9, 1933.

93. A. W. Mitchell to William Green, November 28, 1934, in AFL-CIO Legis-

lative Dept. Records, Box D1/A/27, Folder 1/27/38.

94. George J. Sánchez, *Becoming Mexican American: Ethnicity, Culture, and Identity in Chicano Los Angeles, 1900–1945* (New York: Oxford University Press), p. 211; *SFE*, February 2, 4, 5, 1933. For anti-immigrant sentiments in the 1930s, see also Isaac F. Marcosson, "The Alien in America," *Saturday Evening Post* (April 6, 1935): 22–23, 110, 112–113; Raymond G. Carroll, "The Alien on Relief," *Saturday Evening Post* (January 11, 1936): 16–17, 100–101; Carroll, "Alien Workers in America," *Saturday Evening Post* (January 25, 1936): 23, 82, 84–86, 89; Louis Adamic, "Aliens and Alien-Baiters," *Harpers Magazine* (November 1936): 561–574. My thanks to Anne Woo-Sam for these last references.

95. *SFE*, December 28, 1932.

96. *The Nation* (April 22, 1931): 437; see also *The Nation* (April 29, 1931): 170.

97. Abraham Hoffman, *Unwanted Mexican Americans in the Great Depression: Repatriation Pressures, 1929–1939* (Tucson: University of Arizona Press, 1974), especially pp. 39–40 on Doak; George J. Sánchez, *Becoming Mexican American,* pp. 209–226.

98. Commission on Wartime Relocation and Internment of Civilians, *Personal Justice Denied* (Washington, DC: Commission on the Wartime Relocation and Internment of Civilians, 1982), p. 100.

99. Daniels, *The Politics of Prejudice,* p. 139, fn. 7.

4. No Thanks, Mr. Hearst

1. *Chicago Defender,* January 8, 1933. I am grateful to Eric Arnesen for sharing this citation with me.

2. *Chicago Defender,* February 25, 1933.

3. *Chicago Defender,* February 4, 1933.

4. *Chicago Defender,* March 18, 1933.

5. *Chicago Defender,* January 28, 1933.

6. *Pittsburgh Courier,* January 7, 1933.

7. *Chicago Defender,* February 4, 1933.

8. *Chicago Defender,* January 26, 1933.

9. *Pittsburgh Courier,* January 18, 1933.

10. *Houston Informer,* March 18, 1933. On immigrants, see also *Pittsburgh Courier,* January 7, 1933; *Chicago Defender,* May 29, 25, 1933.

11. Raymond Wolters, *Negroes and the Great Depression* (Westport, CT: Greenwood Press, 1970); Horace Cayton and St. Clair Drake, *Black Metropolis: A Study of Negro Life in a Northern City* (New York: Harcourt Brace & Co., 1945); Mark Naison, *Communists in Harlem During the Depression* (Urbana: University of Illinois, 1983); Cheryl Greenberg, *"Or Does It Explode?" Black Harlem in the Great Depression* (New York: Oxford, 1991); William H. Harris, *The Harder We Run: Black Workers Since the Civil War* (New York, NY: Oxford University Press, 1982), pp. 95–113.

12. Albert Shankman, *Ambivalent Friends: Afro-Americans View the Immigrant* (Westport, CT: Greenwood Press, 1982), p. 49.

13. August Meier and Elliot Rudwick, "The Origins of Nonviolent Direct Action in Afro-American Protest: A Note on Historical Discontinuities," in *Along the Color Line: Explorations in the Black Experience* (Urbana: University of Illinois, 1976), pp. 307–404; Gary Jerome Hunter, " 'Don't Buy From Where You Can't Work': Black Urban Boycott Movements During the Depression, 1929–1941," Ph.D. Diss., University of Michigan, 1977; Kimberley Phillips, "Heaven Bound: Black Migration, Community, and Activism in Cleveland, 1915–1945," Ph.D. Diss., Yale University, 1992, pp. 226–281; Andor Skotnes, " 'Buy Where You Can Work': Boycotting for Jobs in African-American Baltimore, 1933–34," *Journal of Social History,* Vol. 27, No. 4 (Summer 1994): 735–761; Ralph L. Crowder, " 'Don't Buy Where You Can't Work': An Investigation of the Political Forces and Social Conflict Within the

Harlem Boycott of 1934," *Afro-Americans in New York Life and History,* Vol. 15, No. 2 (July 1991): 7–44; Christopher G. Wye, "Merchants of Tomorrow: The Other Side of the 'Don't Spend Your Money Where You Can't Work' Movement," *Ohio History* 93 (Winter-Spring 1984): 40–67; Naison, *Communists in Harlem During the Depression,* pp. 50–51, 102; Greenberg, *"Or Does It Explode?,"* pp. 114–139; Michele Pacifico, " 'Don't Buy Where You Can't Work': The New Negro Alliance of Washington," *Washington History* 6 (Spring/Summer 1994).

14. Hunter, " 'Don't Buy From Where You Can't Work,' " p. 83.

15. Meier and Rudwick, "The Origins of Nonviolent Direct Action," p. 317; Hunter, " 'Don't Buy From Where You Can't Work,' " pp. 77–108.

16. Quoted in Skotnes, " 'Buy Where You Can Work,' " p. 744.

17. Quoted in Skotnes, " 'Buy Where You Can Work,' " p. 744; Skotnes; Hunter, " 'Don't Buy From Where You Can't Work,' " pp. 109–127.

18. Quoted in Meier & Rudwick, "The Origins of Nonviolent Direct Action," p. 323.

19. Quoted in Greenberg, *"Or Does It Explode?,"* p. 118.

20. *Houston Informer,* February 18, 1933.

21. For economic nationalism in the African American community, see Darlene Clark Hine, "The Housewives' League of Detroit: Black Women and Economic Nationalism," in *Hine Sight: Black Women and the Re-Construction of American History* (Brooklyn: Carlson Publishing, 1994), pp. 129–145; Hunter, " 'Don't Buy From Where You Can't Work,' " p. 83.

22. Quoted in Greenberg, *"Or Does It Explode?,"* pp. 117–118.

23. Quoted in Hine, "The Detroit Housewives' League," p. 139.

24. Costonie quotes: in Skotnes, " 'Buy Where You Can Work,' " p. 731;

Hunter, " 'Don't Buy From Where You Can't Work,' " p. 114. On Garvey, see Tony Martin, *Race First: The Ideological and Organizational Struggle of the Marcus Garvey and the Universal Negro Improvement Association* (Dover, MA: Majority Press, 1976); Theodore G. Vincent, *Black Power and the Garvey Movement* (San Francisco: Ramparts Press, 1972); Judith Stein, *The World of Marcus Garvey: Race and Class in Modern Society* (Baton Rouge: Louisiana State University Press, 1986). On Sufi Abdul Hamid and Arthur Reid, other charismatic nationalist leaders, as well as Costonie, see Crowder, " 'Don't Buy Where You Can't Work,' " pp. 14–15, 18–19, 21–22; Hunter, " 'Don't Buy From Where You Can't Work,' " pp. 85–87, 104–105, n. 24, 179–180; Skotnes, " 'Buy Where You Can Work,' " pp. 735–739; Naison, *Communists in Harlem During the Depression,* p. 100; Meier and Rudwick, "The Origins of Nonviolent Direct Action," p. 323; Greenberg, *"Or Does It Explode?,"* pp. 120–123; Roi Ottley, *New World A-Coming: Inside Black America* (Chicago: World Publishing Co., 1943), pp. 118–121.

25. Kimberley Phillips, "Heaven Bound," pp. 226–281.

26. Phillips, "Heaven Bound," pp. 226–281 (quote, p. 253).

27. Phillips, "Heaven Bound," p. 277.

28. E. D. Coblentz to William Randolph Hearst, January 11, 1933, in William Randolph Hearst Papers, Business Correspondence, 77/121, Carton 17 Folder "Samples 1933," Bancroft Library, Berkeley, California; see also Hearst to Coblentz, January 20, 1933. I am grateful to David Nasaw for sharing these materials with me. For the Hearst-Roosevelt exchange, see also Carlisle, *Hearst and the New Deal,* pp. 70–72.

29. On the underconsumptionists and the New Deal, Michael A. Bernstein, *The Great Depression and Economic Change: America, 1929–1939* (Cambridge, England: Cambridge University Press, 1987).

30. Robert H. Zieger, *The CIO, 1935–1955* (Chapel Hill, NC: University of North Carolina Press, 1995), p. 94; Foster Rhea Dulles and Melvyn Dubofsky, *Labor in America: A History,* 4th Ed. (Arlington Heights, IL: Harlan Davidson, 1984), p. 297.

31. Sharon Hartman Strom, "Challenging 'Woman's Place': Feminism, the Left, and Industrial Unionism in the 1930s," *Feminist Studies* 9 (1983): 359–386; on the CIO and women, see Ruth Milkman, *Gender at Work: The Dynamics of Job Segregation by Sex During World War II* (Urbana, IL: University of Illinois Press, 1987); Vicki L. Ruiz, *Cannery Women, Cannery Lives: Mexican Women, Unionization, and the California Food Processing Industry, 1930–1950* (Albuquerque, NM: University of New Mexico Press, 1987). For UCAPAWA, see Ruiz. For an overview of the literature on the CIO's race relations between white and African American men, see Michael Goldfield, "Race and the CIO: The Possibilities for Racial Egalitarianism During the 1930s and 40s," *International Labor and Working-Class History* 44 (1993): 1–32.

32. *NYT,* May 23, 1936.

33. Walter LaFeber, *The American Age: United States' Foreign Policy at Home and Abroad Since 1750* (New York: W. W. Norton, 1989), p. 355.

34. LaFeber, *The American Age,* pp. 355–356; Sidney Lens, *The Forging of the American Empire* (New York: Thomas Y. Crowell, 1971), p. 299; William Appleman Williams, *The Tragedy of American Diplomacy,* Revised and Expanded Edition (New York: Delta, 1962), p. 168.

35. LaFeber, *The American Age,* p. 356; Williams, *Tragedy of American Diplomacy,* pp. 160–200; Thomas Ferguson, "Industrial Conflict and the Coming of the New Deal: The Triumph of Multinational Liberalism in America," in Steve Fraser and Gary Gerstle, eds., *The Rise and Fall of the New Deal Order, 1930–1980* (Princeton,

NJ: Princeton University Press, 1989), pp. 3–31.

36. *NYT,* May 23, 1936.

37. Ferguson, "Industrial Conflict and the Coming of the New Deal," p. 9; *NYT,* December 11, 1933. See also February 19, 1933, letter to the editor from Arthur L. Walker.

38. *San Francisco Chronicle,* January 30, 1933.

39. Maxwell S. Stuart, "Buy American!" *The Nation,* Vol. 136, No. 3527 (February 1933): 142–143.

40. *Cleveland Plain Dealer,* February 7, 1933.

41. *NYT,* February 5, 1933. See also *Cleveland Plain Dealer,* February 8, 1933.

42. *NYT,* January 18, 1932; see also *NYT,* May 25, 1936.

43. Stuart, "Buy American!" pp. 142–143.

44. *NYT,* May 23, 1936.

45. *San Francisco Chronicle,* January 25, 1933. See, for example, Hull's speech, *NYT,* May 23, 1933.

46. "Sure, Buy American!" *Business Week* (February 8, 1933): 32, reprinted in Hodgson, *Economic Nationalism,* pp. 190–191.

47. *NYT,* December 11, 1932.

48. Cordell Hull to William Green, August 8, 1934, AFL-CIO Legislative Dept. Records, Box D1/A/27, Folder 1/27/38, George Meany Archives, Silver Spring, MD.

49. For a summary of the jobs argument, see Helen Hill, *Foreign Trade and the Worker's Job,* Popular Pamphlets on World Problems, No. 1 (January 1935), World Peace Foundation, Boston and New York (in U.S. Labor Department Library).

50. *SFE,* January 7, 1933.

51. *SFE,* January 1, 1933.

52. Quoted in Williams, *Tragedy of American Diplomacy,* p. 170. See Williams, Chapter 5, for the broader argument regarding revolutionary avoidance.

53. See, for example, *SFE,* December

29, 1932. The "believe it or not" quote is from "Always Sell, Never Buy!," *The World Tomorrow*, Vol. 16, No. 2 (January 11, 1933): 31–32.

54. See, for example, *NYT*, December 27, 1932; *Chicago Defender*, May 20, 1933; Oliver Carlson and Ernest Sutherland Bates, *Hearst: Lord of San Simeon* (New York: Viking, 1936).

55. Carlson and Bates, *Hearst: Lord of San Simeon*, pp. 243–244; *National Cyclopedia of American Biography*, Vol. 39 (New York: James T. White Co., 1954), pp. 8–9; " 'Buy American' to Help Prosperity, Says W. R. Hearst," January 14, 1933.

56. C. V. Drew to National Foreign Trade Council, December 29, 1932, Hearings Before the Subcommittee of the Committee on Appropriations of the U.S. Senate on H.R. 13520, Treasury and Post Office Appropriations Bill, 1934 (Washington, DC: Government Printing Office, 1933), p. 106.

57. John Gutmann, "Declaration of Protest," 1934. A reproduction of the photograph appears in Lew Thomas, ed., *The Restless Decade: John Gutmann's Photographs of the Thirties* (New York: Harry Abrams, 1984), p. 60. Thomas lists the date as 1935; the cataloging information accompanying the photograph's exhibition at the San Francisco Museum of Modern Art lists the date as 1934 (Conversation with Doug Nichols, Museum of Modern Art, 1996). See also Gutmann's photograph "Anti-Fascist Posters" (1938), in Thomas, p. 61, which includes a "Boycott Japanese Goods" sign.

58. For more extended analyses of the mobilization of Chinese Americans in support of the war in China, as well as the anti-Japanese boycott in the United States, see Peter Kwong, *Chinatown, New York: Labor and Politics, 1930–1950* (New York: Monthly Review Press, 1979), pp. 95–112; Renqiu Yu, *To Save China, to Save Ourselves: The Chinese Hand Laundry Alliance of New York* (Philadelphia: Temple University Press, 1992), chs. 4–5; and Judy Yung, *Unbound Feet: A Social History*

of Chinese Women in San Francisco (Berkeley: University of California Press, 1995), pp. 224–248. I am grateful to Judy Yung for sharing research materials with me regarding relief activities in San Francisco. The New York citation is from Kwong, pp. 109–110; for unity within the community, see Kwong, pp. 106–107; Yung, p. 227.

59. Quote: "Anti-Japanese Boycott Still Strong at Hong Kong," *China Weekly Review* (May 7, 1932): 312. On the boycott in China, see also Paul K. Whang, "The Anti-Japanese Boycott and Its Effect upon Foreign Trade and Domestic Industry," *China Weekly Review* (September 17, 1932): 108–111; "South-Western China's Anti-Japanese Boycott Intensified," *China Weekly Review* (September 17, 1932): 112–119; and other issues of *China Weekly Review*.

60. Yung, *Unbound Feet*, p. 227.

61. Kwong, *Chinatown, New York*, p. 93.

62. Yu, *To Save China, to Save Ourselves*, pp. 77, 82.

63. Kwong, *Chinatown, New York*, p. 95; see also 93–94.

64. Yu, *To Save China, to Save Ourselves*, p. 102, and chapter 4.

65. Yung, *Unbound Feet*, p. 235.

66. Kwong, *Chinatown, New York*, p. 112. For the Communist Party and the boycott, see *New Masses*, October 5, 1937, p. 9; October 12, 1937, p. 13; February 15, 1938, pp. 13–14; Aug. 9, 1938, p. 11; Sept. 20, 1938, pp. 10–12; Bertram Loeb, "Young America Aids China," *China Today*, Vol. 4 No. 7 (April 1938): 12–13; Vol. 5, No. 6 (March 1939): 19, and passim; see also *Daily Worker*, 1938.

67. "Boycott Japanese Goods!," *The Nation* (August 28, 1937): 211–212; Freda Utley, "Japan Fears a Boycott," *The Nation* (October 2, 1937): 341–342; "Case for the Boycott," *The Nation* (November 6, 1937): 492–493; "The Boycott Is Winning," *The Nation* (January 8, 1938): 33–34; "Does the Boycott Hurt American Labor?" *The Nation* (February 5, 1938);

H. C. Englelbrecht, "America's Gift to Aggressors," *The Nation* (April 9, 1938): 407–410; Freda Kirchwey, "Let's Mind Our Own Business," *The Nation* (February 15, 1939): 421–422.

68. R. A. Howell, "The World's Greatest Boycott," *China Today*, Vol. 4, No. 6 (March 1938); "The Boycott Is Winning," *The Nation* (January 8, 1938): 33; "Did Your Stockings Kill Babies?" pamphlet, Boycott Japanese Goods Committee of Greater Boston, 1938 (Boston, 1938), Vertical File, Taminent Institute Library, New York University, New York, NY.

69. Utley, "Japan Fears a Boycott," p. 341; Leonard Sparks and Mississippi Johnson, "Put Silk in Doghouse," *New Masses* (November 30, 1937): 13.

70. *Time* (January 10, 1938): 42–43; see also *Life* (January 10, 1938): 18.

71. Kwong, *Chinatown, New York,* p. 95.

72. Mary Bein, "Hollywood Chants 'Boycott Japan,' " *China Today,* Vol. 5, No. 4 (January 1939): 8–9, 15.

73. *China Today,* Vol. 4, No. 9 (June 1938): 2.

74. *Time* (January 10, 1938): 42–43.

75. George Kuo, "Japanese Pour Funds into America to Block Silk Boycott," *China Weekly Review* (April 16, 1938): 198; Harry B. Price, "Embargo–A Nationwide Effort," *China Today,* Vol. 5, No. 1 (October 1938): 6.

76. For more sophisticated analyses of Chinese American nationalism, see Yung, *Unbound Feet,* p. 236; Yu, *To Save China, to Save Ourselves,* pp. 82, 87, 101, 118, and passim.

77. Moshe Gottlieb, "The Anti-Nazi Boycott Movement in the United States: An Ideological and Sociological Appreciation," *Jewish Social Studies,* Vol. 35, Nos. 3–4 (July–October 1973): 198–227; William Orbach, "Shattering the Shackles of Powerlessness: The Debate Surrounding the Anti-Nazi Boycott of 1933–41," *Modern Judaism,* Vol. 2, No. 2 (1982): 149–169.

78. Interview by the author with James Shizuru, Los Altos, Calif., February 18, 1998.

5. Making the World Safe for American Products

1. Telephone interview by the author with Larry Russell, July 22, 1997; George Meany to Larry Russell, March 22, 1961, in Records of the AFL-CIO Legislative Department, Box 6, Folder 26, AFL-CIO Records, George Meany Memorial Archives, Silver Spring, Maryland.

2. Meany to Russell, March 22, 1961.

3. Ibid.

4. On the United States' relative position: Barry Bluestone and Bennett Harrison, *The Deindustrialization of America: Plant Closing, Community Abandonment, and the Dismantling of Basic Industry* (New York: Basic Books, 1982), pp. 112–113. My interpretation in the sections that follow draws on Joyce and Gabriel Kolko, *The Limits of Power: The World and United States Foreign Policy, 1945–1954,* especially Chapter 23; Thomas J. McCormick, *America's Half-Century: United States Foreign Policy in the Cold War and After,* 2nd Ed. (Baltimore: The Johns Hopkins University Press, 1995); Walter LaFeber, *The American Age: United States Foreign Policy at Home and Abroad Since 1750* (New York: W. W. Norton, 1989); Philip Armstrong, Andrew Glyn, and John Harrison, *Capitalism Since 1945* (Oxford, England, 1991).

5. Acheson quote: Dean Acheson, "The Marshall Plan; Relief and Reconstruction Are Chiefly Matters of American Self-Interest" (May 8, 1947), excerpted from *Dept. of State Bulletin,* Vol. 16, pp. 991–994, in Walter LaFeber, ed., *America in the Cold War: Twenty Years of Revolutions and Response, 1947–1967* (New York: John Wiley & Sons, 1969).

6. On Bretton Woods, Thomas Ferguson and Joel Rogers, "The Reagan Victory: Corporate Coalitions in the 1980

Campaign," in Ferguson and Rogers, eds., *The Hidden Election: Politics and Economics in the 1980 Presidential Campaign* (New York: Pantheon Books, 1981), p. 11; McCormick, *America's Half-Century*, pp. 32–53; Bluestone and Harrison, *The Deindustrialization of America*, p. 113.

7. Armstrong, Glyn, and Harrison, *Capitalism Since 1945*, pp. 30–31, 154; LaFeber, *The American Age*, p. 556; Alfred E. Eckes, Jr., *Opening America's Market: U.S. Foreign Trade Policy Since 1776* (Chapel Hill, NC: University of North Carolina Press, 1995), pp. 178–229; John W. Evans, *The Kennedy Round in American Trade Policy: Twilight of the GATT?* (Cambridge, MA: Harvard University Press, 1971).

8. Armstrong, Harrison, and Glyn, *Capitalism Since 1945*, p. 161.

9. Anthony DiFilippo, *Military Spending and Industrial Decline: A Study of the American Machine Tool Industry* (Westport, CT: Greenwood Press, 1986), p. 64; for the machine tool industry, see also Max Holland, *When the Machine Stopped: A Cautionary Tale from Industrial America* (Boston: Harvard Business School Press, 1989), p. 38.

10. John Agnew, *The United States in the World-Economy: A Regional Geography* (Cambridge, England: Cambridge University Press, 1987), p. 375.

11. David Brody, *Workers in Industrial America: Essays on the Twentieth Century Struggle* (New York: Oxford University Press, 1980), pp. 172–257; James Green, *The World of the Worker: Labor in Twentieth Century America* (New York: Hill and Wang, 1980), p. 194. For the CIO during World War II, Nelson Lichtenstein, *Labor's War at Home: The CIO in World War II* (New York: Cambridge University Press, 1982).

12. Robert H. Zeiger, *The CIO 1935–1955* (Chapel Hill, NC: University of North Carolina Press, 1995), pp. 211, 214–227; Nelson Lichtenstein, "From Corporatism to Collective Bargaining:

Organized Labor and the Eclipse of Social Democracy in the Postwar Era," in Steve Fraser and Gary Gerstle, eds., *The Rise and Fall of the New Deal Order, 1930–1980* (Princeton, NJ: Princeton University Press, 1989), pp. 122–154; Green, *The World of the Worker*, p. 194; Foster Rhea Dulles and Melvyn Dubofsky, *Labor in America: A History*, 4th Ed. (Arlington Heights, IL: Harlan Davidson, 1984), p. 340.

13. Bert Cochran, *Labor and Communism: The Conflict That Shaped American Unions* (Princeton, NJ: Princeton University Press, 1977); Lichtenstein, *Labor's War at Home*, p. 80; Steve Rosswurm, *The CIO's Left-Led Unions* (New Brunswick, NJ: Rutgers University Press, 1992), p. 2; Ronald L. Filippelli and Mark D. McColloch, *Cold War in the Working Class: The Rise and Decline of the United Electrical Workers* (Albany: State University of New York, 1995).

14. Nelson Lichtenstein, *The Most Dangerous Man in Detroit: Walter Reuther and the Fate of American Labor* (New York: Basic Books, 1995), pp. 277–281; Green, *The World of the Worker*, pp. 194–209; Brody, *Workers in Industrial America*, pp. 188–198.

15. Quoted in Toni Gilpin, "Left by Themselves: A History of the United Farm Equipment and Metal Workers Unions, 1938–1955," Ph.D. Diss., Yale University, 1992, pp. 257–258.

16. Kim Moody, *An Injury to All: The Decline of American Unions* (New York: Verso, 1988), p. 55.

17. Gilpin, "Left by Themselves," (quote, p. 277).

18. Richard A. Lester, *As Unions Mature: An Analysis of the Evolution of American Unionism* (Princeton, NJ: Princeton University Press, 1958), pp. 56–57.

19. On the AFL, CIO, and foreign policy, see Victor Silverman, *Imagining Internationalism in American and British Labor, 1939–1949* (forthcoming, University

of Illinois Press); Ronald Radosh, *American Labor and U.S. Foreign Policy* (New York: Random House, 1969); Jack Scott, *Yankee Unions, Go Home! How the AFL Helped the U.S. Build an Empire in Latin America* (Vancouver, British Columbia: New Star Books, 1978); Beth Sims, *Workers of the World Undermined: American Labor's Role in U.S. Foreign Policy* (Boston: South End Press, 1992); John P. Windmuller, "Foreign Affairs and the AFL-CIO," *Industrial and Labor Relations Review,* Vol. 9 (1956): 419–432; Windmuller, "Labor: A Partner in American Foreign Policy?" *The Annals of the American Academy of Political and Social Science,* Vol. 350 (November 1963): 104–114; Roy Godson, "The AFL Foreign Policy Making Process from the End of World War II to the Merger," *Labor History,* Vol. 16, No. 3 (Summer 1975); Robert Armstrong, Hank Frundt, Hobart Spalding, and Sean Sweeney, *Working Against Us: The American Institute for Free Labor Development (AIFLD) and the International Policy of the AFL-CIO* (New York: North American Congress on Latin America, n.d.).

20. Quoted in Peter Donohue, "From 'Free Trade' to 'Fair Trade': Trade Liberalization's Endorsement and Subsequent Rejection by the American Federation of Labor and Congress of Industrial Organizations, 1934–1975," Ph.D. Diss., University of Texas, Austin, 1986. On AFL, CIO, and AFL-CIO trade policy, Donohue; Charles Vear, "Organized Labor and the Tariff," Ph.D. Diss., Fletcher School of Law and Diplomacy, 1955; Donohue, " 'Free Trade' Unions and the State: Trade Liberalization's Endorsement by the AFL-CIO, 1943–1962," *Research in Political Economy,* Vol. 13 (1992): 1–73; Solomon Barkin, "Labor's Position on Tariff Reduction," *Industrial Relations,* Vol. 1, No. 3 (May 1962): 49–63; Daniel J. B. Mitchell, *Essays on Labor and International Trade* (Los Angeles: Institute of Industrial Relations, University of California, Los Angeles, 1970); Andrew J.

Biermiller to John Hawk, April 24, 1957, in Records of the AFL-CIO Legislative Dept., Box 27, Folder 43, George Meany Memorial Archives, Silver Spring, Maryland; George Meany to Robert Doughton, January 17, 1951, AFL-CIO Legis. Dept., Box D1/B/15 Folder 1/51/34; CIO press release May 19, 1953, "CIO Calls for Year Extension of Reciprocal Trade Agreements," AFL-CIO Legis. Dept. Box 52, Folder 1.

21. "Statement by George Meany, president of American Federation of Labor, Recommendations Regarding Tariff Negotiations Between the United Sates and the Contracting Parties to the *General Agreement on Tariffs and Trade* Submitted to the Committee on Reciprocity Information, November 8, 1955," in AFL-CIO Legis. Dept. Box 42, Folder 1; Donohue, "From 'Free Trade' to 'Fair Trade,' " pp. 53–211; Vear, "Organized Labor and the Tariff," pp. 22–350.

22. *AFL-CIO Looks at Foreign Trade . . . A Policy for the Sixties* (Washington, DC: AFL-CIO Dept. of Research, 1961), p. 126.

23. See, for example, Walter Reuther to John F. Kennedy, July 7, 1954, AFL-CIO Legis. Dept., Box 52, Folder 1.

24. *AFL-CIO Looks at Foreign Trade,* p. 127 (emphasis in original); on the AFL-CIO and the Trade Expansion Act of 1962, see Donohue, "From 'Free Trade' to 'Fair Trade,' " pp. 196–207. On Kennedy's response, see Eckes, Jr., *Opening America's Market,* p. 186; Donohue, "From 'Free Trade' to 'Fair Trade' "; Andrew J. Biermiller to Jacob K. Javits, August 8, 1960, AFL-CIO Legis. Dept., Box D1/A/20 Folder 1/20/41.

25. "The Trade Expansion Drive," *Electrical Workers' Journal* (April 1964): 12–15, 103–104 (quote, p. 12); "The Impact of Foreign Trade on IBEW," *Electrical Workers' Journal* (April 1962): 6–9, 28.

26. "Those Little Foreign Cars," *Electrical Workers' Journal* (November 1958): 22–24.

27. Quoted in Donohue, "From 'Free Trade' to 'Fair Trade,'" p. 131.

28. From the film *The Business of America,* produced and directed by Larry Adelman, Lawrence Daress, and Bruce Schmiechen, San Francisco, California Newsreel, 1984.

29. For Meany and AFL-CIO policy on the Buy American question, see also Memo to George Riley, February 16, 1953, AFL-CIO Legis. Dept., Box 6, Folder 26; Memo, W. C. Hushing re: Buy American Act, February 25, 1953, AFL-CIO Legis. Dept., Box 6, Folder 26.

30. *New York Times,* January 16, 1953.

31. *Wall Street Journal,* December 29, 1952.

32. Mohammad Siddieq Noorzoy, "An Analysis of the Buy American Policy," Ph.D. Diss., University of Washington, 1965; Burton I. Kaufman, *Trade and Aid: Eisenhower's Foreign Economic Policy, 1953–1961* (Baltimore: The Johns Hopkins University Press, 1982), pp. 44–45; New York *Journal of Commerce* (April 16, 20; June 4; September 4; October 19, 1953; December 20, 1954; February 22, 1955; November 17, 1959); *Wall Street Journal,* February 10, 1955. I am grateful to John Logan for sharing materials from the National Archives of Canada on this question.

33. "Copy of a Talk Delivered by Mr. Guy Nunn, Director of Radio and Television UAW on May 18, 1961, over the Detroit Television Station and Seventeen Broadcasting Stations in the United States," in AFL-CIO Legis. Dept., Box 6 Folder 26.

34. Quote: "Statement of Walter P. Reuther, President, United Automobile, Aircraft and Agricultural Implement Workers of America (UAW, AFL-CIO, before the Committee on Ways and Means, U.S. House of Representatives, March 20, 1962," in Records of the United Auto Workers Research Dept., Box 53, Walter Reuther Library, Archives of Labor and Urban Affairs, Wayne State University, Detroit, Michigan; for the United Auto Workers and the import question in the late fifties and early sixties, see "Trade Expansion and Trade Union Tactics," discussion paper, UAW International Affairs Dept., March 15, 1962, United Auto Workers Research Dept., Box 55; "VOLKSWAGEN— RENAULT—OLIVETTI— . . . Foreign Imports and American Jobs!" UAW Education Dept., n.d. [1958], UAW Research Dept., Box 55. For the United Steelworkers of America and the Buy American question, see Vear, "Organized Labor and the Tariff," p. 337.

35. *Oxnard Press-Courier,* July 31, 1959. My thanks to Frank Bardacke for sharing this tidbit with me.

36. Vear, "Organized Labor and the Tariff," pp. 240, 259, 273–274, 307–308, 353–354.

37. Quoted in Donohue, "From 'Free Trade' to 'Fair Trade,'" pp. 168–169; for protests within the AFL, see *Fishery Worker,* February 10, 1950. My thanks to Alan Bérubé for sharing the fish citation with me.

38. "Brief of Display and Smoking Pipe Workers Union, Local No. 21 625— A.F.L., For Submission to United States Tariff Commission," n.d. [1952?], in Records of the New York State Union Label Trades and Service Dept., Box 13, Folder 52, Robert F. Wagner Archives, Tamiment Library, New York University. See also "Hearing on Screen-Printed Silk Scarves," before the U.S. Tariff Commission, February 24, 1953, in New York State Union Label Trades Dept., Box 13, Folder 52.

39. *Justice* (February 1, 15; July 15, 1961; October 1, 1961; June 1–15, 1962; June 15, 1963); "Notes on AFL-CIO Research Directors Meeting on Foreign Trade," October 5, 1960, UAW Research Dept., Box 69, Folder "Foreign Trade— Competition." See also George E. Sokolsky, "Imports Are Threat to American Jobs," 1961, clipping in New York State Label Trades Dept., Box 13, Folder 45.

40. Harry Avrutin to Charles Phillips, September 21, 1955, in New York State

Union Label Trades Dept., Box 6, Folder 1.

41. Martin T. Lacey and James C. Quinn to AFL Local Unions, October 27, 1955, New York State Union Label Trades Dept., Box 6, Folder 1.

42. *The Potters Herald,* East Liverpool, Ohio (September 4, 1958), in Records of the Union Label Trades Department, AFL-CIO, Box 3, Folder 8, George Meany Archives.

43. Press Release, Union Label and Service Trades Department of the State of New York—AFL-CIO, May 24, 1920, in Records of the New York State Union Label Trades Dept., Box 12, Folder 16; Harry Avrutin to Samuel J. Talarico, October 15, 1963, in Records of the Union Label and Service Trades Department, AFL-CIO, Box 12, Folder 18; see the collection for annual programs and correspondence.

44. Radio Talk by Guy Nunn, May 18, 1961.

45. *Electrical Workers' Journal* (April 1962): 6.

46. Joseph Maraia to Harry Avrutin, March 23, 1961, New York State Union Label Trades Dept., Box 13, Folder 45.

47. Sam Johnson to Harry Avrutin, March 22, 1961, New York State Union Label Trades Dept., Box 13, Folder 45. See also Edward Gobey to Gentlemen, n.d.; Russell Post to Union Label and Trade Department of the State of New York, March 23, 1961; William Pekofsky to Union Label and Service Trades Dept. of the State of New York, March 27, 1961; Patrick De Longis to "Dear Sir," March 29, 1961; Rudolph Baisley to Union Label and Service Trades Dept. of the State of N.Y., n.d.; Theodore Raabe to "Dear Sir," April 15, 1961; Philip Bianco to Harry Avrutin, March 30, 1961, all in Box 13, Folder 45, New York State Union Label Trades Dept.

48. Interview with Larry Russell.

49. Carpenters' Local No. 266 to William Green, June 7, 1943, AFL-CIO Legis. Dept. Box 29, Folder 3.

50. Stanislaus County Central Labor Council to American Federation of Labor, December 29, 1944, AFL-CIO Legis. Dept., Box 29, Folder 4.

51. George Collins [Recording Secretary, Central Labor Council, Juneau, Alaska], "Greetings," March 30, 1945, AFL-CIO Legis. Dept., Box 29, Folder 4. For general wartime racism against the Japanese, John W. Dower, *War Without Mercy: Race and Power in the Pacific War* (New York: Pantheon Books, 1986); for both the war and postwar periods, David L. Abney, "Japan Bashing: A History of America's Anti-Japanese Acts, Attitudes and Laws," Ph.D. Diss., Arizona State University, 1995.

52. John J. Kearney to William Green, August 21, 1944, AFL-CIO Legis. Dept., Box 29, Folder 4; "Have Japanese Contributed to the Economic and Spiritual Development of the U.S.?" Address by John J. Kearney, Executive Secretary, Bartenders and Hotel Employees Local 34, Boston, Mass., 1944, AFL-CIO Legis. Dept., Box 29, Folder 4.

53. Arthur A. Rutledge to William Green, July 30, 1943; Rutledge to Green, August 7, 1943; Rutledge to *Catering Industry Employee,* July 31, 1943, all in AFL-CIO Legis. Dept., Box 29, Folder 3.

54. *Union Label,* Official Publication of the Union Label Council of New Jersey, Newark, New Jersey, January 18, 1946, in New York State Union Label Trades Dept., Box 10, Folder 49.

55. Ralph Golden to Members of all AFL Unions, January 18, 1946, New York State Union Label Trades Dept., Box 10, Folder 49.

56. "United States-Japanese Trade," Fact Sheet Prepared by the AFL-CIO Research Department, March 15, 1962, UAW Research Dept., Box 51, Folder "Economic Situation—Foreign vs. U.S., 1962."

57. William S. Borden, *The Pacific Alliance: U.S. Foreign Economic Policy and Japanese Trade Recovery, 1947–1955* (Madison:

University of Wisconsin Press, 1984); Michael Schaller, *The American Occupation of Japan: The Origins of the Cold War in Asia* (New York: Oxford University Press, 1985).

58. Walter B. Edgar, *South Carolina in the Modern Age* (Columbia, SC: University of South Carolina Press, 1992), pp. 91–92. Meany evidently opposed the South Carolina position; see George Meany to Taneo Maeda, July 10, 1946, AFL-CIO Legis. Dept., Box 29, Folder 6. A 1962 AFL-CIO Fact Sheet on "United States–Japanese Trade" wholeheartedly supported increased Japanese trade with the United States—"Japan Must Trade or Die"; "United States-Japanese Trade."

59. Leo Troy, *Trade Union Membership, 1897–1962* (New York: National Bureau of Economic Research, 1965), p. 1.

60. Quoted in Robert H. Zieger, "George Meany: Labor's Organization Man," in Melvyn Dubofsky and Warren Van Tine, *Labor Leaders in America* (Urbana: University of Illinois Press, 1987), p. 342.

61. *Historical Statistics of the United States: Colonial Times to 1970,* Vol. 1 (Washington, DC: United States Department of Commerce, Bureau of the Census, 1975), pp. 131–132.

62. U.S. Bureau of the Census, *Statistical Abstract of the United States: 1975* (Washington, DC: U.S. Dept. of Commerce, 1975), p. 371.

63. On the NAACP suits, see multiple studies by Herbert Hill, beginning with *Black Labor and the American Legal System* (Washington, DC: Bureau of National Affairs, 1977).

64. On the racial politics of the CIO and the purges, see, for example, Vicki L. Ruiz, *Cannery Women, Cannery Lives: Mexican Women, Unionization, and the California Food Processing Industry, 1930–1950* (Albuquerque: University of New Mexico Press, 1987); Nelson Lichtenstein and Robert Korstad, "Opportunities Found and Lost: Labor, Radicals, and the

Early Civil Rights Movement," *Journal of American History,* Vol. 75, No. 3 (December 1988): 786–811; Gilpin, "Left by Themselves"; Michael K. Honey, *Southern Labor and Black Civil Rights: Organizing Memphis Workers* (Urbana: University of Illinois Press, 1993); for an overview, Michael Goldfield, "Race and the CIO: The Possibilities for Racial Egalitarianism During the 1930s and 1940s," *International Labor and Working-Class History,* No. 44 (Fall 1993): 1–32.

65. On the Bracero Program the classic study is Ernesto Galarza, *Merchants of Labor: The Mexican Bracero Study* (Santa Barbara: McNally & Loftin, 1964).

66. Juan R. Garcia, *Operation Wetback: The Mass Deportation of Mexican Undocumented Workers in 1954* (Westport, CT: Greenwood Press, 1980).

67. William Leuchtenberg, *The Perils of Prosperity, 1914–1932* (Chicago: University of Chicago Press, 1958); John Kenneth Galbraith, *The Affluent Society* (Boston: Houghton Mifflin, 1958).

68. For an overview, see Fred Block, *The Origins of International Economic Disorder: A Study of U.S. International Monetary Policy from World War II to the Present* (Berkeley: University of California Press, 1977).

69. Seymour Melman, *The Permanent War Economy: American Capitalism in Decline* (New York: Simon and Schuster, 1974), p. 277.

70. Melman, *The Permanent War Economy;* DeFilippo, *Military Spending and Industrial Decline.*

71. Richard J. Barnet and Ronald E. Müller, *Global Reach: The Power of the Multinational Corporations* (New York: Simon and Schuster, 1974), p. 303.

72. Mira Wilkins, *The Maturing of Multinational Enterprise: American Business Abroad from 1944 to 1970* (Cambridge, MA: Harvard University Press, 1974); Richard J. Barnet and Ronald E. Müller, *Global Reach: The Power of the Multinational Corporations* (New York: Simon and Schuster,

1974); for the longer-term sapping of U.S. industry, Bluestone and Harrison, *The Deindustrialization of America*.

73. Quoted in Donohue, "From 'Free Trade' to 'Fair Trade,'" pp. 188–189.

74. Daniel J. B. Mitchell, "Labor and the Tariff Question," p. 274; "Statement Submitted by Walter P. Reuther, President, United Automobile, Aerospace and Agricultural Implement Workers of America (UAW) to the House Ways and Means Committee In Support of the Continuation of Adjustment Assistance Benefits . . ." July 2, 1968, UAW Research Dept., Box 90, Folder 7/2/68 Adjustment Assistance; Irving Bluestone to W. L. Ginsburg, September 11, 1963, UAW Research Dept., Box 55, Folder Imports and Exports 1962–63; William C. Shelton, "The Changing Attitude of U.S. Labor Unions Toward World Trade," *Monthly Labor Review* 9 (May 1970): 54.

6. So We'll Be Able to Make It in the U.S.A.

1. Leo Troy and Neil Sheflin, *U.S. Union Sourcebook: Membership, Finances, Structure, Directory*, 1st Ed. (West Orange, NJ: Industrial Relations Data and Information Services, 1985), p. 3–16; David Bensman and Roberta Lynch, *Rusted Dreams: Hard Times in a Steel Community* (New York: McGraw-Hill, 1987), p. 91; Bennett Harrison and Barry Bluestone, *The Great U-Turn: Corporate Restructuring and the Polarizing of America* (New York: Basic Books, 1988), p. 37; Barry Bluestone and Bennett Harrison, *The Deindustrialization of America: Plant Closings, Community Abandonment, and the Dismantling of Basic Industry* (New York: Basic Books, 1982).

2. For a summary of this transformation, see Harrison and Bluestone, *The Great U-Turn*.

3. International Ladies' Garment Workers' Union, Membership Census for Period 1902 to 1991, in possession of the author. My thanks to Walter Mankoff of UNITE! for sharing these statistics with me.

4. Richard Rothstein, *Keeping Jobs in Fashion: Alternatives to the Euthanasia of the U.S. Apparel Industry* (Washington, DC: Economic Policy Institute, 1989), pp. 34, 111.

5. On the ILGWU shift, see the Records of the International Ladies' Garment Workers' Union, Kheel Center for Labor-Management Documentation, Martin P. Catherwood Library, New York State School of Industrial and Labor Relations, Cornell University (hereafter ILGWU Records); for example, Wilbur Daniels to Louis Stulberg, July 8, 1971, Louis Stulberg Records (5780–4), Box 32, Folder 5, ILGWU Records; "Preliminary Public Relations Thinking," report amplifying Public Relations Project, 1971, Gus Tyler Records, Box 12, Folder 18, ILGWU Records; Gus Tyler to Henoch Mendelsund, December 21, 1971, and attached report, "A Proposed Strategy for the Import Problem," Stulberg Records (5780–4), Box 7, Folder 3; Report, "Union Label Department, 1972," Records of the New York Cloak Joint Board, Box 16, Folder 4, ILGWU Records; Gus Tyler, *Look for the Union Label: A History of the International Ladies' Garment Workers' Union* (Armonk, NY: M. E. Sharpe, 1995), pp. 262–300; Sol Chick Chaikin, *A Labor Viewpoint: Another Opinion* (New York: Library Research Associates, 1980); *Justice,* throughout the period. On the AFL-CIO, Peter Donohue, "From 'Free Trade' to 'Fair Trade': Trade Liberalization's Endorsement and Subsequent Rejection by the American Federation of Labor and Congress of Industrial Organizations," Ph.D. Diss., University of Texas at Austin, 1986, pp. 283–336.

6. On Burke-Hartke, see Donohue, "From 'Free Trade' to 'Fair Trade,'" pp. 302–335; Records of the AFL-CIO Leg-

islative Department, George Meany Archives, Silver Spring, Maryland. On ILGWU involvement, *Justice* (1971–1972); ILGWU Fair Trade Practices Department, "The Import Crisis: A Speaker's Manual," n.d., Tyler Records, Box 12, Folder 8; on the demonstration, *Los Angeles Times,* November 17, 1971; *Justice* (November 15, 1972).

7. Wilbur Daniels to Louis Stulberg, July 8, 1971, in Stulberg Records (5780–4), Box 32, Folder 5. See also Sol C. Chaikin to Louis Stulberg, August 2, 1971, Sol (Chick) Chaikin Records, Box 28, Folder 5, ILGWU Records; Kitty G. Dickerson, *Textiles and Apparel in the Global Economy,* 2nd Ed. (Englewood Cliffs, NJ: Prentice-Hall, 1995), pp. 349–355.

8. *Justice* (1971–1972); ILGWU Fair Trade Practices Department, "The Import Crisis: A Speaker's Manual," n.d., Tyler Records, Box 12, Folder 8; on the demonstration, *Los Angeles Times,* November 17, 1971; *Justice* (November 15, 1972).

9. "Preliminary Public Relations Thinking," "Amplification of Public Relations Projects," 1971, Tyler Records, Box 12, Folder 8. On local mobilizations, Matthew Schoenwald to All Area Coordinators and Assistants for Imports [sic] Demonstrations, February 8, 1973, Stulberg Records (5780–4), Box 2, Folder 7; Chaikin to Stulberg, August 2, 1971; "Dear _____" and attached "Activity Suggestions" [1972], New York Cloak Joint Board Records, Box 16, Folder 4; ILGWU Fair Trade Practices Department, "The Import Crisis: A Speaker's Manual."

10. For the ILGWU's label promotion program, see ILGWU Records, including memo, "Fourth Meeting, GEB, Montreal, Canada, May 12–15, 1958," in Records of David Dubinsky, Box 281–3B, ILGWU Records; Wilbur Daniels to "Msrs. Hochman, Crone, Glushien, Gronfein, Seaman, Stein, Zimny," June 1, 1959, Dubinsky Records, Box 281, Folder 3A; "Memorandum: 1967 ILGWU

Union Label Advertising Campaign," September 16, 1966," Stulberg Records (5780–4), Box 7, Folder 4B; Pamela V. Ulrich, "'Look for the Label'—The International Ladies' Garment Workers' Union Label Campaign, 1959–1975," *Clothing and Textiles Research Journal,* Vol. 13, No. 1 (1995): 49–56.

11. John Denaro to Louis Stulberg, October 1, 1974, and attached clipping, Denny Griswold, "Case Study No. 1454, How One Union Builds Preference for Its Products," Stulberg Records (5780–4), Box 7, Folder 2; Pamphlets, Eleanor Lambert and Diana Callaway, *College Wardrobe: A Guide to the Right Clothes for Where You Are Going* (1960); Eleanor Lambert and Diana Callaway, *How to Dress Your Little Girl* (1960); Eleanor Lambert and Isabel Brady, *Your Dream Wardrobe and How to Make It Come True: A Fashion Guide to Young America* (1961); Eleanor Lambert and Diana Callaway, *Mother-Daughter Guide to Fashion* (1960), Stulberg Records (5780–3), Box 6, Folder 10; Eleanor Lambert and Diane Papert, *How to Be Well-Dressed* (1959); *Glamour Guide: The Wonderful New World of Lingerie and Loungewear* [n.d., n.a.]; Stulberg Records (5780–3), Box 6, Folder 9.

12. *Fashions, U.S.A.,* various editions, in Records of the ILGWU.

13. Julius Hochman to David Dubinsky, January 5, 1962, Dubinsky Records, Box 280, Folder 4D; *Fashions, U.S.A.,* various editions; leaflet in ILGWU Broadsides collection, ILGWU Records (5780), Box 5, Folder 28.

14. Leaflet in ILGWU Broadsides Collection, ILGWU Records (5780), Box 5, Folder 28.

15. "Baseball. The Great Un-American Game," advertising copy, October 2, 1972; C. C. Johnson Spink, "'Un-American Baseball' Ad Unjustified," November 1972; both in New York Cloak Joint Board Records, Box 16, Folder 4; John Denaro to "Colleague," [October 8, 1974], Stulberg Records (5780–4), Box 7, Folder 2.

16. Copies of ILGWU advertisements in ILGWU Records. On the origins of the TV advertising campaign, Sol Chick Chaiken, "Always Look for the Union Label," in *a Labor Viewpoint: Another Opinion,* pp. 135–136. Union Label Song, written by Paula Green on behalf of the International Ladies' Garment Workers' Union. Permission to quote courtesy of Paula Green. My great thanks to Paula Green for sharing the song's history with me.

17. Union Label Song.

18. Sketch, *Donny and Marie* show, n.d., film clip in Archives of Labor and Urban Affairs, Wayne State University, Detroit, Michigan.

19. *Saturday Night Live,* April 23, 1977. Permission to quote courtesy of Broadway Entertainment and NBC Studios. My thanks to Curt Ford and Louise M. Gallup-Roholt for help with permissions.

20. Asian Americans for Action to Eleanor H. Norton, August 11, 1972 (leaflet attached), in Stulberg Records (5780–4), Box 7, Folder 3; "Made in Japan" advertisement, New York Cloak Joint Board Records, Box 16, Folder 4.

21. Asian Americans for Action to Norton, August 11, 1972.

22. Mitziko Fromartz, George Yuzawa, Mary Kochiyama, Shizu Matsuda, and Aiko Abe to John Denaro, August 23, 1972, in Stulberg Records (5780–4), Folder 7, Folder 3.

23. *Daily World,* October 27, 1972, clipping in Stulberg Records (5780–4), Box 7, Folder 3; "Organizations supporting picket demonstration against ILGWU leadership"; leaflet, "Unemployment and Inflation Are Made in America Not in Japan," October 25, 1972, both in Stulberg Records (5780–4), Box 7, Folder 3; *New York Times,* October 26, 1972, clipping in Stulberg Records (5780–4), Box 16, Folder 4. For additional letters in response to the poster, see Box 16, Folder 4, and Box 7, Folder 3, Stulberg Records (5780–4), including the letters cited in notes to follow.

24. *Wall Street Journal,* September 20, 1972; *New York Times,* September 20, 1972; Fromartz, Yuzawa, Kochiyama, Matsuda, Imai, and Abe to Louis Stulberg, September 28, 1972.

25. Joan Shigekawa to Louis Stulberg, December 4, 1972, in Stulberg Records (5780–4), Box 7, Folder 3.

26. Asian Americans for Action to Norton, August 11, 1972.

27. Stanley K. Abe to Mattie Jackson, [December 6, 1972], in Stulberg Records (5780–4), Box 7, Folder 3.

28. *Wall Street Journal,* September 20, 1972.

29. *New York Times,* August 26, 1972.

30. Bruce Biossat, "ILGWU Is Way Off Base, Unfair," *Jacksonville, Arkansas News,* October 5, 1972, clipping in Records of the New York Cloak Joint Board, Folder 16, Folder 4.

31. Jimmy G. S. Ong to President, International Ladies' Garment Workers' Union, September 13, 1972, Records of the New York Cloak Joint Board, Box 16, Folder 4.

32. Shigekawa to Stulberg, December 4, 1972.

33. *New York Times,* October 26, 1972.

34. Genora Johnson Dollinger to International Ladies Garment Workers [sic], November 16, 1972, Records of the New York Cloak Joint Board, Folder 16, Folder 4. See also personal reply from Gus Tyler that follows. *With Babies and Banners: History of the Women's Emergency Brigade,* Women's Labor History Film Project (Franklin Lakes, NJ: New Day Films, 1978).

35. Marie A. Connelly to Union Label Department, ILGWU, August 14, 1972, Records of the New York Cloak Joint Board, Box 16, Folder 4.

36. Rodney Armstrong to Union Label Department, ILGWU, August 14, 1972, Records of the New York Cloak Joint Board, Box 16, Folder 4,

37. Wilbur Daniels to Louis Stulberg, August 9, 1972, Stulberg Records (5780–4), Box 7, Folder 3.

38. *New York Times,* October 26, 1972.

39. Quoted in John Denaro to Asian Americans for Action, October 6, 1972, Records of the New York Cloak Joint Board, Box 16, Folder 4.

40. Ibid.

41. Advertisement, *New York Times Magazine,* December 24, 1972, p. 36; Louis Stulberg to Joan Shigekawa, December 26, 1972; Stulberg Records (5780–4), Box 7, Folder 3.

42. My argument regarding the evolution of the ILGWU draws on *Justice,* documents in the ILGWU archives, and interviews by the author with Ronald Blackwell (June 3, 1996; New York City), Susan Cowell (August 27, 1997; telephone), May Ying Chen (October 8, 1997; telephone), Muzaffar Chisti (September 8, 1997; telephone), Art Gundersheim (June 4, 1996; New York City), Jeff Hermanson (July 27, 1998; telephone), Herman Starobin (April 22, 1996; Great Neck, New York), and Max Zimny (July 28, 1998; telephone), none of whom is responsible for my interpretation.

43. On the ILGWU's leadership and constituency since its founding, Tyler, *Look for the Union Label;* Joel Seidman, *The Needle Trades* (New York: Farrar and Rinehart, 1942); Alice Kessler-Harris, "Organizing the Unorganizable: Three Jewish Women and Their Union," *Labor History,* Vol. 17, No. 1 (Winter 1976): 5–23; Susan A. Glenn, *Daughters of the Shtetl: Life and Labor in the Immigrant Generation;* Louis Levine (Louis Lorwin), *The Women's Garment Workers: A History of the International Ladies' Garment Workers' Union* (New York: B. W. Huebsch, 1924); Roger D. Waldinger, *Through the Eye of the Needle: Immigrants and Enterprise in New York's Garment Trades* (New York: New York University Press, 1986); Annelise Orleck, *Common Sense and a Little Fire: Women and Working-Class Politics in the United States, 1900–1965;* Altagracia Ortiz, "Puerto Ricans in the Garment Industry of New York City, 1920–1960," in *Labor Divided: Race and Ethnicity in United States Labor Struggles, 1835–1960,* ed. Robert Asher and Charles Stephenson (Albany: State University of New York Press, 1990), pp. 105–125; George N. Green, "The ILGWU in Texas, 1930–70," *Journal of Mexican American History* 1 (Spring 1971): 144–169; Julia Kirk Blackwelder, *Women of the Depression: Caste and Culture in San Antonio, 1929–1939* (College Station, TX: Texas A. & M. University Press, 1984), pp. 86–109; John Laslett and Mary Tyler, *The ILGWU in Los Angeles, 1907–1988* (Inglewood, CA: Ten Speed Press, 1989); Edna Bonacich, "Asians in the Los Angeles Garment Industry," in Paul Ong, Edna Bonacich, and Lucie Cheng, eds., *The New Asian Immigration in Los Angeles and Global Restructuring* (Philadelphia: Temple University Press, 1994), pp. 137–163; Maria Angelina Soldatenko, "The Everyday Lives of Garment Workers in Los Angeles: The Convergence of Gender, Race, Class and Immigration," Ph.D. Diss., University of California, Los Angeles, 1992; Evelyn Blumenberg and Paul Ong, "Labor Squeeze and Ethnic/Racial Recomposition in the U.S. Apparel Industry"; James Loucky, Maria Soldatenko, Gregory Scott, and Edna Bonacich, "Immigrant Enterprise and Labor in the Los Angeles Garment Industry," both in Edna Bonacich, Lucie Cheng, Norma Chinchilla, Nora Hamilton, and Paul Ong, eds., *Global Production: The Apparel Industry in the Pacific Rim* (Philadelphia: Temple University Press, 1994), pp. 309–327, 345–61.

44. Herbert Hill, "Black Workers, Organized Labor, and Title VII of the 1964 Civil Rights Act: Legislative History and Litigation Record," in *Race in America: The Struggle for Equality,* ed. Herbert Hill and James E. Jones, Jr. (Madison, WI: University of Wisconsin Press, 1993), p. 294.

45. ILGWU letterhead, 1972, in Records of the New York Cloak Joint Board,

passim; *Wall Street Journal,* October 18, 1976.

46. Interview with Jeff Hermanson; Herbert Hill, "Black Workers, Organized Labor, and Title VII"; Maria Soldatenko, "The Everyday Lives of Latina Garment Workers in Los Angeles," pp. 281–330.

47. Peter Kwong, *The New Chinatown,* Rev. Ed. (New York: Hill and Wang, 1996), p. 150; see pp. 147–159.

48. Interview by the author with Nick Aiello, April 19, 1996, New Haven, Connecticut; photographs in possession of the author.

49. Interview with Max Zimny; *New York Times,* April 27, 1998; *Women's Wear Daily,* March 27, June 16, 1998; ILGWU Contracts, 1954–1973, in Institution of Industrial Relations Library, University of California, Berkeley.

50. Interviews with Max Zimny, Art Gundersheim, Jeff Hermanson; *New York Times,* April 27, 1998; Robert Fitch, "Sewing Suspicion," *Village Voice,* April 14, 1998; *Wall Street Journal,* October 18, 1976; *Business Week* (September 17, 1979); *Women's Wear Daily,* May 23, 1983.

51. *Wall Street Journal,* October 18, 1976; *Business Week* (September 17, 1979); *Women's Wear Daily,* May 23, 1983; interview with Max Zimny; ILGWU LM-2 Forms, 1959–1995, on file with U.S. Department of Labor, Office of Public Disclosure; my thanks to Phil Goldberg for helping me with these forms.

52. *Newsday,* September 4, 1994; *Business Week* (September 17, 1979); interview with Max Zimny; LM-2 Forms, 1980–89.

53. *New York Times,* April 27, 1998; *Women's Wear Daily,* May 23, 1983; June 16, 1998; Robert Fitch, "Sewing Suspicion"; *Business Week* (September 17, 1979); LM-2 Forms; interview with Max Zimny; interview with Jeff Hermanson; *Apparel Industry Magazine,* Vol. 55, No. 8 (August 1994): 128.

54. *Apparel Industry Magazine,* Vol. 55, No. 8 (August 1994): 128; Robert Fitch, "Sewing Suspicion"; *New York Times,*

April 27, 1998; *Women's Wear Daily,* May 23, 1983; April 8, 1998; June 16, 1998; *Business Week* (September 17, 1979).

55. *Women's Wear Daily,* March 27, 1998.

56. Interview with Jeff Hermanson; LM-2 forms, 1994.

57. Richard Rothstein, *Keeping Jobs in Fashion,* pp. 55–59; Roger Waldinger, *Through the Eye of the Needle,* pp. 76–79; Andrew Ross, ed., *No Sweat: Fashion, Free Trade, and the Rights of Garment Workers* (New York: Verso, 1997).

58. Roger Waldinger, *Through the Eye of the Needle,* pp. 75–77; Andrew Ross, *No Sweat.*

59. Quoted in Richard Rothstein, *Keeping Jobs in Fashion,* p. 52.

60. Richard Rothstein, *Keeping Jobs in Fashion,* p. 51; Edna Bonacich and David V. Waller, "The Rise of U.S. Apparel Manufacturers in the Globalization of the Industry in the Pacific Rim," in Edna Bonacich, et al., *Global Production.*

61. For the strategic goals behind U.S. apparel trade policy, see Richard Rothstein, *Keeping Jobs in Fashion;* Alfred E. Eckes, "Trading American Interests," *Foreign Affairs,* Vol. 71, No. 4 (Fall 1992): 135–153.

62. Edna Bonacich, "Asians in the Los Angeles Garment Industry"; Andrew Ross, *No Sweat;* Tyler, *Look for the Union Label.*

63. Interview with Jeff Hermanson.

64. Maria Soldatenko, "Everyday Lives of Latina Garment Workers in Los Angeles," pp. 287, 306.

65. Interview with Jeff Hermanson.

66. Interview with Jeff Hermanson; LM-2 forms, 1986–1994.

67. Interview with Jeff Hermanson; Waldinger, *Through the Eye of the Needle,* pp. 68–71.

68. Beth Sims, *Workers of the World Undermined: American Labor's Role in U.S. Foreign Policy* (Boston: South End Press, 1992), pp. 46–47; *New America,* 1970s; Paul Buhle, *Taking Care of Business: Sam-*

uel Gompers, George Meany, Lane Kirkland, and the Tragedy of American Labor Leadership (New York: Monthly Review Press, 1999).

69. Beth Sims, *Workers of the World Undermined;* interview with Jeff Hermanson; Robert Armstrong, Hank Frundt, Hobart Spalding, and Sean Sweeney, *Working Against Us: The American Institute for Free Labor Development (AIFLD) and the International Policy of the AFL-CIO* (New York: North American Congress on Latin America, [n.d.]).

70. *Justice* (December 1, 1972).

71. *Justice* (October 1983).

72. Pamphlets, *For Ladies Only* and *Do You Know About the Sweatshops in Vancouver?* [1961], Dubinsky Records, Box 282, Folder 3.

73. *Justice* (July 15, 1969; September 1971; February 1983; and passim); memo, n.a., "Following discussion with Bernard Shane in President's office," October 5, 1961, Dubinsky Records, Box 282, Folder 3; *New York Times,* May 8, 1971.

Puerto Rico was ostensibly simpler, since it was part of the economic borders of United States for trade purposes, if still an unequal protectorate without statehood status. Evading the distinction, ILGWU presidents sometimes spoke of "our 440,000 members in the United States and Puerto Rico," usually when Puerto Ricans were present at conventions. ILGWU members in Puerto Rico joined in the union's coordinated anti-import mobilizations throughout the 1970s and '80s, along with Puerto Ricans from the island residing within the states. The ILGWU targeted the latter with Spanish-language advertisements from the 1960s onward. But Puerto Ricans on the island were another matter altogether. "A number of terms used on union labels are prone to antagonize Puerto Ricans," an internal memo during the 1960s reported. "For example 'American way of life' has little meaning to them. Americans are those foreigners." Moreover, "References

to sweatshops and homework have little meaning in Puerto Rico since homework still continues, even in some union shops and with the sanction of the union." Further, since the union had not attempted to organize shops catering to a local market, "a union label promotion may mean to a lot of Puerto Ricans that we urge them not to buy things produced in Puerto Rico for Puerto Ricans." (ILGWU staffer Jerry Schoen "is not looking forward to having to handle label sales in Puerto Rico," concluded the memo.) Min L. Matheson to Gus Tyler, December 30, 1963, and attached, "Jerry Schoen's Comments on the Union Label Problems in Puerto Rico," ILGWU Records (5780–52), Box 60, Folder 17; "Su Vecina y Amiga Marta Martinez," ILGWU advertisement, n.d. [pre-1972], in ILGWU Broadsides Collection; "Novias Puertoriqueñas: Feliz Matrimonio," ILGWU advertisement copied from *El Mundo,* June 1, 1971, in Stulberg Records (5780–4), Box 7, Folder 3; *Justice* (June 1, 1970; August 1, 1969); report, "Union Label Department, 1972."

74. *Justice* (October 1983).

75. *Justice* (October 1987).

76. Kwong, *The New Chinatown,* p. 156.

77. Interviews with Susan Cowell, Muzzafar Chisti.

78. Interview with May Ying Chen.

79. Laslett and Tyler, *The ILGWU in Los Angeles,* p. 99.

80. Laslett and Tyler, *The ILGWU in Los Angeles,* p. 99; Maria Soldatenko, "Everyday Lives of Latina Garment Workers in Los Angeles," pp. 286–330; Herbert Hill, "Black Workers, Organized Labor, and Title VII."

81. Interviews with Muzzaffar Chisti, Susan Cowell; *Justice* (November 1987 and passim); leaflet, "If You Live in the U.S. It Is Important to Be a Citizen of the United States. The Union Can Help," n.d. [1972–1975], ILGWU Broadsides Collection; Leah Haus, "Openings in the

Wall: Transnational Migrants, Labor Unions and U.S. Immigration Policy," *International Organization,* Vol. 49, No. 2 (Spring 1995): 285–313; Tyler, *Look for the Union Label.*

82. *Justice* (1986 onward); interviews with May Ying Chen, Susan Cowell.

7. Demons in the Parking Lot

1. This scene is a fictional composite drawn from a number of different events. Sources include interview by the author with Jerry Tucker, Seattle, Washington, September 12, 1996; telephone interview by the author August 19, 1998; for visual imagery, see the film *Who Killed Vincent Chin?,* Christine Choy and Renee Tajima, Film News Now Foundation, and WTVS, Detroit (Detroit: WTVS, 1988).

2. "A UAW Factpack on the Domestic Auto Content Bill," in Box 1, Folder 7, UAW Research Department Unprocessed Collection, Records of the United Automobile Workers, Archives of Labor and Urban Affairs, Walter Reuther Library, Wayne State University, Detroit, Michigan.

3. *Solidarity* (April 1975): 2.

4. *Solidarity* (April 22, 1977).

5. UAW Local #598, *Eye Opener,* December 17, 1986, p. 14, in UAW Research Department Unprocessed Collection, Box 1, Folder L. U.'s 500–599.

6. Clipping from the *Milwaukee Journal,* February 1981, attached to Clary Schrubbe to UAW Headquarters, February 15, 1981, in Douglas Fraser Papers, Box 49, Folder 6, UAW Collection, Archives of Labor and Urban Affairs.

7. *San Jose Mercury-News,* February 21, 1992.

8. *Labor Notes* (June 1992): J-6.

9. *Labor Notes* (June 1992): J-6.

10. *Labor Notes* (June 1992): J-6.

11. *Solidarity* (March 18, 1977): 20.

12. *Union Eyes* (Local #696, Dayton, Ohio), December 1986, p. 2, Records of UAW Public Relations Department, Box 1, Folder LU's 600–699.

13. Telephone interview by the author with Dave Elsila, September 11, 1997.

14. *Union Eyes* (Local #696, Dayton, Ohio), December 1986, p. 2, in Records of UAW Public Relations Department, Unprocessed Materials, Box 1, Folder LU's 600–699; for "Jap," see, for example, *Delco Sparks,* December issue II, 1986, p. 4, in UAW Public Relations Dept. Records, Unprocessed Materials, Box 1, Folder LU's 600–699.

15. *Solidarity* (May 1981).

16. *Local 685 News* (February 1987): 2, UAW Public Relations Dept. Records, Unprocessed Materials, Box 1, Folder LU's 600–699.

17. United States Commission on Civil Rights, *Civil Rights Issues Facing Asian Americans in the 1990s* (Washington, DC: United States Commission on Civil Rights, 1992), pp. 25–26; *Who Killed Vincent Chin?*

18. Richard Feldman and Michael Betzold, *End of the Line: Autoworkers and the American Dream* (Urbana, IL: University of Illinois Press, 1990), p. 276.

19. *Union Eyes* (Local #606, Dayton, Ohio), December 1986, p. 2, in UAW Public Relations Dept. Records, Unprocessed Materials, Box 1, Folder LU's 600–699.

20. *Solidarity* (July–August 1975): 2.

21. *Flint UAW News—Local 599 Headlight Edition,* March 1987, p. 2, in UAW Public Relations Dept. Records, Unprocessed Materials, Box 1, Folder LU's 500–599.

22. *Solidarity* (December 16–31, 1980): 21.

23. *The Sparkler* (December 22, 1986): 4.

24. *The Sparkler* (April 15, 1987): 11–15.

25. *Solidarity* (September 1975): 2.

26. *Solidarity* (November 1982): 20.

27. Howard Young to Hank Lacayo, July 15, 1975, in Box 49, Folder 36, Fraser Papers, UAW Records.

28. *Washington Post,* October 29, 1980.

29. Douglas A. Fraser to U.S. Officers and International Executive Board Members, July 2, 1981; Frank James to Dick Martin, February 26, 1981, and attachment; Dick Martin to Al Haener, May 12, 1981, and attachment; all in Fraser Papers, Box 49, Folder 36.

30. Clipping and Associated Press photograph from the *Milwaukee Journal,* February 1981, attached to Clary Schrubbe to UAW Headquarters, February 15, 1981.

31. *American Metal Market/Metalworking News* (July 19, 1982), quoted in Timothy V. Johnson to Dick Martin, August 6, 1982, in Box 49, Folder 36, Fraser Papers. For more on Buy American materials and the UAW leadership, see further correspondence in Box 49, Folder 36, Fraser Papers; *Washington Times,* March 15, 1992; UAW Posters, c. 1981, in Collection of the Political History Department, Smithsonian Institution, Washington, DC.

32. Lee Price to "Several," March 18, 1982, UAW Records Dept. Unprocessed Collection, Box 1, Folder 10.

33. Telephone interview by the author with Lee Price, April 12, 1996; interview with Dave Elsila; telephone interview by the author with Jeff Stansbury, September 2, 1997; interview by the author with Douglas Fraser, Detroit, Michigan, October 15, 1996.

34. *Monthly Labor Review,* Vol. 99, No. 12 (December 1976): 53–54.

35. Nelson Lichtenstein, *The Most Dangerous Man in Detroit: Walter Reuther and the Fate of American Labor* (New York: Basic Books, 1995); telephone interview by the author with Kim Moody, September 5, 1997; interviews with Jeff Stansbury, Dave Elsila, and Lee Price.

36. Kim Moody, *An Injury to All: The Decline of American Unionism* (London and New York: Verso, 1988), pp. 148–149; interview with Jeff Stansbury.

37. Moody, *An Injury to All,* pp. 152–156, 165–166.

38. Bennett Harrison and Barry Bluestone, *The Great U-Turn: Corporate Restructuring and the Polarizing of America* (New York: Basic Books, 1988), pp. 39–41; Moody, *An Injury to All,* pp. 165–191; Jane Slaughter, *Concessions and How to Beat Them* (Detroit: Labor Education and Research Project, 1983).

39. Press Release, "Auto Content Bill Aims for Jobs and Fair Trade Policies . . . ," September 22, 1982, Box 1, Folder 6, UAW Research Dept. Unprocessed Collection.

40. On the push for domestic content legislation, see *Solidarity* (1981–1983); Sheldon Friedman to Doug Fraser, July 17, 1981; Sheldon Friedman to Doug Fraser, June 24, 1981, and attachments; "We Want Jobs—Not Promises!" and attachment; press release, "Fraser Announces Major UAW Legislative Effort . . . ," July 20, 1981; all in UAW Research Dept. Unprocessed Collection, Box 1, Folder 15; press release, "Auto Content Legislation Clears First Hurdle in U.S. Congress," June 10, 1982, Box 1, Folder 9; press release, "UAW Mobilizes Massive Letter Campaign . . . ," October 14, 1983, Box 1, Folder 3; press release, "Auto Content Bill Aims For Jobs and Fair Trade Policies . . . ," September 22, 1982; Lee Price to Research Department Staff, September 10, 1981, Box 1, Folder 14; Howard D. Samuel to "Dear Representative," January 29, 1982, Box 1, Folder 10; *How to Get the Auto Industry Going Again,* "A UAW Factpack on the Domestic Auto Content Bill," Box 1, Folder 7, UAW Research Dept. Unprocessed Collection; *Washington Post,* August 28, October 28, 1982; *New York Times,* August 2, 1982; *Wall Street Journal,* September 17, 1982; *New Republic* (November 15, 1982).

41. Samuel to "Dear Representative," January 29, 1982.

42. Press Release, "Fraser Announces Major UAW Legislative Effort . . . ," July 20, 1981.

43. Donald F. Ephlin, "Labor and the Japanese Challenge," Presentation at University of Michigan Conference on the Auto Industry, January 14, 1981, in UAW Research Dept. Records Unprocessed Collection, Box 2, Folder 2.

44. Mike Parker and Jane Slaughter, *Choosing Sides: Union and the Team Concept* (Boston: South End Press, 1988); Harry C. Katz, *Shifting Gears: Changing Labor Relations in the U.S. Automobile Industry* (Boston: M.I.T. Press, 1985); Mike Parker, "Industrial Relations Myth and Shop-Floor Reality: The 'Team Concept' in the Auto Industry," in *Industrial Democracy in America: The Ambiguous Promise,* ed. Nelson Lichtenstein and Howell John Harris (Cambridge, England: Cambridge University Press, 1993), pp. 249-274.

45. Parker and Slaughter, *Choosing Sides,* p. 4.

46. Agreement between General Motors and the UAW, September 21, 1984, p. 239, in possession of the author.

47. Parker and Slaughter, *Choosing Sides;* for a more positive view of both Saturn and labor-management cooperation, see Barry Bluestone and Irving Bluestone, *Negotiating the Future: A Labor Perspective on American Business* (New York: Basic Books, 1992); Jack O'Toole, *Forming the Future: Lessons from the Saturn Corporation* (Cambridge, MA: Blackwell, 1996).

48. On Moog, LTV, and Tucker, interview with Jerry Tucker; Jack Metzgar, "'Running the Plant Backwards' in UAW Region 5," *Labor Research Review,* No. 7 [n.d.]: 35-43; interview with Jerry Tucker; interview with Jeff Stansbury; Jeff Stansbury, "A Reporter's Notebook on Jerry Tucker," New Directions pamphlet, [n.d.], in possession of the author.

49. Eric Mann, "Keeping GM Van Nuys Open," *Labor Research Review,* No. 9 [n.d.]: 35-44; Eric Mann, *Taking On General Motors: A Case Study of the UAW Campaign to Keep GM Van Nuys Open* (Los Angeles: Center for Labor Research and Education, Institute of Industrial Relations, University of Calif., Los Angeles, 1987).

50. *The Voice of New Directions,* Vol. 1, No. 1 (August 1989): 4-5, in possession of the author. My thanks to Jerry Tucker for sharing documents from New Directions.

51. UAW New Directions, "Constitution and By-Laws," approved October 21, 1989, in possession of the author. On New Directions, interview with Jerry Tucker; Jane Slaughter, "Sparks Among the Auto Workers," *Public Citizen* (September/October 1989): 10-17; David Moberg, "Worried Autoworkers Shy Away From New Directions," *In These Times* (July 5-18, 1989); *Los Angeles Times,* June 21, 1989; Jeff Stansbury, "A Reporter's Notebook on Jerry Tucker"; Jerry Tucker, "Why We Need New Directions in the UAW," pamphlet [n.d.], in possession of the author; *The Voice of New Directions,* issues in possession of the author.

52. Interview with Jerry Tucker.

53. Interviews with Jerry Tucker, Jeff Stansbury.

54. Interview with Jeff Stansbury.

55. Interview with Kim Moody.

56. Interview with Jeff Stansbury.

57. Interview with Jerry Tucker.

58. Interview with Kim Moody.

59. Interview with Jeff Stansbury.

60. Slaughter, *Concessions and How to Beat Them.*

61. Eric Mann, "Keeping GM Van Nuys Open," pp. 123-125.

62. Parker and Slaughter, *Choosing Sides,* p. 8.

63. *Detroit Free Press,* February 4, 1992; thanks to Jane Slaughter for the reference.

64. *Wall Street Journal,* August 4, 1997; February 11, 1998.

65. "Detroit South," *Business Week* (March 16, 1992); Harley Shaiken, with Stephen Herzenberg, *Automation and*

Global Production: Automobile Engine Production in Mexico, the U.S., and Canada (La Jolla, CA: Center for U.S.-Mexican Studies, University of California, San Diego, 1987); Peter Dicken, *Global Shift: The Internationalization of Economic Activity,* 2nd Ed. (New York: Guilford Press, 1992).

66. *Solidarity* (December 1987): 6; Robert Perrucci, *Japanese Auto Transplants in the Heartland: Cooperation and Community* (New York: Aldine DeGruyter, 1994); Choong Soon Kim, *Japanese Industry in the American South* (New York: Routledge, 1995); Dicken, *Global Shift,* pp. 194–195.

67. *Bye! American: The Labor Cartoons of Huck and Konopacki* (Chicago: Charles H. Kerr, 1987), cover and p. 51.

68. Moody, *An Injury to All,* pp. 140–141; American Social History Project, *Who Built America? Working People and the Nation's Economy, Politics, Culture and Society,* Vol. 2 (New York: Pantheon Books, 1992), pp. 652–653.

69. Bluestone and Harrison, *The Great U-Turn,* pp. 21–52; Moody, *An Injury to All,* pp. 119–121.

70. American Federation of Labor and Congress of Industrial Organizations (AFL-CIO), *The Changing Situation of Workers and Their Unions: A Report by the AFL-CIO Committee on the Evolution of Work* (Washington, DC: AFL-CIO, 1985).

71. Beth Sims, *Workers of the World, Undermined: American Labor's Role in U.S. Foreign Policy* (Boston: South End Press, 1992), pp. 22–24, 73; Robert Armstrong, Hank Frundt, Hobert Spalding and Sean Sweeney, *Working Against Us: The American Institute of Free Labor Development (AIFLD) and the International Policy of the AFL-CIO* (New York, NY: North American Congress on Latin America (NACLA), n.d.), p. 15.

72. *Viewpoint,* Vol. 7, No. 2 (1977): 8, 27 (special issue on imports).

73. Earl D. McDavid to Frank James, July 1, 1981, in Fraser Papers, Box 48, Folder 15; poster, "American Is Beautiful"; leaflet, "Hands That Build and Serve America"; plastic bag, "Save Jobs . . . Buy American," all in possession of the author; my thanks to the AFL-CIO Label Trades Department for sharing these materials; *Labeletter,* Vol. 5, No. 6 (June 1981): 3, in Fraser Papers, Box 48, Folder 15. See also graphics for distribution to unions, in Box 3, Folder 4, AFL-CIO Union Label Trades Department Records, George Meany Archives, Silver Spring, Maryland.

74. Paul Garver, "Beyond the Cold War: New Directions for Labor Internationalism," *Labor Research Review,* No. 13 (Vol. 8, No. 1) [n.d.]: 61. My thanks to Dan Ringer for calling my attention to this reference.

75. David McIlwaine to Paul Ornburn, April 25, 1983, in Union Label Dept. Records, Box 1, Folder 2.

76. Photograph of IBEW Local 1205 signs, March 1992, by Robert Zieger; in possession of the author. My thanks to Robert Zieger for sharing this photograph.

77. Bumper stickers in possession of the author, obtained at the Missoula, Montana, Labor Temple, 1991.

78. United Electrical, Radio, and Machine Workers of America, *Policy and Convention Proceedings, 1990* (Pittsburgh: United Electrical, Radio, and Machine Workers of America, 1990), pp. 80–81.

79. Interviews by the author with Chris Townshend, Alexandria, Virginia, April 6 and May 7, 1996.

80. *Policy 1995–1996: Resolutions and Reports Adopted by the 60th Convention of the United Electrical, Radio and Machine Workers of America (UE)* (Pittsburgh, PA: United Electrical, Radio and Machine Workers of America, 1995), p. 35.

81. Interview with Chris Townshend; UE *Policy,* 1960, 1980 (p. 86), 1985 (p. 94), 1990, 1995–1996; United Electrical,

Radio and Machine Workers of America, *How Foreign Is "Foreign Competition,"* reprinted from *UE News* (New York, NY: United Electrical, Radio and Machine Workers of America, 1971).

8. This Label Means Bigger Profits

1. Advertisement, "Crate," sponsored by Crafted With Pride in U.S.A. Council, Inc., February 5, 1992, in possession of Crafted With Pride. My thanks to Robert Swift for sharing video copies of these advertisements with me and for generously sending me printed materials from Crafted With Pride, as well. He is not responsible for the analysis presented here.

2. Interview by the author with Robert Swift, New York, New York, March 28, 1995; *Business Week* (April 9, 1987); Sara U. Douglass and Michelle A. Morganosky, "Textile and Apparel Industry Support for the Crafted with Pride Campaign: A Systems Perspective," *Clothing and Textiles Research Journal,* Vol. 9, No. 1 (Fall 1990): 37–44; Harvard Business School, *Crafted With Pride in U.S.A. Council,* (Cambridge, MA: Harvard Business School, 1987) (9–587–110; Rev. May 13, 1991); Harvard Business School, *It Matters to Me,* (Cambridge, MA: Harvard Business School, 1991) (9–591–067); *Daily News Record,* July 5, 1983, p. 12; July 13, 1983, p. 2; February 15, 1984, p. 2; *International Trade Reporter,* Vol. 8, No. 20 (August 17, 1983): 779; *Women's Wear Daily,* Vol. 146 (July 13, 1983): 21; Vol. 160, No. 47 (September 6, 1990): 6; Vol. 161, No. 64 (April 2, 1991): 15; "Textile Industry Launches 'Buy American' Campaign," UPI story, April 10, 1983; "Milliken Launches Buy-American Campaign," UPI story, March 11, 1983; *Marketing & Media Decisions,* Vol. 20 (November 1985): 68; "U.S. Fights Imports with Star-Studded 'Buy American' Drive," Reuters story, February 23, 1986.

3. Harvard Business School, *Crafted With Pride in U.S.A. Council.*

4. *Women's Wear Daily,* Vol. 150 (September 18, 1985): S12; *Justice* (September 1985): 2; *Washington Post,* September 10, 1985.

5. Quoted in Harvard Business School, *Crafted With Pride in U.S.A. Council,* p. 3.

6. *Women's Wear Daily,* Vol. 150 (September 18, 1985): S12; *Marketing and Media Decisions,* Vol. 20 (November 1985): 68; Harvard Business School, *It Matters to Me.*

7. *The Business Journal,* Charlotte, NC (January 13, 1992).

8. *Women's Wear Daily,* Vol. 160, No. 47 (September 6, 1990): 6.

9. Swift quote: *Women's Wear Daily,* Vol. 160, No. 47 (September 6, 1990): 6; Crafted With Pride in U.S.A. Council, Inc., "Highlights of Holiday 1993 Advertising Tracking, Crafted With Pride in U.S.A. Council, Inc.," in possession of the author; Crafted With Pride advertisements, including "Line" (December 14, 1990) and "Moving" (December 14, 1990), lent to the author by Robert Swift; for other advertisements, *Women's Wear Daily,* Vol. 161, No. 64 (February 2, 1991): 15.

10. Crafted With Pride in U.S.A. Council, Inc., pamphlet, *This Label Means Bigger Profits,* in possession of the author.

11. Interview with Robert Swift; *Women's Wear Daily,* Vol. 47 (September 6, 1984): 42. For examples, *New York Times,* June 4, 1993; March 25, 1994; *Journal of Commerce,* May 21, 1993; *Charlotte Observer,* March 6, 1992.

12. Interview by the author with Art Gundersheim, June 4, 1996, New York, New York; *Women's Wear Daily,* Vol. 150 (September 18, 1985): S13; Harvard Business School, *Crafted With Pride in U.S.A. Council,* p. 4; Crafted With Pride in U.S.A. Council, Inc., "Quick Response: Facts at a Glance," document in possession of the author. For the retailers' initial response, see *Women's Wear Daily,* Vol.

145, No. 2 (May 16, 1983); "Quick Response: Now for the Hard Part," *Material Handling Engineering,* Vol. 45, No. 3 (March 1990): 67–78.

13. Crafted With Pride in U.S.A. Council, Inc., *Update,* No. 21 (November 1989).

14. Ibid.

15. *Update,* No. 22 (February 1990).

16. *Update,* No. 23 (June 1990).

17. *Update,* No. 29 (September 1991) (quotes). *Update,* Nos. 20–23 29, 32, 35; *Daily News Record,* Vol. 21, No. 83 (August 29, 1991): 20.

18. Interview with Art Gundersheim; Fiber, Fabric & Apparel Coalition for Trade (FFACT) press release, "FFACT Pledges Strong Support for New Textile and Apparel Bill," February 19, 1987; FFACT press release, "Textile, Apparel, Footwear Leader to Ways & Means: 'We Need Effective Legislative Help,'" February 27, 1987; FFACT, "The Textile & Apparel Trade Act of 1987"; FFACT, "Talking Points: Textile & Apparel Trade Act of 1987"; FFACT, "Why Support Import Controls," January 1987; FFACT, "Fact Sheet: Textile & Apparel Trade Act of 1987: How It Is Compatible with GATT"; list of affiliates, FFACT; Nick Aiello private collection; copies in possession of the author; my thanks to Nick Aiello for sharing these materials with me; *Justice* (September 1986): 16; (June 1987): 1, 3.

19. *Update,* No. 21 (November 1989).

20. *Fortune* (October 12, 1987).

21. Visit by the author to Crafted With Pride, March 28, 1995.

22. *Business Week* (January 19, 1981).

23. Alyssa A. Lappen, "Can Roger Milliken Emulate William Randolph Hearst?" *Forbes* (May 29, 1989).

24. Interview with Art Gundersheim; Alyssa Lappen, "Can Roger Milliken Emulate William Randolph Hearst?"

25. *Business Week* (January 19, 1981).

26. Alyssa Lappen, "Can Roger Milliken Emulate William Randolph Hearst?";

Fortune (September 10, 1990): 135; *Business Week* (January 19, 1981): 62; *Business Week* (May 28, 1990): 27.

27. *Business Week* (January 19, 1981); Alyssa Lappen, "Can Roger Milliken Emulate William Randolph Hearst?"

28. Alyssa Lappen, "Can Roger Milliken Emulate William Randolph Hearst?"

29. Ibid.

30. "Fat Cats: GOPAC's Ten Biggest Spenders," Mojo Wire (*Mother Jones* Web page), October 6, 1997, http://www. mojones.com/coinop_congress/eye_ on_newt/fat_cat.html; Alyssa Lappen, "Can Roger Milliken Emulate William Randolph Hearst?"; "Under the Influence: The 1996 Presidential Candidates and Their Campaign Advisers: Pat Buchanan," June 3, 1996, http://www. essential.org/cpi/uti/buchanan.html.

31. "Statement by Roger Milliken on Behalf of Patrick J. Buchanan," October 6, 1997, http://www.buchanan.org/ rogerm.html.

32. "Under the Influence"; David Corn, "Pat's Big Laborer," *Nation,* Vol. 262, No. 11 (March 1996): 5; David Corn, "A Potent Trinity—God, Country & Me," *The Nation,* Vol. 260, No. 25 (June 26,1995): 913–916; Patrick J. Buchanan, speech delivered before the Manchester Institute of Arts and Sciences, Manchester, New Hampshire, March 20, 1995, *Vital Speeches of the Day,* Vol. 61, No. 15 (May 15, 1995): 461–463; "The Election Is About Who We Are: Taking Back Our Country," speech delivered at the Republican National Convention, Houston, Texas, August 17, 1992, *Vital Speeches of the Day,* Vol. 58, No. 23 (September 15, 1992): 712–715.

33. David Corn, "Pat's Big Laborer," p. 5; "Statement by Roger Milliken on Behalf of Patrick J. Buchanan," October 6, 1997; "Cotton King: Roger Milliken" (#215), Mojo Wire (*Mother Jones* Web page), http://www.motherjones.com/ coinop_congress/96mojo_400/milliken.html; Ira Stoll, "Foe of Unions Plays

Big Role on Pat's Team," *Forward* Web page, October 6, 1997, http://www.forward.com/BACK/96.03.01/news.buch.html; Karen Gullo, "Between Presidential Bids, Buchanan Raised $2 Million Through Group" (Associated Press story, *Daily Iowan*), http://www.uiowa.edu/~dlyiowan/issue/v127/i177/stores/A0501N.html; "Buchanan Campaign Announces National Advisory Committee," press release, June 7, 1995, Buchanan for President Web page, June 3, 1996, http://www.buchanan.org/nac.html; "Under the Influence."

34. *Business Week* (January 19, 1981).

35. *Women's Wear Daily,* Vol. 150 (September 18, 1985).

36. *Daily News Record,* Vol. 19, No. 217 (November 3, 1989): 1.

37. "Milliken & Company: 1988 Award Winner," June 3, 1989, http:/www.benchnet.com/awards/mbmilli.txt; *Textile Industry,* Vol. 140, No. 12 (December 1990): 42–48.

38. *Business Week* (January 19, 1981).

39. *Women's Wear Daily,* Vol. 158, No. 86 (November 3, 1989): 25.

40. *PR Newswire,* July 26, 1994; August 15, 1995; *Women's Wear Daily,* Vol. 159, No. 157 (March 22, 1990): 9.

41. Larry Kramer, "Darlington Workers Still Seeking Justice 21 Years After Illegal Closing," *Labor Unity* (August 1977): 3–4; Philip Sparks, "The Darlington Case: Justice Delayed Is Justice Denied," *Labor Law Journal* (December 1975): 759–766; David Corn, "Pat's Big Laborer." My thanks to Mike Donovan of UNITE! and Keir Jorgensen, formerly of ACTWU and now with the AFL-CIO, for helping me with Darlington materials.

42. David Corn, "Pat's Big Laborer"; Philip Sparks, "The Darlington Case"; Larry Kramer, "Darlington Workers Still Seeking Justice." My thanks to David Corn for helping me with research on Milliken.

43. Interview by the author with Herman Starobin, Great Neck, Long Island,

April 22, 1996; interview with Art Gundersheim; interview with Robert Swift; telephone interview by the author with Susan Cowell, August 27, 1997; telephone interview by the author with Keir Jorgenson, October 30, 1997; *Justice* (September 1983): 2; (July–August 1983): 2, 16; (September 1986): 16; (June 1987): 1, 3; Dewey L. Trogdon to Sol Chaiken, May 23, 1986 in Records of Sol (Chick) Chaiken, Box 28, Folder 4, Records of the International Ladies' Garment Workers' Union, Labor-Management Documentation Center, Catherwood Library, New York State School of Industrial and Labor Relations, Cornell University; James H. Martin, Jr., to Sol Chaiken, March 14, 1986, Chaiken Records, Box 18, Folder 26; FFACT documents in possession of Nick Aiello, cited previously; *International Trade Report,* Vol. 8, No. 20 (August 17, 1983): 779.

44. *Justice* (September 1993): 2.

45. Interview with Art Gundersheim.

46. Interview with Susan Cowell.

47. *Business Journal* (Charlotte, NC), Vol. 6, No. 39 (January 13, 1992); *Women's Wear Daily,* Vol. 166, No. 29 (August 11, 1993); *Atlanta Journal and Constitution,* September 24, 1992; *Women's Wear Daily/Global* (March 1998); *Daily News Record,* March 18, 1998; Kitty G. Dickerson, *Textiles and Apparel in the World Economy,* 2nd Ed. (Englewood Cliffs, NJ: Prentice-Hall, 1995), pp. 439–442. My thanks to Desma Holcomb for help with sources.

48. *USA Today* (March 5, 1996); Anna Kochan, "Second European Quality Award," *Quality,* Vol. 33, No. 1 (January 1994): 8; Simon Caulkin, "The Road to Peerless Wigan," *Management Today* (March 1994): 28–32.

49. *Washington Post,* September 10, 1985; interview with Art Gundersheim; *Business Week* (October 14, 1985): 142.

50. *Discount Store News,* December 9, 1985, p. 74.

51. UPI story, February 17, 1986.

52. *Discount Store News,* April 15, 1985

(quote); *Housewares* (February 7, 1990): 7; *Discount Store News* (March 17, 1986): 1; *Children's Business,* Vol. 8 No. 4 (April 1993): 31; *New York Times,* April 10, 1985.

53. *Discount Store News* (December 9, 1985); Wal-Mart, *1989 Annual Report,* p. 9; UPI story, December 22, 1992.

54. *Business Week* (October 12, 1985): 142; *Drug Topics,* Vol. 135 No. 7 (April 8, 1991): 70; *Advertising Age* (December 23, 30, 1991); UPI story, December 22, 1992; *Wall Street Journal,* August 8, 1997; Wal-Mart, *1994 Annual Report.*

55. Sam Walton with John Huey, *Sam Walton, Made in America: My Story* (New York: Doubleday, 1992); *San Jose Mercury-News,* September 29, 1997; UPI story, February 17, 1986; *Forbes* (October 28, 1985): 108; *Los Angeles Times,* June 22, 1998.

56. UPI story, December 22, 1992; *Dateline NBC,* December 22, 1992.

57. UPI story, December 22, 1992.

58. *Wall Street Journal,* January 4, 1993.

59. *Business Dateline/Northeastern Wisconsin Business Review* (January 22, 1993); *Bergen Record,* December 24, 1992; *Editor & Publisher* Vol. 126, No. 1 (January 16, 1993): 26–27; *New York Times,* December 25, 1992.

60. *Wall Street Journal,* November 13, 1989; *Editor & Publisher* (January 16, 1993): 26–27; *Children's Business,* Vol. 8, No. 4 (April 1993): 31; Matthew Schifrin, "The Big Squeeze," *Forbes* (March 11, 1996): 45–46.

61. *Boston Globe,* December 19, 1996. For additional evidence of Wal-Mart's clout, see *Wall Street Journal,* October 22, 1997.

62. Wal-Mart, *Annual Report,* 1994, p. 5.

63. Albert Norman, "Eight Ways to Stop the Store: Up Against Wal-Mart," *Nation,* Vol. 258, No. 12 (March 28, 1994): 418.

64. Kenneth Stone, "Impact of Wal-Mart Stores on Iowa Communities, 1983–1993," *Economic Development,* Vol. 13, No. 2 (Spring 1995): 60–69.

65. Kai Mander and Alex Boston, "Wal-Mart Worldwide: The Making of a Global Retailer," *Ecologist,* Vol. 26, No. 6 (November–December 1995): 238–241.

66. Albert Norman, "Eight Ways to Stop the Store"; *Editor & Publisher,* Vol. 126, No. 3 (January 16, 1993): 27; Constance E. Beaumont, *How Superstore Sprawl Can Harm Communities and What Citizens Can Do About It* (Washington, DC: National Trust for Historic Preservation, 1994); Sarah Anderson, "Wal-Mart's War on Main Street," *The Progressive,* Vol. 48, No. 11 (November 1994): 19–22.

67. Walton with Huey, *Sam Walton,* p. 126.

68. *Advertising Age* (December 23/ December 30, 1991).

69. Walton with Huey, *Sam Walton,* pp. 129, 242 (quotes); *Business Week* (March 16, 1992); Kai Mander and Alex Boston, "Wal-Mart Worldwide."

70. Union Label and Service Trades Department, AFL-CIO, *Label Letter,* Vol. 22, No. 3 (May/June 1997): 4.

71. Mander and Boston, "Wal-Mart Worldwide," *Santa Cruz Sentinel,* August 9, 1987. For Wal-Mart's anti-union activities, see also *Toronto Global and Mail,* February 13, 15, 1997.

72. Mander and Boston, "Wal-Mart Worldwide," *Wall Street Journal,* October 21, 1997.

73. *Business Week* (March 16, 1992): 86.

74. UPI story, June 2, 1992.

75. *Discount Store News* (March 17, 1986); for Wal-Mart's imports, see also *Charleston Gazette,* September 21, 1995.

76. *Discount Store News* (June 15, 1992): 127.

77. *Nation's Business,* Vol. 8, No. 4 (April 1993): 31.

78. *Chain Store Age Executive* (June 1985): 47.

79. *Business Week* (March 16, 1992).

80. *Business Week* (March 16, 1992).

81. *Wall Street Journal,* August 8, 1997.

82. Wal-Mart, *Annual Report,* 1994, p. 9; *Chicago Sun-Times,* November 17,

1993; *Wall Street Journal,* August 8, 1997; *San Jose Mercury-News,* June 4, 1997; *Discount Store News* (June 15, 1996): 1, 16; *Forbes* (March 25, 1986): 37–38; Mander and Boston, "Wal-Mart Worldwide;" Wal-Mart Stores, Inc., Form 10-K Annual Report for the Year Ending 1996.

83. Mander and Boston, "Wal-Mart Worldwide."

84. Wal-Mart, *Annual Report, 1994.*

85. *Chicago Sun-Times,* February 3, 1992.

86. Ibid.

87. *USA Today,* July 16, 1992.

88. *Footwear News,* Vol. 48, No. 7 (February 17, 1992): 68.

89. *U.S. News and World Report,* June 5, 1995 (quote); *USA Today,* July 14, 1995; *Washington Post,* September 21, 1994.

90. *Washington Post,* September 21, 1994; *Boston Herald,* September 21, 1994; *Business Week* (December 12, 1994): 86, 90; *USA Today,* July 14, 1995.

91. *Washington Post,* September 21, 1994.

92. *Boston Herald,* September 21, 1994; September 7, 1996; *Chicago Sun-Times,* February 3, 1992; *Footwear News,* Vol. 50, No. 20 (July 16, 1994): 12; Sallie Tisdale, "Shoe and Tell," *The New Republic* (September 12, 1994): 10–11; *Washington Post,* May 21, 1994; *Business Week* (December 12, 1994): 86, 90.

93. *Providence Business News,* Vol. 10, No. 11 (June 26, 1995).

94. *Business Week* (December 12, 1994): 86.

95. *Boston Herald,* July 10, 1995; September 7, 1996; *Christian Science Monitor,* July 17, 1995; *Providence Business Journal* (June 26, 1995); *Washington Post,* September 21, 1994.

96. *Providence Business News,* June 26, 1995; "Made in the U.S.A.," *Dateline NBC,* October 12, 1997.

97. *Footwear News,* Vol. 50, No. 20 (May 16, 1994): 12.

98. *Sportstyle* (July 1996): 30; *Boston Globe,* February 23, 1993; Sallie Tisdale,

"Shoe and Tell"; transcript of speech by Jim Davis to New Balance employees, 1993, in possession of UNITE! and the author; my thanks to Jerry Fishbein for sharing documents with me.

99. *Los Angeles Times,* May 5, 1997; *Journal of Commerce* (July 13, 1995); *Christian Science Monitor* (July 17, 1995).

100. Official Transcript, Proceedings before Federal Trade Commission, Docket/Case No. P894219, "Made in U.S.A.," Washington DC, March 26 and 27, 1996 (Washington, DC: Heritage Reporting Corporation, 1996).

101. Federal Trade Commission, "Made in U.S.A.," p. 266.

102. Federal Trade Commission, "Made in U.S.A.," p. 12.

103. Federal Trade Commission, "Made in U.S.A.," p. 263.

104. Federal Trade Commission, "Made in U.S.A.," p. 557.

105. Patricia Stamm to Robert Pitofsky, December 4, 1995, in Federal Trade Commission, "Made in U.S.A." Policy Comments, FTC File No. P894219, list of public comment documents received.

106. Herbert W. Samenfeld to Office of the Secretary, Federal Trade Commission, in Federal Trade Commission, "Made in U.S.A." Policy Comments.

107. Harold Tuchel to Federal Trade Commission, November 17, 1995, Federal Trade Commission, "Made in U.S.A." Policy Comments.

108. *Los Angeles Times,* May 6, 1997; Union Label and Service Trades Department, AFL-CIO, *Label Letter,* Vol. 22, No. 4 (July/August 1977): 1; Vol. 22, No. 5 (September/October 1997): 1; Extra issue, "Save 'Made in USA' Focuses on Congress," *Label Letter* [n.d.] (Fall 1997); Made in USA Coalition Website, November 23, 1997, http://www.usamade.org/coalition.html; *Wall Street Journal,* December 2, 1997; *San Jose Mercury-News,* December 2, 1997; *New York Times,* December 2, 6, 1997.

109. *Boston Herald,* September 7, 1996; *Orange County Register,* September 7, 1996.

9. Nationalism from the Bottom Up

1. *New York Times,* January 9, 10, 1992.

2. *New York Times,* January 22, 1992.

3. Nancy Folbre and the Center for Popular Economics, *The New Field Guide to the U.S. Economy* (New York: The New Press, 1995), p. 2:15; *Economic Report of President, 1992* (Washington, DC: Government Printing Office, February 1992).

4. *San Francisco Chronicle,* February 3, 1992.

5. *Chicago Tribune,* August 7, 1993; *St. Louis Post-Dispatch,* July 25, 1993.

6. *Philadelphia Inquirer,* January 5, 1992.

7. *Newsweek* (February 3, 1992).

8. *San Jose Mercury-News,* November 25, 1991.

9. Albany, N.Y. *Times Union,* September 25, 1994.

10. *USA Today,* January 24, 1992.

11. *New Yorker* (May 11, 1992): 31.

12. *St. Louis Post-Dispatch,* June 2, 1990.

13. *St. Petersburg Times,* January 8, 1987. For another example, *Houston Chronicle,* May 24, 1993.

14. American Pride, *Made in the U.S.A. Product News* (Fairhope, Alabama, 1994), p. 3; *Journal of Commerce* (June 29, 1995). Other, more extensive guidebooks include Annette Donoho, *Buy American: Who Owns What in the United States* (Waikoloa, HI: Annette LaBonte Donoho, 1991); Made in the USA Foundation, *Made in the USA: The Complete Guide to America's Finest Products,* several editions, including 4th Ed. (Bethesda, MD: National Press, 1993); Anne Grant and Web Burrell, *The Patriotic Consumer* (Kansas City, MO: Andrews and McMeel, 1992).

15. American Pride, *Made in the U.S.A. Product News.*

16. Telephone interview by the author with Phyllis Manrod, April 9, 1996.

17. *Buy America Newsletter,* Vol. 6, No. 3 (Summer 1997): 7; Vol. 3, No. 3 (Summer 1994): 7.

18. Jog suit: *Buy America Newsletter,* Vol. 5, No. 3 (Summer 1996): 2. On the Buy America Foundation, *Buy America Newsletter* (1992–1997), and fundraising cover letter, in possession of the author; William J. Lynott, *Why Buy American?,* pamphlet in possession of the author (Abington, PA: Buy America Foundation, 1993); Craig Stock, "Home Remedy for Unfair Trade," *Philadelphia Inquirer,* January 5, 1992; *USA Weekend,* April 2–4, 1993; *Chicago Tribune,* April 20, 1992; *Cleveland Plain Dealer,* January 12, 1992; *New York Times,* January 23, 1992.

19. *Buy America Newsletter,* Vol. 5, No. 4 (Fall 1996): 6.

20. *Buy America Newsletter* Vol. 5, No. 2 (Spring 1996): 6.

21. *Buy America Newsletter,* Vol. 5, No. 3 (Summer 1996): 6.

22. *Buy America Newsletter,* Vol. 6, No. 4 (Fall 1997): 6.

23. Interview with Phyllis Manrod.

24. There was at least one exception, however: when one reader wrote in to complain about lack of trade union support for buying American, Lynott did insert in tiny, tiny letters: "Ed. note: Many union locals are strong supporters of BAF [Buy America Foundation], and we are most appreciative." *Buy America Newsletter,* Vol. 5, No. 2 (Spring 1996): 6.

25. Interview by the author with Joel Joseph, Washington, DC, June 6, 1996; *Made in the USA Reports,* Vol. 7, No. 2 (Summer 1996), in possession of the author; *Made in the USA Foundation,* pamphlet in possession of the author [n.d.]; *Capital Times,* July 16, 1992; *San Francisco Chronicle,* November 2, 1992.

26. Interview with Phyllis Manrod; interview with Joel Joseph.

27. Quote: Interview by the author with Paul Marcone, Washington, DC, May 23, 1996. On federal Buy American Legislation, Rep. James A. Traficant, Jr., "The Buy American Act: Past, Present and Future," November 16, 1994, in possession of the author; Stanley N. Sherman, *Government Procurement Management,* 2nd Ed. (Gaithersburg, MD: Wordcrafters Publications, 1985), pp. 346–349; United States Congress, House Committee on Government Operations, *Buy American Act of 1987: Hearing Before a Subcommittee of the Committee on Government Operations,* March 25, 1987 (Washington, DC: Government Printing Office, 1988); United States Congress, House Committee on Government Operations, *Buy American Act of 1987: Report Together with Additional and Dissenting Views* (Washington, DC: Government Printing Office, 1987); Robert C. Turner and Kermit Gordon, "Memorandum for Mr. Feldman: Subject: Procurement Policies Giving Preference to Domestic Producers," June 25, 1962, Kermit Gordon Papers, Box 25, Folder "Buy American," John F. Kennedy Library, Boston, Massachusetts (thanks to Jim Wooten for sharing this document); Michael R. Gordon, "Buy-American Weapons Drive—Another Thorn in Trans-Atlantic Relations," *National Journal* (August 14, 1982): 1416–1420; *Business Week* (September 24, 1979; June 28, 1982); *Jane's Defense Weekly* (October 14, 1989); *Washington Post,* October 22, 1978, August 10, 1982; *International Trade Reporter,* June 23, 1982, July 18, 1990; *Forbes* (August 6, 1979). American Auto Labelling Act: *Consumer Reports* (October 1994): 620; *U.S. News & World Report* (October 10, 1994); Peritz Avram, "US Car Makers Collide over a Window Sticker," *Professional Engineering,* Vol. 7, No. 16 (September 21, 1994): 17. National Buy American Week: Public Law 99–127, 99th Congress, Joint Resolution October 18, 1985 (99 STAT. 521).

28. Interview by the author with Rep.

James Traficant, Washington, DC, May 23, 1996; interview with Paul Marcone; James A. Traficant, "The Buy American Act"; *News from Congressman James Traficant,* press releases 1987–1996, in possession of the author; my thanks to Rep. Traficant and Paul Marcone for generously sharing materials with me; *International Trade Reporter,* July 7, 1993, December 21, 1994, February 15, 1995; *Federal Contracts Report,* July 5, 1993; *Phoenix Gazette,* May 20, 1994; *Export Control News,* May 31, 1994; *Cleveland Plain Dealer,* May 20, 1994.

29. *U.S. News & World Report* (July 3, 1978). On state and local Buy American laws, United States–Japan Trade Council, *State 'Buy American' Policies: The Protectionist Drive for Closed Bidding Laws,* 1967; United States–Japan Trade Council, *State Barriers to World Trade,* 1973, both in Records of the Union Label Trades Department, AFL-CIO, Box 1, Folder 14, George Meany Archives, Silver Spring, Maryland; American Federation of Labor and Congress of Industrial Organizations (AFL-CIO), *States Should Keep Their 'Buy America' Laws Intact,* n.d. [c. 1990]; document fragment "State Precedents," Union Label Trades Department, Box 1, Folder 14; "States with Some Type of 'Buy American' Policy," 1981, Union Label Trades Department, Box 1, Folder 14; see also miscellaneous correspondence from American Iron and Steel Institute, United Steelworkers of America, Bethlehem Steel Corporation, and others, in Box 1, Folder 14; Thomas R. Donohue to Principal Officers of State Federation, Principal Officers of Central Labor Councils, November 30, 1990, August 26, 1991, in possession of the author; *Journal of Commerce* (May 2, 1968); *U.S. News & World Report* (July 3, 1978); *New York Times,* June 21, 1981, August 15, 1983, June 24, 1985; *Washington Post,* June 14, 1981; *Los Angeles Times,* December 1, 1985; March 26, 1992; February 9, 1992; *Bergen Record,* March 17, 1985; *Chicago Tribune,* August

7, 1986; *New Jersey Law Journal* (January
3, 1991): 12 (October 10, 1991): 47
(November 14, 1991): 5; Allentown,
Pennsylvania, *Morning Call,* June 7, 10,
1994; *Justice* (September 1984): 6. For
background on California's Buy Ameri-
can legislation, California Assembly Sub-
Committee on Governmental Efficiency
and Economy, *Buy American,* hearing, Los
Angeles, November 6, 1959 (Sacramento:
California State Legislature, 1959); Cali-
fornia State Assembly, Economic Devel-
opment Subcommittee, Assembly Interim
Committee on Ways and Means, "The
California Buy American Act: A Back-
ground Paper," prepared by Frederick A.
Breier, 1964, in California State Assembly
Office of Research Library; California
State Legislature, Joint Legislative Budget
Committee, *The Effect of the Buy-American
Policy on State Auto Procurement,* Novem-
ber 1982 (Sacramento: State of California,
1982); California State Legislature,
Assembly Interim Committee on Ways
and Means, *Report of the Subcommittee on
Economic Development on the California Buy
American Act: Issues and Alternatives,* Cali-
fornia State Legislature Reports, Vol. 21,
No. 16 (1967).

30. *Orlando Sentinel,* January 17, 1995.

31. *Buy America Newsletter,* Vol. 5, No.
3 (Summer 1996): 2; *Chicago Tribune,*
March 24, 1986. For the environmentalist
argument, see, for example, Herman E.
Daly, "Free Trade: The Perils of Deregu-
lation," and Helena Norberg-Hodge,
"Shifting Direction: From Global Depen-
dence to Local Interdependence," in Jerry
Mander and Edward Goldsmith, *The Case
Against the Global Economy and for a Turn
Toward the Local* (San Francisco: Sierra
Club Books, 1996), pp. 229–238, 393–
406.

32. *Los Angeles Times,* February 6,
1992.

33. *Daily Yomiuri,* June 4, 1992; *Los
Angeles Times,* January 7, 23, 24, 1992;
February 1, 5, 6, 7, 25, 27, 29, 1992; May
27, 1992; June 4, 1992; August 19, 1992.

34. *Los Angeles Times,* May 25, 1992.

35. Ibid.

36. *Los Angeles Times,* February 7,
1992.

37. *St. Louis Post-Dispatch,* November
27, 1994.

38. *New York Times,* January 12, 1991.

39. *New York Times,* January 27, 1992.
For earlier opposition, see June 24, 1985.

40. *Buffalo News,* July 2, 1995.

41. *Washington Post,* March 12, 1992.

42. *Oakland Tribune,* July 25, 1993.

43. *San Jose Mercury-News,* May 14,
1993.

44. See also *Oakland Tribune,* March
16, May 14, July 25, September 2, 1993;
Chicago Tribune, July 25, August 7, 1993;
St. Louis Post-Dispatch, September 28,
1995.

45. For accessible analyses of this
process, see Richard J. Barnet and John
Cavanagh, *Global Dreams: Imperial Corporations and the New World Order* (New
York: Simon & Schuster, 1994); William Greider, *One World, Ready or Not:
The Manic Logic of Global Capitalism*
(New York: Simon & Schuster,
1997).

46. For the debate on GATT overrid-
ing state-level Buy American laws, see
International Trade Reporter, Vol. 4, No.
20 (May 20, 1987): 674; Vol. 5, No. 11
(March 16, 1988): 357; Vol. 9, No. 21
(May 20, 1992): 871; *European Report,*
May 16, 1992; *American Metal Market,*
Vol. 99, No. 167 (August 30, 1991): 4.

47. *Drug Topics,* Vol. 135, No. 6 (March
23, 1992).

48. *Wall Street Journal,* August 8, 1972;
Congressional Record, Vol. 117, Part 19,
July 15, 1971 (Washington, DC: Govern-
ment Printing Office, 1971), p. 25466.

49. Japanese American Citizens League
(JACL), "Comments from Across the
United States That Engage in or Contribute to Japan Bashing," n.d. [1992–1993],
p. 2.

50. *San Jose Mercury-News,* November
1, 1991.

51. *Wall Street Journal,* August 8, 1982.

52. Japanese American Citizens League, "Comments from Across the United States," p. 2.

53. Japanese American Citizens League, "Comments from Across the United States," p. 6.

54. Japanese American Citizens League, "Comments from Across the United States," p. 5.

55. *Washington Post,* February 2, 1992.

56. Japanese American Citizens League, "Comments from Across the United States," p. 3.

57. Japanese American Citizens League, "Comments from Across the United States," p. 7; United States Commission on Civil Rights, *Civil Rights Issues Facing Asian Americans in the 1990s* (Washington, DC: United States Commission on Civil Rights, 1992), p. 44.

58. Japanese American Citizens League, "Comments from Across the United States"; United States Commission on Civil Rights, *Civil Rights Issues Facing Asian Americans in the 1990s;* Japanese American Citizens League, "Japan-Bashing, 'Buy American' and Japanese Americans," leaflet, 1992.

59. *New York Times,* October 31, November 1, 1989.

60. *San Jose Mercury-News,* January 24, 1992.

61. Michael Crichton, *Rising Sun,* paperback edition (New York: Ballantine Books, 1992), pp. 258, 252, 393.

62. Michael Crichton, *Rising Sun,* Ballantine paperback edition, pp. 393–394, 397–399.

63. Michael Crichton, *Rising Sun,* Ballantine paperback edition, front matter.

64. *Congressional Record,* 100th Con., 2d Sess., 134 (October 5, 1988, daily edition), H9583, quoted in David L. Abney, "Japan Bashing: A History of America's Anti-Japanese Acts, Attitudes and Laws," Ph.D. Diss., Arizona State University, 1995, p. 347.

65. "My comment is very simply this: We will have a rice paddy in the East Lawn of the White House. . . . Let me say it to you again. This is my quote: The way we've operated after all these threats from Japan, we will have a rice paddy on the East Lawn of the White House." Interview by the author with James Traficant, May 23, 1996.

66. *New York Times,* March 16, 1982.

67. *Washington Post,* February 2, 1992.

68. Michael Crichton, *Rising Sun,* Ballantine paperback edition, front matter.

69. William J. Lynott, *Why Buy American?*

70. *Buy America Newsletter,* Vol. 5, No. 2 (Spring 1996): 2.

71. Japanese American Citizens League, "Japan-Bashing, 'Buy American' and Japanese Americans."

72. *Labor Notes* (June 1992): J6.

73. Japanese American Citizens League, "Japan-Bashing, 'Buy American' and Japanese Americans."

74. *New York Times,* January 27, 1992.

75. *San Francisco Chronicle,* February 25, 1992.

76. Julianne Malveaux, *Sex, Lies and Stereotypes: Perspectives of a Mad Economist* (Los Angeles: Pines One Publishing, 1994), pp. 56–58.

77. *San Diego Union-Tribune,* February 18, 1992.

78. The Hosiery Corporation of America, logo stamped on back of envelope, 1995, with an eagle and the slogan "Products Made by Americans for Americans," in possession of the author.

79. *St. Louis Post-Dispatch,* September 28, 1995.

80. *Chicago Sun-Times,* March 11, 1992.

81. *Automotive News,* September 7, 1992.

82. Telephone interview by the author with Jan Beyers, January 17, 1998.

83. Japanese American Citizens League, "Comments from Across the United States."

84. Japanese American Citizens

League, "Japan-Bashing, 'Buy American' and Japanese Americans."

85. Christine Choy and Renee Tajima, *Who Killed Vincent Chin?* Film News Now and WTVS, Detroit (Detroit: WTVS, 1988).

86. *Chicago Sun-Times,* March 11, 1992.

87. Karl Taro Greenfeld, "Return of the Yellow Peril," *The Nation* (May 11, 1992): 636; see also Anthony LeJeune, *National Review,* Vol. 44 (August 17, 1992): 40–41, quoted, with Greenfeld, in Abney, "Japan Bashing," p. 338.

88. *New York Times,* March 16, 1992.

89. *Labor Notes,* special report, "Are These Our Enemies . . . or Our Friends?" (June 1992): J1–8.

90. *Los Angeles Times,* June 14, 1992.

91. Abney, "Japan Bashing."

92. *San Francisco Chronicle,* January 29, 1992; *Minneapolis Star Tribune,* February 1, 1992; *Los Angeles Times,* February 16, 1992; Reuter Business Report wire story, February 16, 1992; Louisville, Kentucky *Courier-Journal,* March 8, 1992.

93. *Contractor,* Vol. 39, No. 5 (May 1992): 54.

94. *Chicago Tribune,* January 25, 1992; *Newsweek* (February 3, 1992).

95. *Atlanta Journal and Constitution,* March 15, 1992.

96. *San Francisco Chronicle,* April 13, 1994.

97. *San Jose Mercury-News,* October 6, 1991; January 3, May 8, 1992.

98. *Consumer Reports* (July 1994): 3.

99. *Orlando Sentinel Tribune,* March 30, 1990; see also *Detroit News,* January 14, 1992.

100. *Crain's Chicago Business,* January 6, 1986.

101. *Bergen Record,* November 21, 1991.

102. *Wall Street Journal,* September 8, 1997; advertisement on radio station KPIG, Freedom, California, October 22, 1996.

103. *Chicago Tribune,* November 27, 1994; *Autoweek* (April 13, 1992).

104. *Los Angeles Times,* January 25, 1992; *Autoweek* (March 16, 1992); *Atlanta Journal and Constitution,* May 29, 1992.

105. Harvard Business School, *Crafted With Pride in U.S.A. Council,* Report #9-587-110, May 13, 1991, revision (Boston: President and Fellows of Harvard College, 1987), p. 14.

106. Harvard Business School, *Crafted With Pride in U.S.A. Council,* p. 5; Crafted With Pride in U.S.A., Inc., "Summary of Research Findings (1984–1986)," document in possession of the author.

107. *San Diego Business Journal* (October 4, 1993): 1; *Orlando Sentinel Tribune,* October 8, 1992; Gannett News Service wire story, October 29, 1992; *Crain's Chicago Business,* February 3, 1992; *Housewares* (February 7, 1990): 7; *Advertising Age,* Vol. 62, No. 16 (April 15, 1991); *Bergen Record,* February 14, 1992. Behind these news stories lay a sea of academic articles assessing consumer behavior regarding country of origin, with particular concern over methodological issues. See, for example, Richard Ettenson, Janet Wagner, and Gary Gaeth, "Evaluating the Effect of Country of Origin and the 'Made in the USA' Campaign: A Conjoint Approach," *Journal of Retailing,* Vol. 64, No. 1 (Spring 1988): 85–100; Ronald J. Dornoff, Clint B. Tankersley, and Gregory P. White, "Consumers' Perceptions of Imports," *Akron Business and Economic Review,* Vol. 5, No. 2 (1974): 26–29; "Understanding How American Consumers Formulate Their Attitudes About Foreign Products," Donald G. Howard, *Journal of International Consumer Marketing,* Vol. 2, No. 2 (1990): 7–23.

108. *Bergen Record,* February 14, 1992; *Advertising Age,* Vol. 62, No. 16 (May 15, 1991; *Daily News Record,* May 10, 1993; *Los Angeles Times,* February 21, 1991; Harvard Business School, *Crafted with Pride in U.S.A Council,* p. 5.

109. *Buy America Newsletter,* 1992–1997; interview with Joel Joseph.

110. *Adweek* (November 6, 1989).

111. *Adweek* (November 6, 1989; March 18, 1991); *San Francisco Chronicle,* May 25, 1992; *Crain's Chicago Business,* February 3, 1992; *Washington Times,* February 18, 1992; *Automotive News* (June 22, 1992); *AutoWeek* (July 6, 1992).

112. Interview by the author with Art Gundersheim, New York, New York, June 6, 1996.

113. *Advertising Age,* Vol. 63, No. 5 (February 3, 1992): 44.

114. *Forbes* (August 17, 1992).

115. *Investor's Business Daily,* February 2, 1992.

116. *Crain's Chicago Business,* February 3, 1992.

117. *Advertising Age,* Vol. 63, No. 2 (February 3, 1992).

118. *Charleston Gazette,* May 24, 1994; *Discount Store News,* Vol. 33, No. 12 (June 20, 1994): 23. The most influential and revealing study, often cited, was International Mass Retail Association and the Gallup Organization, *Consumer Attitudes Toward Product Sourcing* (Washington, DC: International Mass Retail Association, 1994).

119. *Crain's Chicago Business,* January 6, 1986.

120. *Children's Business,* Vol. 8, No. 4 (April 1993): 31.

121. *Housewares* (February 7, 1990); see also *Los Angeles Times,* February 21, 1991.

122. *Housewares* (February 7, 1990); *Los Angeles Times,* February 21, 1991.

123. *Adweek* (November 6, 1989); interview with Art Gundersheim.

Conclusion

1. Telephone interview by the author with Harley Shaiken, March 5, 1998.

2. Terry Davis, "Cross-Border Organizing Comes Home: UE and FAT in Mexico and Milwaukee," *Labor Research Review,* No. 23 (1995): 23–29; Kim Moody, *Workers in a Lean World: Unions in the International Economy* (London: Verso, 1997), pp. 240–242; Jeremy Brecher and Timothy Costello, *Global Village or Global Pillage? Economic Reconstruction from the Bottom Up* (Boston: South End Press, 1994); Kim Moody and Mary McGinn, *Unions and Free Trade: Solidarity vs. Competition* (Detroit: Labor Notes Books, 1992), pp. 48–49.

3. Kenneth S. Zinn, "Labor Solidarity in the New and World Order: The UMWA Program in Colombia," *Labor Research Review,* No. 23 (1995): 35–43; (quote, p. 38).

4. Ibid.

5. Jeremy Brecher and Timothy Costello, *Global Village or Global Pillage?;* John Cavanagh, John Gershman, Karen Baker, and Gretchen Helmke, eds., *Trading Freedom: How Free Trade Affects Our Lives, Work and Environment* (San Francisco: Institute for Food and Development Policy, 1992).

6. For a summary of the new administration and its initiatives in the first year, see Jeremy Brecher and Tim Costello, "A 'New Labor Movement' in the Shell of the Old?" and responses by John Sweeney, Ron Carey, and Jane Slaughter, *Labor Research Review,* No. 24 (1996): 5–37.

7. Kim Moody, "American Labor: A Movement Again?" *Monthly Review,* Vol. 49, No. 3 (July, 1997).

8. *Los Angeles Times,* February 22, April 30, June 1, 14, August 23, 1996; *Washington Post,* May 12, 30, 1996; *New York Times,* May 24, 1996; Eyal Press, "Kathie Lee's Slip," *The Nation,* Vol. 262, No. 24 (June 17, 1996): 6–7; Nancy Gibbs, "Cause Celeb: Two High-Profile Endorsers Are Props in a Worldwide Debate Over Sweatshops and the Use of Child Labor," *Time* (June 17, 1996); Andrew Ross, ed., *No Sweat: Fashion, Free Trade, and the Rights of Garment Workers* (New York: Verso, 1997), especially contributions by Ross, John Cavanagh, and Kitty Krupat.

9. Andrew Ross, *No Sweat.*

10. Quoted in David E. Sanger, "'Asian Money,' American Fears," *New York Times,* January 5, 1997.

11. For the new anti-globalization Buchanan, see Patrick J. Buchanan, *The Great Betrayal: How American Sovereignty and Social Justice Are Being Sacrificed to the Gods of the Global Economy* (Boston: Little, Brown, 1998).

12. See, for example, Joe Uehlein, "Using Labor's Trade Secretariats," and Joy Anne Grune, "Working Women & the Food Secretariat," both in *Labor Research Review,* No. 13 (Spring 1989): 31–41, 42–47, respectively.

13. For proposals about the progressive uses of protectionism, see Tim Lang and Colin Hines, *The New Protectionism: Protecting the Future Against Free Trade* (New York: The New Press, 1993).

ACKNOWLEDGMENTS

When I started this project, I had no clear sense of the chronology of Buy American campaigns or of their extent. I was able to research and write the book only because dozens of people sent me tidbits of information, tipped me off about collections, or helped me with obscure references at the last minute. My great thanks to Eric Arnesen, Barbara Bair, Frank Bardacke, Deborah Bernhart, Alan Bérubé, Paul Buhle, Tom Berry, Donna Del Blasio, Mike Donovan, John Dower, Jerry Fishbein, Phil Goldberg, Andrew Herod, Desma Holcomb, Jonathan Holloway, Julius Jacobson, Phyllis Jacobson, Keir Jorgensen, Debra Lindsey, John Logan, Staughton Lynd, Walter Mankoff, Congresswoman Patsy Takemoto Mink, David Montgomery, Alice Yang Murray, Amy Newell, Hope Nisly, Peter Olney, Kimberley Phillips, Mary Beth Pudup, Peter Rachleff, Dan Ringer, Harry Rubenstein, Jane Slaughter, Heather Thompson, Lori Wallach, Anne Woo-Sam, Jim Wooten, Robert Zieger, and the New Directions Solidarity School in Ben Lomond. My special thanks to Mary Blewett, Thomas Ferguson, David Nasaw, and Judy Yung for generously sharing their original research.

I also want to thank all the people whom I interviewed for the book, none of whom is responsible for its conclusions: Nick Aiello, Mark Anderson, Ronald Blackwell, May Ying Chen, Muzzafar Chisti, Bill Cunningham, Susan Cowell, Dave Elsila, Douglas Fraser, Art Gundersheim, Jeff Hermanson, Keir Jorgensen, Joel Joseph, Phyllis Manrod, Paul Marcone, Kim Moody, Lee Price, Larry Russell, James Shizuru, Jeff Stansbury, Robert Swift, Chris Townshend, Congressman James Traficant, Jerry Tucker, Max Zimny, and the late Herman Starobin. Thanks, also, to all the interviewees who shared original documents with me.

Thank you to the many people whose often invisible labor behind the scenes made this book possible: Thanks to the archivists and staff at the Wayne State Archives of Labor and Urban Affairs, the George Meany Archives, the Robert Wagner Archives, and the Kheel Center for Labor-Management Documentation at the New York State School for Industrial and Labor Relations. Thanks to the dozens of people working in the library at the University of California, Santa Cruz, especially the staffs of the government documents collection, interlibrary loan office, and the reference desk; and to Dwight Frey, Cheryl Gomez, and Debbie Turner for making library visits fun. My thanks to Kim Jackson and Deb Reed, in American Studies; and to Kathy Durcan, Henrietta Brown, Zoe Sodja, and Cheryl Van De Veer for transcribing interviews and helping with the manuscript during various crunches. Huge thanks to Cherie Turner, who miraculously made it physically possible for me to finish it.

This book exists only because of a series of generous grants from the National Endowment for the Humanities. I want to thank deeply the staff of the endowment, along with the anonymous peers who awarded a Fellowship for College Teachers and Independent Scholars, a Summer Stipend, and a Travel to Collections Grant. My thanks, as well, to the UCSC Academic Senate for yearly grants that kept the project going.

It's hard to get right all the proper thanks to my friends, colleagues, and loved ones, but I'll try. For support and friendship along the way, thanks to Eric Arnesen, David Brundage, Cathy Buller, Adriana Craciun, Ulrika Dahl, Peter Dimmock, Miriam Frank, Steve Fraser, Toni Gilpin, Julie Greene, Martha Hodes, Tera Hunter, John Logan, Roz Spafford, Laura Tabili, Helen Wallis, and the American Studies Program at UCSC, epecially Michael Cowan, John Dizikes, Yvette Huginnie, Ann Lane, and Judy Yung. Thanks to Dave Roediger and Leon Fink for supporting the project in its early stages, and beyond. Thanks to Frank Bardacke for years of sharing the agonizing and exhilarating daily process of writing our books; to Lisbeth Haas, with whom it was once again "a delight to share writing books together"; and to Alan Bérubé for so many instructive and enjoyable discussions of how to write for a popular audience. Thanks to Kim Moody for comradeship in figuring out the messy politics of trade policy. My special thanks to Ann E. Kingsolver, Gwendolyn Mink, Priscilla Murolo, Mary Beth Pudup, and Dana Takagi for comradeship in figuring out the politics of the book, as well as great friendship. My deepest thanks, as always, to the folks who make daily life possible, meaningful, and fun, and who held my hand throughout the project: Barbara Bair, Gerri Dayharsh, Steve McCabe, Becky Dayharsh McCabe, Ramona Dayharsh McCabe, Hamsa Heinrich, Gwendolyn Mink, Gerda Ray, and Karin Stallard.

As ever, I want to thank my parents, Joseph and Carolyn Frank, and my sister, Laura Frank, for their ongoing loving support and for their endless faith in my intellectual endeavors. My deepest thanks to Judy, James, and Kiyo Shizuru as well, for teaching me about racism against Asian Americans, beginning with that first "Remember Pearl Harbor" bumper sticker thirty-nine years ago. I hope this book contributes some measure of reparation.

My life has been inspired, challenged, and shaped immeasurably by the two wise, wonderful women, Marge Frantz and Eleanor Engstrand, to whom this book is dedicated. I'll never be able to pay them back, express my gratitude properly, or change the world in all the ways they'd want it to be changed, but here's a start.

Dozens of people helped me—and the book—immensely by reading drafts of the original book proposal or of individual chapters. My great thanks go to Frank Bardacke, Jeremy Brecher, Leon Fink, Yvette Huginnie, Ann Lane, Arthur MacEwan, Amy Newell, Mary Beth Pudup, Gerda Ray, Karin Stallard, Barbara Clark Smith, Thompson Smith, Jeff Stansbury, and the UCSC reading group on Race, Nation, and Colonialism, including Pedro Castillo, Alan Christy, Lisbeth Haas, Bruce Levine, Alice Yang Murray, and Tyler Stovall. My particular thanks to David Montgomery for help on sources, for reading Chapter 2, and for his vision of workers' empowerment, always abiding in my work. Thanks to my personal council of economic advisers, John Willoughby, for reading the entire manuscript and making sure I got things right. I also want to thank Kimberley Phillips, Marcus Rediker, and Judy Yung for their generosity in supporting my use of their research, and especially Barbara Clark Smith, on whom I am immensely dependent, not only for her research but for her broader insights into, and knowledge of, the American Revolution.

Beacon Press still seems like a blessing from the sky, and I am endlessly grateful to them for publishing my book and for their commitment to politically engaged scholarship. Thanks to Robin D. G. Kelley and Marcus Rediker for making it possible; to Andrew Hrycyna for support and advice in the early stages; to Margaret Park Bridges and the production department; to Patricia Waldygo for great copyediting; and to Elizabeth Elsas for the spectacular cover. Most of all, my thanks to Deb Chasman, for believing in this project, for all her wonderful advice and sharp insights, and for such a lovely friendship along the way.

Two more friends read the manuscript and made the whole thing possible. My deepest gratitude to Nelson Lichtenstein for his endless faith that I could pull off this messy project with its thorny politics and offbeat style, for his vast enthusiasm for (almost) anything I wrote, and for his advice on how to make it better at every turn. Thanks, finally, to my glorious research assistant, Vanessa Tait, who took time out of her own impressive dissertation on community involvement in the labor movement to help with this book for over five years. She conducted enormous amounts of primary research for this book, ran hundreds of research errands, and was a superb critic of the entire manuscript, both stylistically and politically. Last but not least, it was always fun working together. Thanks!

INDEX

Abbott, Robert, 79–81
Abe, Stanley L., 140
Abney, David, 236
Acheson, Dean, 105
Adams, Abigail, 16–17, 18, 19
Adams, John, 7, 16
Adams, Samuel, 3, 4, 22, 31
AFL-CIO Looks at Foreign Trade, 112
African American Labor Institute, 111
African American press, 79–82
African Americans: Buy American movement of 1930s and, 79–82; Buy American movement of 1970s–80s and, 79–82; Don't Buy Where You Can't Work movement, 81–83; immigrants and, 1930s, 81–83. *See also* Future Outlook League; Montgomery Bus Boycott; segregation; slaves
Agricultural workers, 88, 125
Agriculture, 41, 42
Aiello, Nick 145
Alameda County (California) Supervisors, 64
Alaska, 43, 222
Aldis, N., 16
Alien actors bill, 71, 76
Alien Land Laws, 74, 235
Amalgamated Association of Iron and Steel Workers, 47, 51–52
Amalgamated Clothing and Textile Workers' Union (ACTWU), 133, 134, 144, 196, 197–98; merger into UNITE!, 249
Amalgamated Meat Cutters' Union, 118
American Apparel Management Association (AAMA), 197
American Association of Importers and Exporters, 211
American Automobile Labeling Act, 221

American Center for International Solidarity, 248
American Century, 103, 124–26, 131
American Committee Against War and Fascism, 98
American Federation of Labor (AFL): Buy American movement of 1930s and, 67–70; in 1880s, 45, 47, 50; endorses 1930s boycott of Japanese products, 98; loyalty oaths, 108; merger with CIO, 110; nativism and, 72, 78; racism in 1930s, 68; trade policy, 111, 116; Union Label Trades Department, 69–70, 118; World War II gains, 108
American Federation of Labor and Congress of Industrial Organizations (AFL-CIO): attitudes toward organizing, 124, 182; Buy American campaigns and, 102–4; decline, 182; Industrial Union Department, 183; International Department, 182; label department, 69–70, 110; and "Made in U.S.A." standard, 21, 212; merger with CIO, 110, 124; overseas operations, 127–28, 153, 182–83; racism in, 105; Sweeney administration, 248–49; trade policy, 11, 116, 123, 127, 133, 182; Union Label and Service Trades Department, 118, 183–84, 211
American Fiber, Textile, Apparel Coalition, 197
American Flint Glass Workers, 69
American Institute for Free Labor Development (AIFLD), 153, 183, 248
American Institute of Steel Construction, 66
American Match Institute, 66
American Pride, Inc., 217